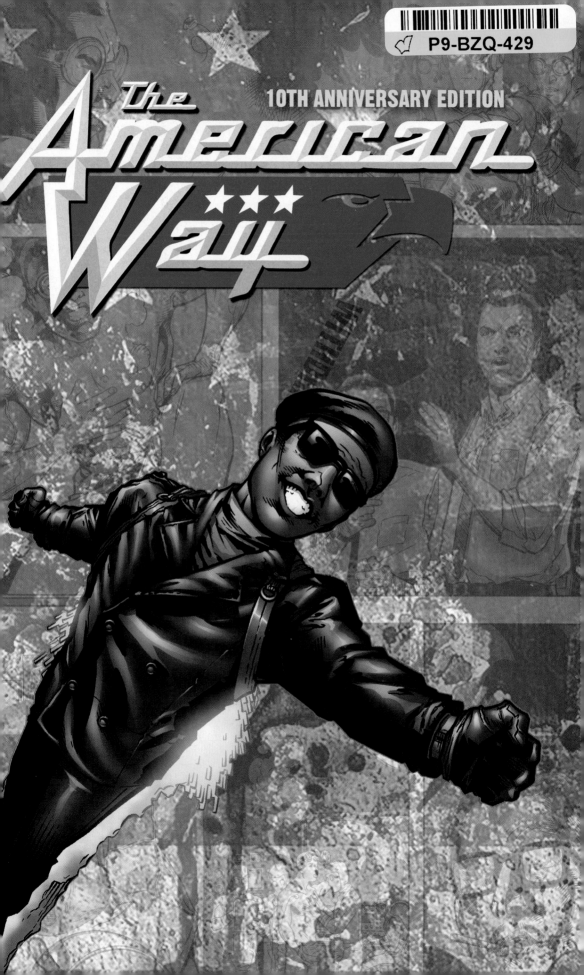

10TH ANNIVERSARY EDITION

The American Way

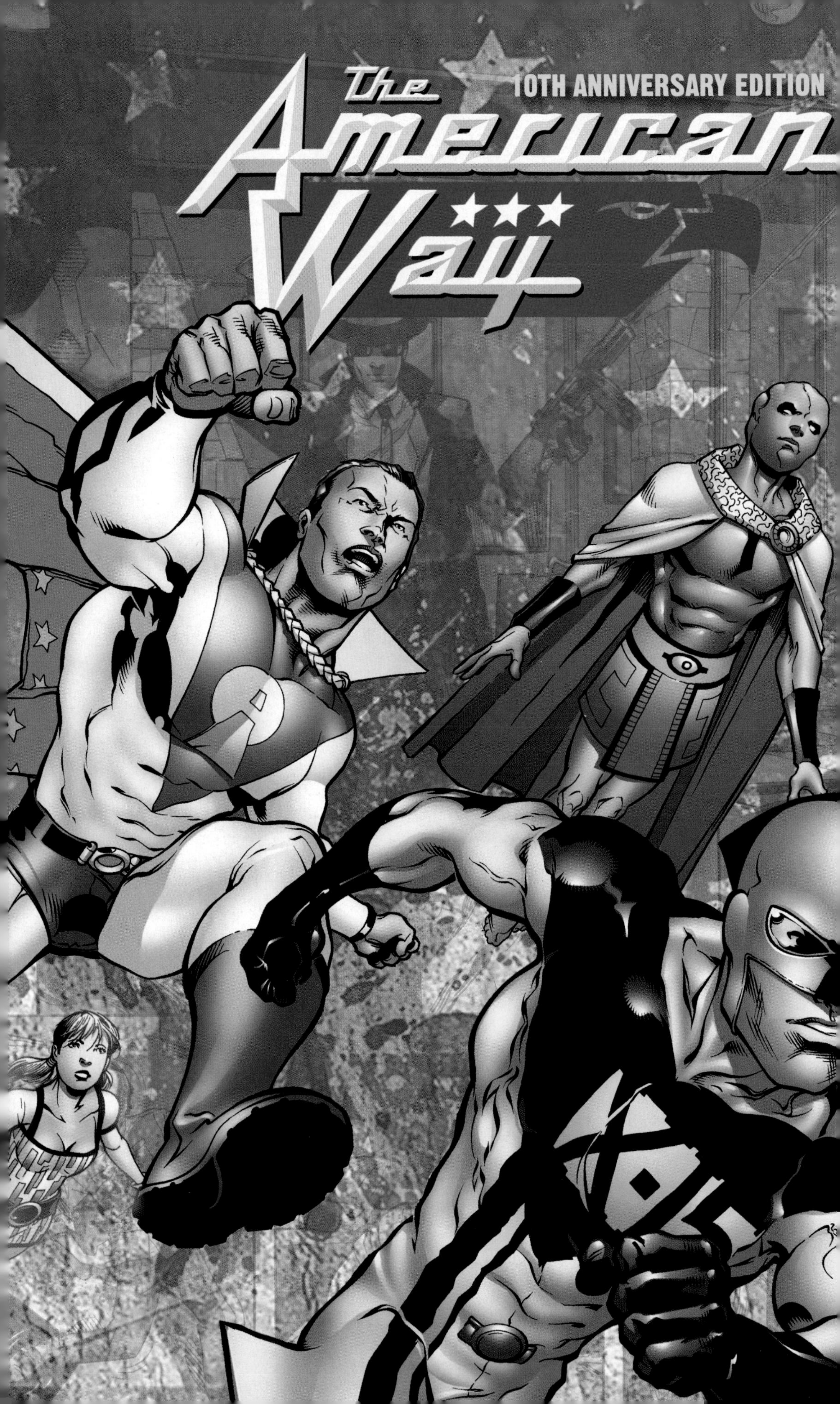

The American Way
10TH ANNIVERSARY EDITION

JOHN RIDLEY
writer

GEORGES JEANTY
penciller

KARL STORY
RAY SNYDER
inkers

WILDSTORM FX
colorist

PAT BROSSEAU **TRAVIS LANHAM** **ROB LEIGH**
letterers

GEORGES JEANTY **KARL STORY** **RANDY MAYOR**
series and collection cover artists

THE AMERICAN WAY 10TH ANNIVERSARY EDITION

Published by DC Comics. Compilation, character and cover sketches, and all new material Copyright © 2017 D
Comics. All Rights Reserved. Originally published by Wildstorm Productions in single magazine form in
THE AMERICAN WAY #1-8. Copyright © 2006 DC Comics. All Rights Reserved. All characters, their distinctive
likenesses and related elements featured in this publication are trademarks of DC Comics. VERTIGO is tradem
of DC Comics. The stories, characters and incidents featured in this publication are entirely fictional. DC Comic
does not read or accept unsolicited submissions of ideas, stories or artwork.
DC Comics, 2900 West Alameda Ave., Burbank, CA 91505
Printed in The United States. 5/5/17. First Printing.
ISBN: 978-1-4012-7354-5

Library of Congress Cataloging-in-Publication Data is available.

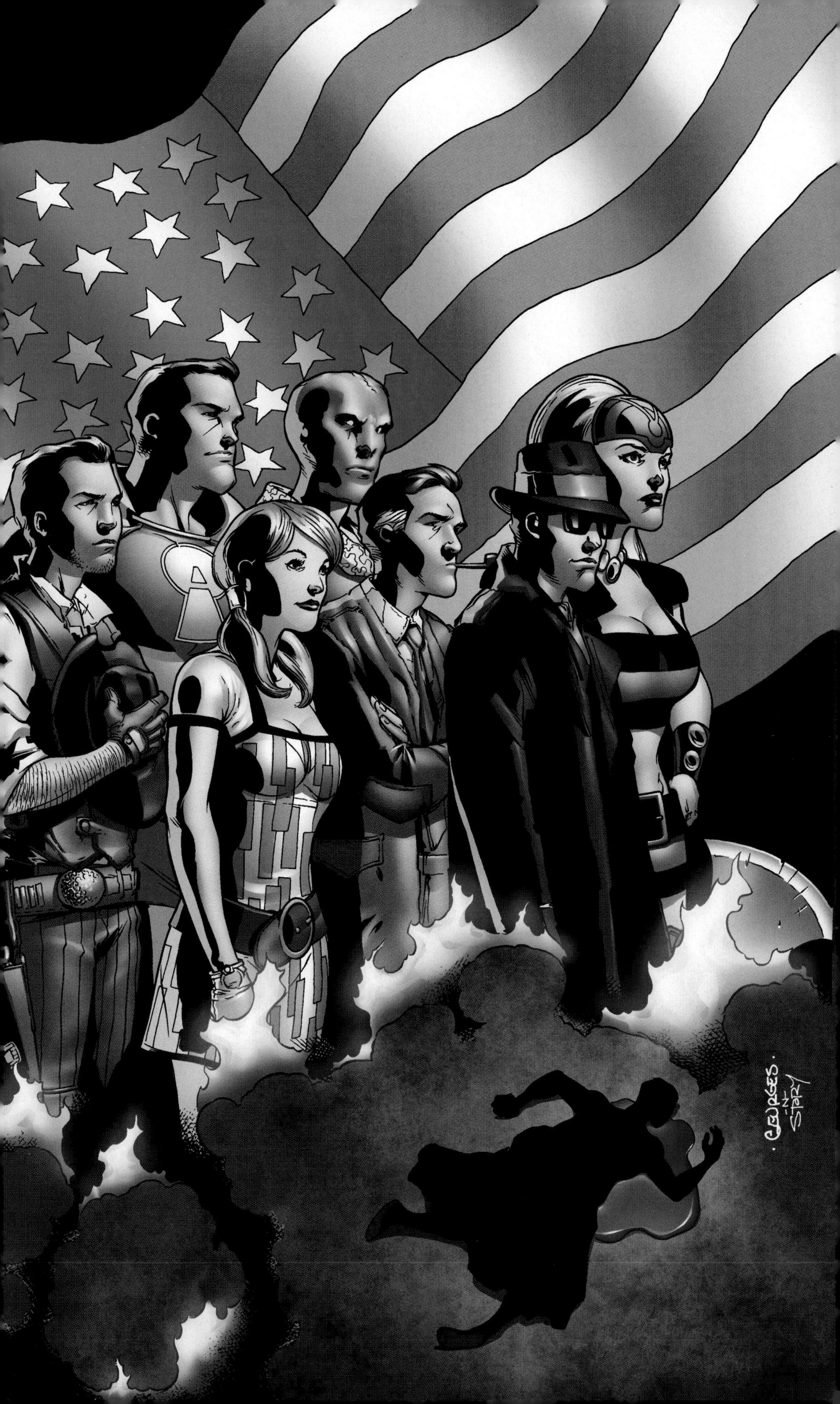

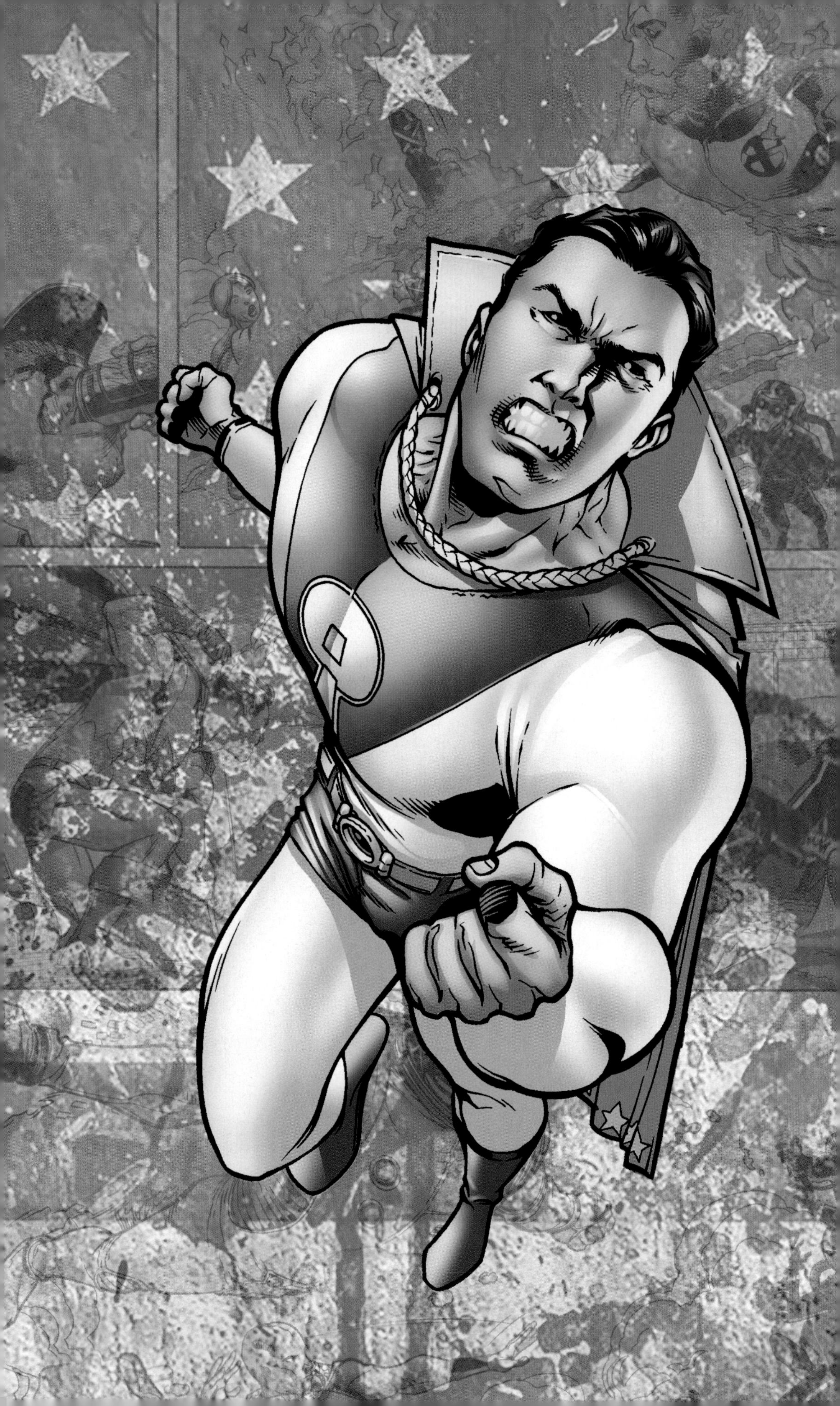

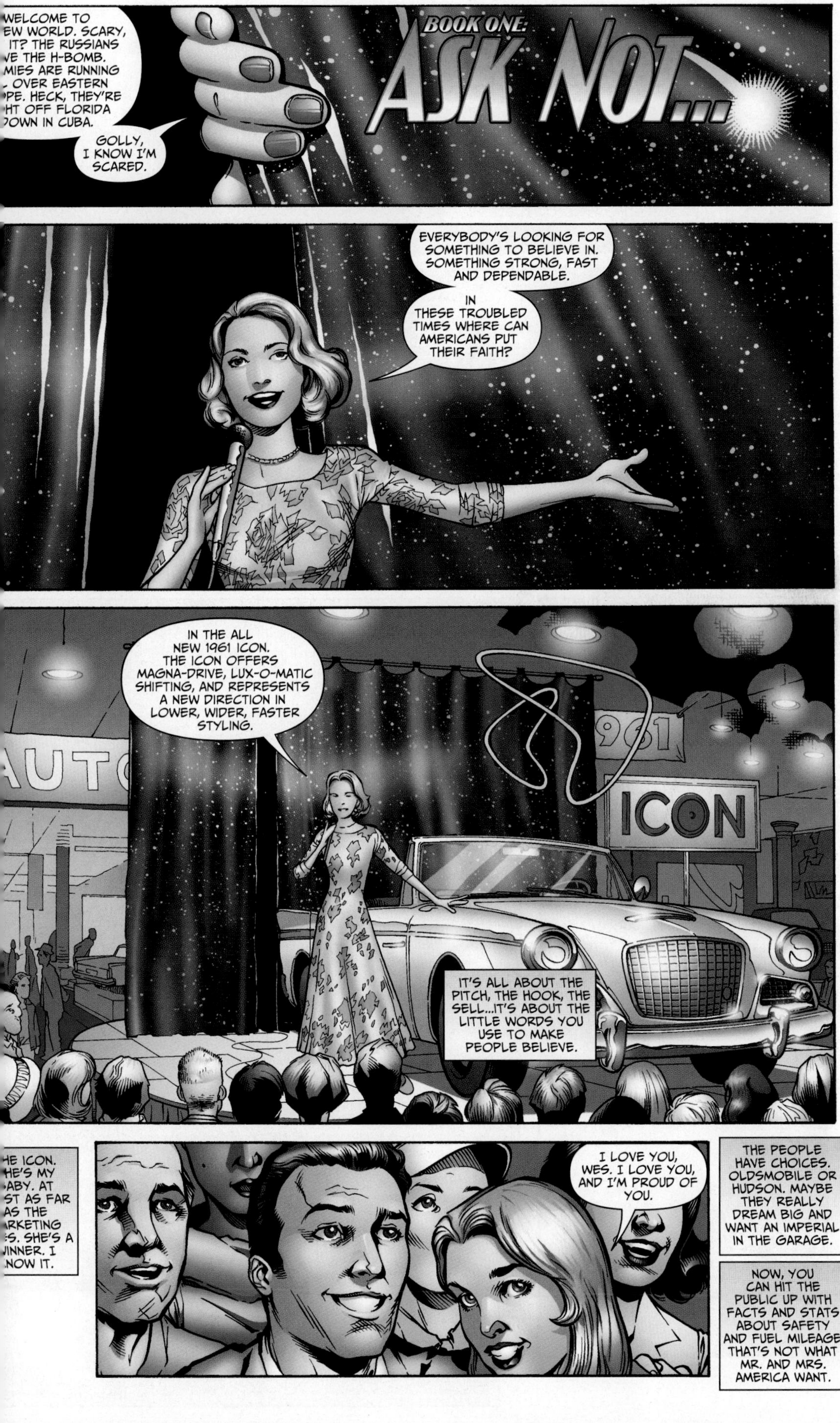
WELCOME TO EW WORLD. SCARY, IT? THE RUSSIANS VE THE H-BOMB. MIES ARE RUNNING OVER EASTERN PE. HECK, THEY'RE HT OFF FLORIDA DOWN IN CUBA.
GOLLY, I KNOW I'M SCARED.
BOOK ONE:
ASK NOT...
EVERYBODY'S LOOKING FOR SOMETHING TO BELIEVE IN. SOMETHING STRONG, FAST AND DEPENDABLE.
IN THESE TROUBLED TIMES WHERE CAN AMERICANS PUT THEIR FAITH?
IN THE ALL NEW 1961 ICON. THE ICON OFFERS MAGNA-DRIVE, LUX-O-MATIC SHIFTING, AND REPRESENTS A NEW DIRECTION IN LOWER, WIDER, FASTER STYLING.
AUTO
ICON
IT'S ALL ABOUT THE PITCH, THE HOOK, THE SELL...IT'S ABOUT THE LITTLE WORDS YOU USE TO MAKE PEOPLE BELIEVE.
HE ICON. HE'S MY ABY. AT ST AS FAR AS THE ARKETING ES. SHE'S A WINNER. I NOW IT.
I LOVE YOU, WES. I LOVE YOU, AND I'M PROUD OF YOU.
THE PEOPLE HAVE CHOICES. OLDSMOBILE OR HUDSON. MAYBE THEY REALLY DREAM BIG AND WANT AN IMPERIAL IN THE GARAGE.
NOW, YOU CAN HIT THE PUBLIC UP WITH FACTS AND STATS ABOUT SAFETY AND FUEL MILEAGE. THAT'S NOT WHAT MR. AND MRS. AMERICA WANT.

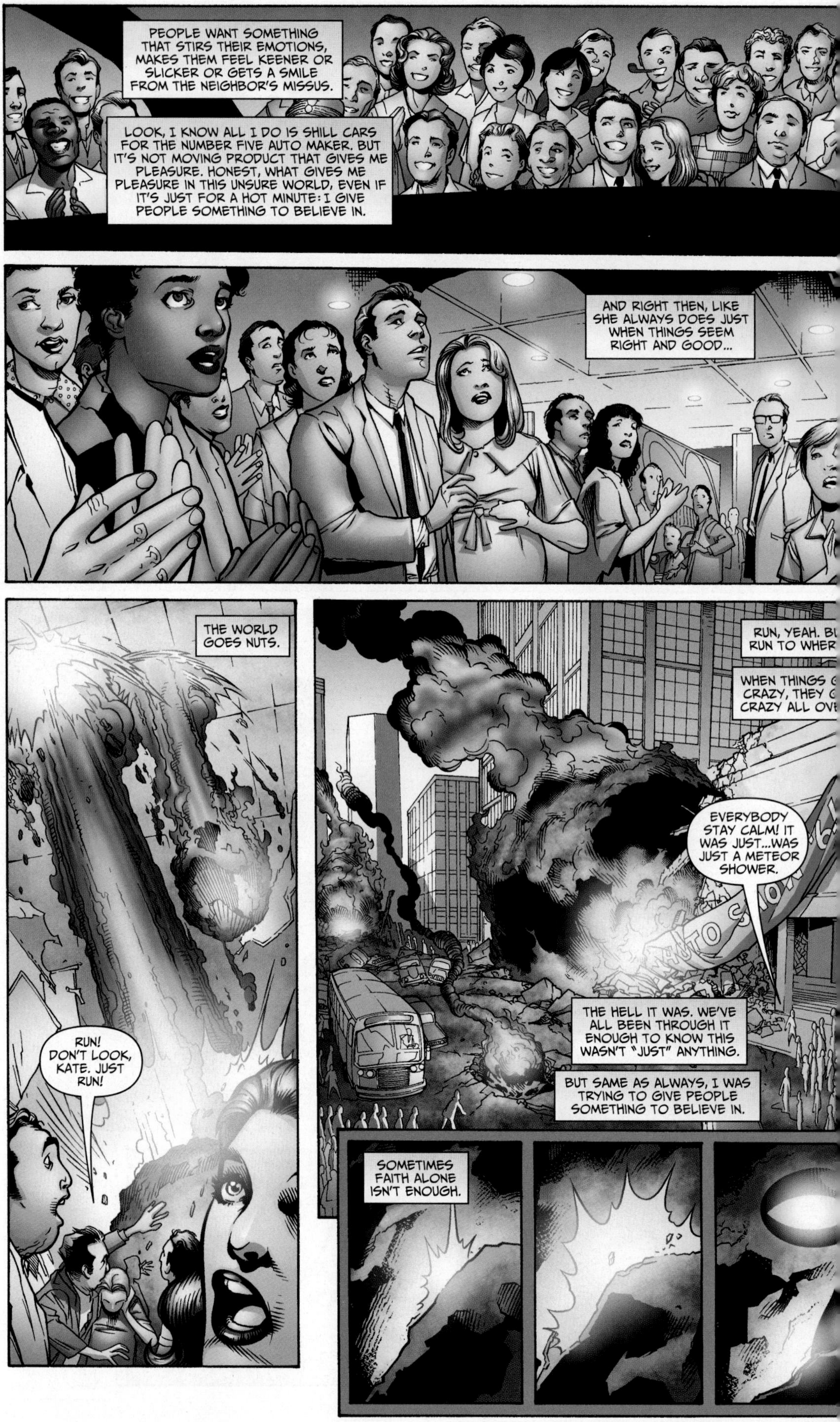
PEOPLE WANT SOMETHING THAT STIRS THEIR EMOTIONS, MAKES THEM FEEL KEENER OR SLICKER OR GETS A SMILE FROM THE NEIGHBOR'S MISSUS.
LOOK, I KNOW ALL I DO IS SHILL CARS FOR THE NUMBER FIVE AUTO MAKER. BUT IT'S NOT MOVING PRODUCT THAT GIVES ME PLEASURE. HONEST, WHAT GIVES ME PLEASURE IN THIS UNSURE WORLD, EVEN IF IT'S JUST FOR A HOT MINUTE: I GIVE PEOPLE SOMETHING TO BELIEVE IN.
AND RIGHT THEN, LIKE SHE ALWAYS DOES JUST WHEN THINGS SEEM RIGHT AND GOOD...
THE WORLD GOES NUTS.
RUN! DON'T LOOK, KATE. JUST RUN!
WHEN THINGS
EVERYBODY STAY CALM! IT WAS JUST...WAS JUST A METEOR SHOWER.
THE HELL IT WAS. WE'VE ALL BEEN THROUGH IT ENOUGH TO KNOW THIS WASN'T "JUST" ANYTHING.
BUT SAME AS ALWAYS, I WAS TRYING TO GIVE PEOPLE SOMETHING TO BELIEVE IN.
SOMETIMES FAITH ALONE ISN'T ENOUGH.

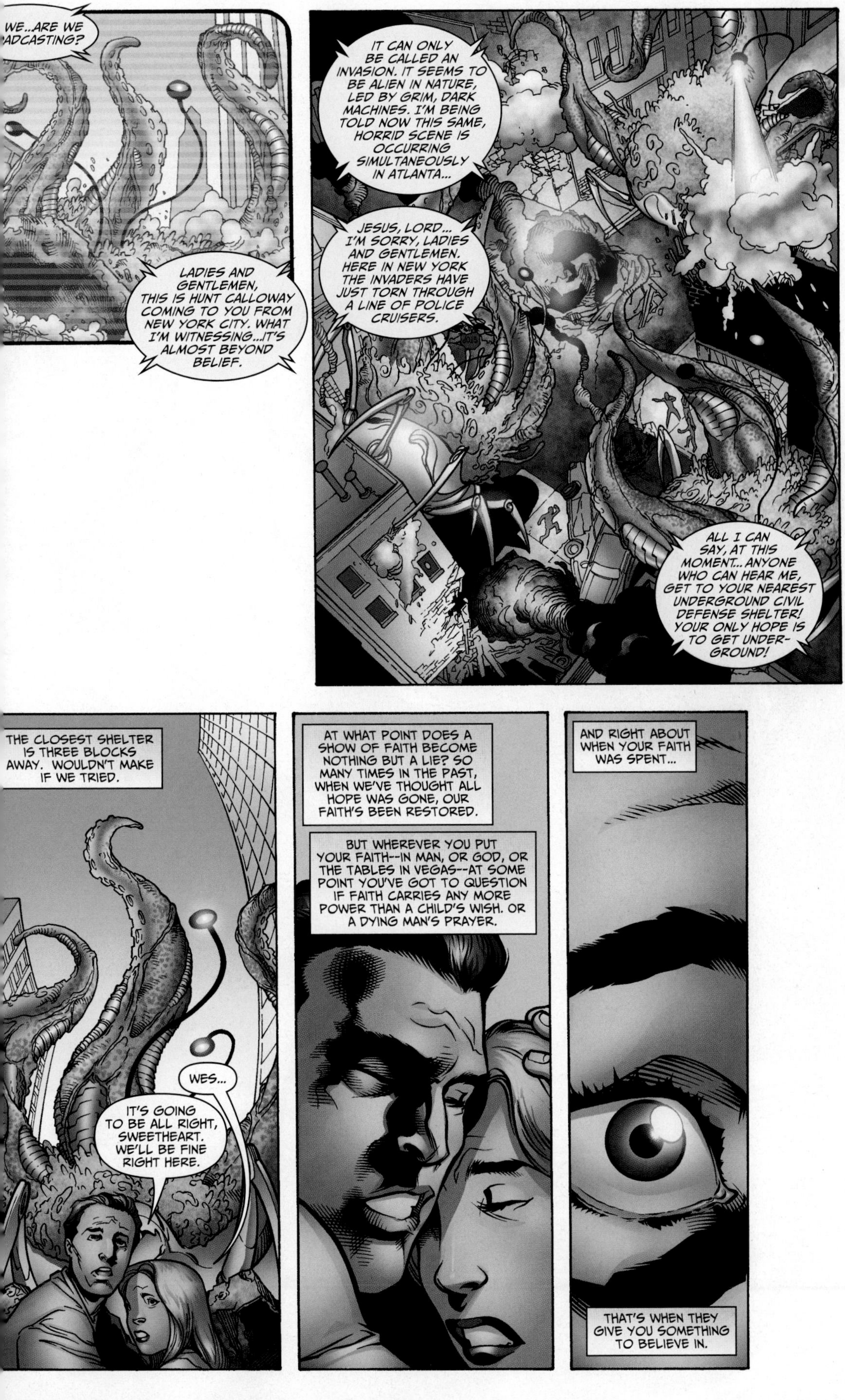
WE...ARE WE ...ADCASTING?
LADIES AND GENTLEMEN, THIS IS HUNT CALLOWAY COMING TO YOU FROM NEW YORK CITY. WHAT I'M WITNESSING...IT'S ALMOST BEYOND BELIEF.
IT CAN ONLY BE CALLED AN INVASION. IT SEEMS TO BE ALIEN IN NATURE, LED BY GRIM, DARK MACHINES. I'M BEING TOLD NOW THIS SAME, HORRID SCENE IS OCCURRING SIMULTANEOUSLY IN ATLANTA...
JESUS, LORD... I'M SORRY, LADIES AND GENTLEMEN. HERE IN NEW YORK THE INVADERS HAVE JUST TORN THROUGH A LINE OF POLICE CRUISERS.
ALL I CAN SAY, AT THIS MOMENT... ANYONE WHO CAN HEAR ME, GET TO YOUR NEAREST UNDERGROUND CIVIL DEFENSE SHELTER! YOUR ONLY HOPE IS TO GET UNDER-GROUND!
THE CLOSEST SHELTER IS THREE BLOCKS AWAY. WOULDN'T MAKE IF WE TRIED.
WES...
IT'S GOING TO BE ALL RIGHT, SWEETHEART. WE'LL BE FINE RIGHT HERE.
AT WHAT POINT DOES A SHOW OF FAITH BECOME NOTHING BUT A LIE? SO MANY TIMES IN THE PAST, WHEN WE'VE THOUGHT ALL HOPE WAS GONE, OUR FAITH'S BEEN RESTORED.
BUT WHEREVER YOU PUT YOUR FAITH--IN MAN, OR GOD, OR THE TABLES IN VEGAS--AT SOME POINT YOU'VE GOT TO QUESTION IF FAITH CARRIES ANY MORE POWER THAN A CHILD'S WISH. OR A DYING MAN'S PRAYER.
AND RIGHT ABOUT WHEN YOUR FAITH WAS SPENT...
THAT'S WHEN THEY GIVE YOU SOMETHING TO BELIEVE IN.

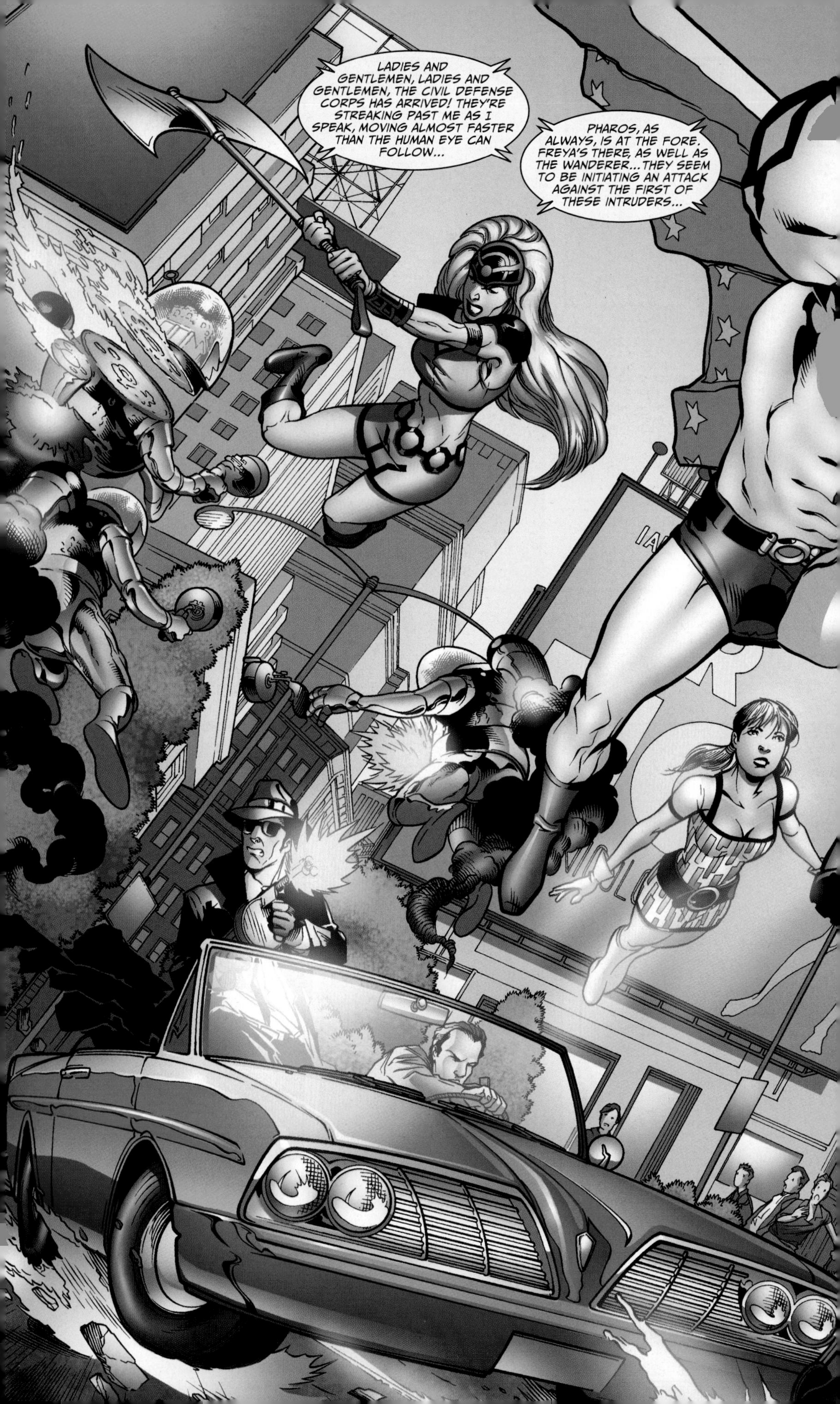

LADIES AND GENTLEMEN, LADIES AND GENTLEMEN, THE CIVIL DEFENSE CORPS HAS ARRIVED! THEY'RE STREAKING PAST ME AS I SPEAK, MOVING ALMOST FASTER THAN THE HUMAN EYE CAN FOLLOW...
PHAROS, AS ALWAYS, IS AT THE FORE. FREYA'S THERE, AS WELL AS THE WANDERER...THEY SEEM TO BE INITIATING AN ATTACK AGAINST THE FIRST OF THESE INTRUDERS...

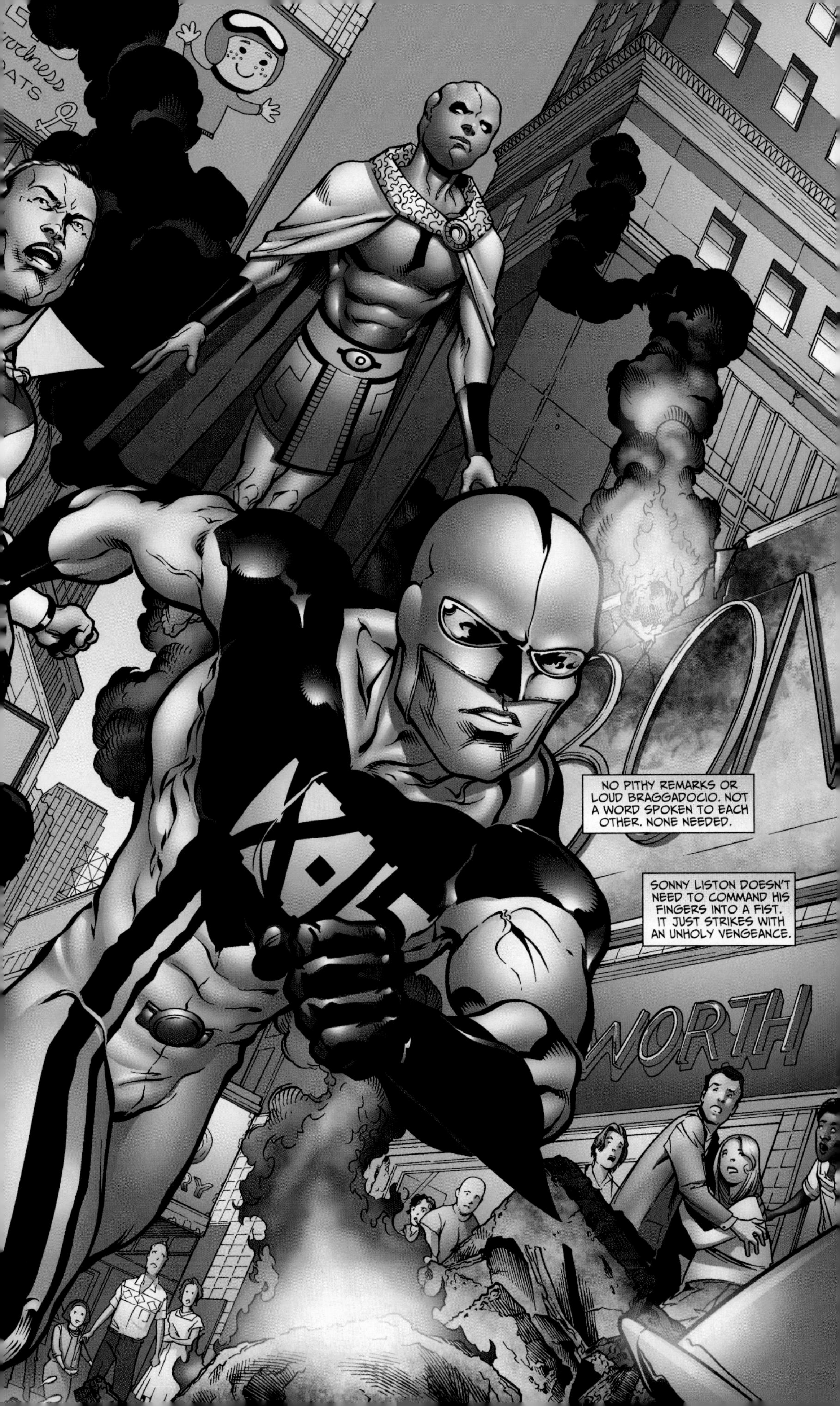
NO PITHY REMARKS OR LOUD BRAGGADOCIO. NOT A WORD SPOKEN TO EACH OTHER. NONE NEEDED.
SONNY LISTON DOESN'T NEED TO COMMAND HIS FINGERS INTO A FIST. IT JUST STRIKES WITH AN UNHOLY VENGEANCE.
WORTH

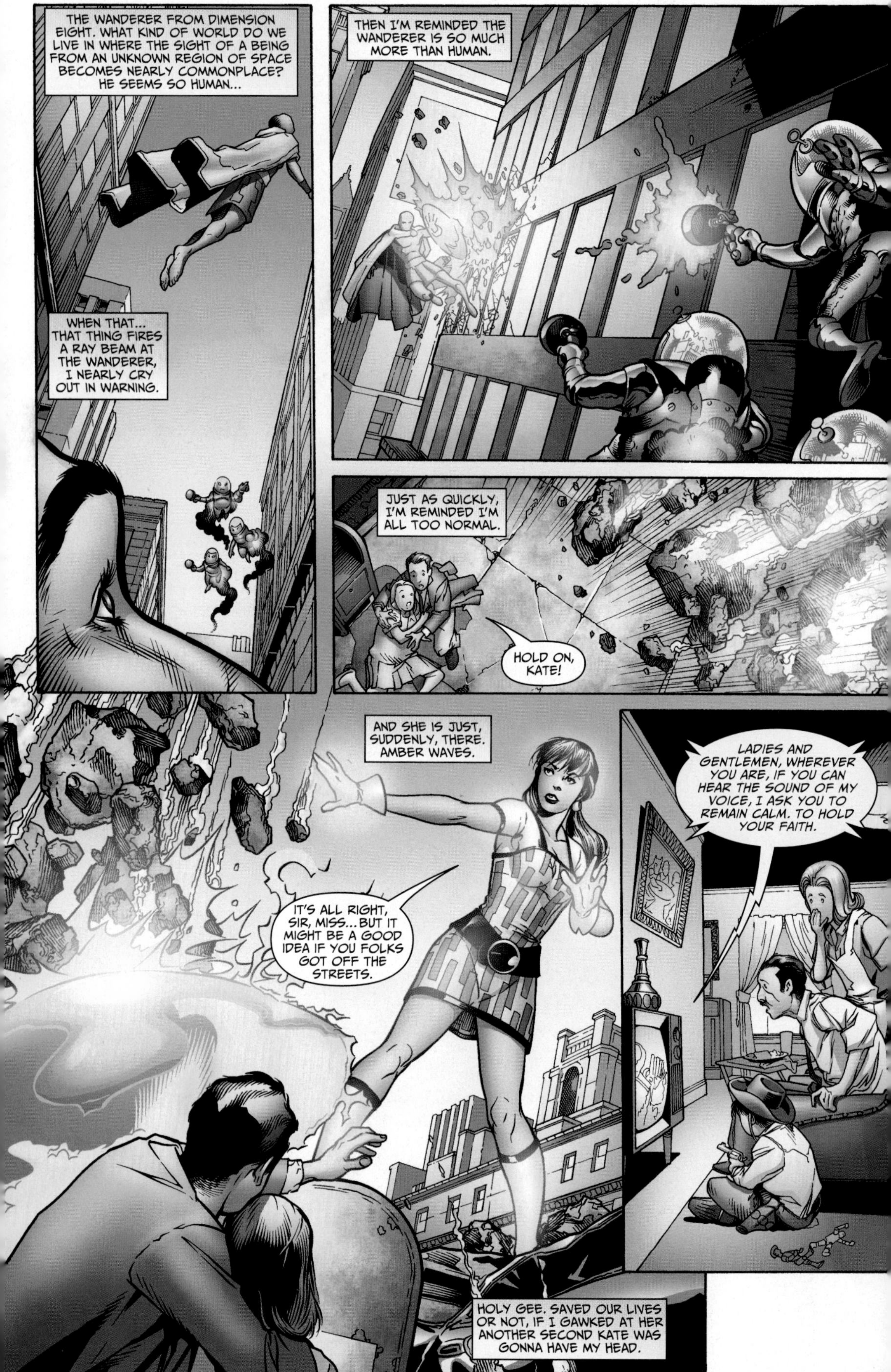
THE WANDERER FROM DIMENSION EIGHT. WHAT KIND OF WORLD DO WE LIVE IN WHERE THE SIGHT OF A BEING FROM AN UNKNOWN REGION OF SPACE BECOMES NEARLY COMMONPLACE? HE SEEMS SO HUMAN...
WHEN THAT... THAT THING FIRES A RAY BEAM AT THE WANDERER, I NEARLY CRY OUT IN WARNING.
THEN I'M REMINDED THE WANDERER IS SO MUCH MORE THAN HUMAN.
JUST AS QUICKLY, I'M REMINDED I'M ALL TOO NORMAL.
HOLD ON, KATE!
AND SHE IS JUST, SUDDENLY, THERE. AMBER WAVES.
IT'S ALL RIGHT, SIR, MISS... BUT IT MIGHT BE A GOOD IDEA IF YOU FOLKS GOT OFF THE STREETS.
LADIES AND GENTLEMEN, WHEREVER YOU ARE, IF YOU CAN HEAR THE SOUND OF MY VOICE, I ASK YOU TO REMAIN CALM. TO HOLD YOUR FAITH.
HOLY GEE. SAVED OUR LIVES OR NOT, IF I GAWKED AT HER ANOTHER SECOND KATE WAS GONNA HAVE MY HEAD.

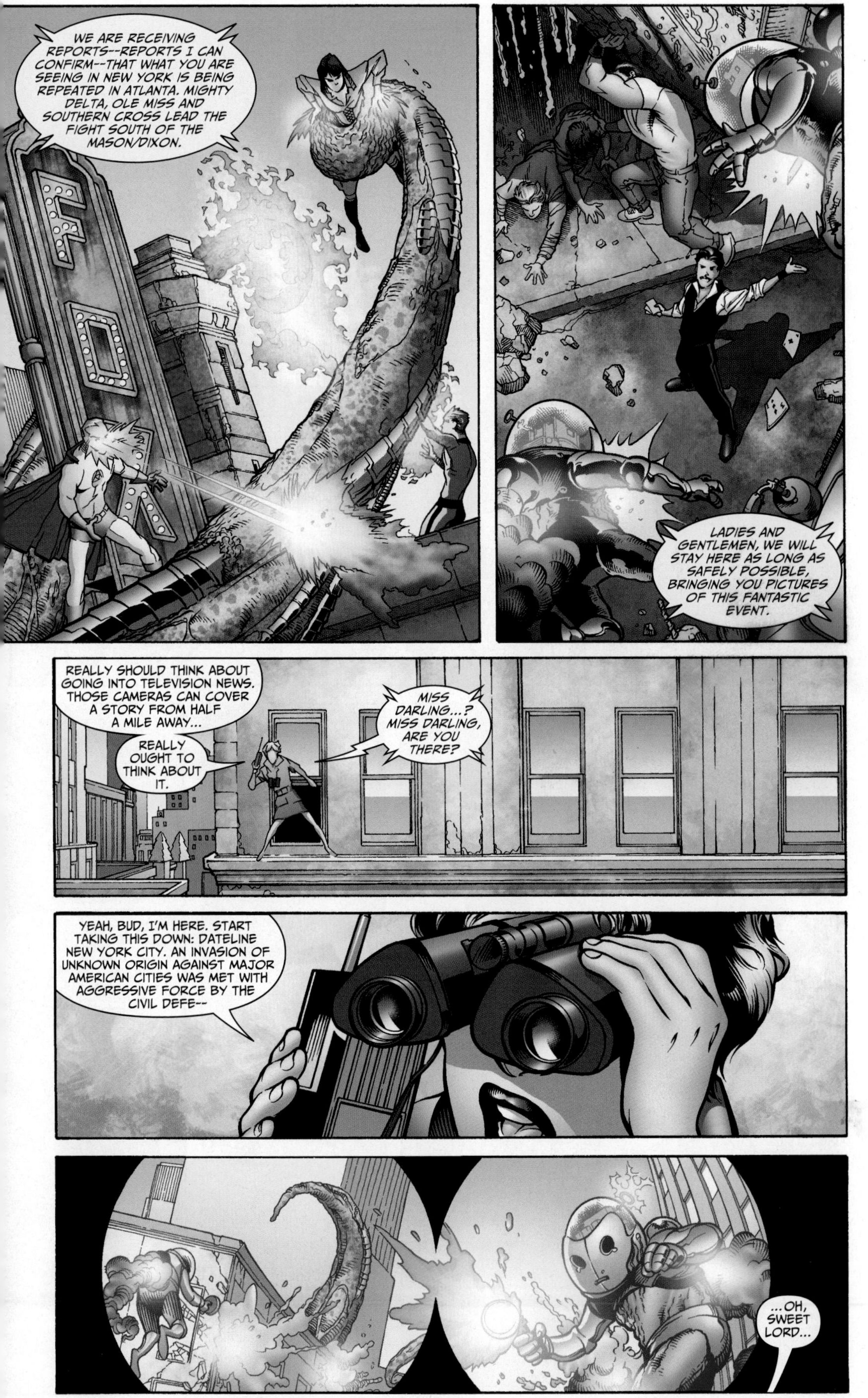
WE ARE RECEIVING REPORTS--REPORTS I CAN CONFIRM--THAT WHAT YOU ARE SEEING IN NEW YORK IS BEING REPEATED IN ATLANTA. MIGHTY DELTA, OLE MISS AND SOUTHERN CROSS LEAD THE FIGHT SOUTH OF THE MASON/DIXON.
LADIES AND GENTLEMEN, WE WILL STAY HERE AS LONG AS SAFELY POSSIBLE, BRINGING YOU PICTURES OF THIS FANTASTIC EVENT.
REALLY SHOULD THINK ABOUT GOING INTO TELEVISION NEWS. THOSE CAMERAS CAN COVER A STORY FROM HALF A MILE AWAY...
REALLY OUGHT TO THINK ABOUT IT.
MISS DARLING...? MISS DARLING, ARE YOU THERE?
YEAH, BUD, I'M HERE. START TAKING THIS DOWN: DATELINE NEW YORK CITY. AN INVASION OF UNKNOWN ORIGIN AGAINST MAJOR AMERICAN CITIES WAS MET WITH AGGRESSIVE FORCE BY THE CIVIL DEFE--
...OH, SWEET LORD...

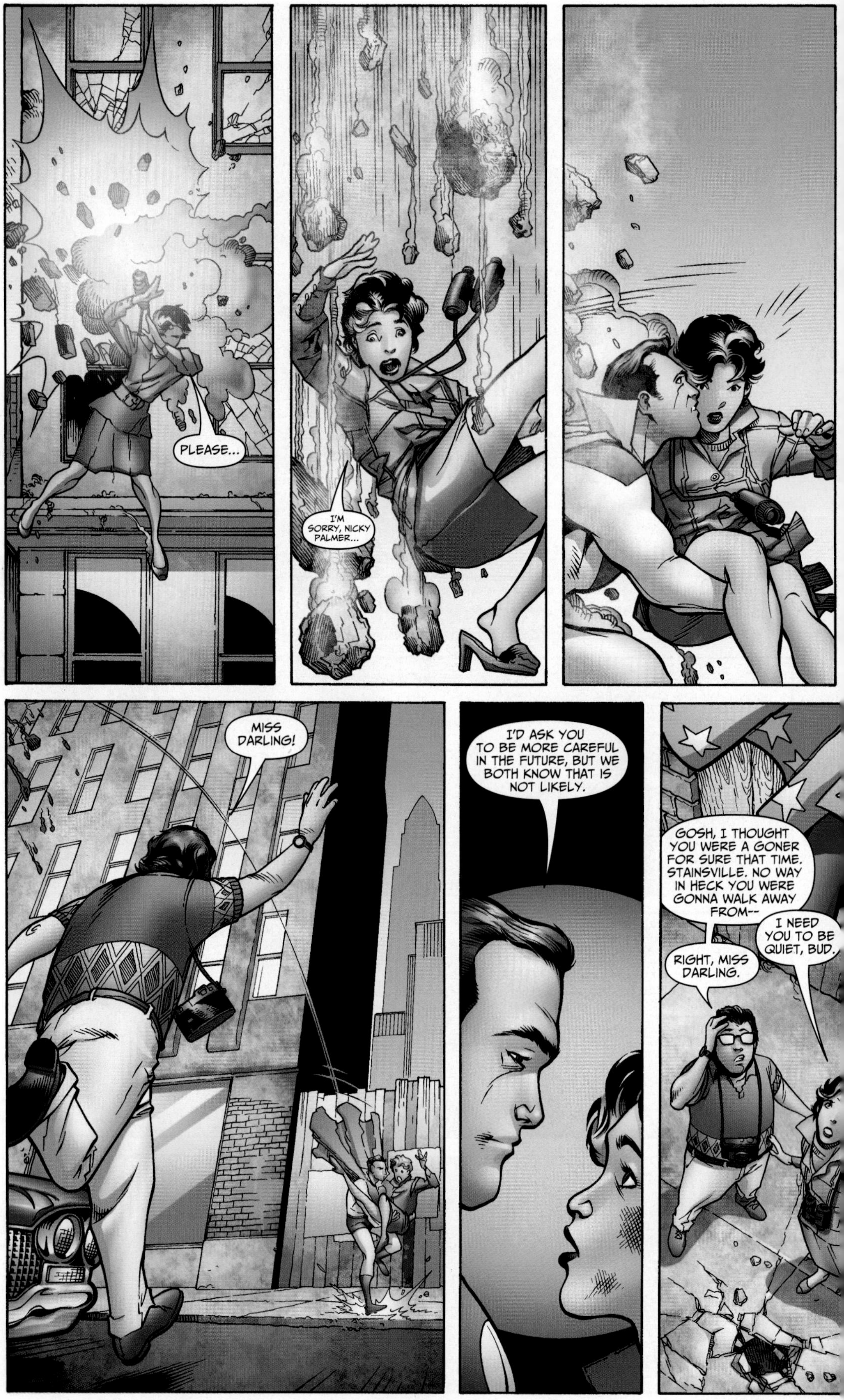
PLEASE...
I'M SORRY, NICKY PALMER...
MISS DARLING!
I'D ASK YOU TO BE MORE CAREFUL IN THE FUTURE, BUT WE BOTH KNOW THAT IS NOT LIKELY.
GOSH, I THOUGHT YOU WERE A GONER FOR SURE THAT TIME. STAINSVILLE. NO WAY IN HECK YOU WERE GONNA WALK AWAY FROM--
I NEED YOU TO BE QUIET, BUD.
RIGHT, MISS DARLING.

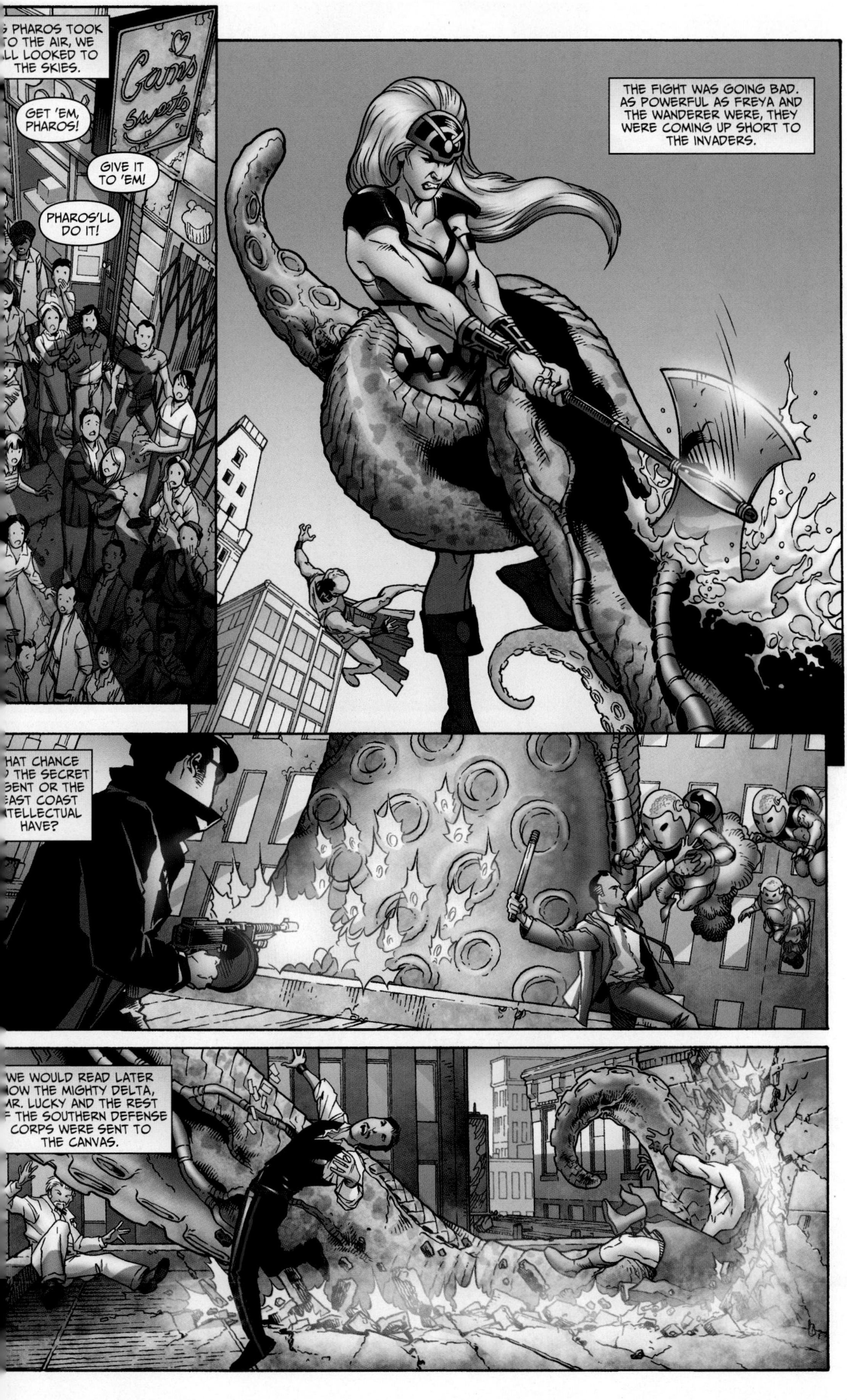

S PHAROS TOOK TO THE AIR, WE ALL LOOKED TO THE SKIES.
GET 'EM, PHAROS!
GIVE IT TO 'EM!
PHAROS'LL DO IT!
THE FIGHT WAS GOING BAD. AS POWERFUL AS FREYA AND THE WANDERER WERE, THEY WERE COMING UP SHORT TO THE INVADERS.
HAT CHANCE D THE SECRET GENT OR THE EAST COAST NTELLECTUAL HAVE?
WE WOULD READ LATER OW THE MIGHTY DELTA, MR. LUCKY AND THE REST F THE SOUTHERN DEFENSE CORPS WERE SENT TO THE CANVAS.

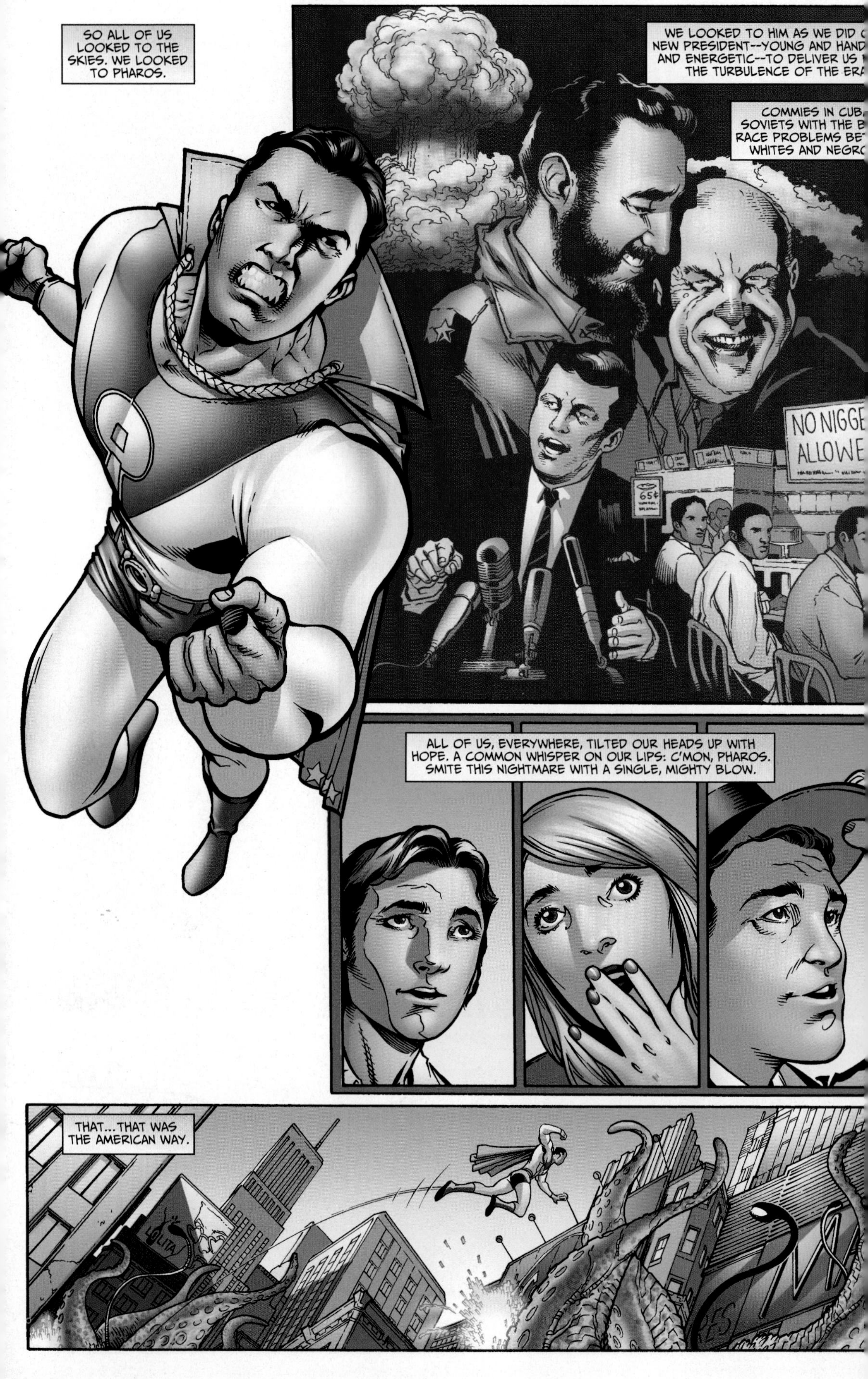
SO ALL OF US LOOKED TO THE SKIES. WE LOOKED TO PHAROS.
WE LOOKED TO HIM AS WE DID
NEW PRESIDENT--YOUNG AND HAND
AND ENERGETIC--TO DELIVER US
THE TURBULENCE OF THE ERA
COMMIES IN CUB
SOVIETS WITH THE B
RACE PROBLEMS BET
WHITES AND NEGRO
NO NIGGE
ALLOWE
65¢
ALL OF US, EVERYWHERE, TILTED OUR HEADS UP WITH HOPE. A COMMON WHISPER ON OUR LIPS: C'MON, PHAROS. SMITE THIS NIGHTMARE WITH A SINGLE, MIGHTY BLOW.
THAT...THAT WAS THE AMERICAN WAY.
LOLITA

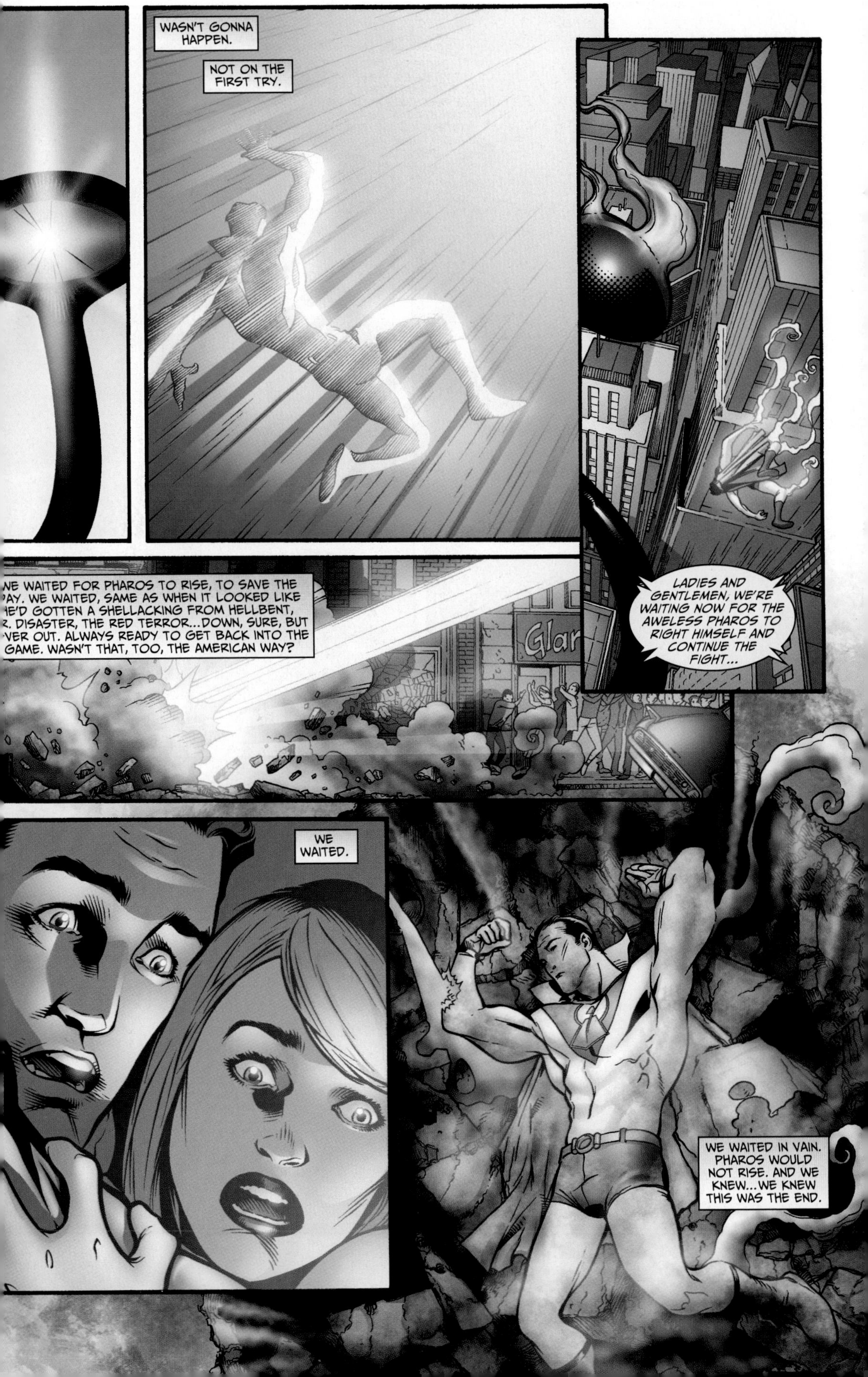

WASN'T GONNA HAPPEN.
NOT ON THE FIRST TRY.
LADIES AND GENTLEMEN, WE'RE WAITING NOW FOR THE AWELESS PHAROS TO RIGHT HIMSELF AND CONTINUE THE FIGHT...
WE WAITED FOR PHAROS TO RISE, TO SAVE THE DAY. WE WAITED, SAME AS WHEN IT LOOKED LIKE HE'D GOTTEN A SHELLACKING FROM HELLBENT, DR. DISASTER, THE RED TERROR...DOWN, SURE, BUT NEVER OUT. ALWAYS READY TO GET BACK INTO THE GAME. WASN'T THAT, TOO, THE AMERICAN WAY?
WE WAITED.
WE WAITED IN VAIN. PHAROS WOULD NOT RISE. AND WE KNEW...WE KNEW THIS WAS THE END.

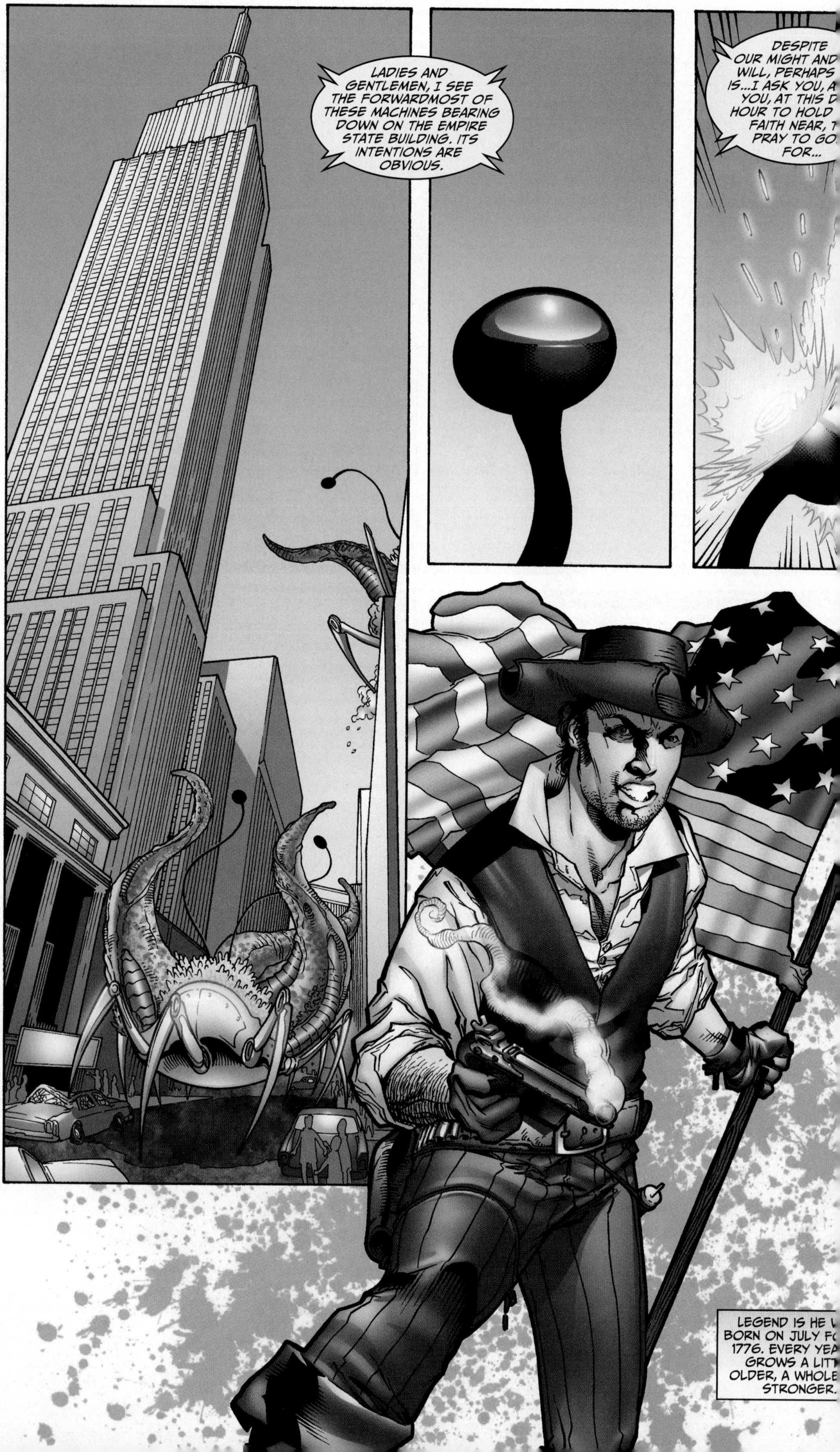
LADIES AND GENTLEMEN, I SEE THE FORWARDMOST OF THESE MACHINES BEARING DOWN ON THE EMPIRE STATE BUILDING. ITS INTENTIONS ARE OBVIOUS.
DESPITE OUR MIGHT AND WILL, PERHAPS IS...I ASK YOU, A YOU, AT THIS D HOUR TO HOLD FAITH NEAR, T PRAY TO GO FOR...
LEGEND IS HE BORN ON JULY F 1776. EVERY YEA GROWS A LIT OLDER, A WHOLE STRONGER.

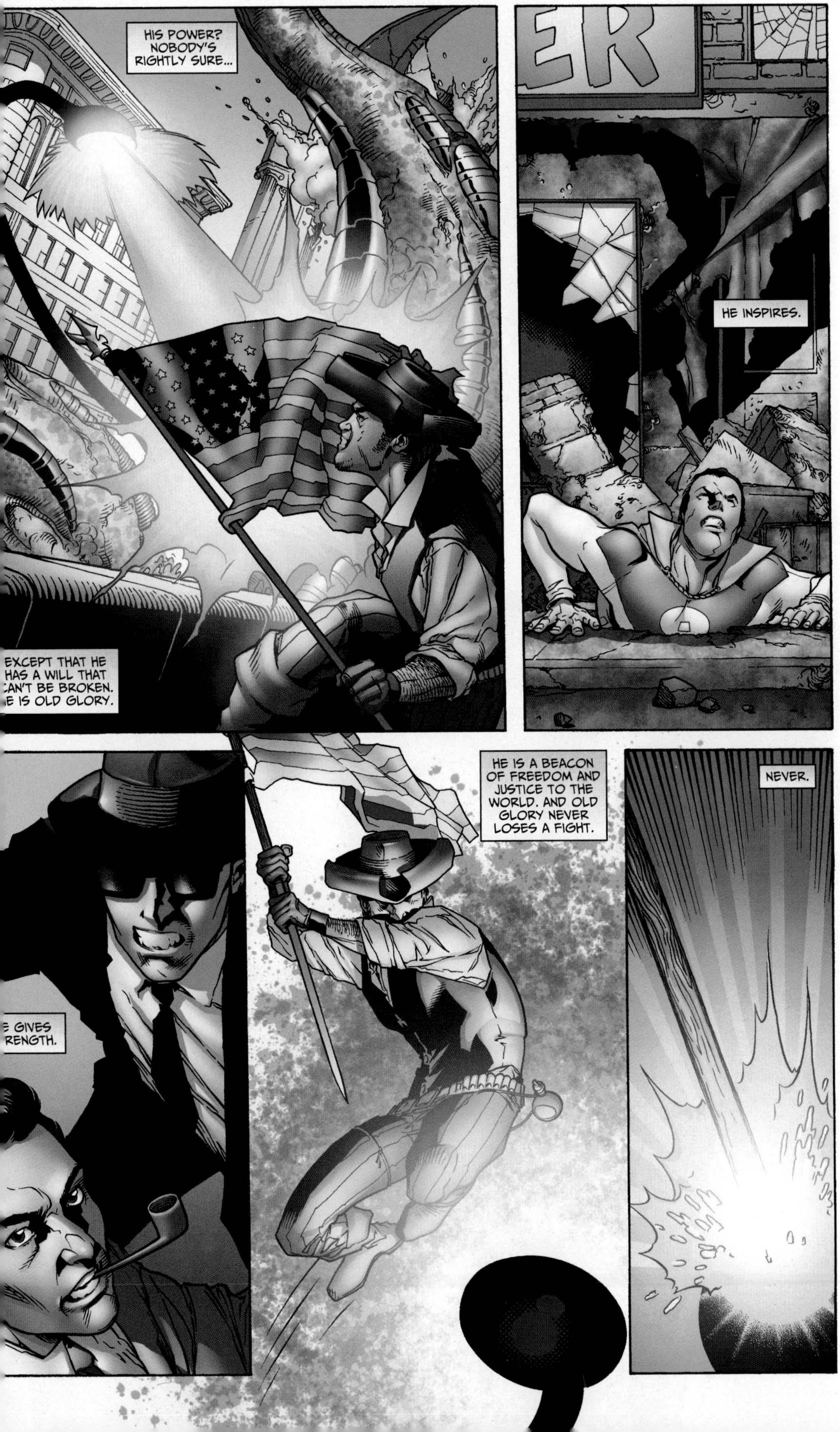
HIS POWER? NOBODY'S RIGHTLY SURE...
EXCEPT THAT HE HAS A WILL THAT CAN'T BE BROKEN. E IS OLD GLORY.
HE INSPIRES.
E GIVES RENGTH.
HE IS A BEACON OF FREEDOM AND JUSTICE TO THE WORLD. AND OLD GLORY NEVER LOSES A FIGHT.
NEVER.

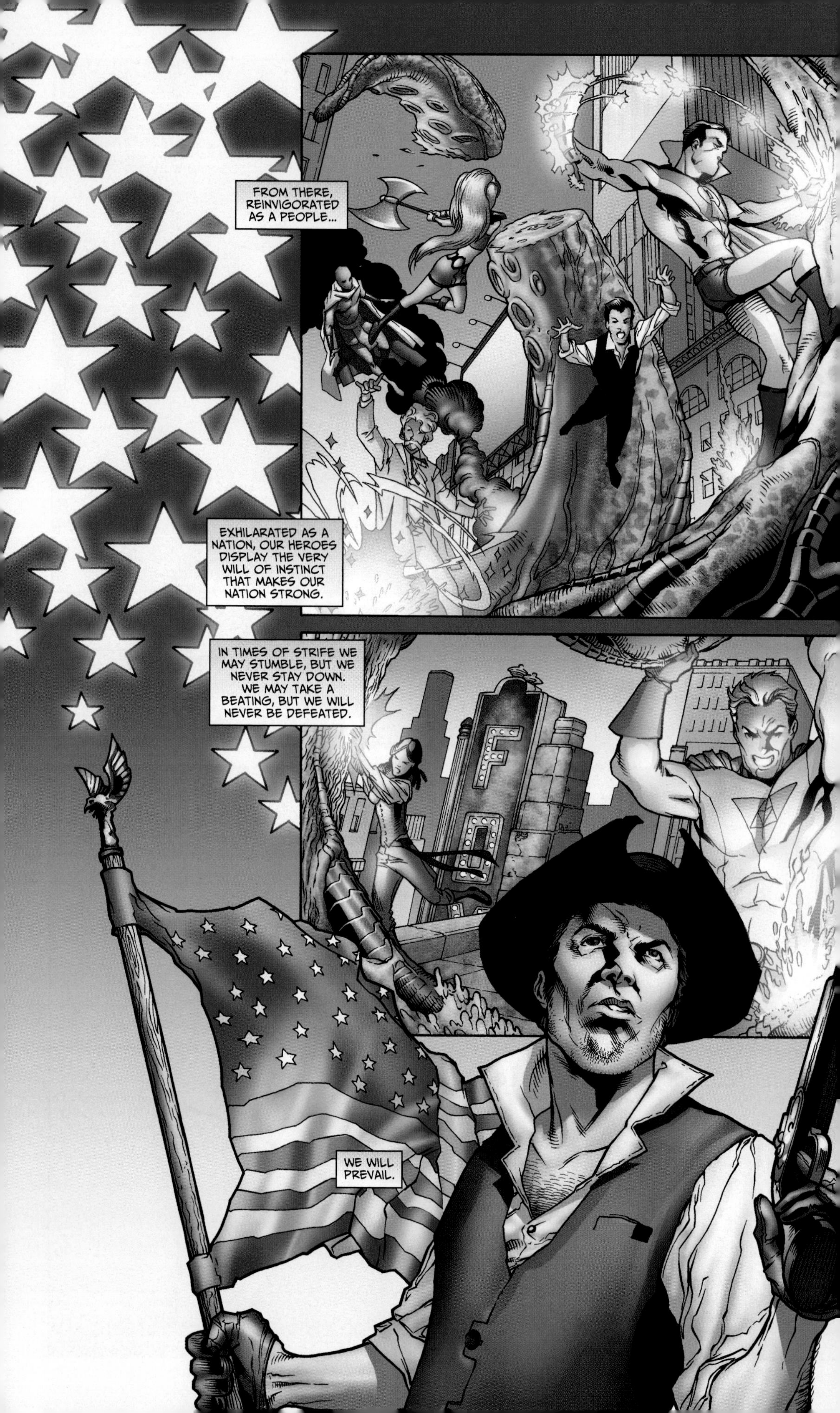
FROM THERE, REINVIGORATED AS A PEOPLE...
EXHILARATED AS A NATION, OUR HEROES DISPLAY THE VERY WILL OF INSTINCT THAT MAKES OUR NATION STRONG.
IN TIMES OF STRIFE WE MAY STUMBLE, BUT WE NEVER STAY DOWN. WE MAY TAKE A BEATING, BUT WE WILL NEVER BE DEFEATED.
WE WILL PREVAIL.

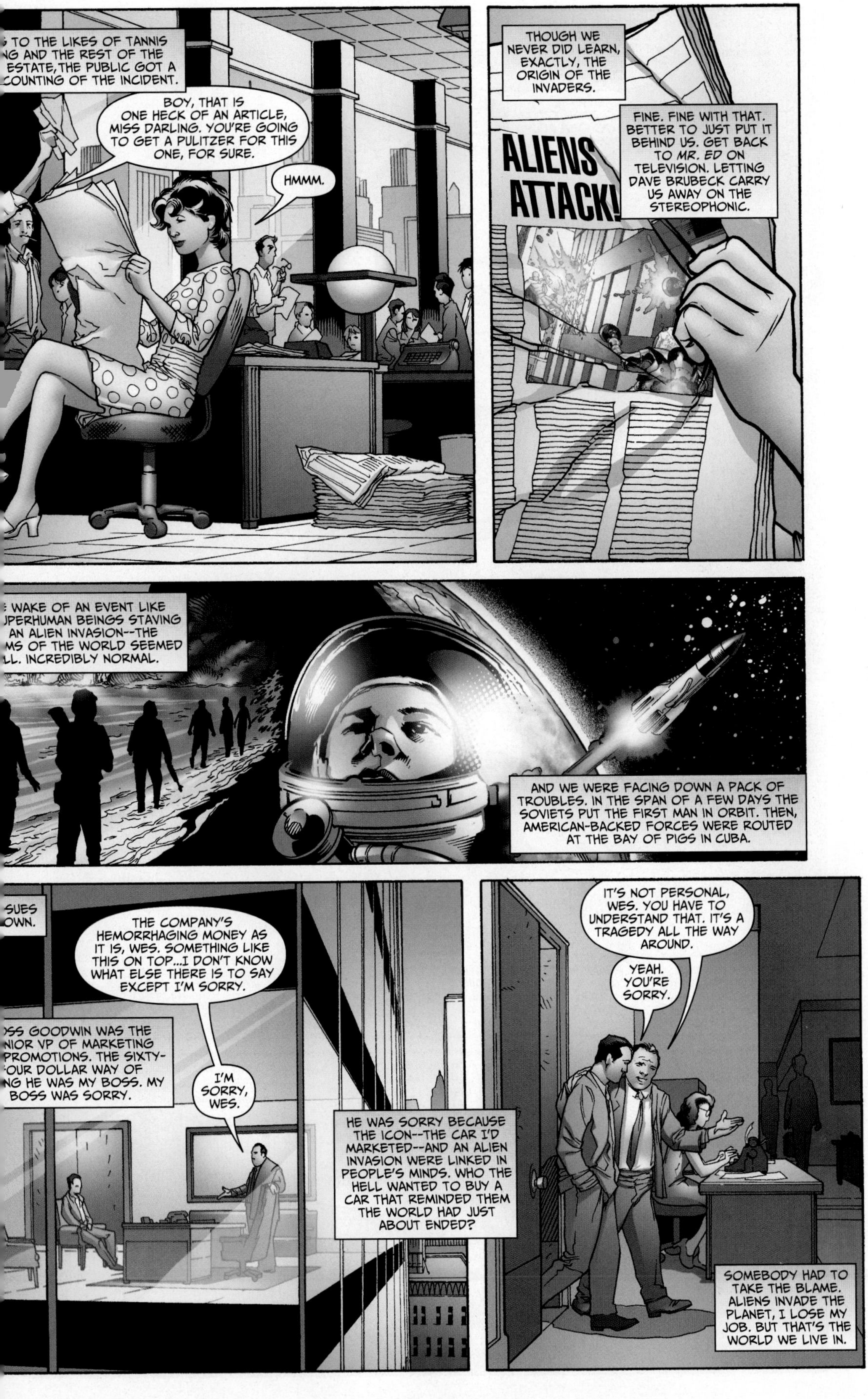

TO THE LIKES OF TANNIS
G AND THE REST OF THE
ESTATE, THE PUBLIC GOT A
COUNTING OF THE INCIDENT.
BOY, THAT IS ONE HECK OF AN ARTICLE, MISS DARLING. YOU'RE GOING TO GET A PULITZER FOR THIS ONE, FOR SURE.
HMMM.
THOUGH WE NEVER DID LEARN, EXACTLY, THE ORIGIN OF THE INVADERS.
ALIENS ATTACK!
FINE. FINE WITH THAT. BETTER TO JUST PUT IT BEHIND US. GET BACK TO MR. ED ON TELEVISION. LETTING DAVE BRUBECK CARRY US AWAY ON THE STEREOPHONIC.
WAKE OF AN EVENT LIKE
UPERHUMAN BEINGS STAVING
AN ALIEN INVASION--THE
MS OF THE WORLD SEEMED
LL. INCREDIBLY NORMAL.
AND WE WERE FACING DOWN A PACK OF TROUBLES. IN THE SPAN OF A FEW DAYS THE SOVIETS PUT THE FIRST MAN IN ORBIT. THEN, AMERICAN-BACKED FORCES WERE ROUTED AT THE BAY OF PIGS IN CUBA.
SUES
OWN.
THE COMPANY'S HEMORRHAGING MONEY AS IT IS, WES. SOMETHING LIKE THIS ON TOP...I DON'T KNOW WHAT ELSE THERE IS TO SAY EXCEPT I'M SORRY.
OSS GOODWIN WAS THE
NIOR VP OF MARKETING
PROMOTIONS. THE SIXTY-
FOUR DOLLAR WAY OF
NG HE WAS MY BOSS. MY
BOSS WAS SORRY.
I'M SORRY, WES.
HE WAS SORRY BECAUSE THE ICON--THE CAR I'D MARKETED--AND AN ALIEN INVASION WERE LINKED IN PEOPLE'S MINDS. WHO THE HELL WANTED TO BUY A CAR THAT REMINDED THEM THE WORLD HAD JUST ABOUT ENDED?
IT'S NOT PERSONAL, WES. YOU HAVE TO UNDERSTAND THAT. IT'S A TRAGEDY ALL THE WAY AROUND.
YEAH. YOU'RE SORRY.
SOMEBODY HAD TO TAKE THE BLAME. ALIENS INVADE THE PLANET, I LOSE MY JOB. BUT THAT'S THE WORLD WE LIVE IN.

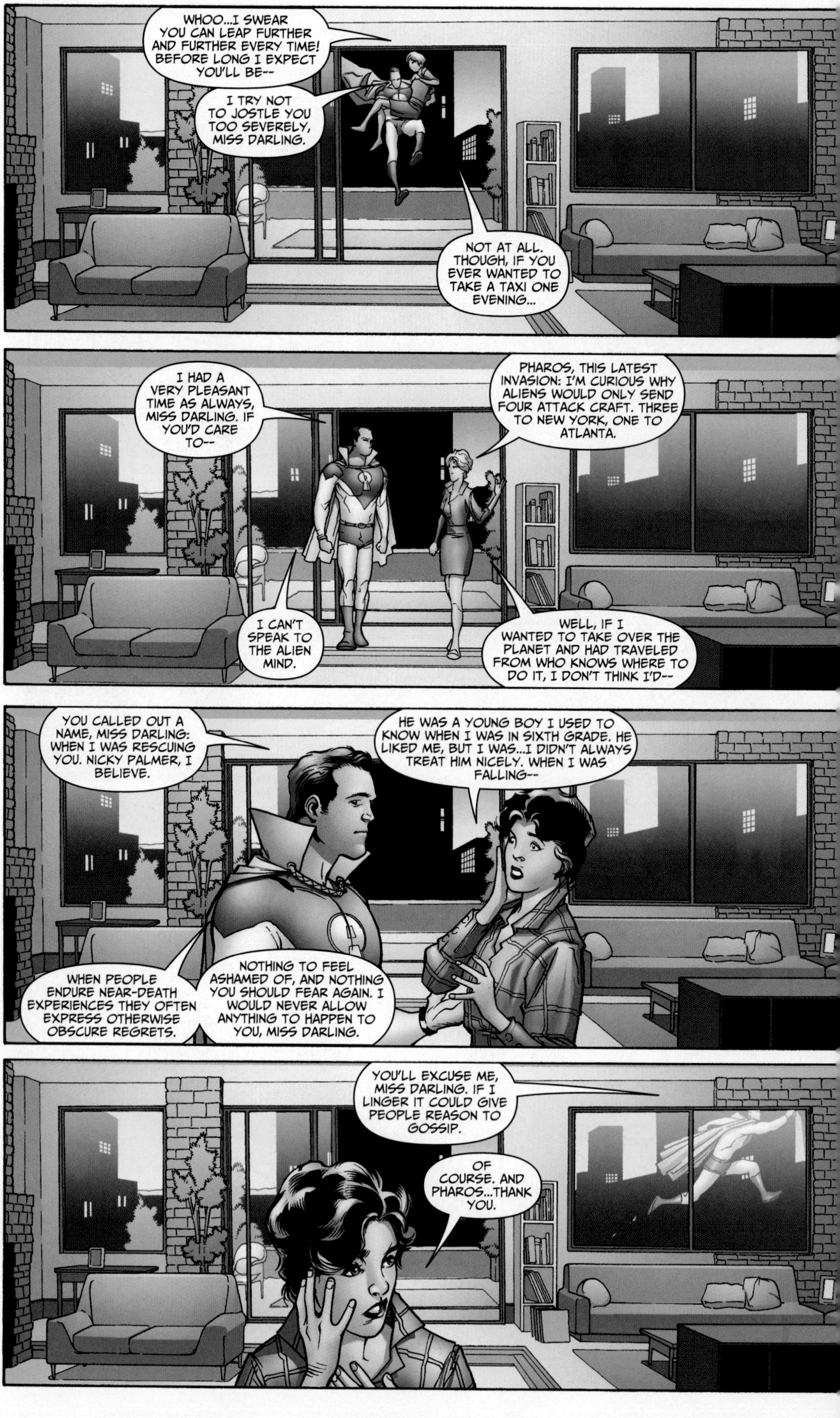
WHOO...I SWEAR YOU CAN LEAP FURTHER AND FURTHER EVERY TIME! BEFORE LONG I EXPECT YOU'LL BE--
I TRY NOT TO JOSTLE YOU TOO SEVERELY, MISS DARLING.
NOT AT ALL. THOUGH, IF YOU EVER WANTED TO TAKE A TAXI ONE EVENING...
I HAD A VERY PLEASANT TIME AS ALWAYS, MISS DARLING. IF YOU'D CARE TO--
PHAROS, THIS LATEST INVASION: I'M CURIOUS WHY ALIENS WOULD ONLY SEND FOUR ATTACK CRAFT. THREE TO NEW YORK, ONE TO ATLANTA.
I CAN'T SPEAK TO THE ALIEN MIND.
WELL, IF I WANTED TO TAKE OVER THE PLANET AND HAD TRAVELED FROM WHO KNOWS WHERE TO DO IT, I DON'T THINK I'D--
YOU CALLED OUT A NAME, MISS DARLING: WHEN I WAS RESCUING YOU. NICKY PALMER, I BELIEVE.
HE WAS A YOUNG BOY I USED TO KNOW WHEN I WAS IN SIXTH GRADE. HE LIKED ME, BUT I WAS...I DIDN'T ALWAYS TREAT HIM NICELY. WHEN I WAS FALLING--
WHEN PEOPLE ENDURE NEAR-DEATH EXPERIENCES THEY OFTEN EXPRESS OTHERWISE OBSCURE REGRETS.
NOTHING TO FEEL ASHAMED OF, AND NOTHING YOU SHOULD FEAR AGAIN. I WOULD NEVER ALLOW ANYTHING TO HAPPEN TO YOU, MISS DARLING.
YOU'LL EXCUSE ME, MISS DARLING. IF I LINGER IT COULD GIVE PEOPLE REASON TO GOSSIP.
OF COURSE. AND PHAROS...THANK YOU.

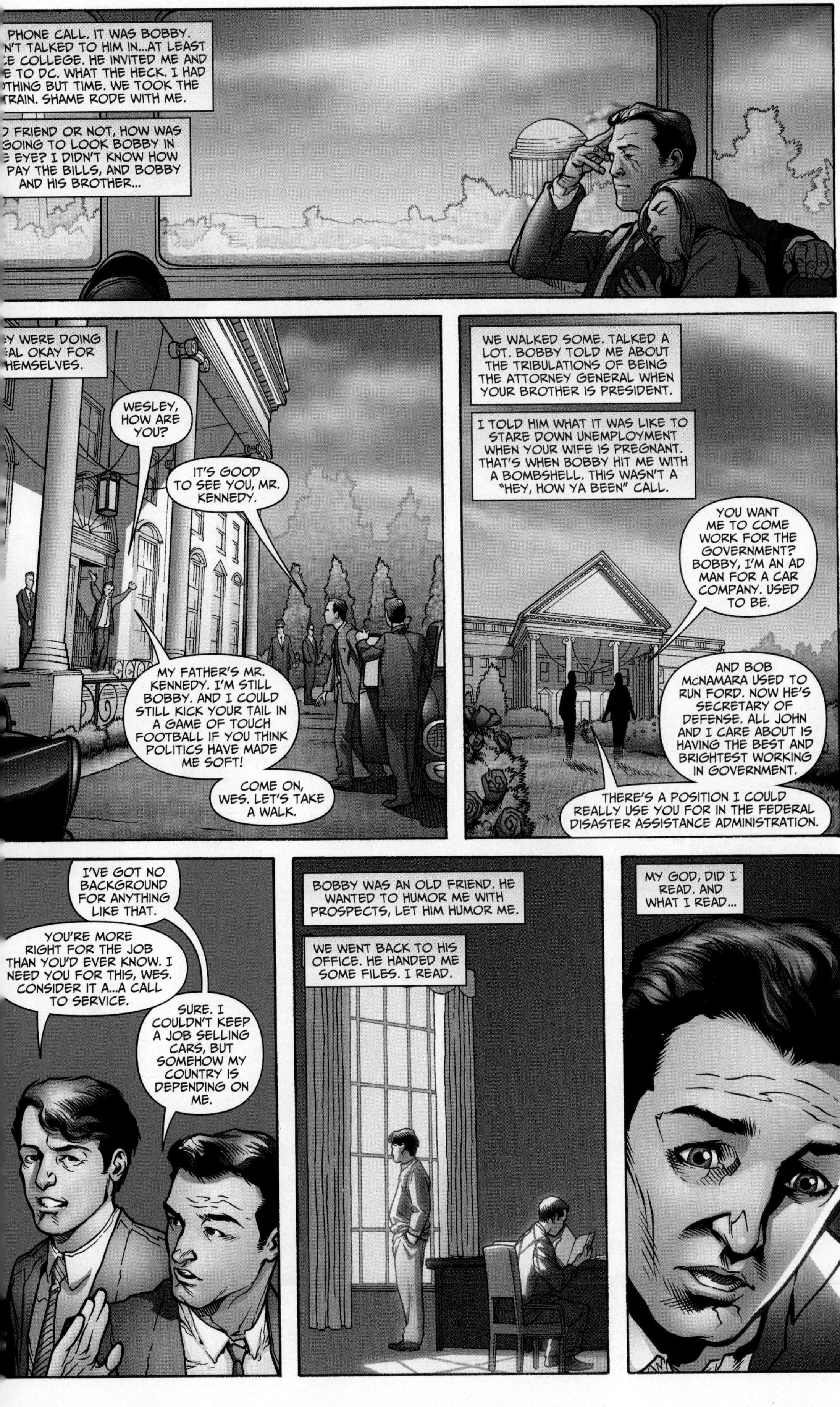

PHONE CALL. IT WAS BOBBY. N'T TALKED TO HIM IN...AT LEAST CE COLLEGE. HE INVITED ME AND E TO DC. WHAT THE HECK. I HAD OTHING BUT TIME. WE TOOK THE TRAIN. SHAME RODE WITH ME.
D FRIEND OR NOT, HOW WAS GOING TO LOOK BOBBY IN E EYE? I DIDN'T KNOW HOW PAY THE BILLS, AND BOBBY AND HIS BROTHER...
EY WERE DOING EAL OKAY FOR HEMSELVES.
WESLEY, HOW ARE YOU?
IT'S GOOD TO SEE YOU, MR. KENNEDY.
MY FATHER'S MR. KENNEDY. I'M STILL BOBBY. AND I COULD STILL KICK YOUR TAIL IN A GAME OF TOUCH FOOTBALL IF YOU THINK POLITICS HAVE MADE ME SOFT!
COME ON, WES. LET'S TAKE A WALK.
WE WALKED SOME. TALKED A LOT. BOBBY TOLD ME ABOUT THE TRIBULATIONS OF BEING THE ATTORNEY GENERAL WHEN YOUR BROTHER IS PRESIDENT.
I TOLD HIM WHAT IT WAS LIKE TO STARE DOWN UNEMPLOYMENT WHEN YOUR WIFE IS PREGNANT. THAT'S WHEN BOBBY HIT ME WITH A BOMBSHELL. THIS WASN'T A "HEY, HOW YA BEEN" CALL.
YOU WANT ME TO COME WORK FOR THE GOVERNMENT? BOBBY, I'M AN AD MAN FOR A CAR COMPANY. USED TO BE.
AND BOB McNAMARA USED TO RUN FORD. NOW HE'S SECRETARY OF DEFENSE. ALL JOHN AND I CARE ABOUT IS HAVING THE BEST AND BRIGHTEST WORKING IN GOVERNMENT.
THERE'S A POSITION I COULD REALLY USE YOU FOR IN THE FEDERAL DISASTER ASSISTANCE ADMINISTRATION.
I'VE GOT NO BACKGROUND FOR ANYTHING LIKE THAT.
YOU'RE MORE RIGHT FOR THE JOB THAN YOU'D EVER KNOW. I NEED YOU FOR THIS, WES. CONSIDER IT A...A CALL TO SERVICE.
SURE. I COULDN'T KEEP A JOB SELLING CARS, BUT SOMEHOW MY COUNTRY IS DEPENDING ON ME.
BOBBY WAS AN OLD FRIEND. HE WANTED TO HUMOR ME WITH PROSPECTS, LET HIM HUMOR ME.
WE WENT BACK TO HIS OFFICE. HE HANDED ME SOME FILES. I READ.
MY GOD, DID I READ. AND WHAT I READ...

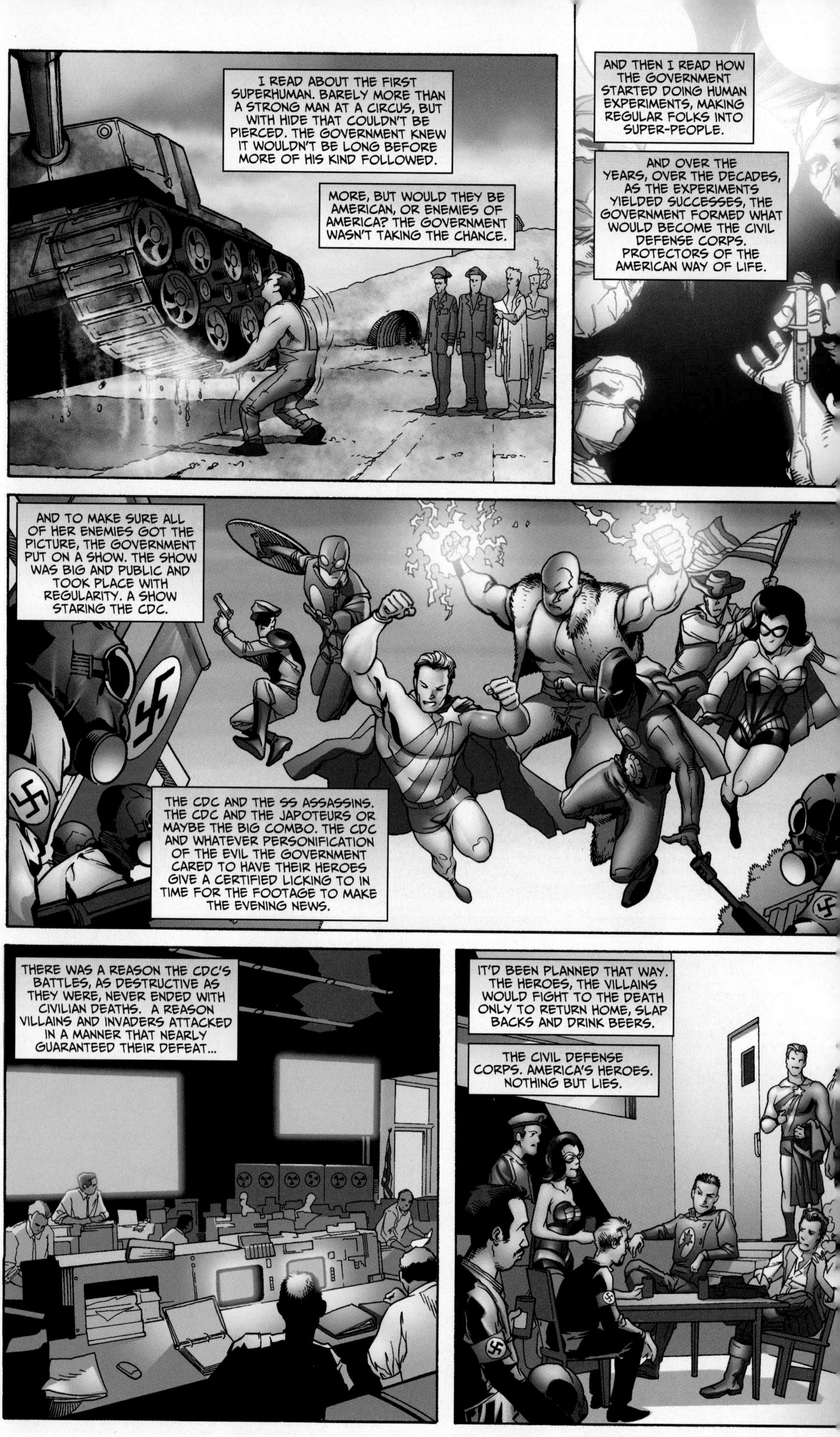
I READ ABOUT THE FIRST SUPERHUMAN. BARELY MORE THAN A STRONG MAN AT A CIRCUS, BUT WITH HIDE THAT COULDN'T BE PIERCED. THE GOVERNMENT KNEW IT WOULDN'T BE LONG BEFORE MORE OF HIS KIND FOLLOWED.
MORE, BUT WOULD THEY BE AMERICAN, OR ENEMIES OF AMERICA? THE GOVERNMENT WASN'T TAKING THE CHANCE.
AND THEN I READ HOW THE GOVERNMENT STARTED DOING HUMAN EXPERIMENTS, MAKING REGULAR FOLKS INTO SUPER-PEOPLE.
AND OVER THE YEARS, OVER THE DECADES, AS THE EXPERIMENTS YIELDED SUCCESSES, THE GOVERNMENT FORMED WHAT WOULD BECOME THE CIVIL DEFENSE CORPS. PROTECTORS OF THE AMERICAN WAY OF LIFE.
AND TO MAKE SURE ALL OF HER ENEMIES GOT THE PICTURE, THE GOVERNMENT PUT ON A SHOW. THE SHOW WAS BIG AND PUBLIC AND TOOK PLACE WITH REGULARITY. A SHOW STARING THE CDC.
THE CDC AND THE SS ASSASSINS. THE CDC AND THE JAPOTEURS OR MAYBE THE BIG COMBO. THE CDC AND WHATEVER PERSONIFICATION OF THE EVIL THE GOVERNMENT CARED TO HAVE THEIR HEROES GIVE A CERTIFIED LICKING TO IN TIME FOR THE FOOTAGE TO MAKE THE EVENING NEWS.
THERE WAS A REASON THE CDC'S BATTLES, AS DESTRUCTIVE AS THEY WERE, NEVER ENDED WITH CIVILIAN DEATHS. A REASON VILLAINS AND INVADERS ATTACKED IN A MANNER THAT NEARLY GUARANTEED THEIR DEFEAT...
IT'D BEEN PLANNED THAT WAY. THE HEROES, THE VILLAINS WOULD FIGHT TO THE DEATH ONLY TO RETURN HOME, SLAP BACKS AND DRINK BEERS.
THE CIVIL DEFENSE CORPS. AMERICA'S HEROES. NOTHING BUT LIES.

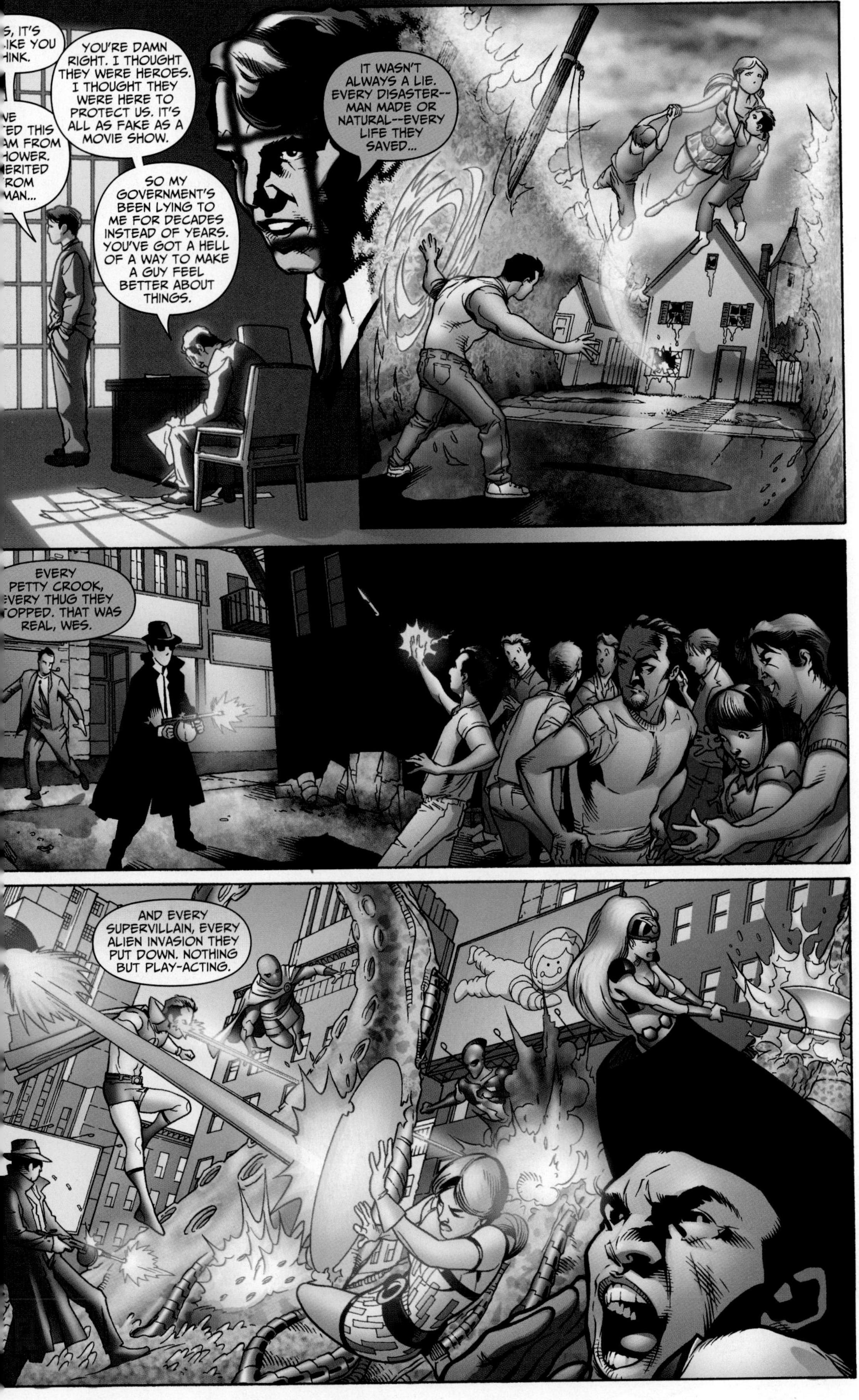
S, IT'S IKE YOU HINK.
WE TED THIS AM FROM HOWER. ERITED FROM MAN...
YOU'RE DAMN RIGHT. I THOUGHT THEY WERE HEROES. I THOUGHT THEY WERE HERE TO PROTECT US. IT'S ALL AS FAKE AS A MOVIE SHOW.
SO MY GOVERNMENT'S BEEN LYING TO ME FOR DECADES INSTEAD OF YEARS. YOU'VE GOT A HELL OF A WAY TO MAKE A GUY FEEL BETTER ABOUT THINGS.
IT WASN'T ALWAYS A LIE. EVERY DISASTER-- MAN MADE OR NATURAL--EVERY LIFE THEY SAVED...
EVERY PETTY CROOK, EVERY THUG THEY TOPPED. THAT WAS REAL, WES.
AND EVERY SUPERVILLAIN, EVERY ALIEN INVASION THEY PUT DOWN. NOTHING BUT PLAY-ACTING.

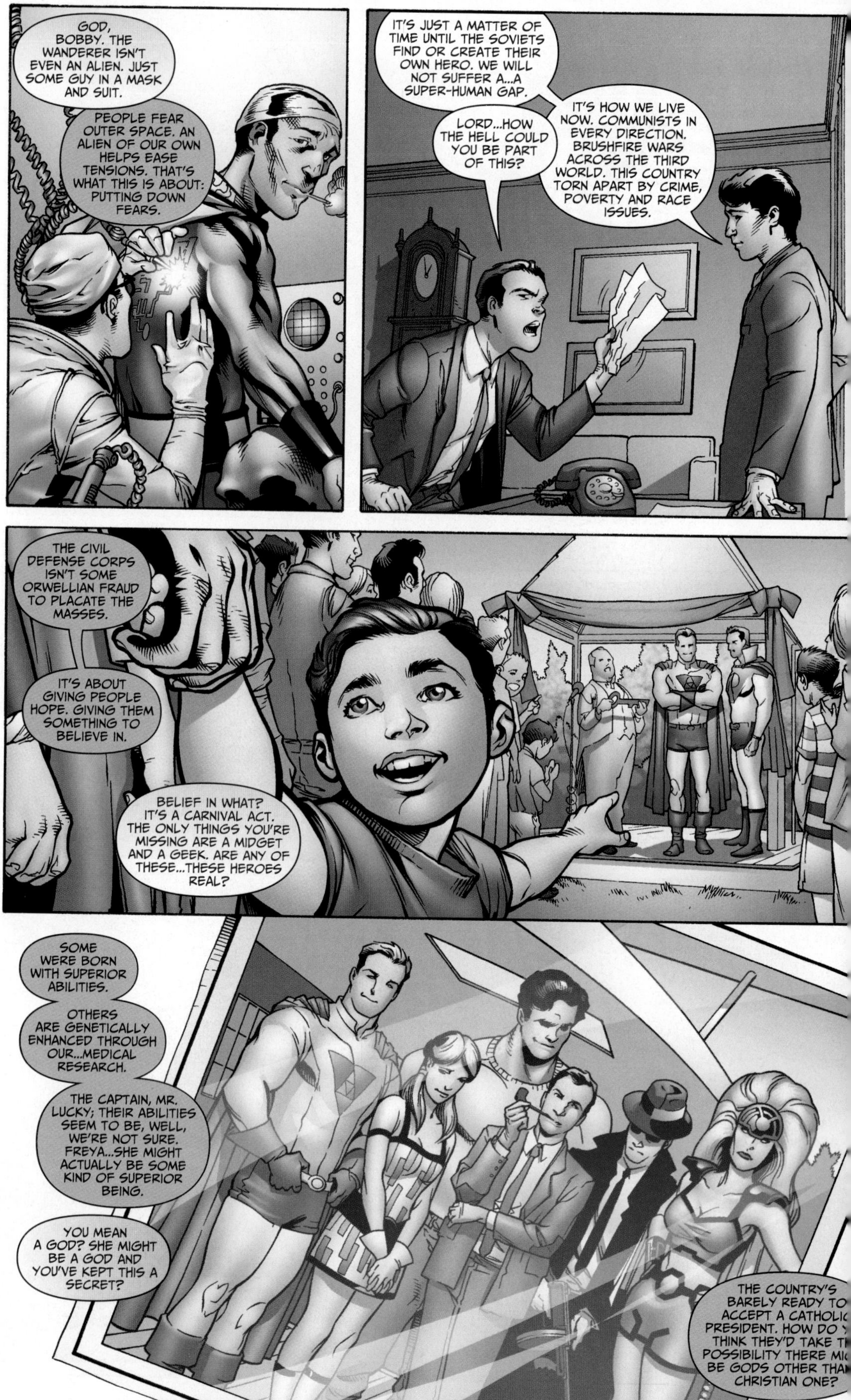

GOD, BOBBY. THE WANDERER ISN'T EVEN AN ALIEN. JUST SOME GUY IN A MASK AND SUIT.
PEOPLE FEAR OUTER SPACE. AN ALIEN OF OUR OWN HELPS EASE TENSIONS. THAT'S WHAT THIS IS ABOUT: PUTTING DOWN FEARS.
IT'S JUST A MATTER OF TIME UNTIL THE SOVIETS FIND OR CREATE THEIR OWN HERO. WE WILL NOT SUFFER A...A SUPER-HUMAN GAP.
LORD...HOW THE HELL COULD YOU BE PART OF THIS?
IT'S HOW WE LIVE NOW. COMMUNISTS IN EVERY DIRECTION. BRUSHFIRE WARS ACROSS THE THIRD WORLD. THIS COUNTRY TORN APART BY CRIME, POVERTY AND RACE ISSUES.
THE CIVIL DEFENSE CORPS ISN'T SOME ORWELLIAN FRAUD TO PLACATE THE MASSES.
IT'S ABOUT GIVING PEOPLE HOPE. GIVING THEM SOMETHING TO BELIEVE IN.
BELIEF IN WHAT? IT'S A CARNIVAL ACT. THE ONLY THINGS YOU'RE MISSING ARE A MIDGET AND A GEEK. ARE ANY OF THESE...THESE HEROES REAL?
SOME WERE BORN WITH SUPERIOR ABILITIES.
OTHERS ARE GENETICALLY ENHANCED THROUGH OUR...MEDICAL RESEARCH.
THE CAPTAIN, MR. LUCKY; THEIR ABILITIES SEEM TO BE, WELL, WE'RE NOT SURE. FREYA...SHE MIGHT ACTUALLY BE SOME KIND OF SUPERIOR BEING.
YOU MEAN A GOD? SHE MIGHT BE A GOD AND YOU'VE KEPT THIS A SECRET?
THE COUNTRY'S BARELY READY TO ACCEPT A CATHOLIC PRESIDENT. HOW DO Y THINK THEY'D TAKE T POSSIBILITY THERE MI BE GODS OTHER THA CHRISTIAN ONE?

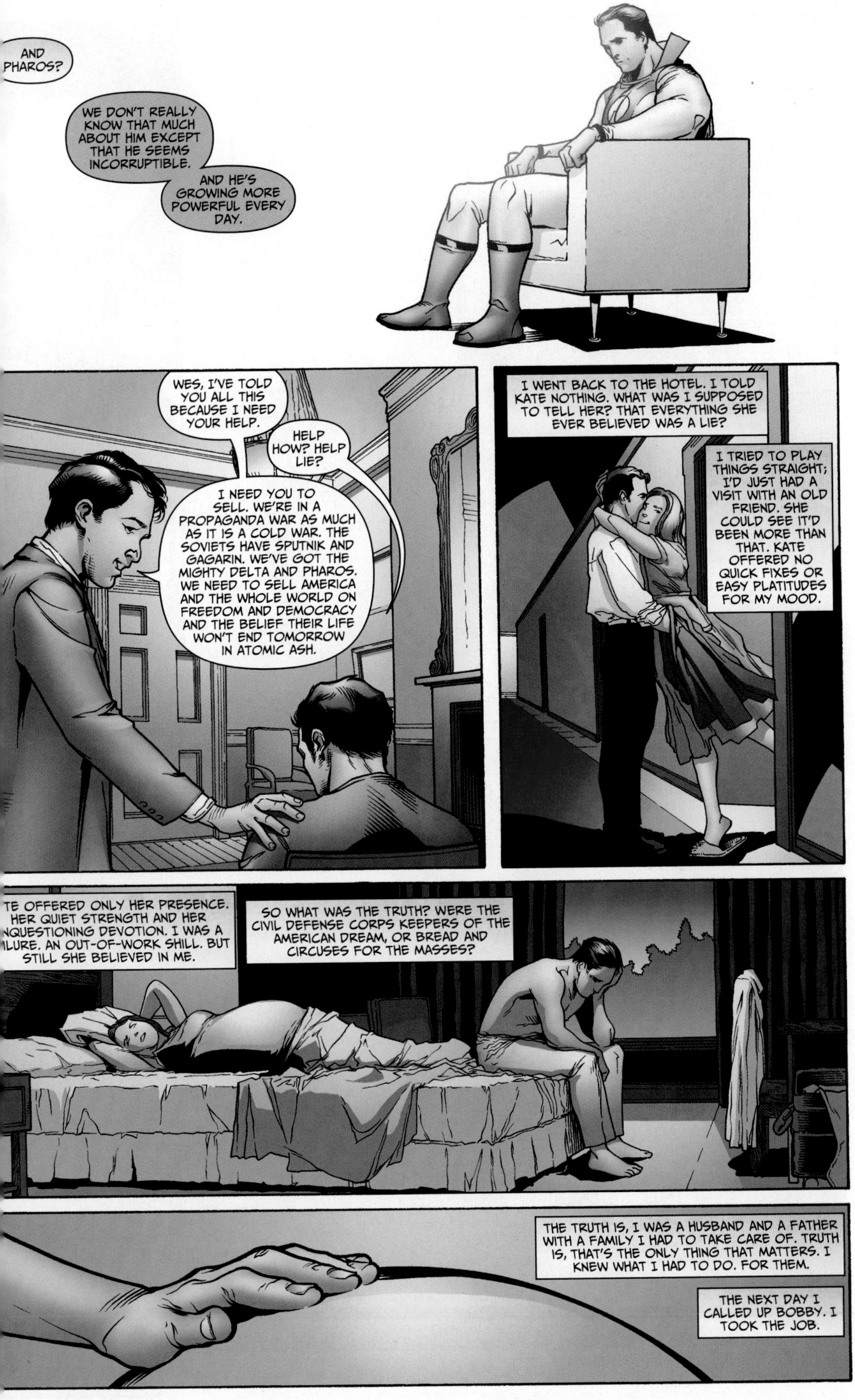
AND PHAROS?
WE DON'T REALLY KNOW THAT MUCH ABOUT HIM EXCEPT THAT HE SEEMS INCORRUPTIBLE.
AND HE'S GROWING MORE POWERFUL EVERY DAY.
WES, I'VE TOLD YOU ALL THIS BECAUSE I NEED YOUR HELP.
HELP HOW? HELP LIE?
I NEED YOU TO SELL. WE'RE IN A PROPAGANDA WAR AS MUCH AS IT IS A COLD WAR. THE SOVIETS HAVE SPUTNIK AND GAGARIN. WE'VE GOT THE MIGHTY DELTA AND PHAROS. WE NEED TO SELL AMERICA AND THE WHOLE WORLD ON FREEDOM AND DEMOCRACY AND THE BELIEF THEIR LIFE WON'T END TOMORROW IN ATOMIC ASH.
I WENT BACK TO THE HOTEL. I TOLD KATE NOTHING. WHAT WAS I SUPPOSED TO TELL HER? THAT EVERYTHING SHE EVER BELIEVED WAS A LIE?
I TRIED TO PLAY THINGS STRAIGHT; I'D JUST HAD A VISIT WITH AN OLD FRIEND. SHE COULD SEE IT'D BEEN MORE THAN THAT. KATE OFFERED NO QUICK FIXES OR EASY PLATITUDES FOR MY MOOD.
TE OFFERED ONLY HER PRESENCE. HER QUIET STRENGTH AND HER NQUESTIONING DEVOTION. I WAS A ILURE. AN OUT-OF-WORK SHILL. BUT STILL SHE BELIEVED IN ME.
SO WHAT WAS THE TRUTH? WERE THE CIVIL DEFENSE CORPS KEEPERS OF THE AMERICAN DREAM, OR BREAD AND CIRCUSES FOR THE MASSES?
THE TRUTH IS, I WAS A HUSBAND AND A FATHER WITH A FAMILY I HAD TO TAKE CARE OF. TRUTH IS, THAT'S THE ONLY THING THAT MATTERS. I KNEW WHAT I HAD TO DO. FOR THEM.
THE NEXT DAY I CALLED UP BOBBY. I TOOK THE JOB.

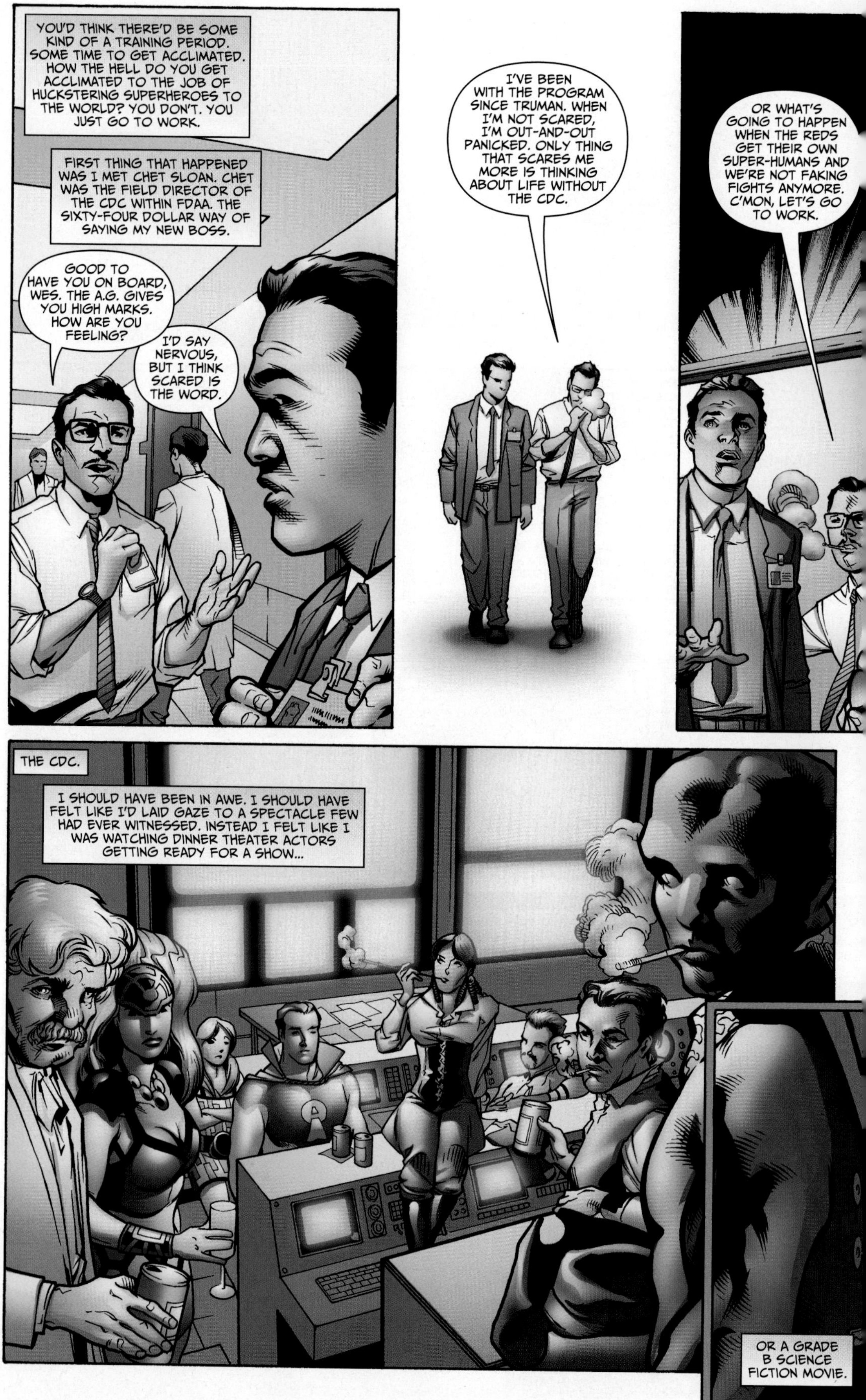
YOU'D THINK THERE'D BE SOME KIND OF A TRAINING PERIOD. SOME TIME TO GET ACCLIMATED. HOW THE HELL DO YOU GET ACCLIMATED TO THE JOB OF HUCKSTERING SUPERHEROES TO THE WORLD? YOU DON'T. YOU JUST GO TO WORK.
FIRST THING THAT HAPPENED WAS I MET CHET SLOAN. CHET WAS THE FIELD DIRECTOR OF THE CDC WITHIN FDAA. THE SIXTY-FOUR DOLLAR WAY OF SAYING MY NEW BOSS.
GOOD TO HAVE YOU ON BOARD, WES. THE A.G. GIVES YOU HIGH MARKS. HOW ARE YOU FEELING?
I'D SAY NERVOUS, BUT I THINK SCARED IS THE WORD.
I'VE BEEN WITH THE PROGRAM SINCE TRUMAN. WHEN I'M NOT SCARED, I'M OUT-AND-OUT PANICKED. ONLY THING THAT SCARES ME MORE IS THINKING ABOUT LIFE WITHOUT THE CDC.
OR WHAT'S GOING TO HAPPEN WHEN THE REDS GET THEIR OWN SUPER-HUMANS AND WE'RE NOT FAKING FIGHTS ANYMORE. C'MON, LET'S GO TO WORK.
THE CDC.
I SHOULD HAVE BEEN IN AWE. I SHOULD HAVE FELT LIKE I'D LAID GAZE TO A SPECTACLE FEW HAD EVER WITNESSED. INSTEAD I FELT LIKE I WAS WATCHING DINNER THEATER ACTORS GETTING READY FOR A SHOW...
OR A GRADE B SCIENCE FICTION MOVIE.

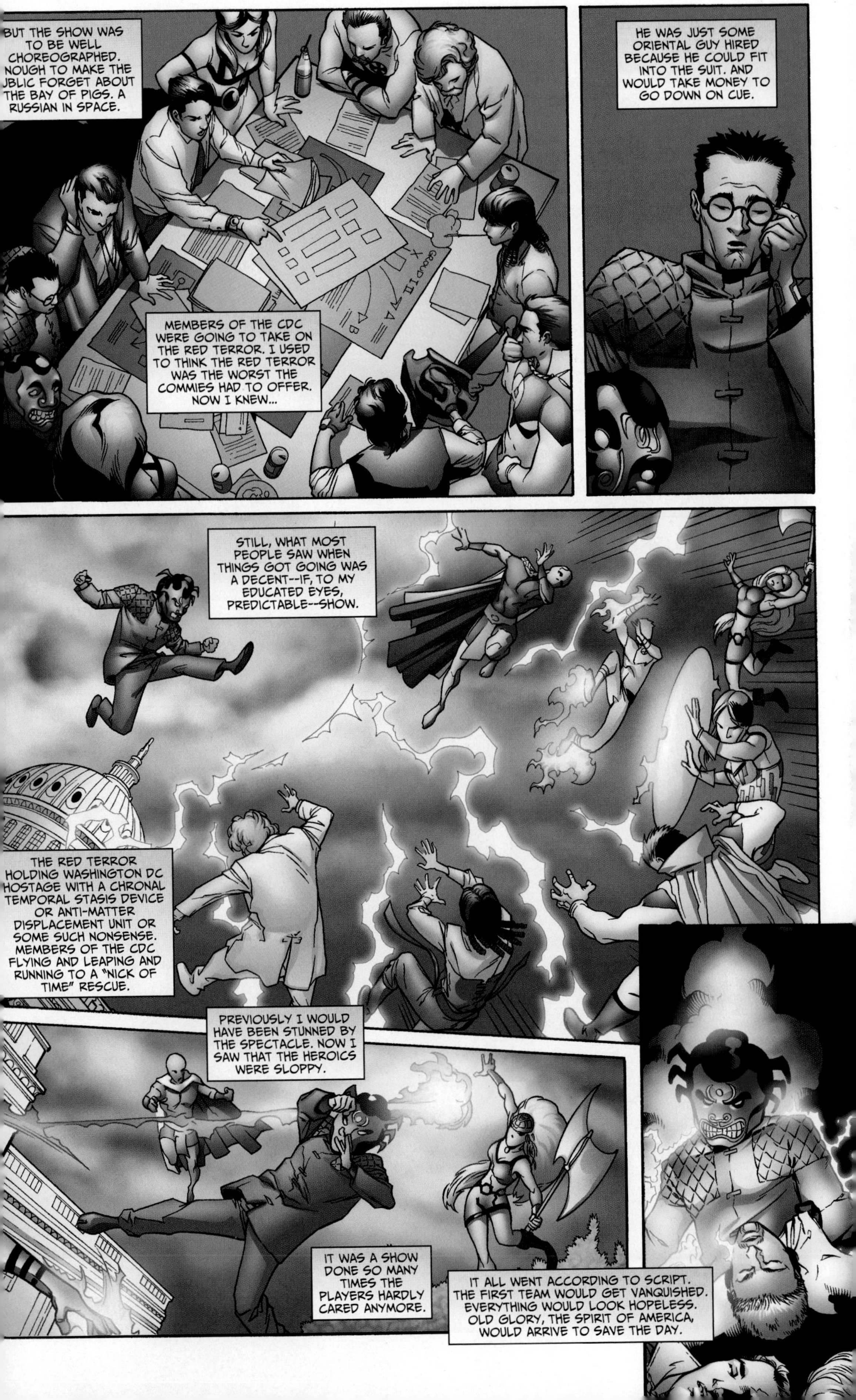
BUT THE SHOW WAS TO BE WELL CHOREOGRAPHED. NOUGH TO MAKE THE JBLIC FORGET ABOUT THE BAY OF PIGS. A RUSSIAN IN SPACE.
MEMBERS OF THE CDC WERE GOING TO TAKE ON THE RED TERROR. I USED TO THINK THE RED TERROR WAS THE WORST THE COMMIES HAD TO OFFER. NOW I KNEW...
HE WAS JUST SOME ORIENTAL GUY HIRED BECAUSE HE COULD FIT INTO THE SUIT. AND WOULD TAKE MONEY TO GO DOWN ON CUE.
STILL, WHAT MOST PEOPLE SAW WHEN THINGS GOT GOING WAS A DECENT--IF, TO MY EDUCATED EYES, PREDICTABLE--SHOW.
THE RED TERROR HOLDING WASHINGTON DC HOSTAGE WITH A CHRONAL TEMPORAL STASIS DEVICE OR ANTI-MATTER DISPLACEMENT UNIT OR SOME SUCH NONSENSE. MEMBERS OF THE CDC FLYING AND LEAPING AND RUNNING TO A "NICK OF TIME" RESCUE.
PREVIOUSLY I WOULD HAVE BEEN STUNNED BY THE SPECTACLE. NOW I SAW THAT THE HEROICS WERE SLOPPY.
IT WAS A SHOW DONE SO MANY TIMES THE PLAYERS HARDLY CARED ANYMORE.
IT ALL WENT ACCORDING TO SCRIPT. THE FIRST TEAM WOULD GET VANQUISHED. EVERYTHING WOULD LOOK HOPELESS. OLD GLORY, THE SPIRIT OF AMERICA, WOULD ARRIVE TO SAVE THE DAY.

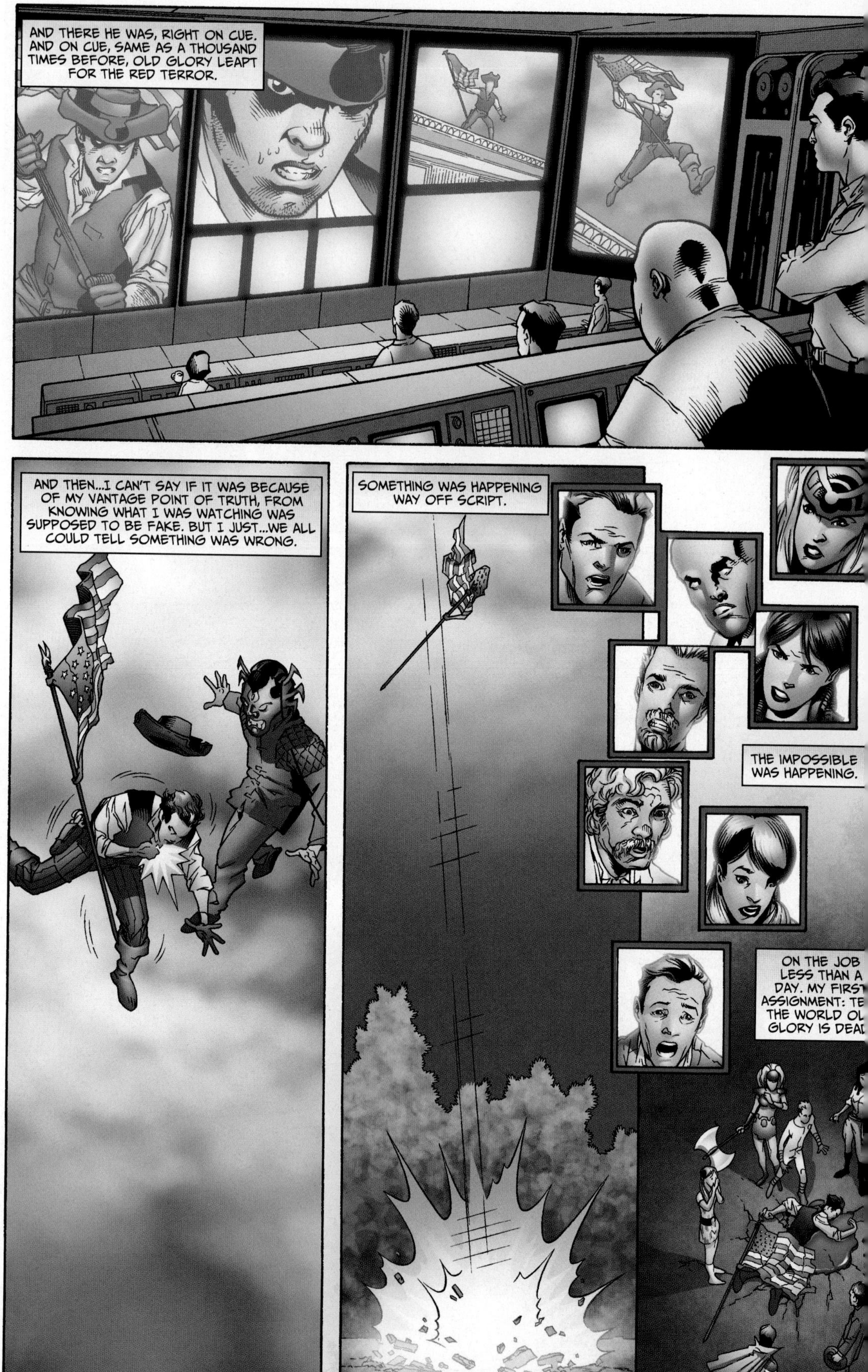
AND THERE HE WAS, RIGHT ON CUE. AND ON CUE, SAME AS A THOUSAND TIMES BEFORE, OLD GLORY LEAPT FOR THE RED TERROR.
AND THEN...I CAN'T SAY IF IT WAS BECAUSE OF MY VANTAGE POINT OF TRUTH, FROM KNOWING WHAT I WAS WATCHING WAS SUPPOSED TO BE FAKE. BUT I JUST...WE ALL COULD TELL SOMETHING WAS WRONG.
SOMETHING WAS HAPPENING WAY OFF SCRIPT.
THE IMPOSSIBLE WAS HAPPENING.
ON THE JOB LESS THAN A DAY. MY FIRS ASSIGNMENT: TE THE WORLD OL GLORY IS DEA

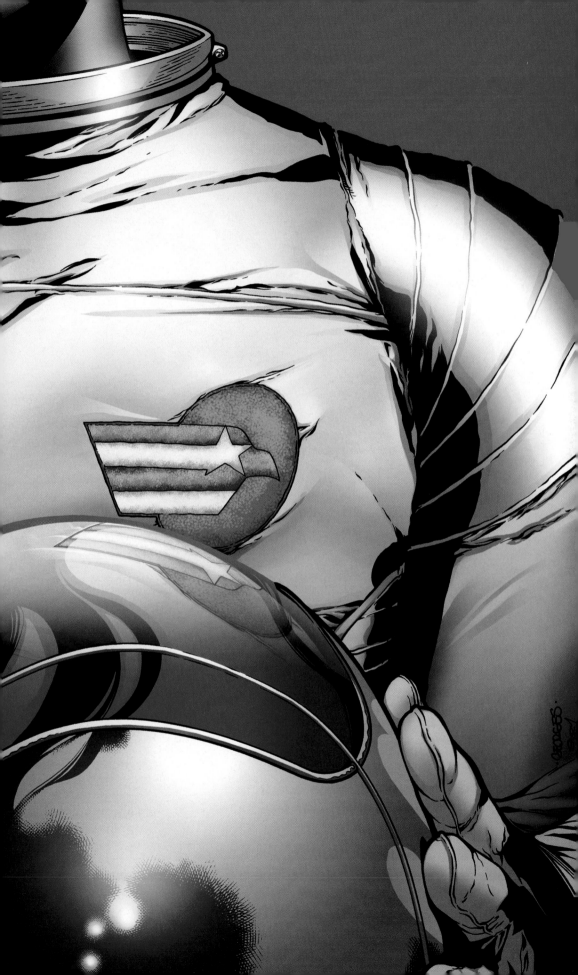

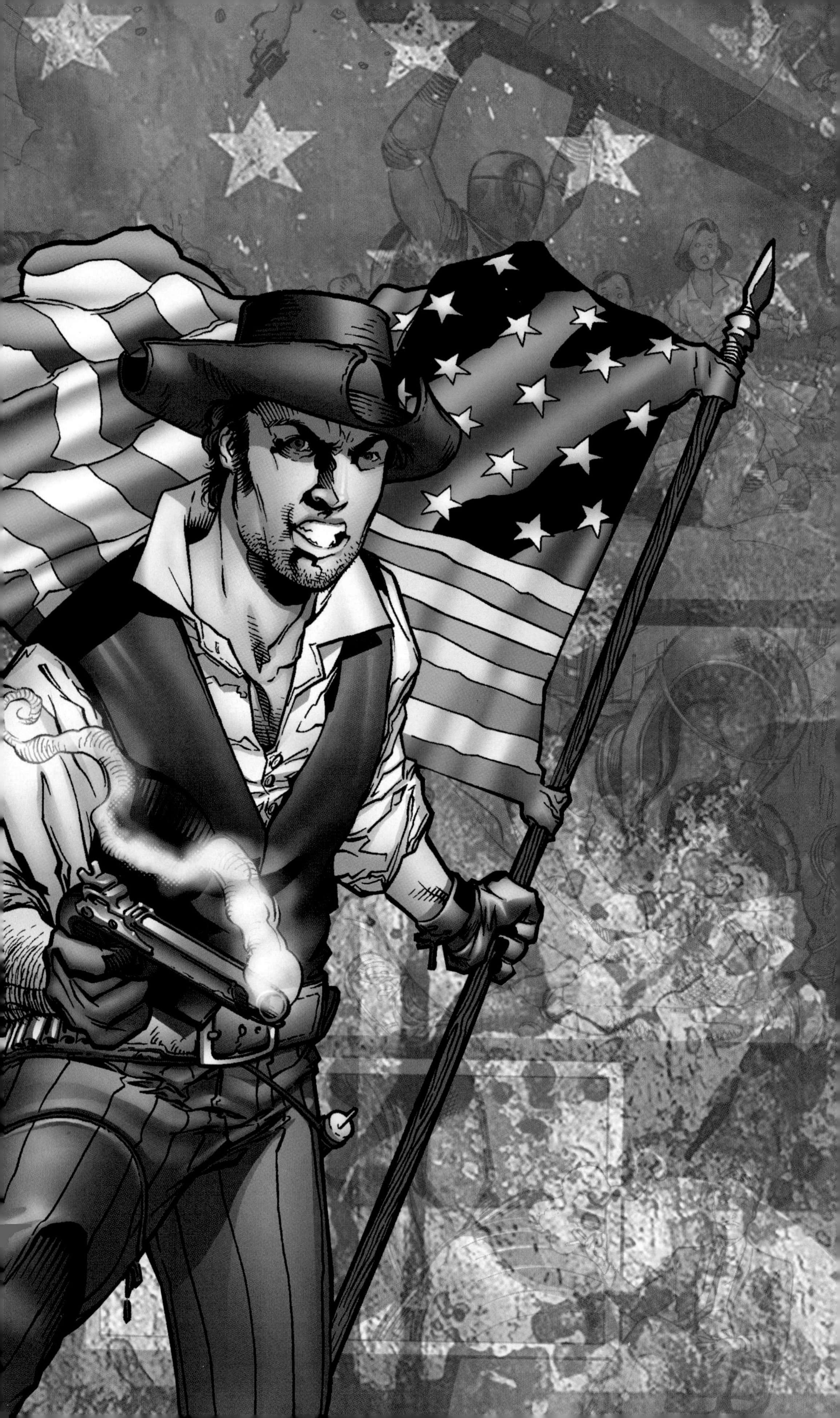

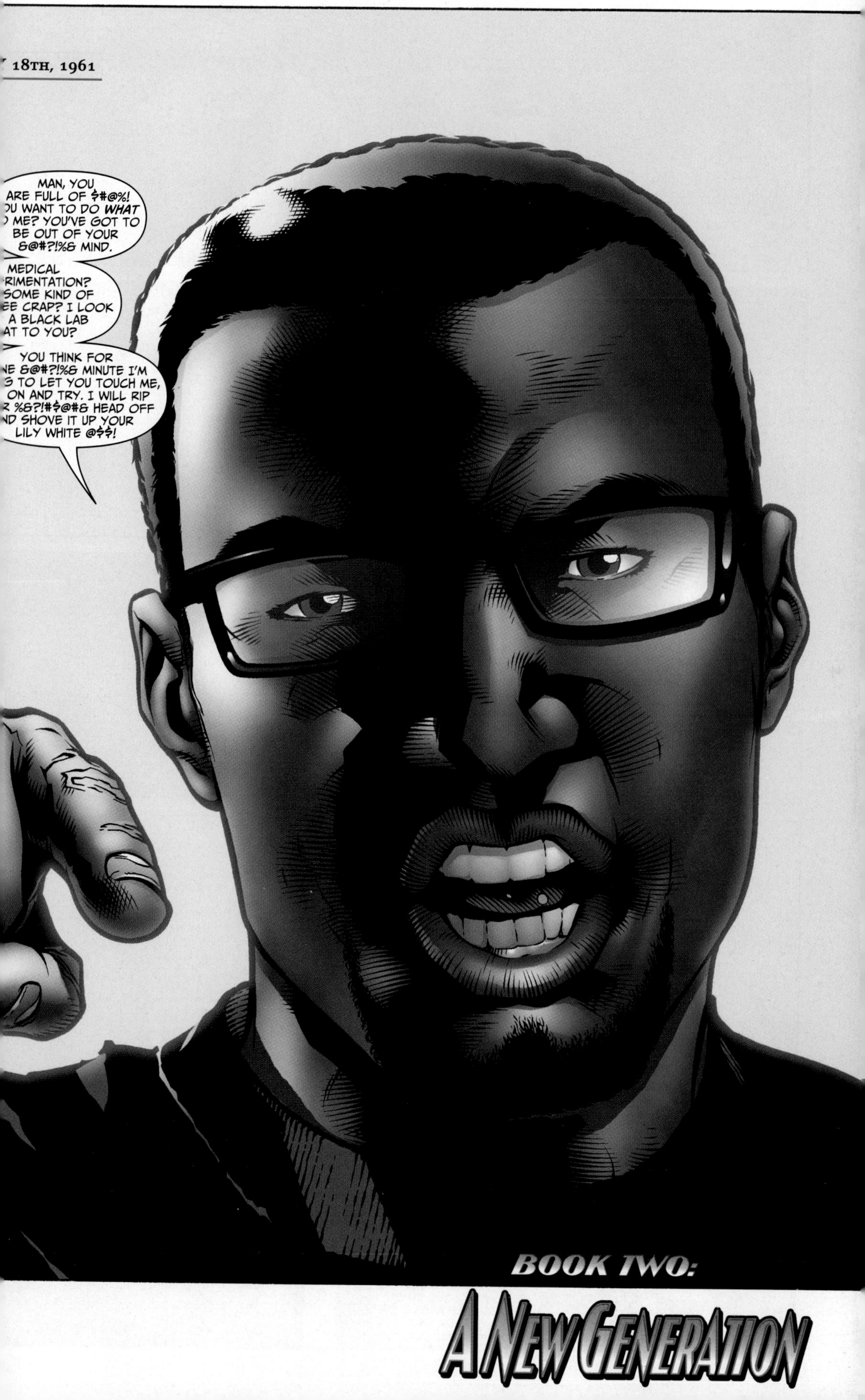
18TH, 1961
MAN, YOU ARE FULL OF $#@%! OU WANT TO DO WHAT) ME? YOU'VE GOT TO BE OUT OF YOUR &@#?!%& MIND.
MEDICAL RIMENTATION? SOME KIND OF EE CRAP? I LOOK A BLACK LAB AT TO YOU?
YOU THINK FOR NE &@#?!%& MINUTE I'M G TO LET YOU TOUCH ME, ON AND TRY. I WILL RIP R %&?!#$@#& HEAD OFF ND SHOVE IT UP YOUR LILY WHITE @$$!
BOOK TWO:
A NEW GENERATION

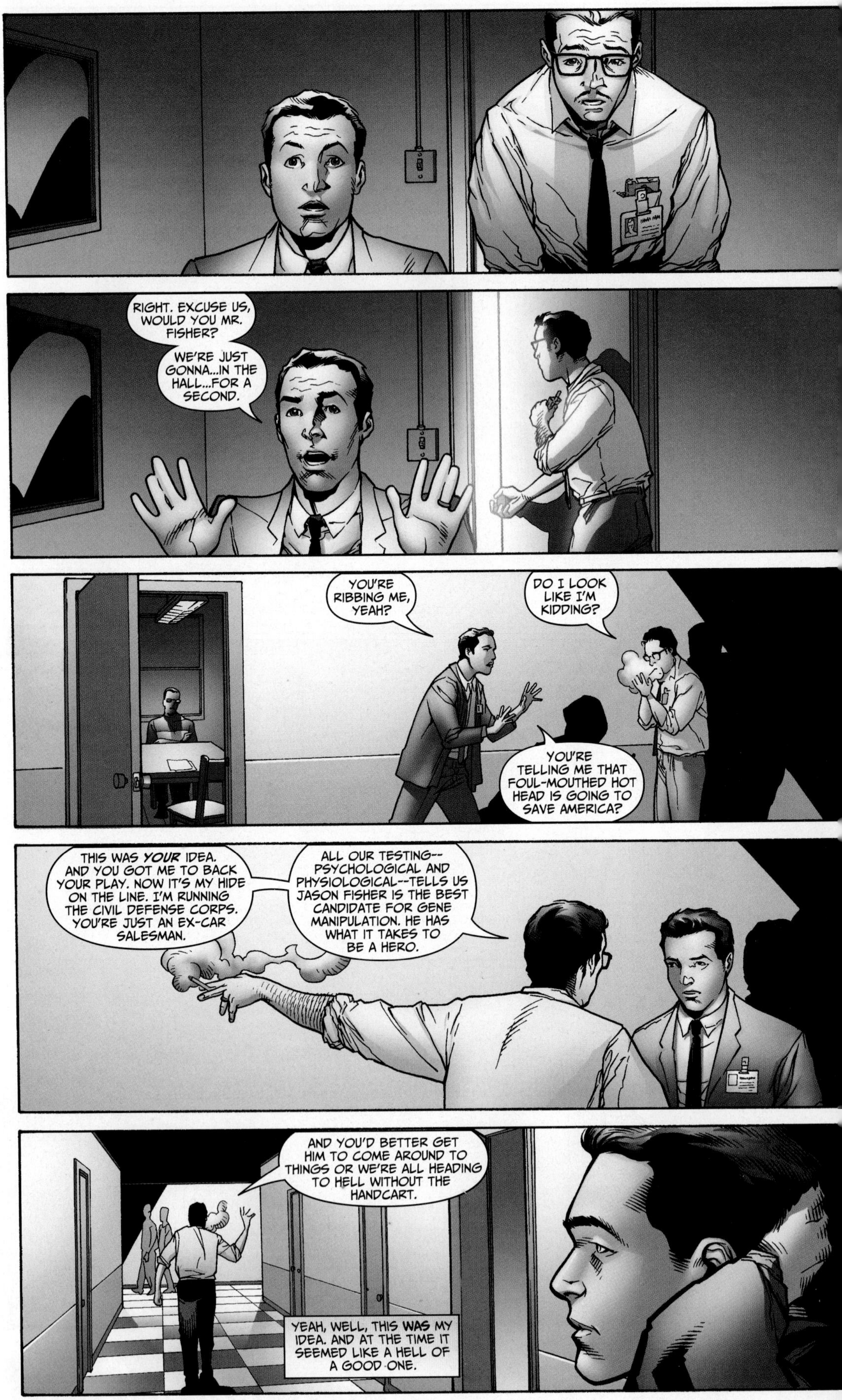
RIGHT. EXCUSE US, WOULD YOU MR. FISHER?
WE'RE JUST GONNA...IN THE HALL...FOR A SECOND.
YOU'RE RIBBING ME, YEAH?
DO I LOOK LIKE I'M KIDDING?
YOU'RE TELLING ME THAT FOUL-MOUTHED HOT HEAD IS GOING TO SAVE AMERICA?
ALL OUR TESTING--PSYCHOLOGICAL AND PHYSIOLOGICAL--TELLS US JASON FISHER IS THE BEST CANDIDATE FOR GENE MANIPULATION. HE HAS WHAT IT TAKES TO BE A HERO.
THIS WAS YOUR IDEA. AND YOU GOT ME TO BACK YOUR PLAY. NOW IT'S MY HIDE ON THE LINE. I'M RUNNING THE CIVIL DEFENSE CORPS. YOU'RE JUST AN EX-CAR SALESMAN.
AND YOU'D BETTER GET HIM TO COME AROUND TO THINGS OR WE'RE ALL HEADING TO HELL WITHOUT THE HANDCART.
YEAH, WELL, THIS WAS MY IDEA. AND AT THE TIME IT SEEMED LIKE A HELL OF A GOOD ONE.

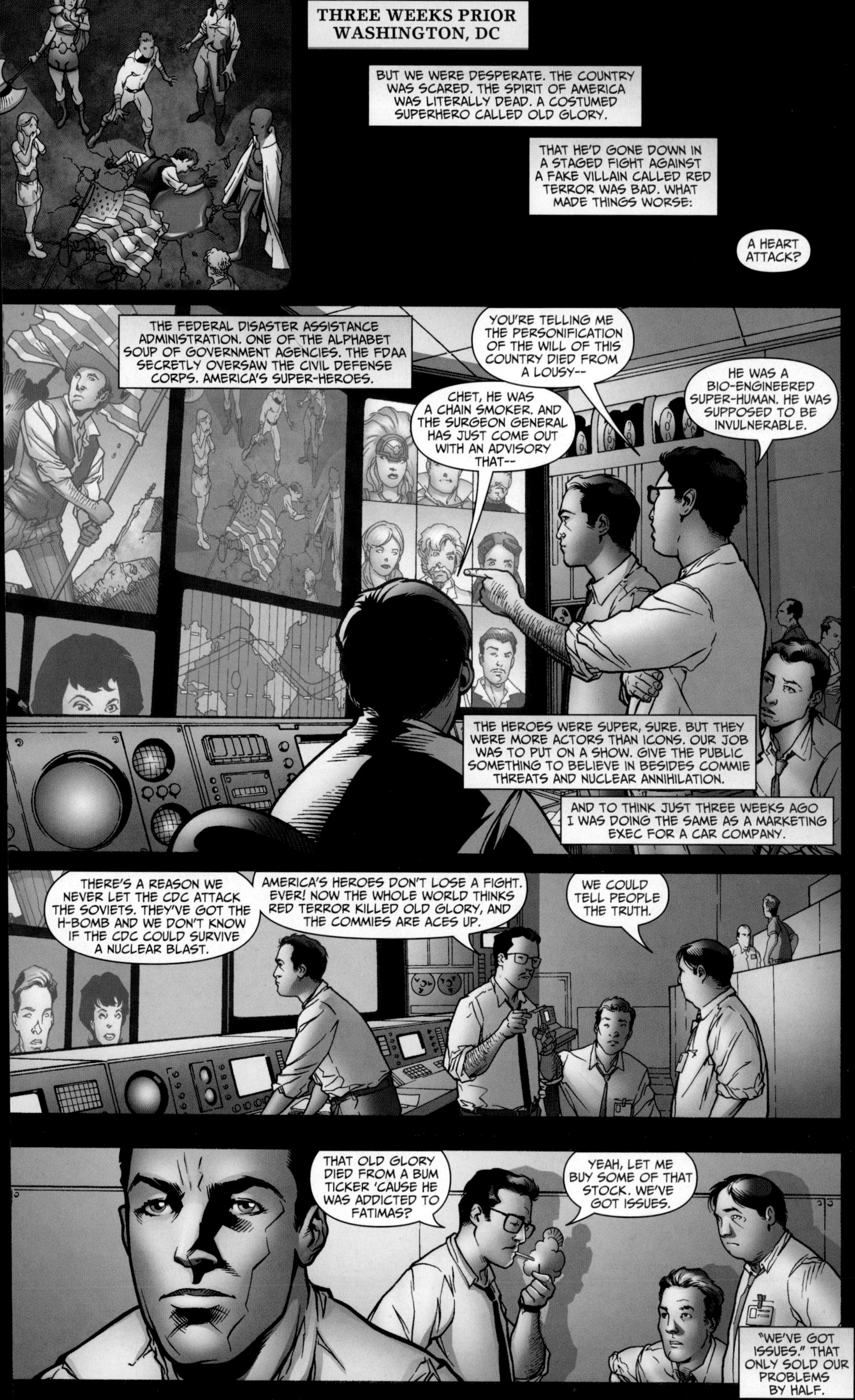
THREE WEEKS PRIOR
WASHINGTON, DC
BUT WE WERE DESPERATE. THE COUNTRY WAS SCARED. THE SPIRIT OF AMERICA WAS LITERALLY DEAD. A COSTUMED SUPERHERO CALLED OLD GLORY.
THAT HE'D GONE DOWN IN A STAGED FIGHT AGAINST A FAKE VILLAIN CALLED RED TERROR WAS BAD. WHAT MADE THINGS WORSE:
A HEART ATTACK?
THE FEDERAL DISASTER ASSISTANCE ADMINISTRATION. ONE OF THE ALPHABET SOUP OF GOVERNMENT AGENCIES. THE FDAA SECRETLY OVERSAW THE CIVIL DEFENSE CORPS. AMERICA'S SUPER-HEROES.
YOU'RE TELLING ME THE PERSONIFICATION OF THE WILL OF THIS COUNTRY DIED FROM A LOUSY--
CHET, HE WAS A CHAIN SMOKER. AND THE SURGEON GENERAL HAS JUST COME OUT WITH AN ADVISORY THAT--
HE WAS A BIO-ENGINEERED SUPER-HUMAN. HE WAS SUPPOSED TO BE INVULNERABLE.
THE HEROES WERE SUPER, SURE. BUT THEY WERE MORE ACTORS THAN ICONS. OUR JOB WAS TO PUT ON A SHOW. GIVE THE PUBLIC SOMETHING TO BELIEVE IN BESIDES COMMIE THREATS AND NUCLEAR ANNIHILATION.
AND TO THINK JUST THREE WEEKS AGO I WAS DOING THE SAME AS A MARKETING EXEC FOR A CAR COMPANY.
THERE'S A REASON WE NEVER LET THE CDC ATTACK THE SOVIETS. THEY'VE GOT THE H-BOMB AND WE DON'T KNOW IF THE CDC COULD SURVIVE A NUCLEAR BLAST.
AMERICA'S HEROES DON'T LOSE A FIGHT. EVER! NOW THE WHOLE WORLD THINKS RED TERROR KILLED OLD GLORY, AND THE COMMIES ARE ACES UP.
WE COULD TELL PEOPLE THE TRUTH.
THAT OLD GLORY DIED FROM A BUM TICKER 'CAUSE HE WAS ADDICTED TO FATIMAS?
YEAH, LET ME BUY SOME OF THAT STOCK. WE'VE GOT ISSUES.
"WE'VE GOT ISSUES." THAT ONLY SOLD OUR PROBLEMS BY HALF.

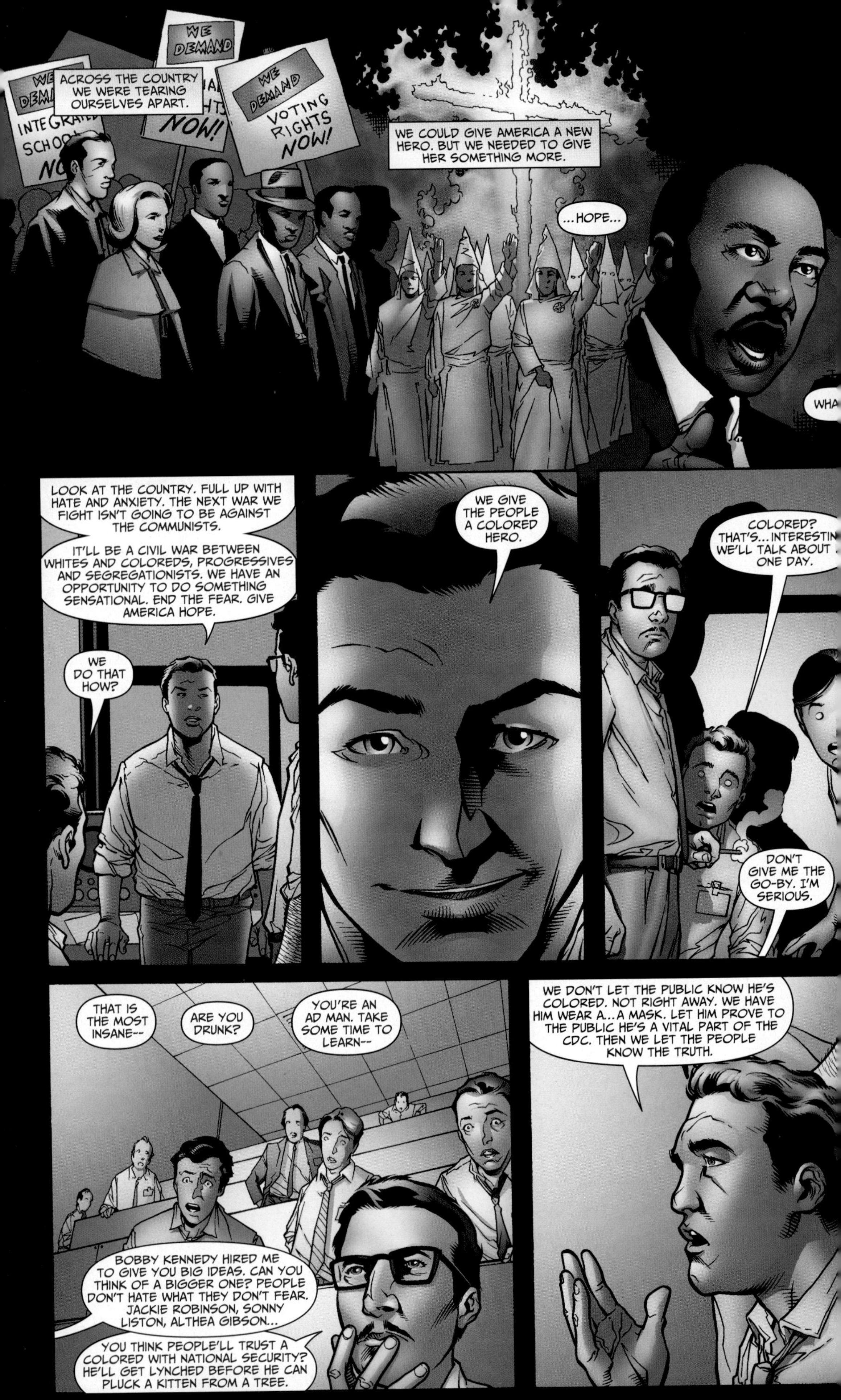
WE DEMAND
INTEGRATED SCHOOLS NOW
WE DEMAND
NOW!
ACROSS THE COUNTRY WE WERE TEARING OURSELVES APART.
WE DEMAND
VOTING RIGHTS NOW!
WE COULD GIVE AMERICA A NEW HERO. BUT WE NEEDED TO GIVE HER SOMETHING MORE.
...HOPE...
WHA
LOOK AT THE COUNTRY. FULL UP WITH HATE AND ANXIETY. THE NEXT WAR WE FIGHT ISN'T GOING TO BE AGAINST THE COMMUNISTS.
IT'LL BE A CIVIL WAR BETWEEN WHITES AND COLOREDS, PROGRESSIVES AND SEGREGATIONISTS. WE HAVE AN OPPORTUNITY TO DO SOMETHING SENSATIONAL. END THE FEAR. GIVE AMERICA HOPE.
WE DO THAT HOW?
WE GIVE THE PEOPLE A COLORED HERO.
COLORED? THAT'S...INTERESTIN WE'LL TALK ABOUT ONE DAY.
DON'T GIVE ME THE GO-BY. I'M SERIOUS.
THAT IS THE MOST INSANE--
ARE YOU DRUNK?
YOU'RE AN AD MAN. TAKE SOME TIME TO LEARN--
BOBBY KENNEDY HIRED ME TO GIVE YOU BIG IDEAS. CAN YOU THINK OF A BIGGER ONE? PEOPLE DON'T HATE WHAT THEY DON'T FEAR. JACKIE ROBINSON, SONNY LISTON, ALTHEA GIBSON...
YOU THINK PEOPLE'LL TRUST A COLORED WITH NATIONAL SECURITY? HE'LL GET LYNCHED BEFORE HE CAN PLUCK A KITTEN FROM A TREE.
WE DON'T LET THE PUBLIC KNOW HE'S COLORED. NOT RIGHT AWAY. WE HAVE HIM WEAR A...A MASK. LET HIM PROVE TO THE PUBLIC HE'S A VITAL PART OF THE CDC. THEN WE LET THE PEOPLE KNOW THE TRUTH.

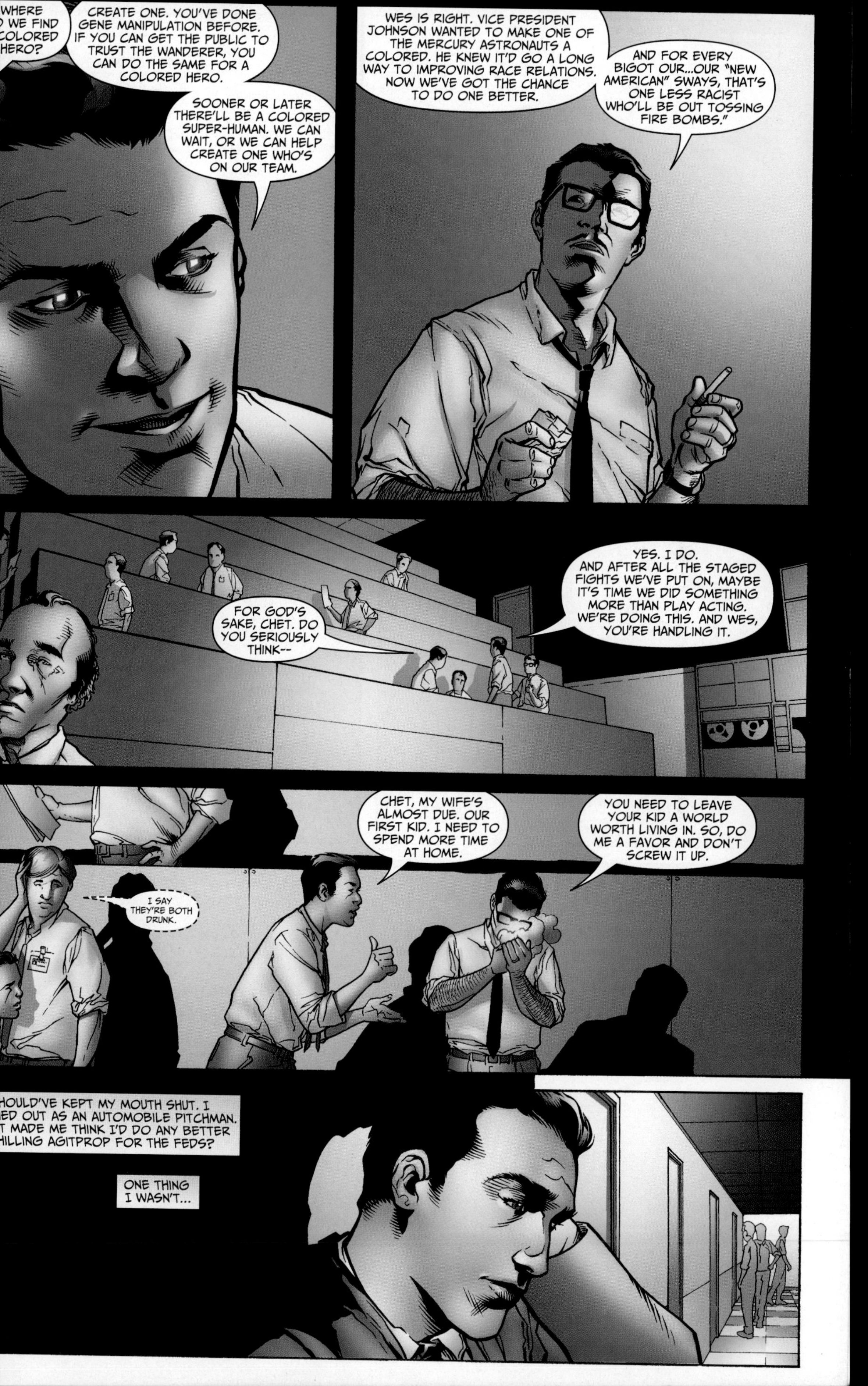

WHERE D WE FIND COLORED HERO?
CREATE ONE. YOU'VE DONE GENE MANIPULATION BEFORE. IF YOU CAN GET THE PUBLIC TO TRUST THE WANDERER, YOU CAN DO THE SAME FOR A COLORED HERO.
SOONER OR LATER THERE'LL BE A COLORED SUPER-HUMAN. WE CAN WAIT, OR WE CAN HELP CREATE ONE WHO'S ON OUR TEAM.
WES IS RIGHT. VICE PRESIDENT JOHNSON WANTED TO MAKE ONE OF THE MERCURY ASTRONAUTS A COLORED. HE KNEW IT'D GO A LONG WAY TO IMPROVING RACE RELATIONS. NOW WE'VE GOT THE CHANCE TO DO ONE BETTER.
AND FOR EVERY BIGOT OUR...OUR "NEW AMERICAN" SWAYS, THAT'S ONE LESS RACIST WHO'LL BE OUT TOSSING FIRE BOMBS."
FOR GOD'S SAKE, CHET. DO YOU SERIOUSLY THINK--
YES. I DO. AND AFTER ALL THE STAGED FIGHTS WE'VE PUT ON, MAYBE IT'S TIME WE DID SOMETHING MORE THAN PLAY ACTING. WE'RE DOING THIS. AND WES, YOU'RE HANDLING IT.
I SAY THEY'RE BOTH DRUNK.
CHET, MY WIFE'S ALMOST DUE. OUR FIRST KID. I NEED TO SPEND MORE TIME AT HOME.
YOU NEED TO LEAVE YOUR KID A WORLD WORTH LIVING IN. SO, DO ME A FAVOR AND DON'T SCREW IT UP.
HOULD'VE KEPT MY MOUTH SHUT. I ED OUT AS AN AUTOMOBILE PITCHMAN. T MADE ME THINK I'D DO ANY BETTER HILLING AGITPROP FOR THE FEDS?
ONE THING I WASN'T...

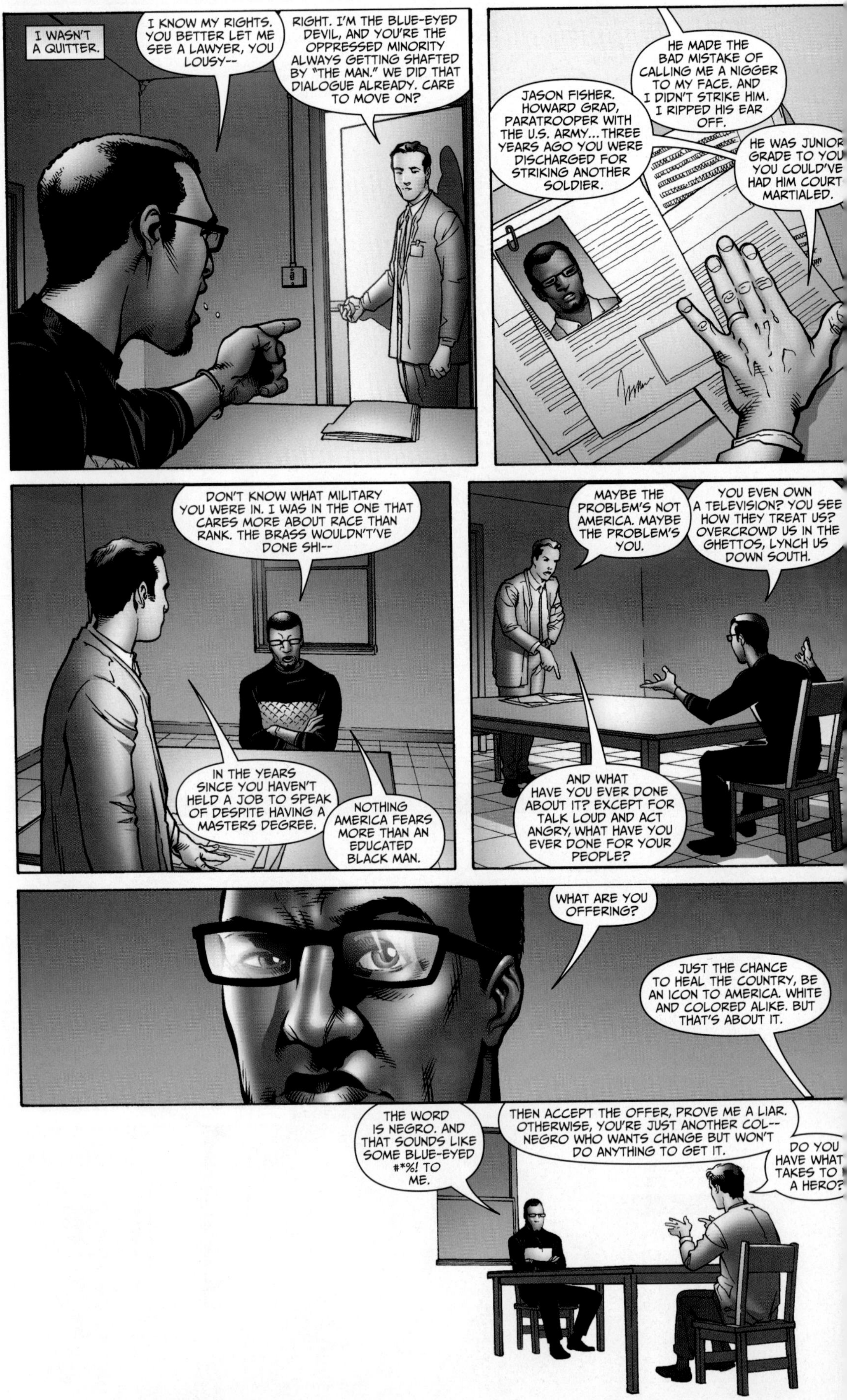

I WASN'T A QUITTER.
I KNOW MY RIGHTS. YOU BETTER LET ME SEE A LAWYER, YOU LOUSY--
RIGHT. I'M THE BLUE-EYED DEVIL, AND YOU'RE THE OPPRESSED MINORITY ALWAYS GETTING SHAFTED BY "THE MAN." WE DID THAT DIALOGUE ALREADY. CARE TO MOVE ON?
JASON FISHER. HOWARD GRAD, PARATROOPER WITH THE U.S. ARMY... THREE YEARS AGO YOU WERE DISCHARGED FOR STRIKING ANOTHER SOLDIER.
HE MADE THE BAD MISTAKE OF CALLING ME A NIGGER TO MY FACE. AND I DIDN'T STRIKE HIM. I RIPPED HIS EAR OFF.
HE WAS JUNIOR GRADE TO YOU YOU COULD'VE HAD HIM COURT MARTIALED.
DON'T KNOW WHAT MILITARY YOU WERE IN. I WAS IN THE ONE THAT CARES MORE ABOUT RACE THAN RANK. THE BRASS WOULDN'T'VE DONE SHI--
IN THE YEARS SINCE YOU HAVEN'T HELD A JOB TO SPEAK OF DESPITE HAVING A MASTERS DEGREE.
NOTHING AMERICA FEARS MORE THAN AN EDUCATED BLACK MAN.
MAYBE THE PROBLEM'S NOT AMERICA. MAYBE THE PROBLEM'S YOU.
YOU EVEN OWN A TELEVISION? YOU SEE HOW THEY TREAT US? OVERCROWD US IN THE GHETTOS, LYNCH US DOWN SOUTH.
AND WHAT HAVE YOU EVER DONE ABOUT IT? EXCEPT FOR TALK LOUD AND ACT ANGRY, WHAT HAVE YOU EVER DONE FOR YOUR PEOPLE?
WHAT ARE YOU OFFERING?
JUST THE CHANCE TO HEAL THE COUNTRY, BE AN ICON TO AMERICA. WHITE AND COLORED ALIKE. BUT THAT'S ABOUT IT.
THE WORD IS NEGRO. AND THAT SOUNDS LIKE SOME BLUE-EYED #*%! TO ME.
THEN ACCEPT THE OFFER, PROVE ME A LIAR. OTHERWISE, YOU'RE JUST ANOTHER COL-- NEGRO WHO WANTS CHANGE BUT WON'T DO ANYTHING TO GET IT.
DO YOU HAVE WHAT TAKES TO A HERO?

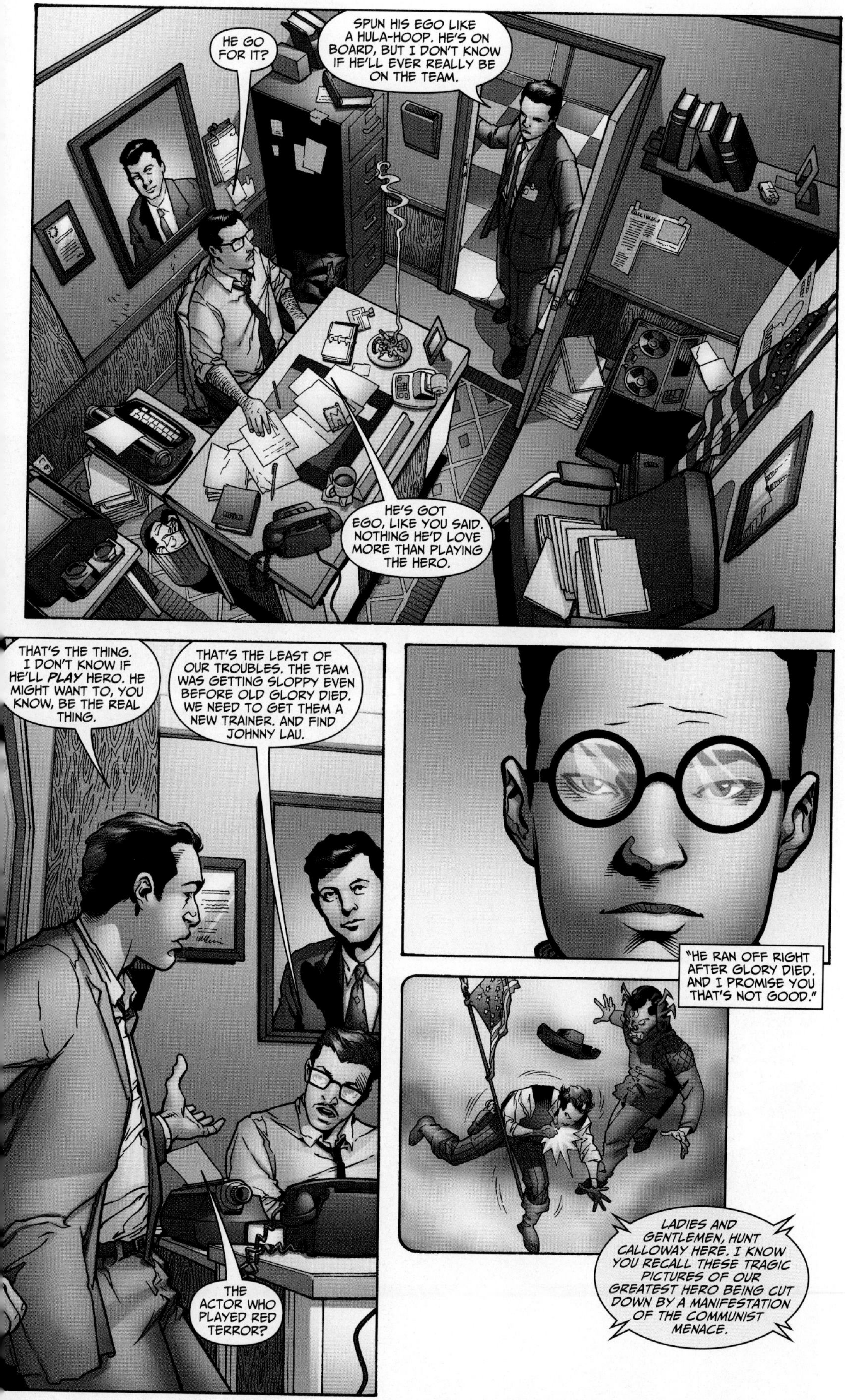
HE GO FOR IT?
SPUN HIS EGO LIKE A HULA-HOOP. HE'S ON BOARD, BUT I DON'T KNOW IF HE'LL EVER REALLY BE ON THE TEAM.
HE'S GOT EGO, LIKE YOU SAID. NOTHING HE'D LOVE MORE THAN PLAYING THE HERO.
THAT'S THE THING. I DON'T KNOW IF HE'LL *PLAY* HERO. HE MIGHT WANT TO, YOU KNOW, BE THE REAL THING.
THAT'S THE LEAST OF OUR TROUBLES. THE TEAM WAS GETTING SLOPPY EVEN BEFORE OLD GLORY DIED. WE NEED TO GET THEM A NEW TRAINER. AND FIND JOHNNY LAU.
THE ACTOR WHO PLAYED RED TERROR?
"HE RAN OFF RIGHT AFTER GLORY DIED. AND I PROMISE YOU THAT'S NOT GOOD."
LADIES AND GENTLEMEN, HUNT CALLOWAY HERE. I KNOW YOU RECALL THESE TRAGIC PICTURES OF OUR GREATEST HERO BEING CUT DOWN BY A MANIFESTATION OF THE COMMUNIST MENACE.

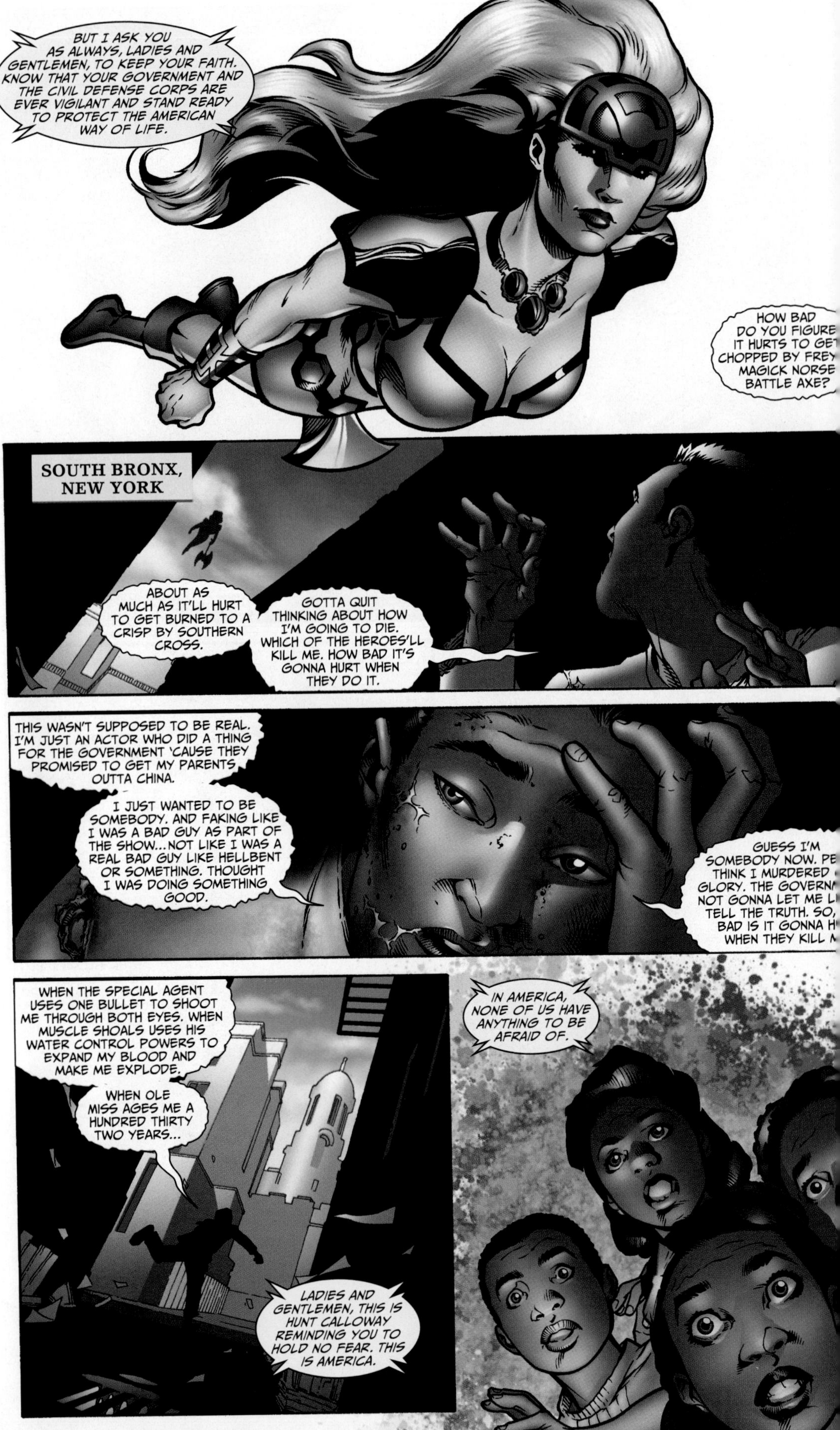
BUT I ASK YOU AS ALWAYS, LADIES AND GENTLEMEN, TO KEEP YOUR FAITH. KNOW THAT YOUR GOVERNMENT AND THE CIVIL DEFENSE CORPS ARE EVER VIGILANT AND STAND READY TO PROTECT THE AMERICAN WAY OF LIFE.
HOW BAD DO YOU FIGURE IT HURTS TO GET CHOPPED BY FREY MAGICK NORSE BATTLE AXE?
SOUTH BRONX, NEW YORK
ABOUT AS MUCH AS IT'LL HURT TO GET BURNED TO A CRISP BY SOUTHERN CROSS.
GOTTA QUIT THINKING ABOUT HOW I'M GOING TO DIE. WHICH OF THE HEROES'LL KILL ME. HOW BAD IT'S GONNA HURT WHEN THEY DO IT.
THIS WASN'T SUPPOSED TO BE REAL. I'M JUST AN ACTOR WHO DID A THING FOR THE GOVERNMENT 'CAUSE THEY PROMISED TO GET MY PARENTS OUTTA CHINA.
I JUST WANTED TO BE SOMEBODY. AND FAKING LIKE I WAS A BAD GUY AS PART OF THE SHOW...NOT LIKE I WAS A REAL BAD GUY LIKE HELLBENT OR SOMETHING. THOUGHT I WAS DOING SOMETHING GOOD.
GUESS I'M SOMEBODY NOW. PE THINK I MURDERED GLORY. THE GOVERN NOT GONNA LET ME L TELL THE TRUTH. SO, BAD IS IT GONNA H WHEN THEY KILL
WHEN THE SPECIAL AGENT USES ONE BULLET TO SHOOT ME THROUGH BOTH EYES. WHEN MUSCLE SHOALS USES HIS WATER CONTROL POWERS TO EXPAND MY BLOOD AND MAKE ME EXPLODE.
WHEN OLE MISS AGES ME A HUNDRED THIRTY TWO YEARS...
IN AMERICA, NONE OF US HAVE ANYTHING TO BE AFRAID OF.
LADIES AND GENTLEMEN, THIS IS HUNT CALLOWAY REMINDING YOU TO HOLD NO FEAR. THIS IS AMERICA.

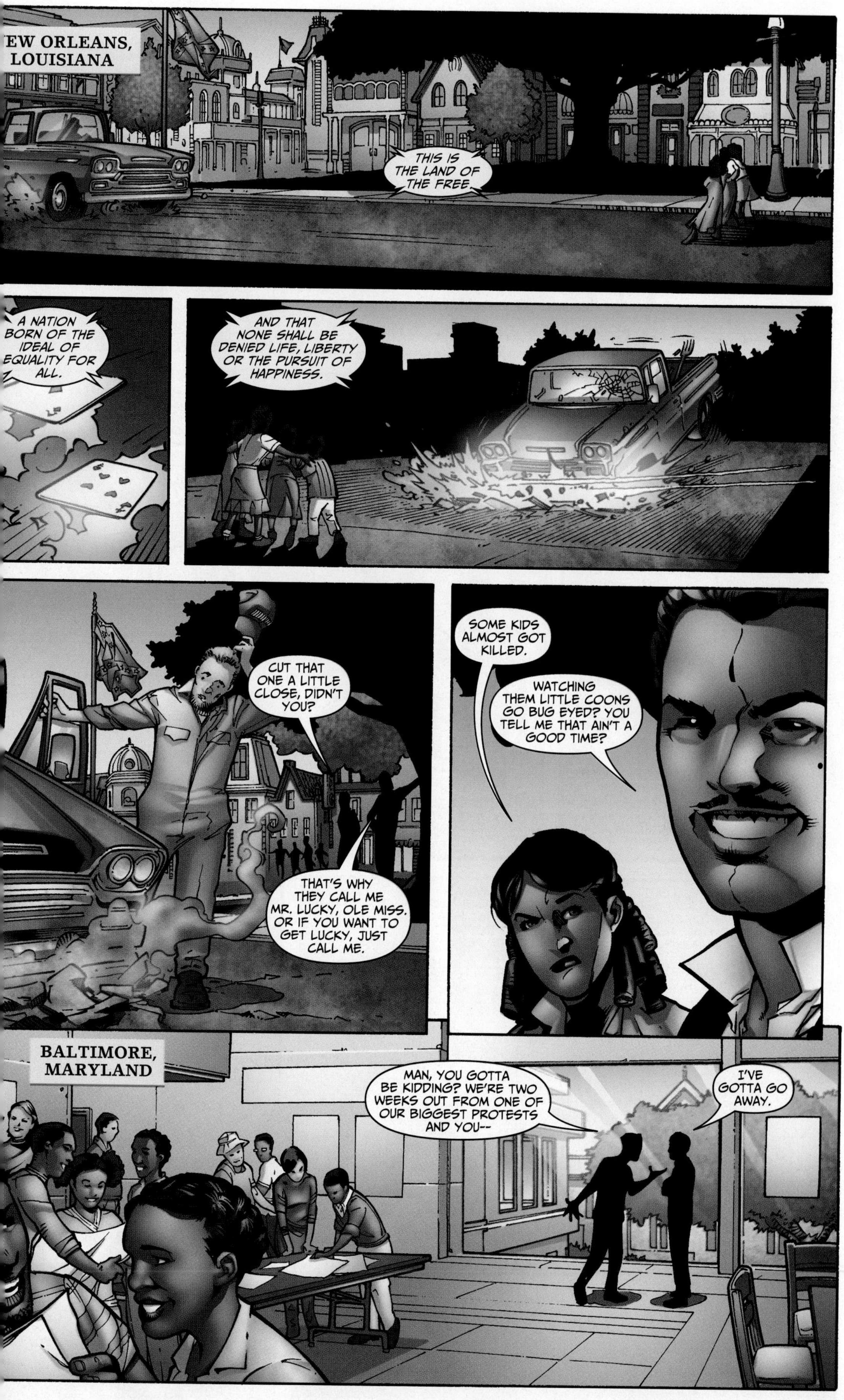

EW ORLEANS, LOUISIANA
THIS IS THE LAND OF THE FREE.
A NATION BORN OF THE IDEAL OF EQUALITY FOR ALL.
AND THAT NONE SHALL BE DENIED LIFE, LIBERTY OR THE PURSUIT OF HAPPINESS.
CUT THAT ONE A LITTLE CLOSE, DIDN'T YOU?
THAT'S WHY THEY CALL ME MR. LUCKY, OLE MISS. OR IF YOU WANT TO GET LUCKY, JUST CALL ME.
SOME KIDS ALMOST GOT KILLED.
WATCHING THEM LITTLE COONS GO BUG EYED? YOU TELL ME THAT AIN'T A GOOD TIME?
BALTIMORE, MARYLAND
MAN, YOU GOTTA BE KIDDING? WE'RE TWO WEEKS OUT FROM ONE OF OUR BIGGEST PROTESTS AND YOU--
I'VE GOTTA GO AWAY.

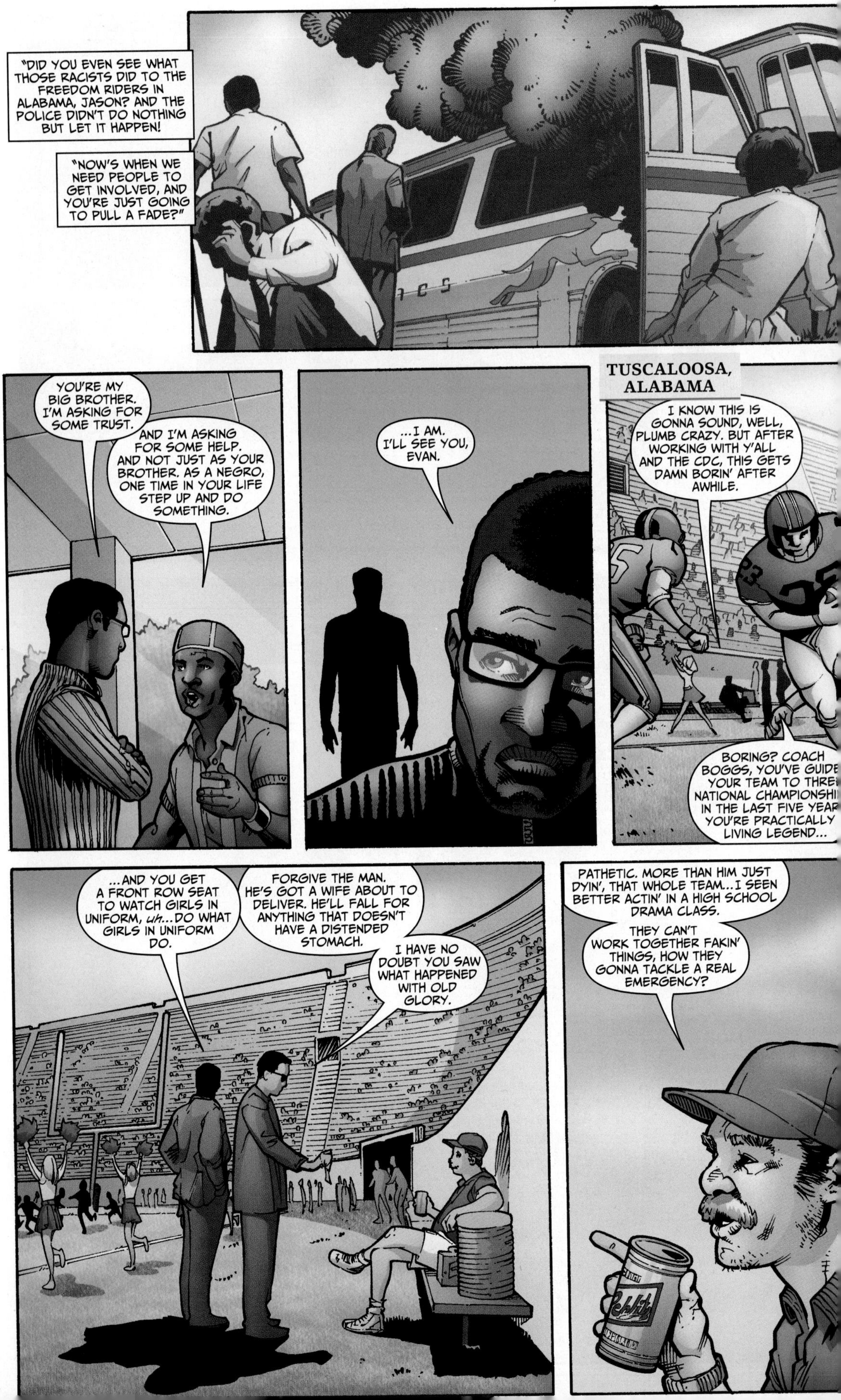
"DID YOU EVEN SEE WHAT THOSE RACISTS DID TO THE FREEDOM RIDERS IN ALABAMA, JASON? AND THE POLICE DIDN'T DO NOTHING BUT LET IT HAPPEN!
"NOW'S WHEN WE NEED PEOPLE TO GET INVOLVED, AND YOU'RE JUST GOING TO PULL A FADE?"
YOU'RE MY BIG BROTHER. I'M ASKING FOR SOME TRUST.
AND I'M ASKING FOR SOME HELP. AND NOT JUST AS YOUR BROTHER. AS A NEGRO, ONE TIME IN YOUR LIFE STEP UP AND DO SOMETHING.
...I AM. I'LL SEE YOU, EVAN.
TUSCALOOSA, ALABAMA
I KNOW THIS IS GONNA SOUND, WELL, PLUMB CRAZY. BUT AFTER WORKING WITH Y'ALL AND THE CDC, THIS GETS DAMN BORIN' AFTER AWHILE.
BORING? COACH BOGGS, YOU'VE GUIDE YOUR TEAM TO THRE NATIONAL CHAMPIONSHI IN THE LAST FIVE YEAR YOU'RE PRACTICALLY LIVING LEGEND...
...AND YOU GET A FRONT ROW SEAT TO WATCH GIRLS IN UNIFORM, *uh*...DO WHAT GIRLS IN UNIFORM DO.
FORGIVE THE MAN. HE'S GOT A WIFE ABOUT TO DELIVER. HE'LL FALL FOR ANYTHING THAT DOESN'T HAVE A DISTENDED STOMACH.
I HAVE NO DOUBT YOU SAW WHAT HAPPENED WITH OLD GLORY.
PATHETIC. MORE THAN HIM JUST DYIN', THAT WHOLE TEAM...I SEEN BETTER ACTIN' IN A HIGH SCHOOL DRAMA CLASS.
THEY CAN'T WORK TOGETHER FAKIN' THINGS, HOW THEY GONNA TACKLE A REAL EMERGENCY?

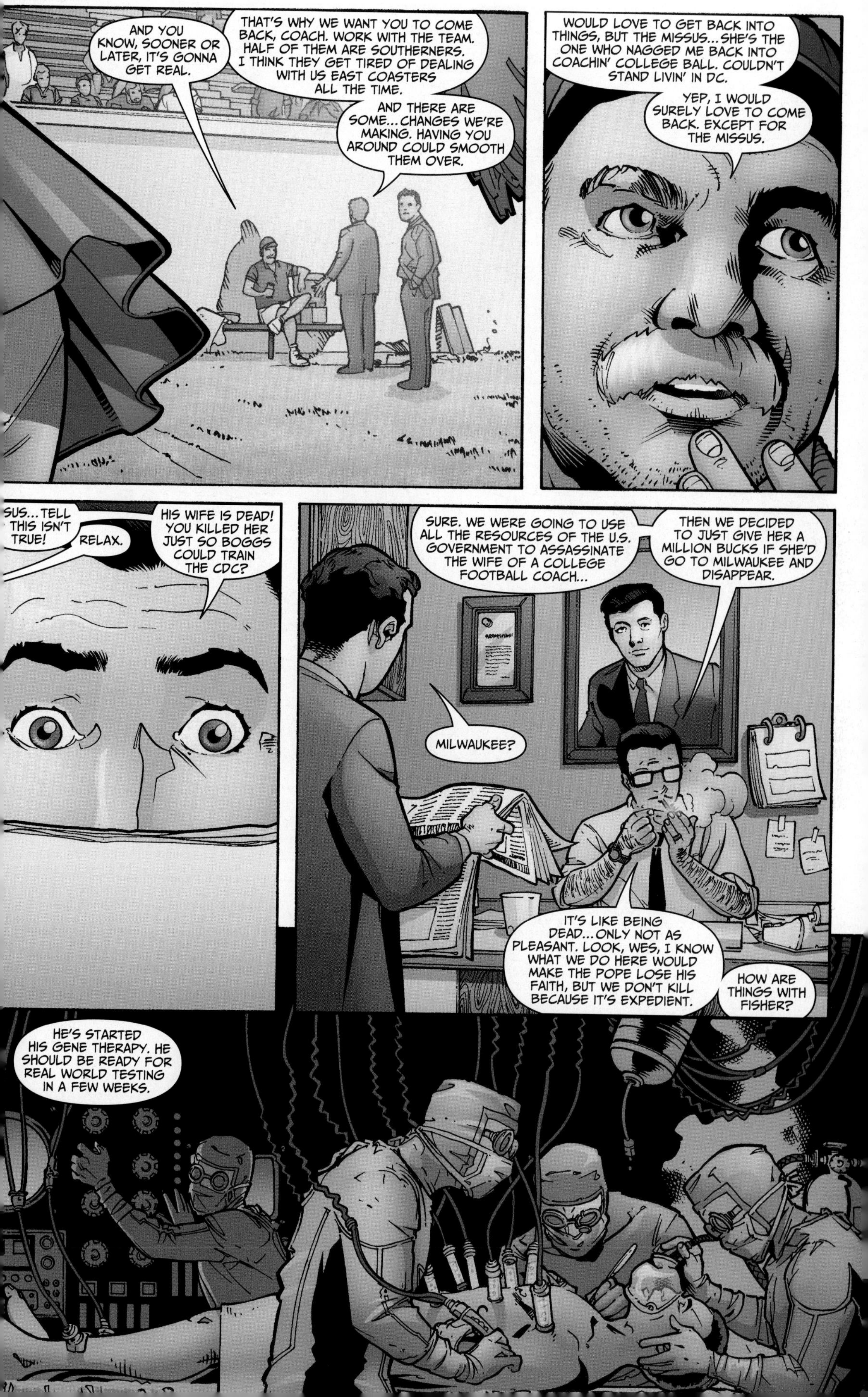
AND YOU KNOW, SOONER OR LATER, IT'S GONNA GET REAL.
THAT'S WHY WE WANT YOU TO COME BACK, COACH. WORK WITH THE TEAM. HALF OF THEM ARE SOUTHERNERS. I THINK THEY GET TIRED OF DEALING WITH US EAST COASTERS ALL THE TIME.
AND THERE ARE SOME... CHANGES WE'RE MAKING. HAVING YOU AROUND COULD SMOOTH THEM OVER.
WOULD LOVE TO GET BACK INTO THINGS, BUT THE MISSUS... SHE'S THE ONE WHO NAGGED ME BACK INTO COACHIN' COLLEGE BALL. COULDN'T STAND LIVIN' IN DC.
YEP, I WOULD SURELY LOVE TO COME BACK. EXCEPT FOR THE MISSUS.
SUS... TELL THIS ISN'T TRUE!
RELAX.
HIS WIFE IS DEAD! YOU KILLED HER JUST SO BOGGS COULD TRAIN THE CDC?
SURE. WE WERE GOING TO USE ALL THE RESOURCES OF THE U.S. GOVERNMENT TO ASSASSINATE THE WIFE OF A COLLEGE FOOTBALL COACH...
THEN WE DECIDED TO JUST GIVE HER A MILLION BUCKS IF SHE'D GO TO MILWAUKEE AND DISAPPEAR.
MILWAUKEE?
IT'S LIKE BEING DEAD... ONLY NOT AS PLEASANT. LOOK, WES, I KNOW WHAT WE DO HERE WOULD MAKE THE POPE LOSE HIS FAITH, BUT WE DON'T KILL BECAUSE IT'S EXPEDIENT.
HOW ARE THINGS WITH FISHER?
HE'S STARTED HIS GENE THERAPY. HE SHOULD BE READY FOR REAL WORLD TESTING IN A FEW WEEKS.

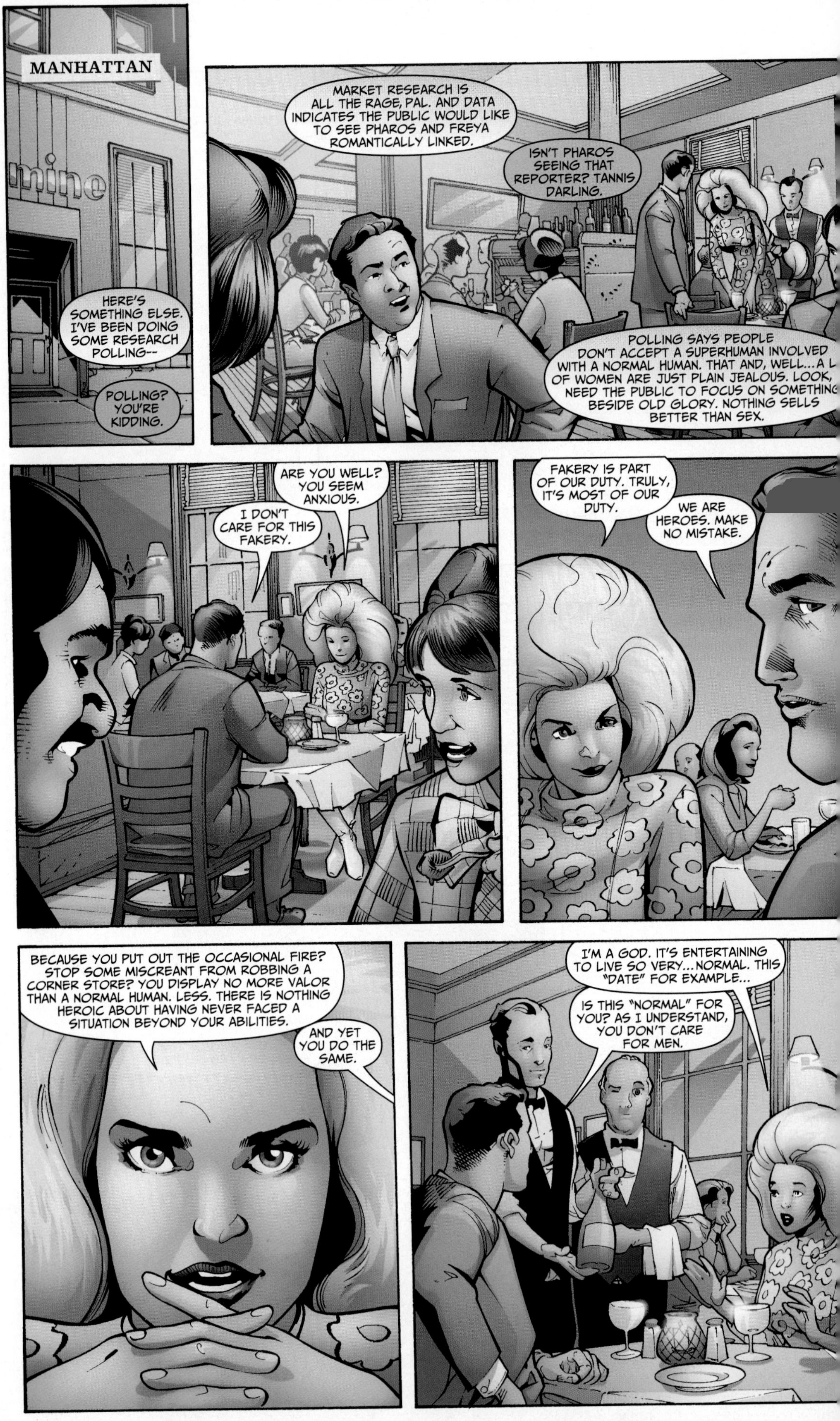
MANHATTAN
mine
HERE'S SOMETHING ELSE. I'VE BEEN DOING SOME RESEARCH POLLING--
POLLING? YOU'RE KIDDING.
MARKET RESEARCH IS ALL THE RAGE, PAL. AND DATA INDICATES THE PUBLIC WOULD LIKE TO SEE PHAROS AND FREYA ROMANTICALLY LINKED.
ISN'T PHAROS SEEING THAT REPORTER? TANNIS DARLING.
POLLING SAYS PEOPLE DON'T ACCEPT A SUPERHUMAN INVOLVED WITH A NORMAL HUMAN. THAT AND, WELL...A L OF WOMEN ARE JUST PLAIN JEALOUS. LOOK, NEED THE PUBLIC TO FOCUS ON SOMETHING BESIDE OLD GLORY. NOTHING SELLS BETTER THAN SEX.
I DON'T CARE FOR THIS FAKERY.
ARE YOU WELL? YOU SEEM ANXIOUS.
FAKERY IS PART OF OUR DUTY. TRULY, IT'S MOST OF OUR DUTY.
WE ARE HEROES. MAKE NO MISTAKE.
BECAUSE YOU PUT OUT THE OCCASIONAL FIRE? STOP SOME MISCREANT FROM ROBBING A CORNER STORE? YOU DISPLAY NO MORE VALOR THAN A NORMAL HUMAN. LESS. THERE IS NOTHING HEROIC ABOUT HAVING NEVER FACED A SITUATION BEYOND YOUR ABILITIES.
AND YET YOU DO THE SAME.
I'M A GOD. IT'S ENTERTAINING TO LIVE SO VERY...NORMAL. THIS "DATE" FOR EXAMPLE...
IS THIS "NORMAL" FOR YOU? AS I UNDERSTAND, YOU DON'T CARE FOR MEN.

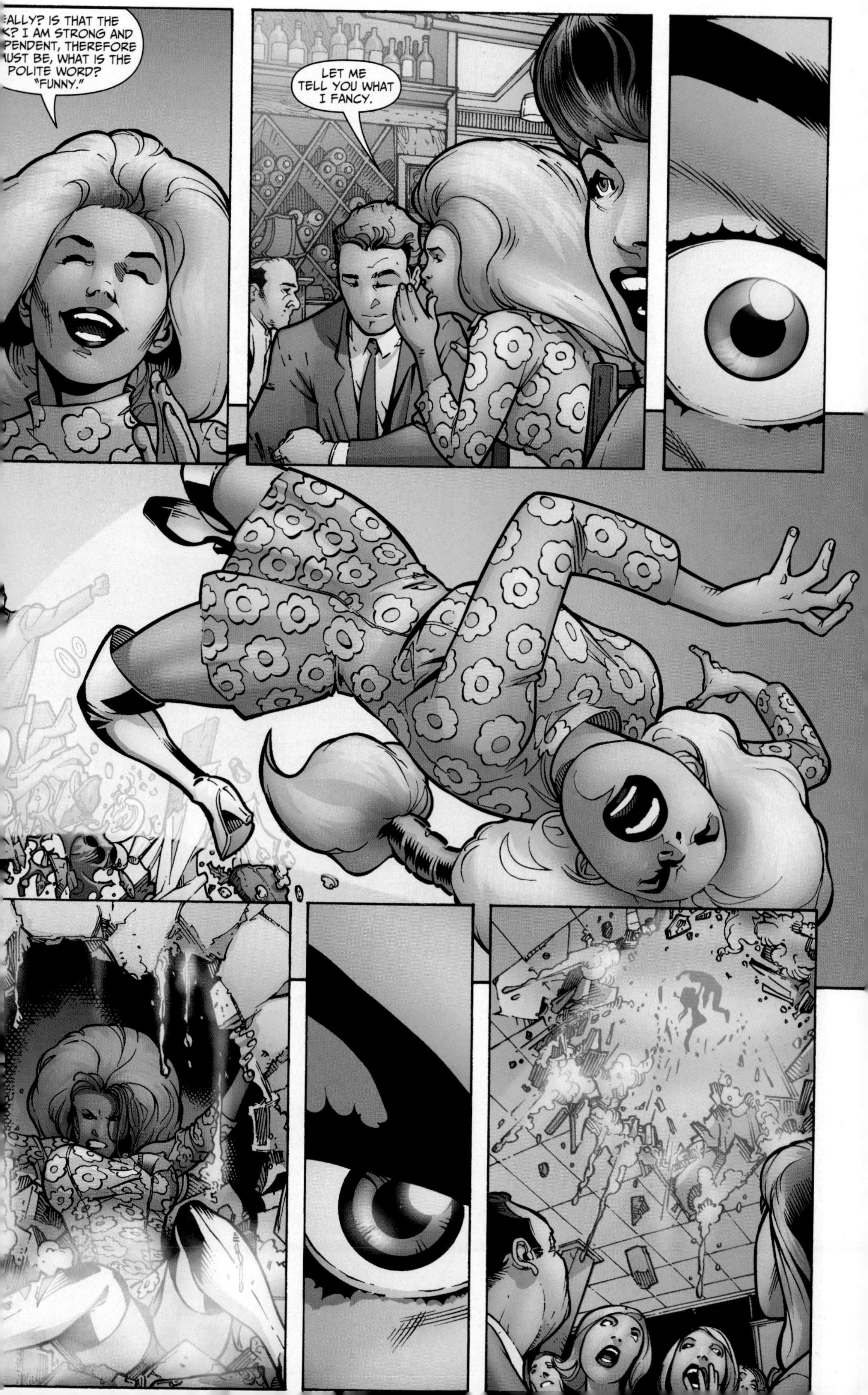
EALLY? IS THAT THE
K? I AM STRONG AND
PENDENT, THEREFORE
MUST BE, WHAT IS THE
POLITE WORD?
"FUNNY."
LET ME
TELL YOU WHAT
I FANCY.

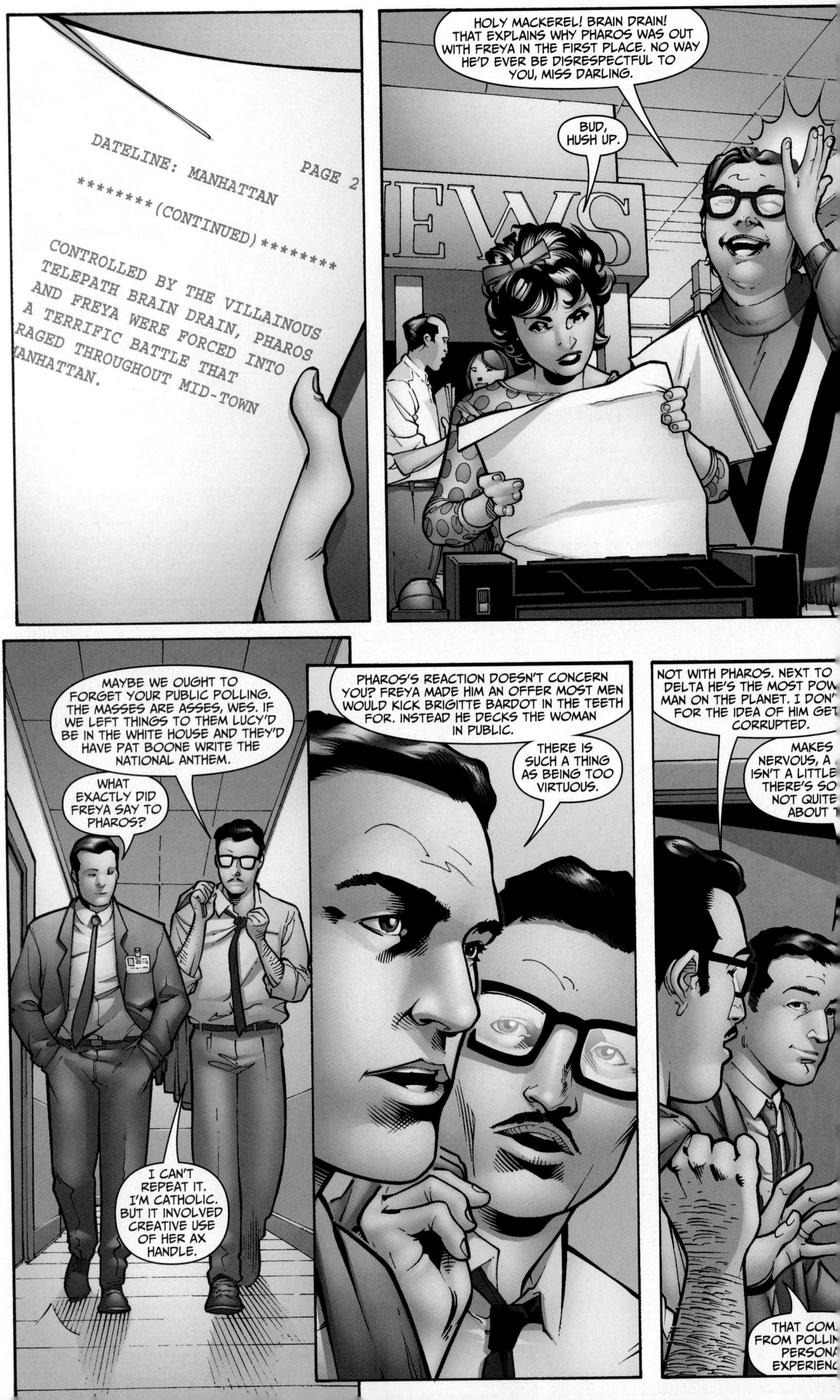
DATELINE: MANHATTAN
PAGE 2
********(CONTINUED)********
CONTROLLED BY THE VILLAINOUS TELEPATH BRAIN DRAIN, PHAROS AND FREYA WERE FORCED INTO A TERRIFIC BATTLE THAT RAGED THROUGHOUT MID-TOWN MANHATTAN.
HOLY MACKEREL! BRAIN DRAIN! THAT EXPLAINS WHY PHAROS WAS OUT WITH FREYA IN THE FIRST PLACE. NO WAY HE'D EVER BE DISRESPECTFUL TO YOU, MISS DARLING.
BUD, HUSH UP.
MAYBE WE OUGHT TO FORGET YOUR PUBLIC POLLING. THE MASSES ARE ASSES, WES. IF WE LEFT THINGS TO THEM LUCY'D BE IN THE WHITE HOUSE AND THEY'D HAVE PAT BOONE WRITE THE NATIONAL ANTHEM.
WHAT EXACTLY DID FREYA SAY TO PHAROS?
I CAN'T REPEAT IT. I'M CATHOLIC. BUT IT INVOLVED CREATIVE USE OF HER AX HANDLE.
PHAROS'S REACTION DOESN'T CONCERN YOU? FREYA MADE HIM AN OFFER MOST MEN WOULD KICK BRIGITTE BARDOT IN THE TEETH FOR. INSTEAD HE DECKS THE WOMAN IN PUBLIC.
THERE IS SUCH A THING AS BEING TOO VIRTUOUS.
NOT WITH PHAROS. NEXT TO
DELTA HE'S THE MOST POW
MAN ON THE PLANET. I DON'
FOR THE IDEA OF HIM GET
CORRUPTED.
MAKES
NERVOUS, A
ISN'T A LITTLE
THERE'S SO
NOT QUITE
ABOUT
THAT COM
FROM POLLIN
PERSONA
EXPERIENC

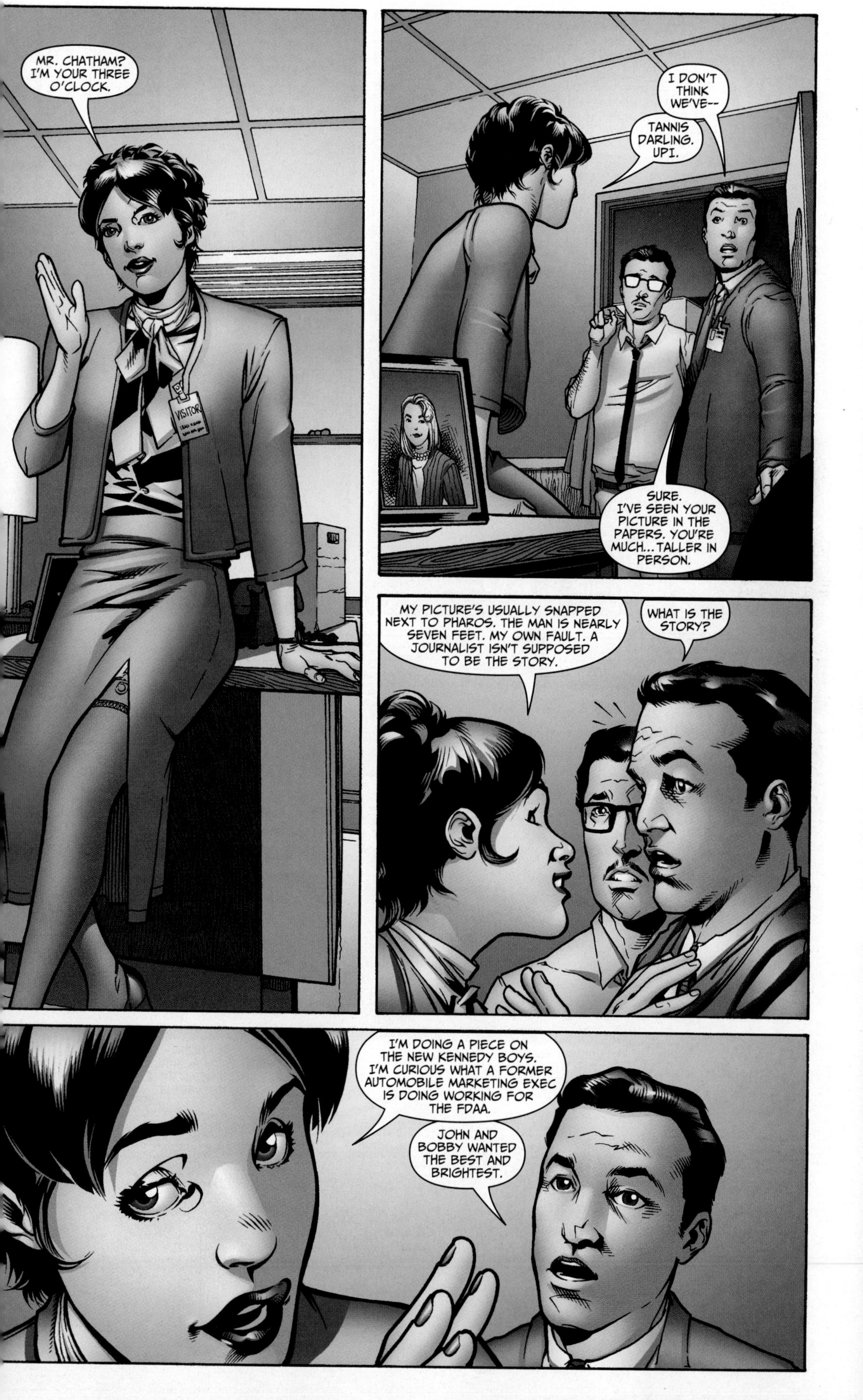
MR. CHATHAM? I'M YOUR THREE O'CLOCK.
I DON'T THINK WE'VE--
TANNIS DARLING. UPI.
SURE. I'VE SEEN YOUR PICTURE IN THE PAPERS. YOU'RE MUCH... TALLER IN PERSON.
MY PICTURE'S USUALLY SNAPPED NEXT TO PHAROS. THE MAN IS NEARLY SEVEN FEET. MY OWN FAULT. A JOURNALIST ISN'T SUPPOSED TO BE THE STORY.
WHAT IS THE STORY?
I'M DOING A PIECE ON THE NEW KENNEDY BOYS. I'M CURIOUS WHAT A FORMER AUTOMOBILE MARKETING EXEC IS DOING WORKING FOR THE FDAA.
JOHN AND BOBBY WANTED THE BEST AND BRIGHTEST.

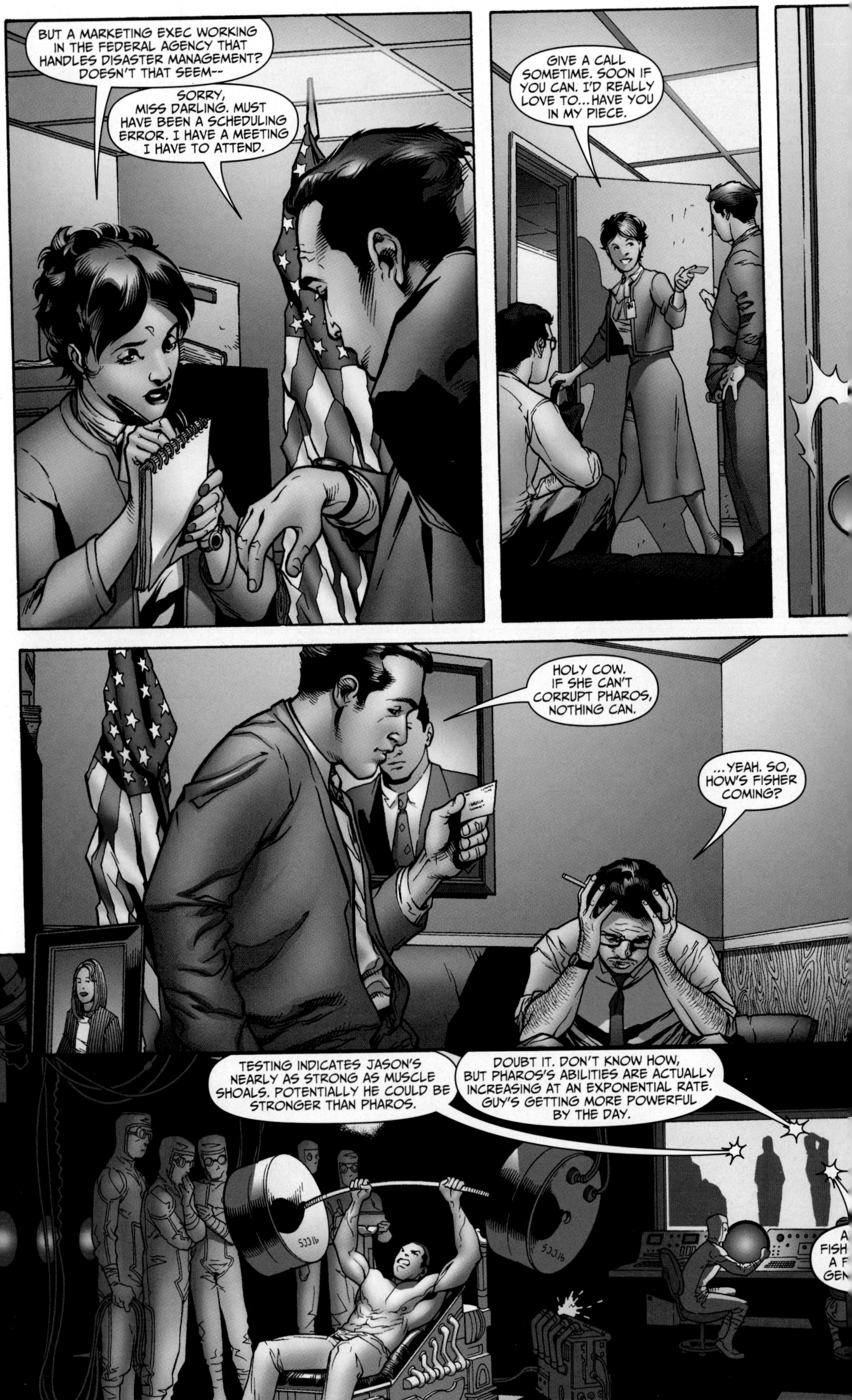
BUT A MARKETING EXEC WORKING IN THE FEDERAL AGENCY THAT HANDLES DISASTER MANAGEMENT? DOESN'T THAT SEEM--
SORRY, MISS DARLING. MUST HAVE BEEN A SCHEDULING ERROR. I HAVE A MEETING I HAVE TO ATTEND.
GIVE A CALL SOMETIME. SOON IF YOU CAN. I'D REALLY LOVE TO...HAVE YOU IN MY PIECE.
HOLY COW. IF SHE CAN'T CORRUPT PHAROS, NOTHING CAN.
...YEAH. SO, HOW'S FISHER COMING?
TESTING INDICATES JASON'S NEARLY AS STRONG AS MUSCLE SHOALS. POTENTIALLY HE COULD BE STRONGER THAN PHAROS.
DOUBT IT. DON'T KNOW HOW, BUT PHAROS'S ABILITIES ARE ACTUALLY INCREASING AT AN EXPONENTIAL RATE. GUY'S GETTING MORE POWERFUL BY THE DAY.

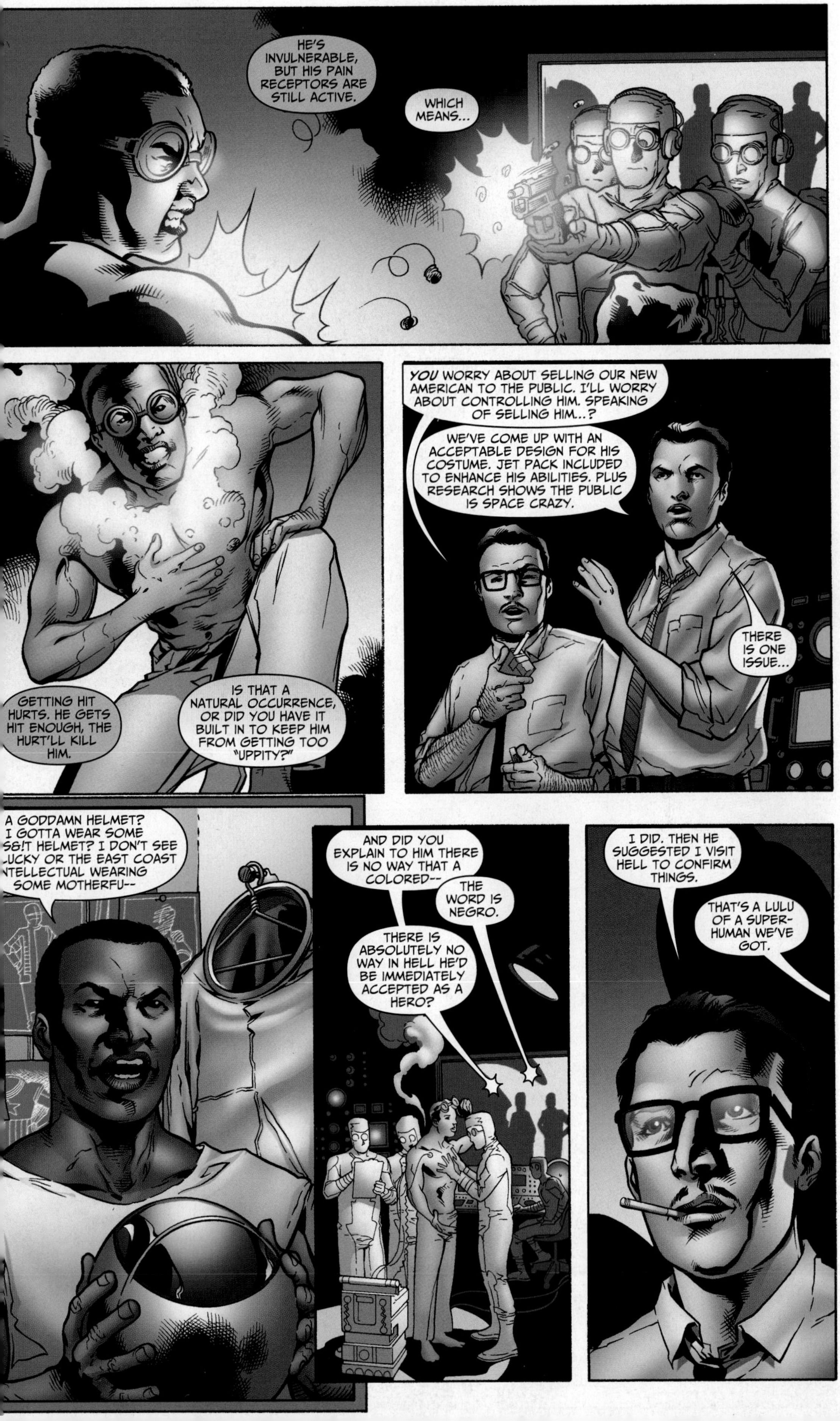
HE'S INVULNERABLE, BUT HIS PAIN RECEPTORS ARE STILL ACTIVE.
WHICH MEANS...
GETTING HIT HURTS. HE GETS HIT ENOUGH, THE HURT'LL KILL HIM.
IS THAT A NATURAL OCCURRENCE, OR DID YOU HAVE IT BUILT IN TO KEEP HIM FROM GETTING TOO "UPPITY?"
YOU WORRY ABOUT SELLING OUR NEW AMERICAN TO THE PUBLIC. I'LL WORRY ABOUT CONTROLLING HIM. SPEAKING OF SELLING HIM...?
WE'VE COME UP WITH AN ACCEPTABLE DESIGN FOR HIS COSTUME. JET PACK INCLUDED TO ENHANCE HIS ABILITIES. PLUS RESEARCH SHOWS THE PUBLIC IS SPACE CRAZY.
THERE IS ONE ISSUE...
A GODDAMN HELMET? I GOTTA WEAR SOME S&!T HELMET? I DON'T SEE LUCKY OR THE EAST COAST INTELLECTUAL WEARING SOME MOTHERFU--
AND DID YOU EXPLAIN TO HIM THERE IS NO WAY THAT A COLORED--
THE WORD IS NEGRO.
THERE IS ABSOLUTELY NO WAY IN HELL HE'D BE IMMEDIATELY ACCEPTED AS A HERO?
I DID. THEN HE SUGGESTED I VISIT HELL TO CONFIRM THINGS.
THAT'S A LULU OF A SUPER-HUMAN WE'VE GOT.

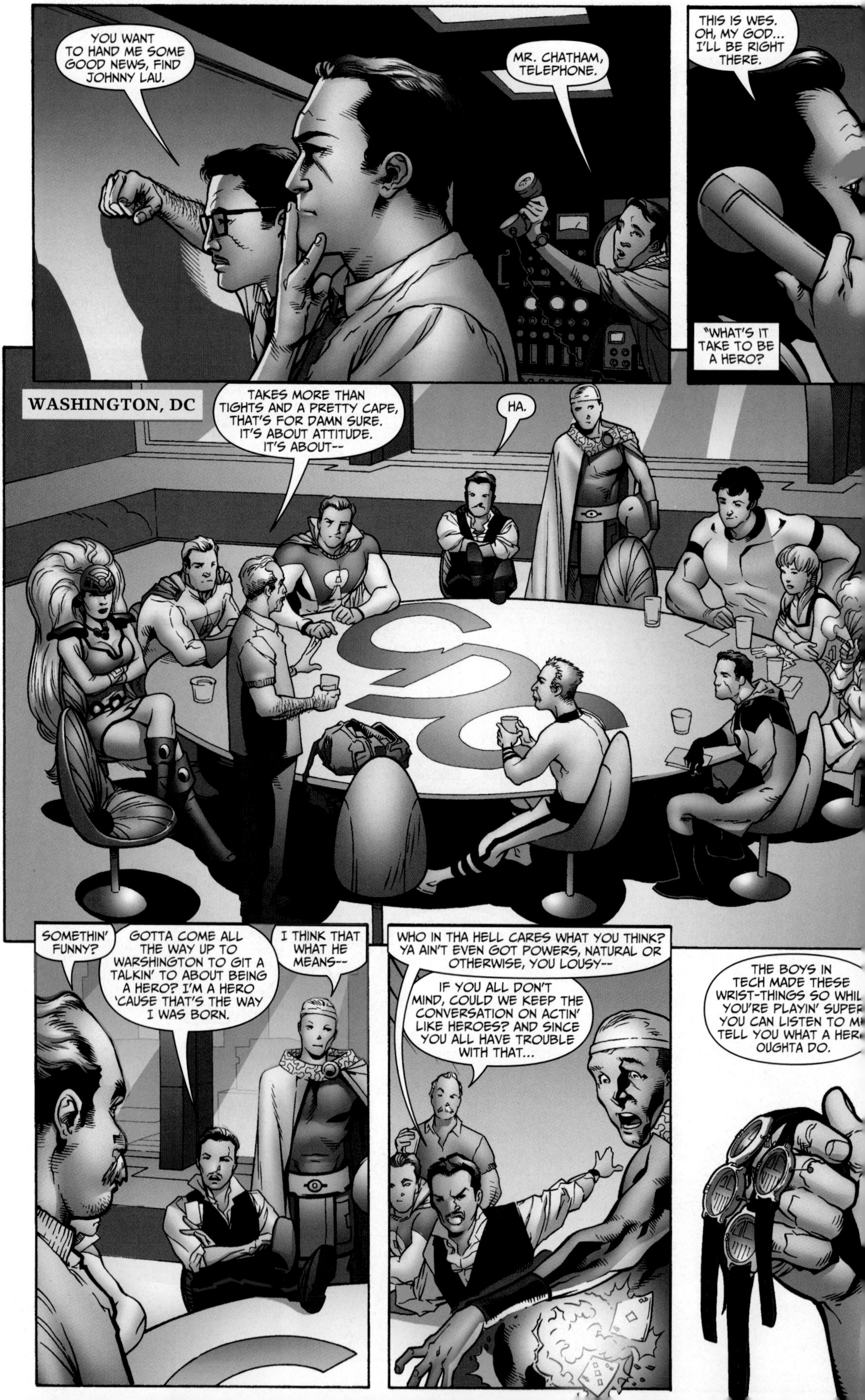
YOU WANT TO HAND ME SOME GOOD NEWS, FIND JOHNNY LAU.
MR. CHATHAM, TELEPHONE.
THIS IS WES. OH, MY GOD... I'LL BE RIGHT THERE.
"WHAT'S IT TAKE TO BE A HERO?
WASHINGTON, DC
TAKES MORE THAN TIGHTS AND A PRETTY CAPE, THAT'S FOR DAMN SURE. IT'S ABOUT ATTITUDE. IT'S ABOUT--
HA.
SOMETHIN' FUNNY?
GOTTA COME ALL THE WAY UP TO WARSHINGTON TO GIT A TALKIN' TO ABOUT BEING A HERO? I'M A HERO 'CAUSE THAT'S THE WAY I WAS BORN.
I THINK THAT WHAT HE MEANS--
WHO IN THA HELL CARES WHAT YOU THINK? YA AIN'T EVEN GOT POWERS, NATURAL OR OTHERWISE, YOU LOUSY--
IF YOU ALL DON'T MIND, COULD WE KEEP THE CONVERSATION ON ACTIN' LIKE HEROES? AND SINCE YOU ALL HAVE TROUBLE WITH THAT...
THE BOYS IN TECH MADE THESE WRIST-THINGS SO WHIL YOU'RE PLAYIN' SUPER YOU CAN LISTEN TO M TELL YOU WHAT A HER OUGHTA DO.

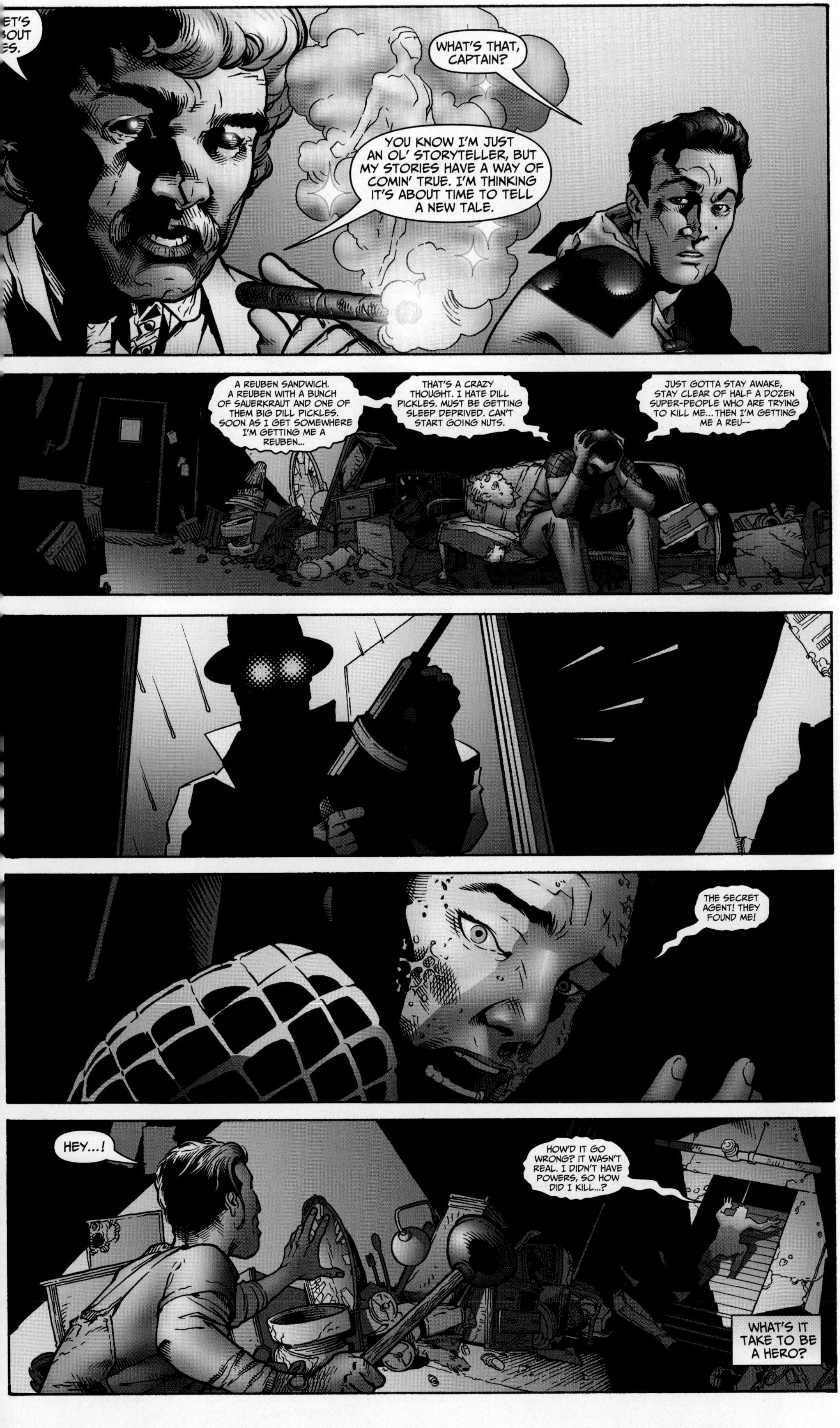

ET'S
BOUT
ES.
WHAT'S THAT, CAPTAIN?
YOU KNOW I'M JUST AN OL' STORYTELLER, BUT MY STORIES HAVE A WAY OF COMIN' TRUE. I'M THINKING IT'S ABOUT TIME TO TELL A NEW TALE.
A REUBEN SANDWICH. A REUBEN WITH A BUNCH OF SAUERKRAUT AND ONE OF THEM BIG DILL PICKLES. SOON AS I GET SOMEWHERE I'M GETTING ME A REUBEN...
THAT'S A CRAZY THOUGHT. I HATE DILL PICKLES. MUST BE GETTING SLEEP DEPRIVED. CAN'T START GOING NUTS.
JUST GOTTA STAY AWAKE, STAY CLEAR OF HALF A DOZEN SUPER-PEOPLE WHO ARE TRYING TO KILL ME...THEN I'M GETTING ME A REU--
THE SECRET AGENT! THEY FOUND ME!
HEY...!
HOW'D IT GO WRONG? IT WASN'T REAL. I DIDN'T HAVE POWERS, SO HOW DID I KILL...?
WHAT'S IT TAKE TO BE A HERO?

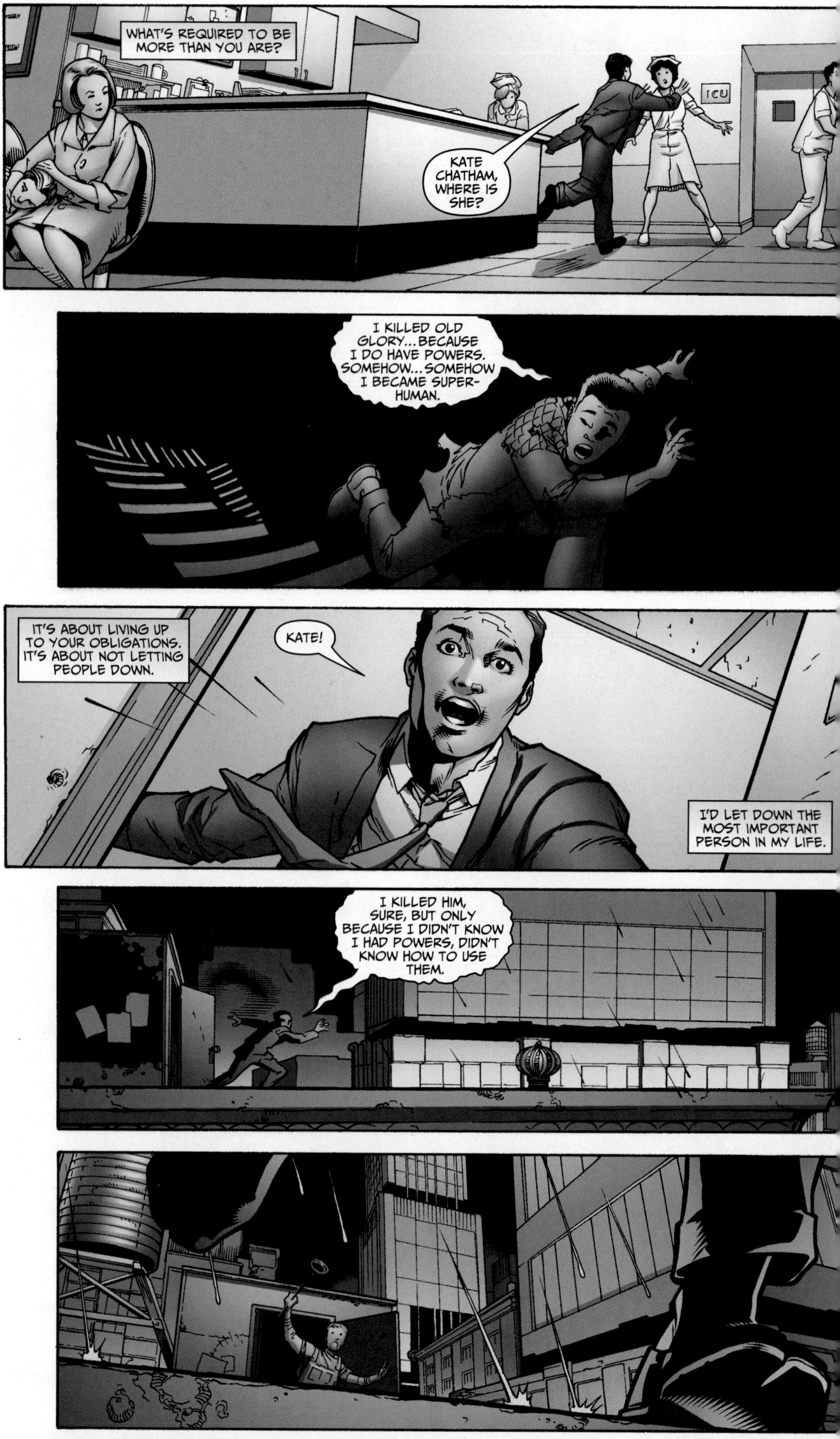
WHAT'S REQUIRED TO BE MORE THAN YOU ARE?
ICU
KATE CHATHAM, WHERE IS SHE?
I KILLED OLD GLORY...BECAUSE I DO HAVE POWERS. SOMEHOW...SOMEHOW I BECAME SUPER-HUMAN.
IT'S ABOUT LIVING UP TO YOUR OBLIGATIONS. IT'S ABOUT NOT LETTING PEOPLE DOWN.
KATE!
I'D LET DOWN THE MOST IMPORTANT PERSON IN MY LIFE.
I KILLED HIM, SURE, BUT ONLY BECAUSE I DIDN'T KNOW I HAD POWERS, DIDN'T KNOW HOW TO USE THEM.

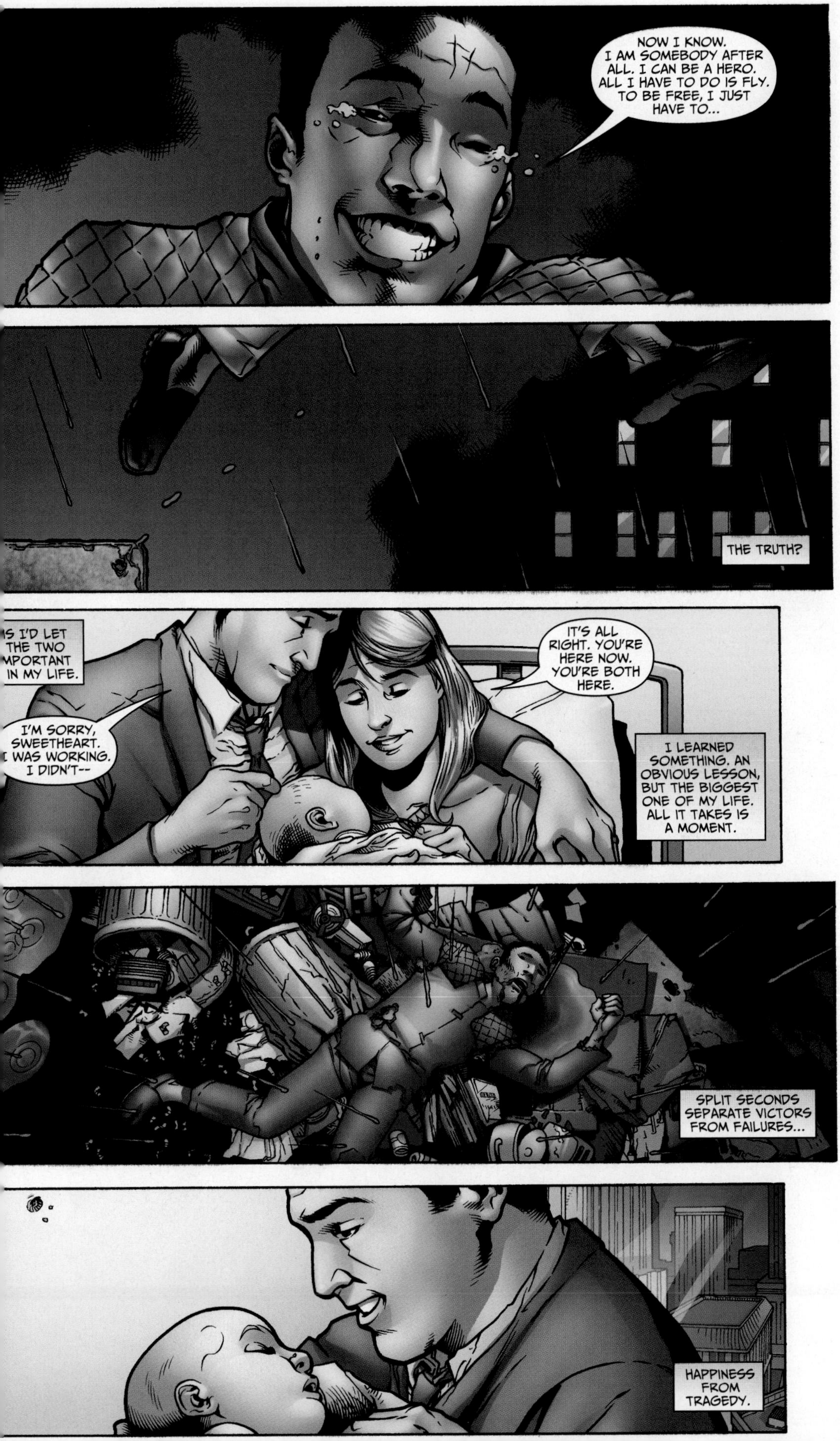
NOW I KNOW. I AM SOMEBODY AFTER ALL. I CAN BE A HERO. ALL I HAVE TO DO IS FLY. TO BE FREE, I JUST HAVE TO...
THE TRUTH?
S I'D LET THE TWO MPORTANT IN MY LIFE.
I'M SORRY, SWEETHEART. I WAS WORKING. I DIDN'T--
IT'S ALL RIGHT. YOU'RE HERE NOW. YOU'RE BOTH HERE.
I LEARNED SOMETHING. AN OBVIOUS LESSON, BUT THE BIGGEST ONE OF MY LIFE. ALL IT TAKES IS A MOMENT.
SPLIT SECONDS SEPARATE VICTORS FROM FAILURES...
HAPPINESS FROM TRAGEDY.

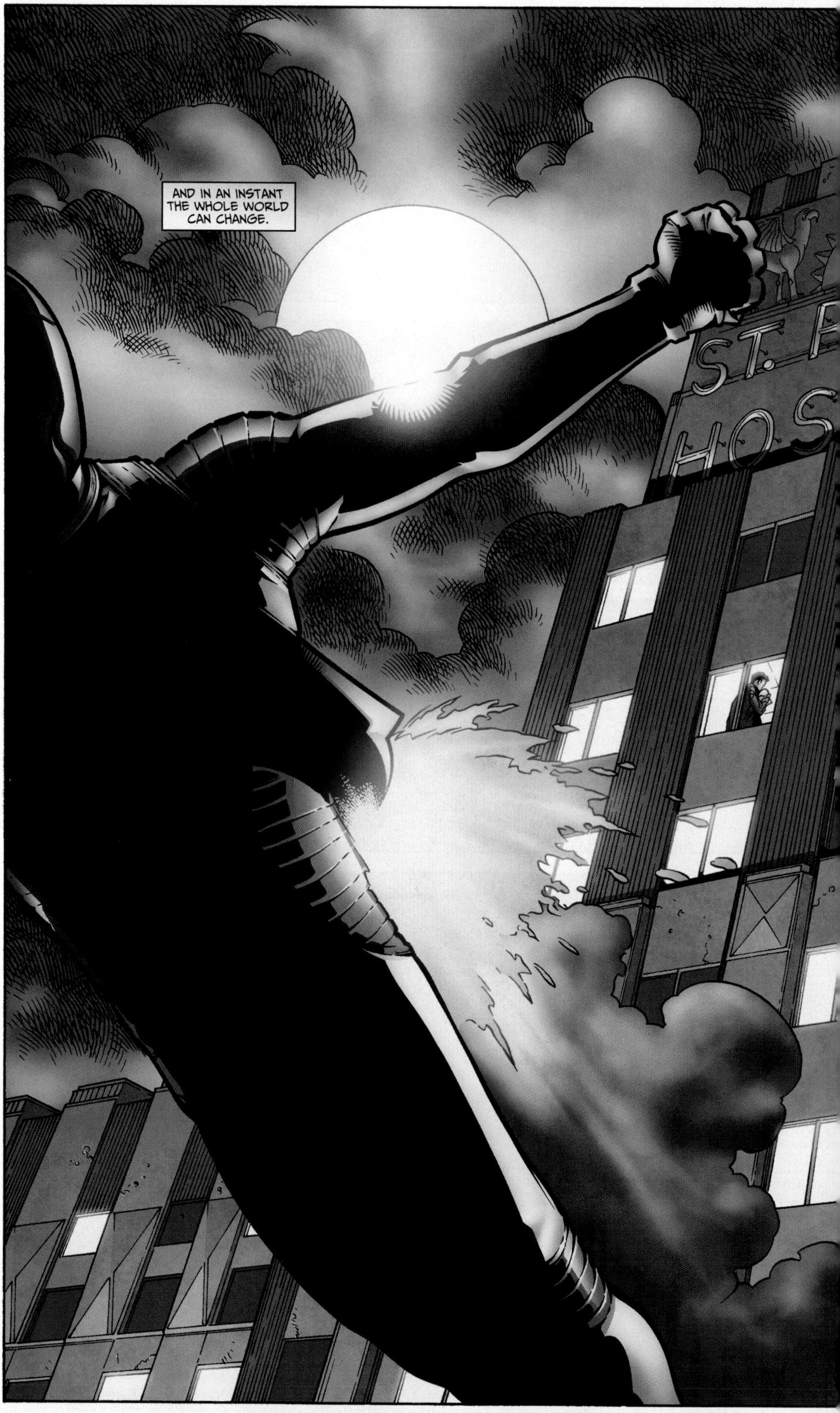
AND IN AN INSTANT THE WHOLE WORLD CAN CHANGE.
ST. F
HOS

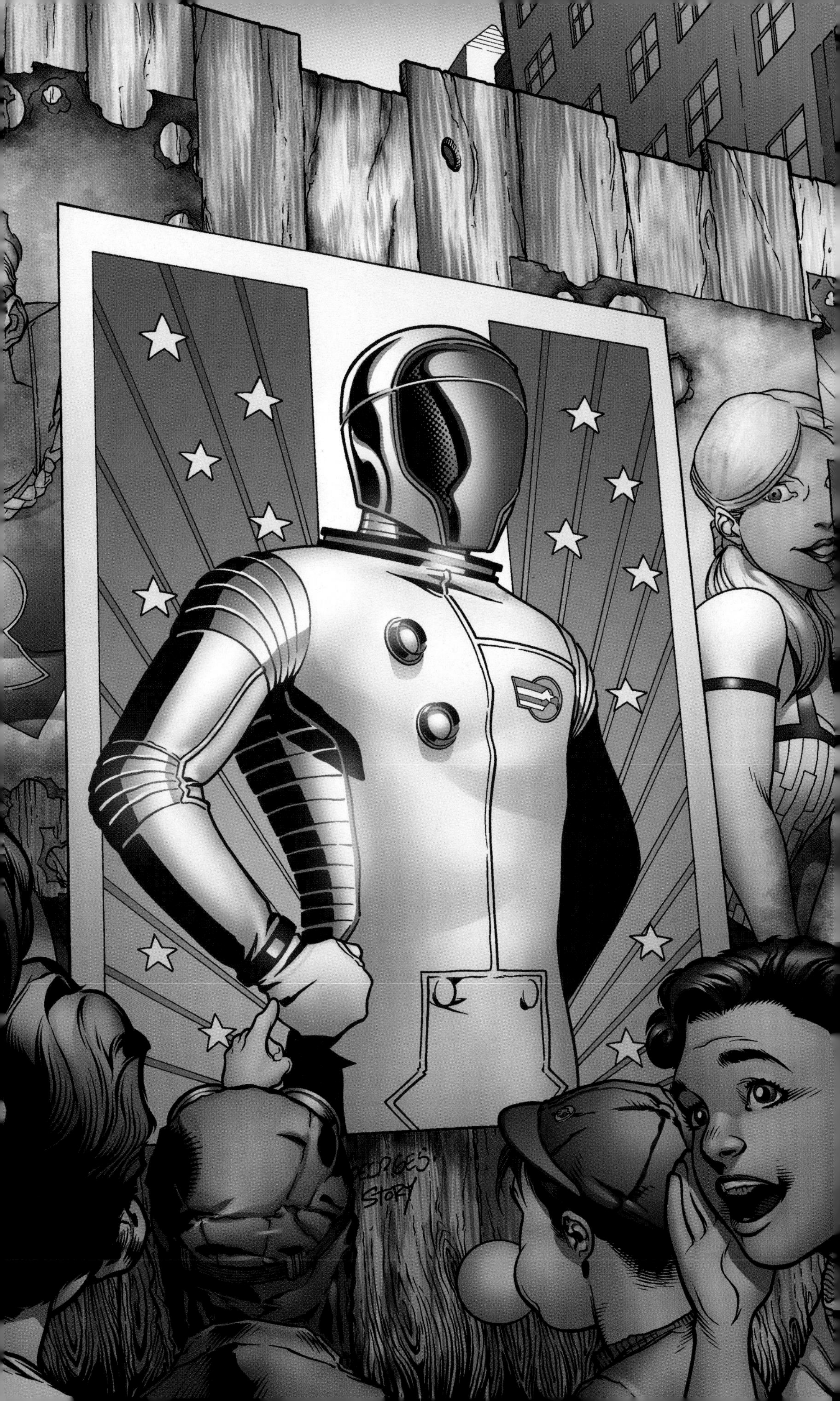

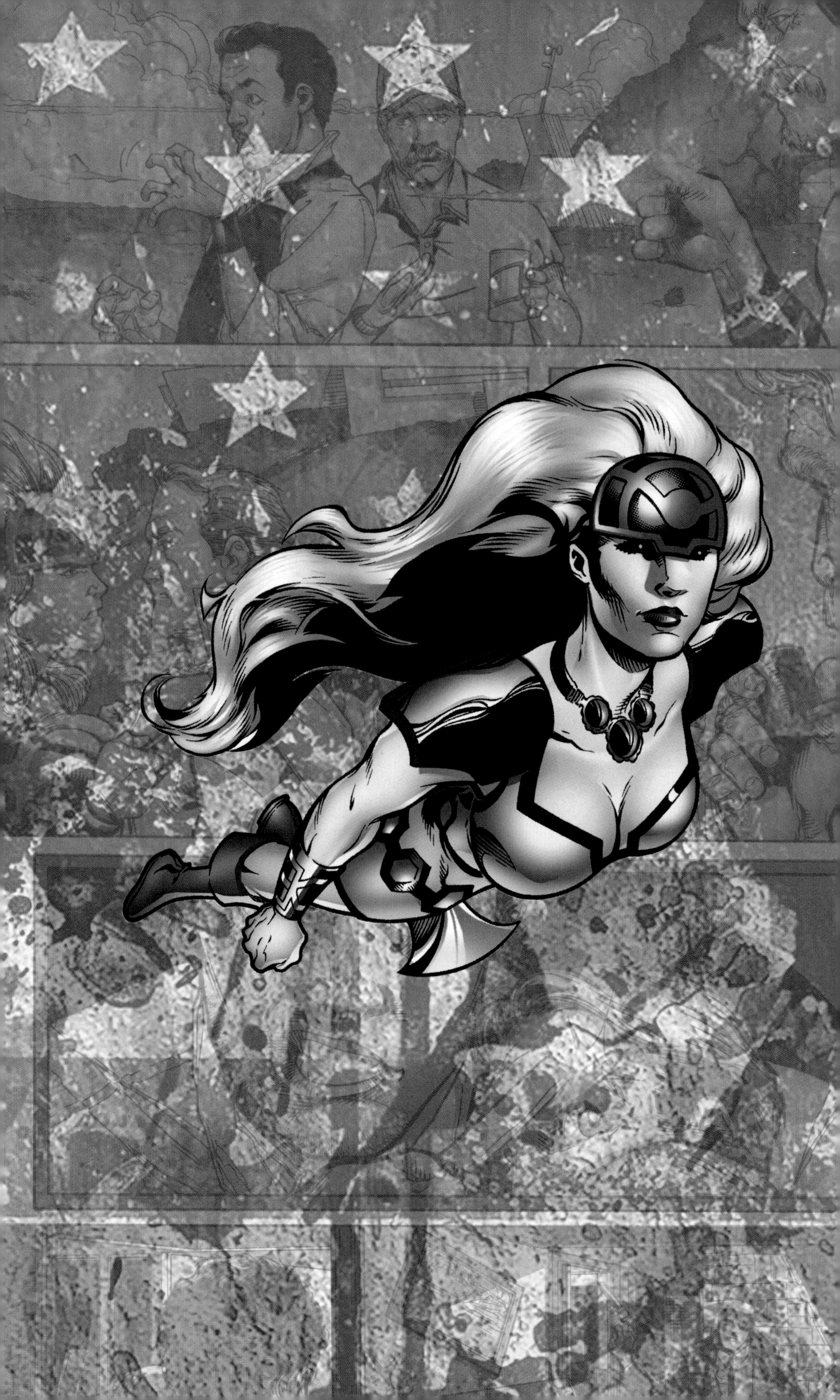

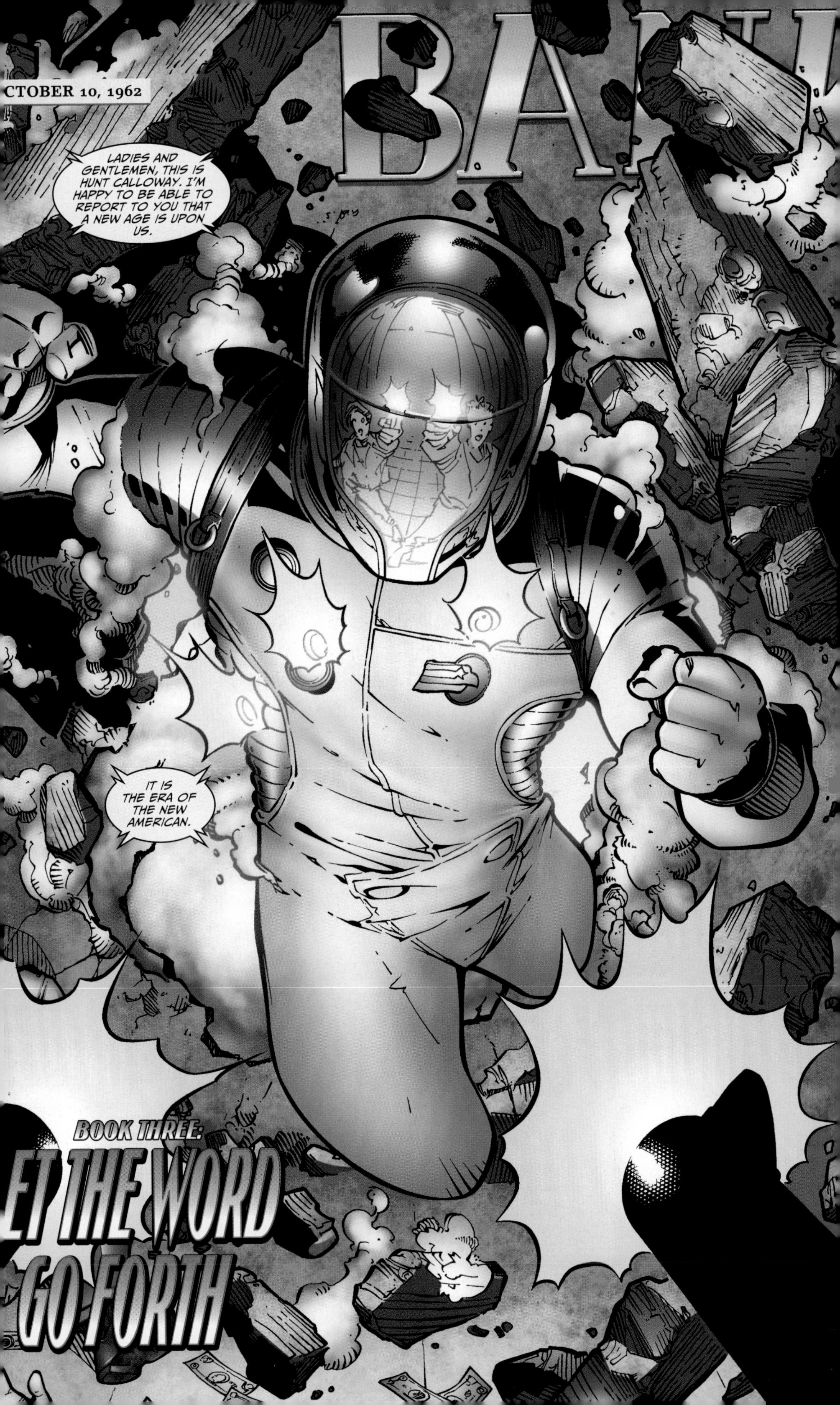
CTOBER 10, 1962
LADIES AND GENTLEMEN, THIS IS HUNT CALLOWAY. I'M HAPPY TO BE ABLE TO REPORT TO YOU THAT A NEW AGE IS UPON US.
IT IS THE ERA OF THE NEW AMERICAN.
BOOK THREE:
ET THE WORD GO FORTH

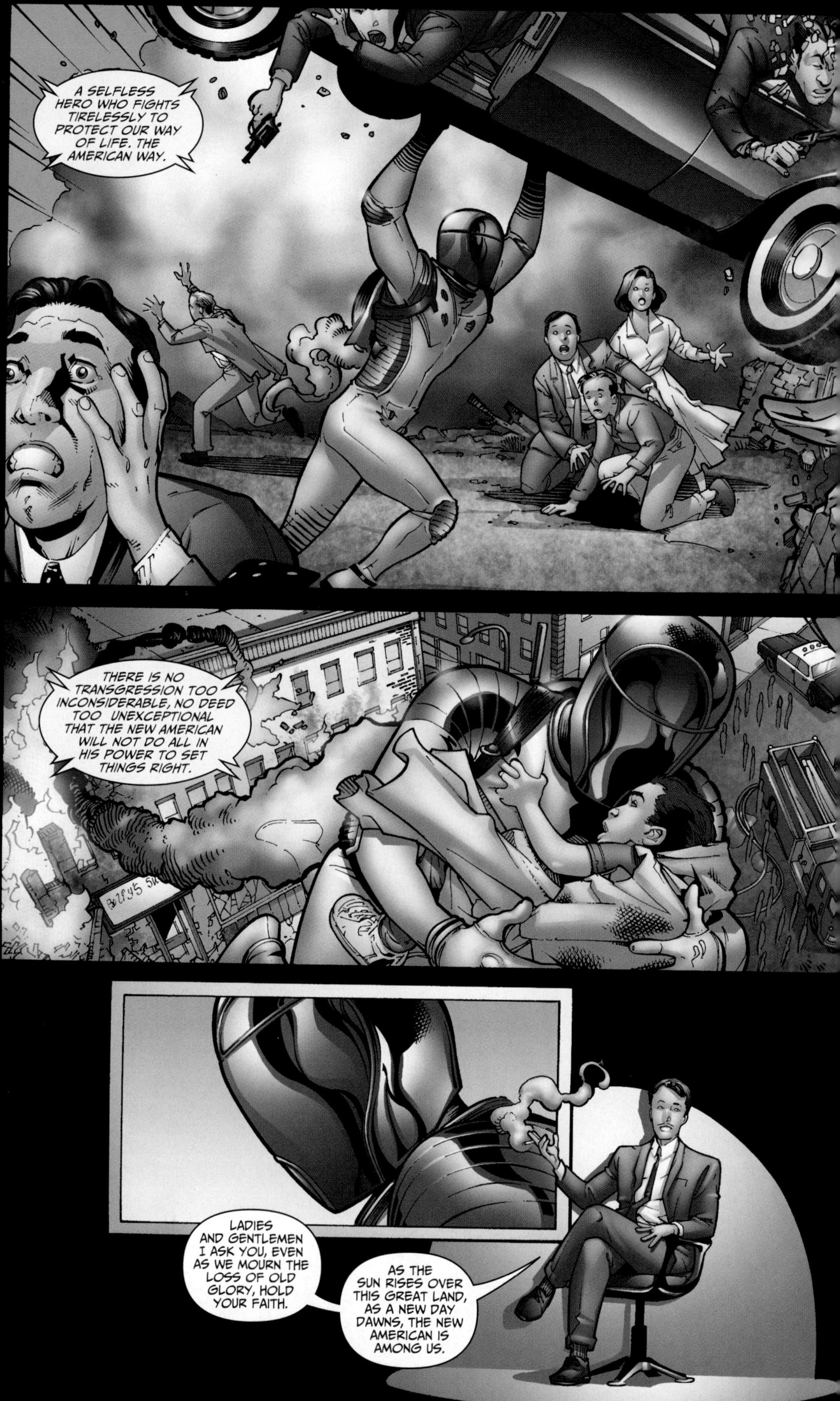
A SELFLESS HERO WHO FIGHTS TIRELESSLY TO PROTECT OUR WAY OF LIFE. THE AMERICAN WAY.
THERE IS NO TRANSGRESSION TOO INCONSIDERABLE, NO DEED TOO UNEXCEPTIONAL THAT THE NEW AMERICAN WILL NOT DO ALL IN HIS POWER TO SET THINGS RIGHT.
LADIES AND GENTLEMEN I ASK YOU, EVEN AS WE MOURN THE LOSS OF OLD GLORY, HOLD YOUR FAITH.
AS THE SUN RISES OVER THIS GREAT LAND, AS A NEW DAY DAWNS, THE NEW AMERICAN IS AMONG US.

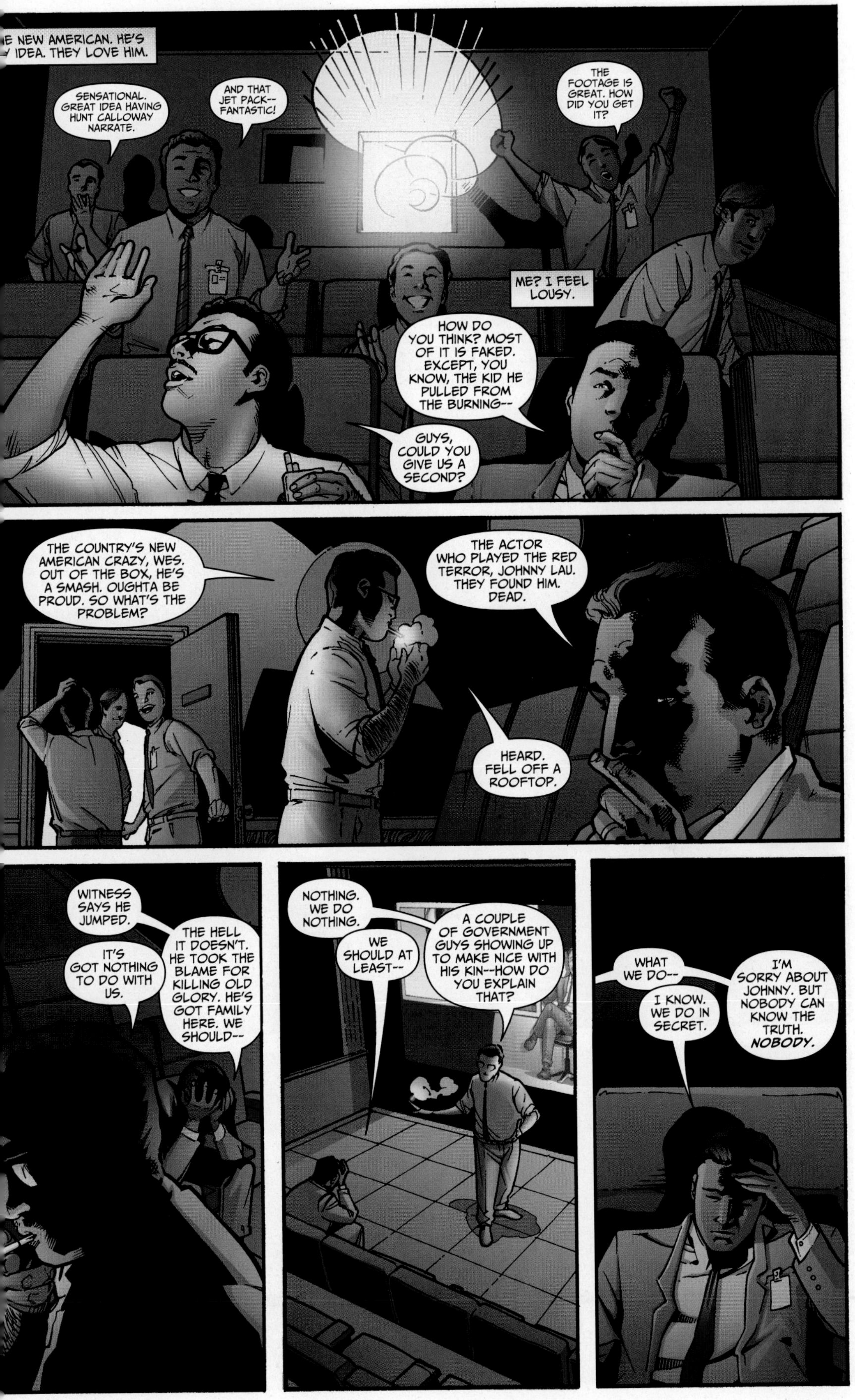
E NEW AMERICAN. HE'S
Y IDEA. THEY LOVE HIM.
SENSATIONAL. GREAT IDEA HAVING HUNT CALLOWAY NARRATE.
AND THAT JET PACK-- FANTASTIC!
THE FOOTAGE IS GREAT. HOW DID YOU GET IT?
ME? I FEEL LOUSY.
HOW DO YOU THINK? MOST OF IT IS FAKED. EXCEPT, YOU KNOW, THE KID HE PULLED FROM THE BURNING--
GUYS, COULD YOU GIVE US A SECOND?
THE COUNTRY'S NEW AMERICAN CRAZY, WES. OUT OF THE BOX, HE'S A SMASH. OUGHTA BE PROUD. SO WHAT'S THE PROBLEM?
THE ACTOR WHO PLAYED THE RED TERROR, JOHNNY LAU. THEY FOUND HIM. DEAD.
HEARD. FELL OFF A ROOFTOP.
WITNESS SAYS HE JUMPED.
IT'S GOT NOTHING TO DO WITH US.
THE HELL IT DOESN'T. HE TOOK THE BLAME FOR KILLING OLD GLORY. HE'S GOT FAMILY HERE. WE SHOULD--
NOTHING. WE DO NOTHING.
WE SHOULD AT LEAST--
A COUPLE OF GOVERNMENT GUYS SHOWING UP TO MAKE NICE WITH HIS KIN--HOW DO YOU EXPLAIN THAT?
WHAT WE DO--
I KNOW. WE DO IN SECRET.
I'M SORRY ABOUT JOHNNY. BUT NOBODY CAN KNOW THE TRUTH. *NOBODY.*

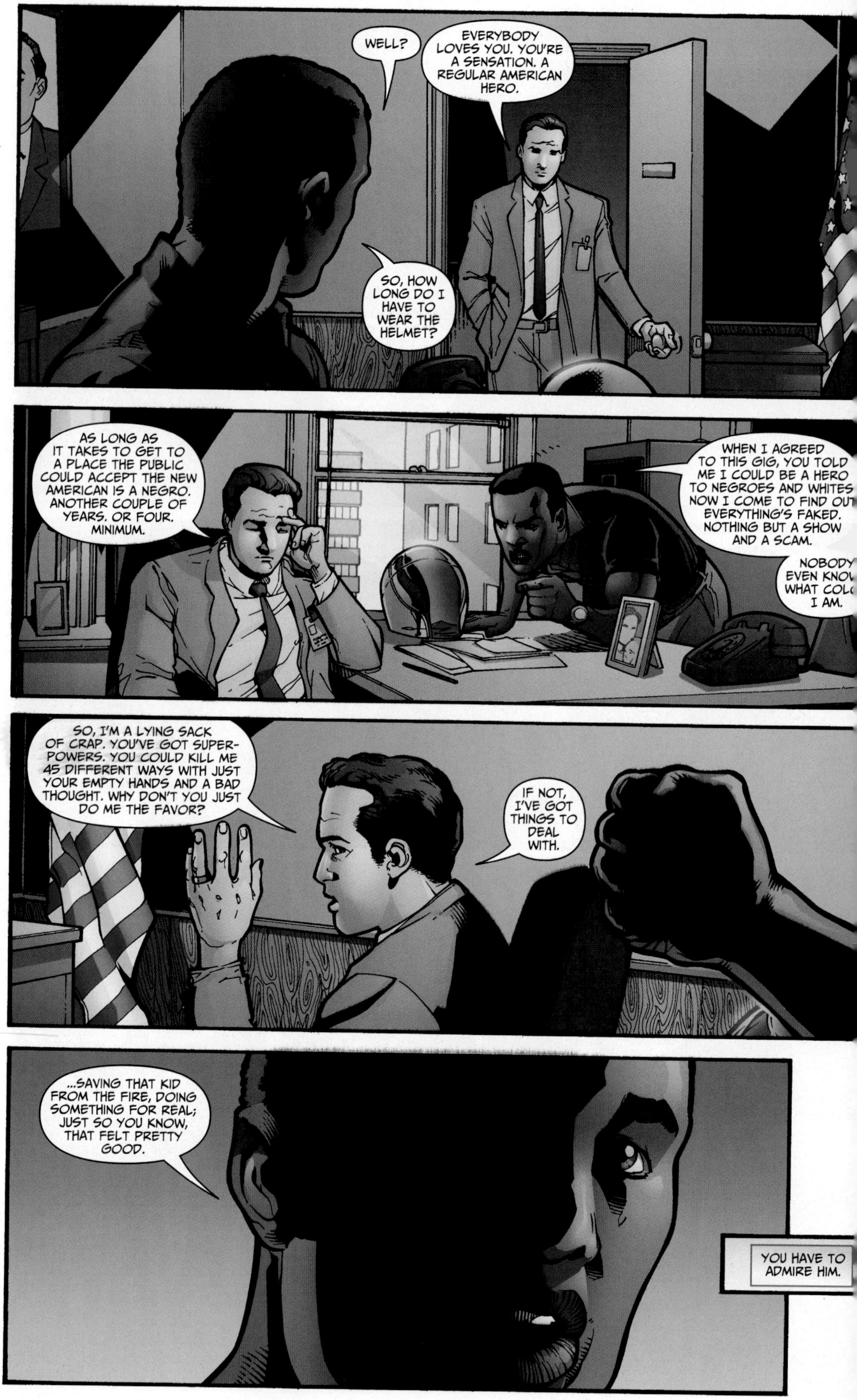
WELL?
EVERYBODY LOVES YOU. YOU'RE A SENSATION. A REGULAR AMERICAN HERO.
SO, HOW LONG DO I HAVE TO WEAR THE HELMET?
AS LONG AS IT TAKES TO GET TO A PLACE THE PUBLIC COULD ACCEPT THE NEW AMERICAN IS A NEGRO. ANOTHER COUPLE OF YEARS. OR FOUR. MINIMUM.
WHEN I AGREED TO THIS GIG, YOU TOLD ME I COULD BE A HERO TO NEGROES AND WHITES NOW I COME TO FIND OUT EVERYTHING'S FAKED. NOTHING BUT A SHOW AND A SCAM.
NOBODY EVEN KNOW WHAT COL I AM.
SO, I'M A LYING SACK OF CRAP. YOU'VE GOT SUPER-POWERS. YOU COULD KILL ME 45 DIFFERENT WAYS WITH JUST YOUR EMPTY HANDS AND A BAD THOUGHT. WHY DON'T YOU JUST DO ME THE FAVOR?
IF NOT, I'VE GOT THINGS TO DEAL WITH.
...SAVING THAT KID FROM THE FIRE, DOING SOMETHING FOR REAL; JUST SO YOU KNOW, THAT FELT PRETTY GOOD.
YOU HAVE TO ADMIRE HIM.

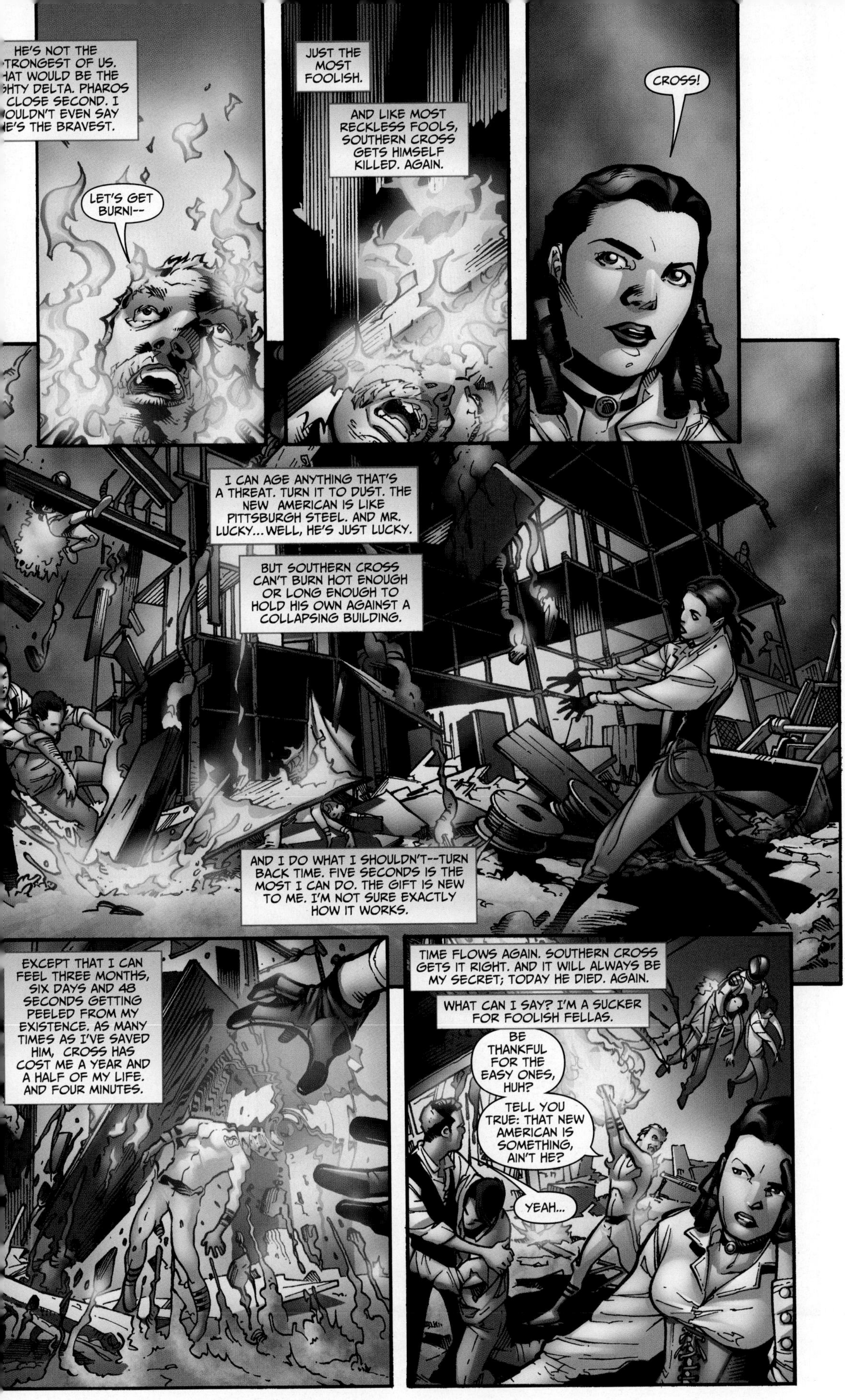
HE'S NOT THE
TRONGEST OF US.
HAT WOULD BE THE
GHTY DELTA. PHAROS
CLOSE SECOND. I
OULDN'T EVEN SAY
E'S THE BRAVEST.
LET'S GET BURNI--
JUST THE MOST FOOLISH.
AND LIKE MOST RECKLESS FOOLS, SOUTHERN CROSS GETS HIMSELF KILLED. AGAIN.
CROSS!
I CAN AGE ANYTHING THAT'S A THREAT. TURN IT TO DUST. THE NEW AMERICAN IS LIKE PITTSBURGH STEEL. AND MR. LUCKY...WELL, HE'S JUST LUCKY.
BUT SOUTHERN CROSS CAN'T BURN HOT ENOUGH OR LONG ENOUGH TO HOLD HIS OWN AGAINST A COLLAPSING BUILDING.
AND I DO WHAT I SHOULDN'T--TURN BACK TIME. FIVE SECONDS IS THE MOST I CAN DO. THE GIFT IS NEW TO ME. I'M NOT SURE EXACTLY HOW IT WORKS.
EXCEPT THAT I CAN FEEL THREE MONTHS, SIX DAYS AND 48 SECONDS GETTING PEELED FROM MY EXISTENCE. AS MANY TIMES AS I'VE SAVED HIM, CROSS HAS COST ME A YEAR AND A HALF OF MY LIFE. AND FOUR MINUTES.
TIME FLOWS AGAIN. SOUTHERN CROSS GETS IT RIGHT. AND IT WILL ALWAYS BE MY SECRET; TODAY HE DIED. AGAIN.
WHAT CAN I SAY? I'M A SUCKER FOR FOOLISH FELLAS.
BE THANKFUL FOR THE EASY ONES, HUH?
TELL YOU TRUE: THAT NEW AMERICAN IS SOMETHING, AIN'T HE?
YEAH...

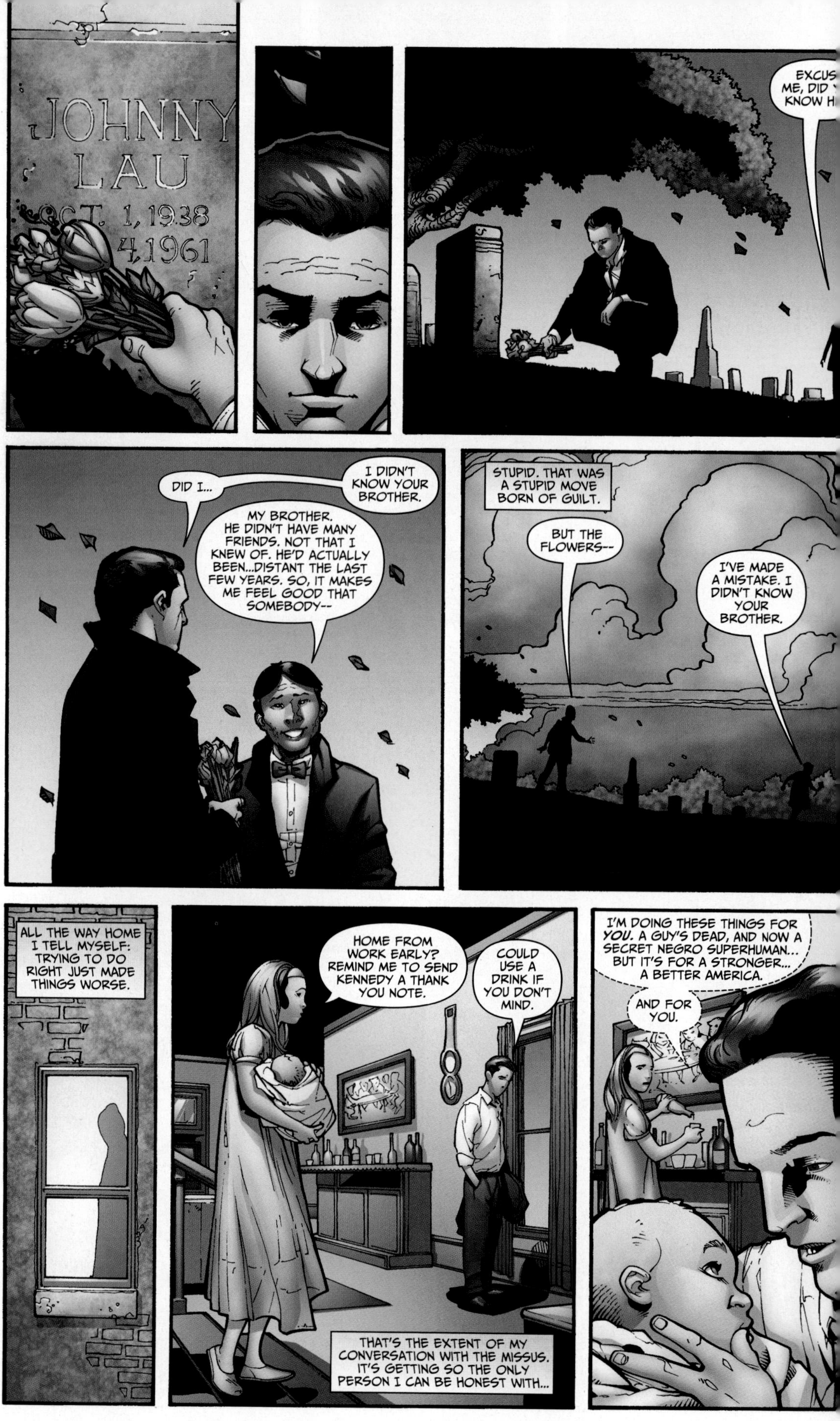
JOHNNY
LAU
OCT. 1, 1938
4, 1961
EXCUS
ME, DID
KNOW H
DID I...
I DIDN'T KNOW YOUR BROTHER.
MY BROTHER. HE DIDN'T HAVE MANY FRIENDS. NOT THAT I KNEW OF. HE'D ACTUALLY BEEN...DISTANT THE LAST FEW YEARS. SO, IT MAKES ME FEEL GOOD THAT SOMEBODY--
STUPID. THAT WAS A STUPID MOVE BORN OF GUILT.
BUT THE FLOWERS--
I'VE MADE A MISTAKE. I DIDN'T KNOW YOUR BROTHER.
ALL THE WAY HOME I TELL MYSELF: TRYING TO DO RIGHT JUST MADE THINGS WORSE.
HOME FROM WORK EARLY? REMIND ME TO SEND KENNEDY A THANK YOU NOTE.
COULD USE A DRINK IF YOU DON'T MIND.
THAT'S THE EXTENT OF MY CONVERSATION WITH THE MISSUS. IT'S GETTING SO THE ONLY PERSON I CAN BE HONEST WITH...
I'M DOING THESE THINGS FOR YOU. A GUY'S DEAD, AND NOW A SECRET NEGRO SUPERHUMAN... BUT IT'S FOR A STRONGER... A BETTER AMERICA.
AND FOR YOU.

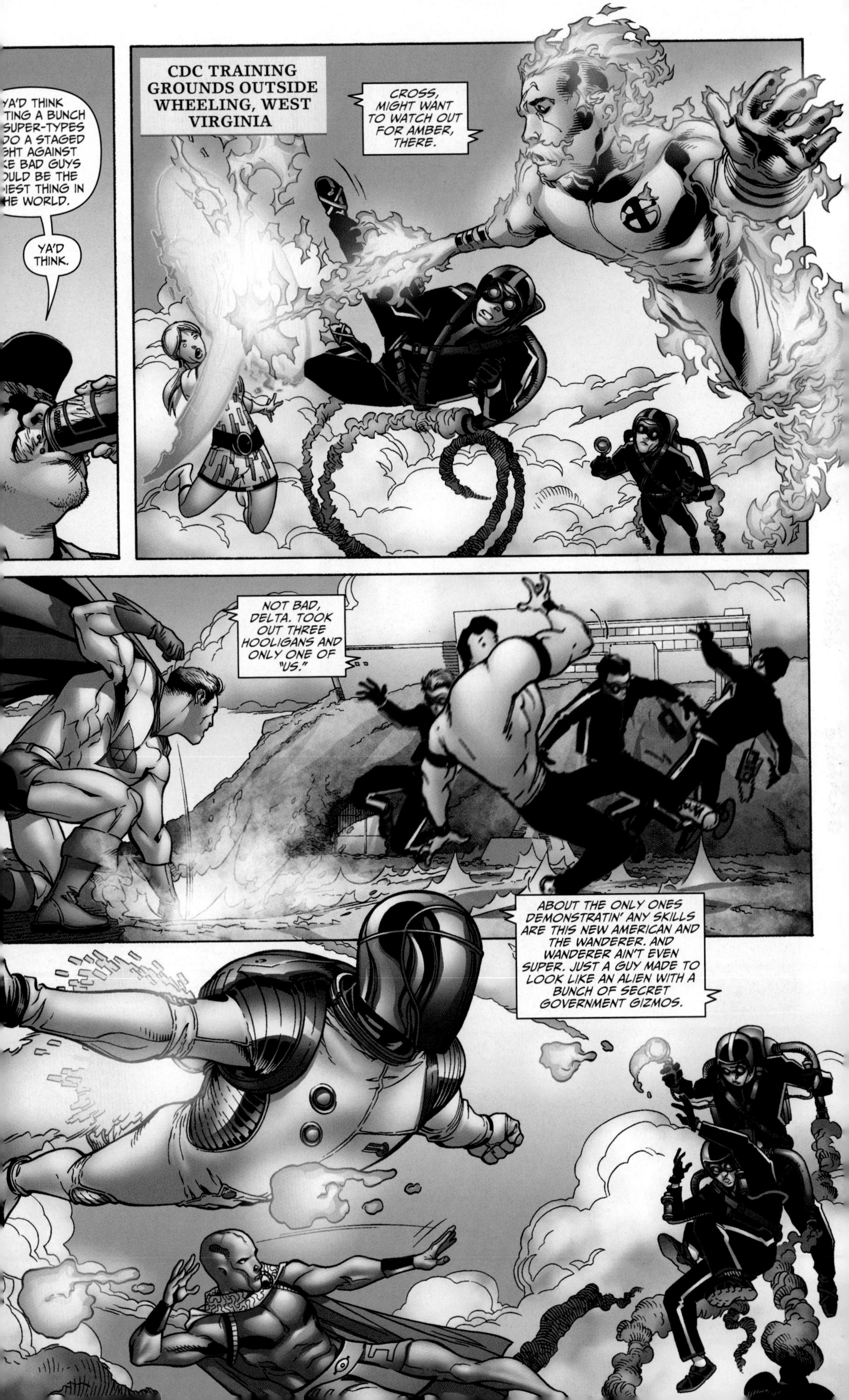

YA'D THINK TING A BUNCH SUPER-TYPES DO A STAGED GHT AGAINST KE BAD GUYS OULD BE THE PIEST THING IN HE WORLD.
YA'D THINK.
CDC TRAINING GROUNDS OUTSIDE WHEELING, WEST VIRGINIA
CROSS, MIGHT WANT TO WATCH OUT FOR AMBER, THERE.
NOT BAD, DELTA. TOOK OUT THREE HOOLIGANS AND ONLY ONE OF "US."
ABOUT THE ONLY ONES DEMONSTRATIN' ANY SKILLS ARE THIS NEW AMERICAN AND THE WANDERER. AND WANDERER AIN'T EVEN SUPER. JUST A GUY MADE TO LOOK LIKE AN ALIEN WITH A BUNCH OF SECRET GOVERNMENT GIZMOS.

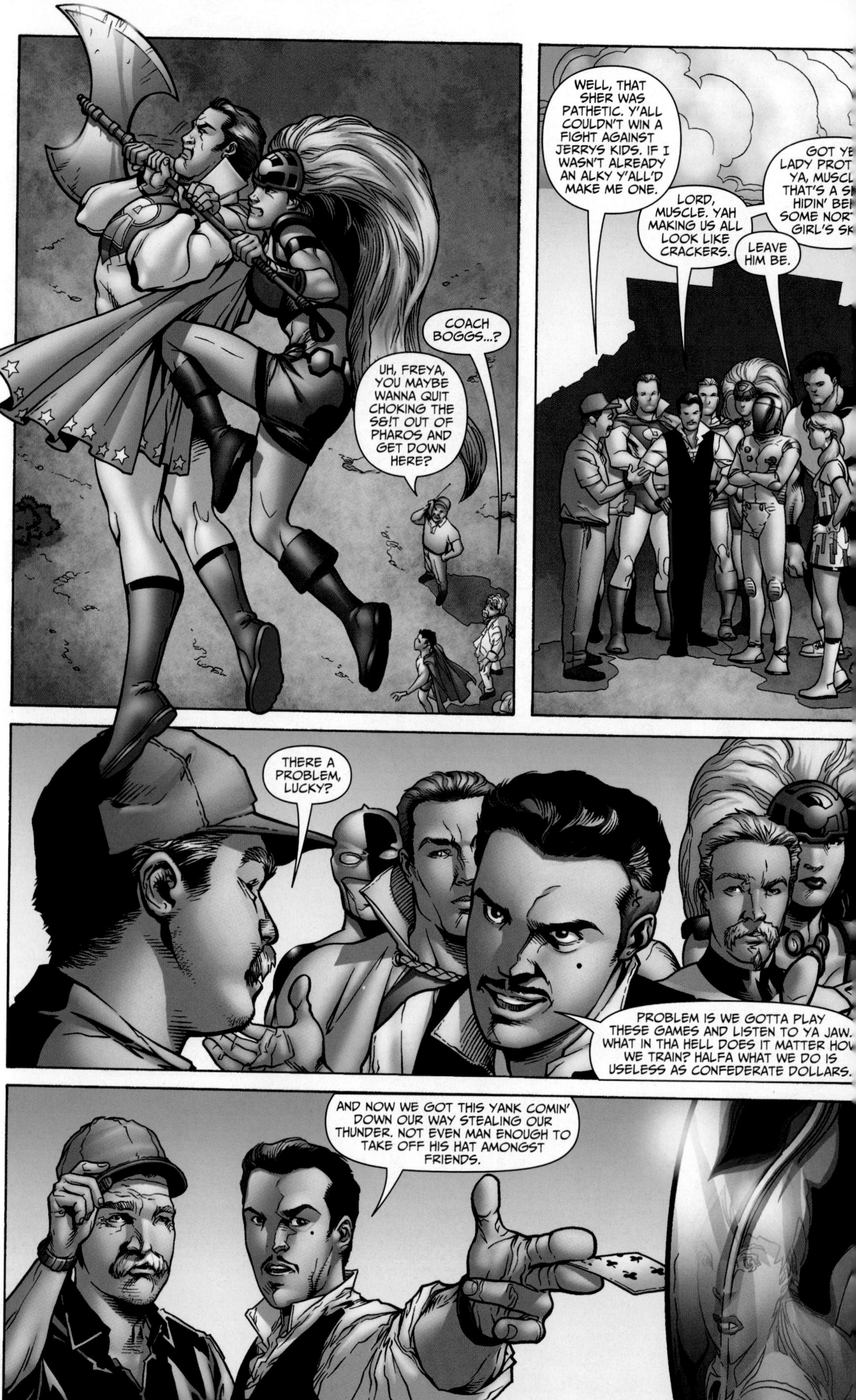
COACH BOGGS...?
UH, FREYA, YOU MAYBE WANNA QUIT CHOKING THE S&!T OUT OF PHAROS AND GET DOWN HERE?
WELL, THAT SHER WAS PATHETIC. Y'ALL COULDN'T WIN A FIGHT AGAINST JERRYS KIDS. IF I WASN'T ALREADY AN ALKY Y'ALL'D MAKE ME ONE.
LORD, MUSCLE. YAH MAKING US ALL LOOK LIKE CRACKERS.
LEAVE HIM BE.
THERE A PROBLEM, LUCKY?
PROBLEM IS WE GOTTA PLAY THESE GAMES AND LISTEN TO YA JAW. WHAT IN THA HELL DOES IT MATTER HOW WE TRAIN? HALFA WHAT WE DO IS USELESS AS CONFEDERATE DOLLARS.
AND NOW WE GOT THIS YANK COMIN' DOWN OUR WAY STEALING OUR THUNDER. NOT EVEN MAN ENOUGH TO TAKE OFF HIS HAT AMONGST FRIENDS.

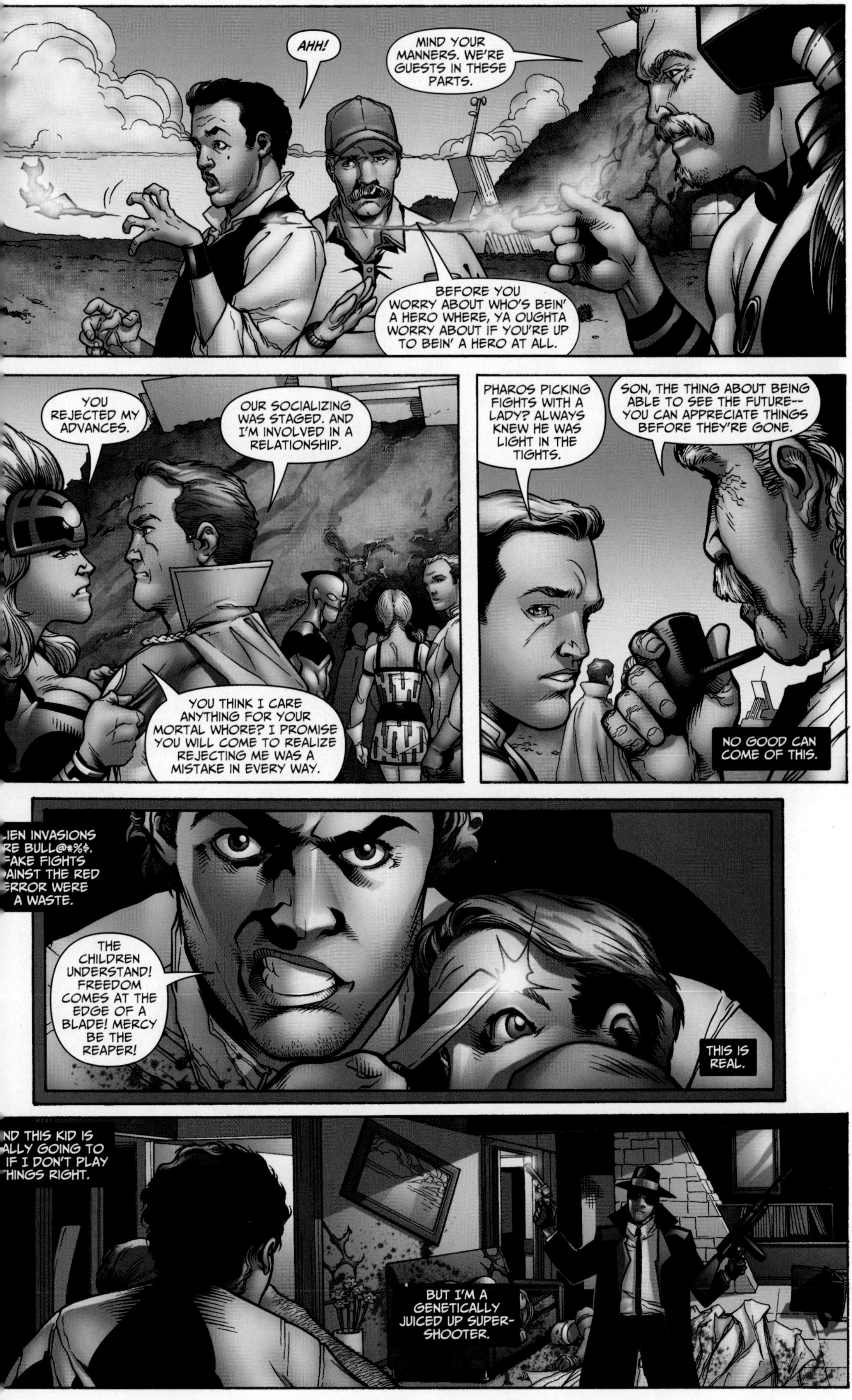
AHH!
MIND YOUR MANNERS. WE'RE GUESTS IN THESE PARTS.
BEFORE YOU WORRY ABOUT WHO'S BEIN' A HERO WHERE, YA OUGHTA WORRY ABOUT IF YOU'RE UP TO BEIN' A HERO AT ALL.
YOU REJECTED MY ADVANCES.
OUR SOCIALIZING WAS STAGED. AND I'M INVOLVED IN A RELATIONSHIP.
YOU THINK I CARE ANYTHING FOR YOUR MORTAL WHORE? I PROMISE YOU WILL COME TO REALIZE REJECTING ME WAS A MISTAKE IN EVERY WAY.
PHAROS PICKING FIGHTS WITH A LADY? ALWAYS KNEW HE WAS LIGHT IN THE TIGHTS.
SON, THE THING ABOUT BEING ABLE TO SEE THE FUTURE-- YOU CAN APPRECIATE THINGS BEFORE THEY'RE GONE.
NO GOOD CAN COME OF THIS.
THE CHILDREN UNDERSTAND! FREEDOM COMES AT THE EDGE OF A BLADE! MERCY BE THE REAPER!
THIS IS REAL.
BUT I'M A GENETICALLY JUICED UP SUPER-SHOOTER.

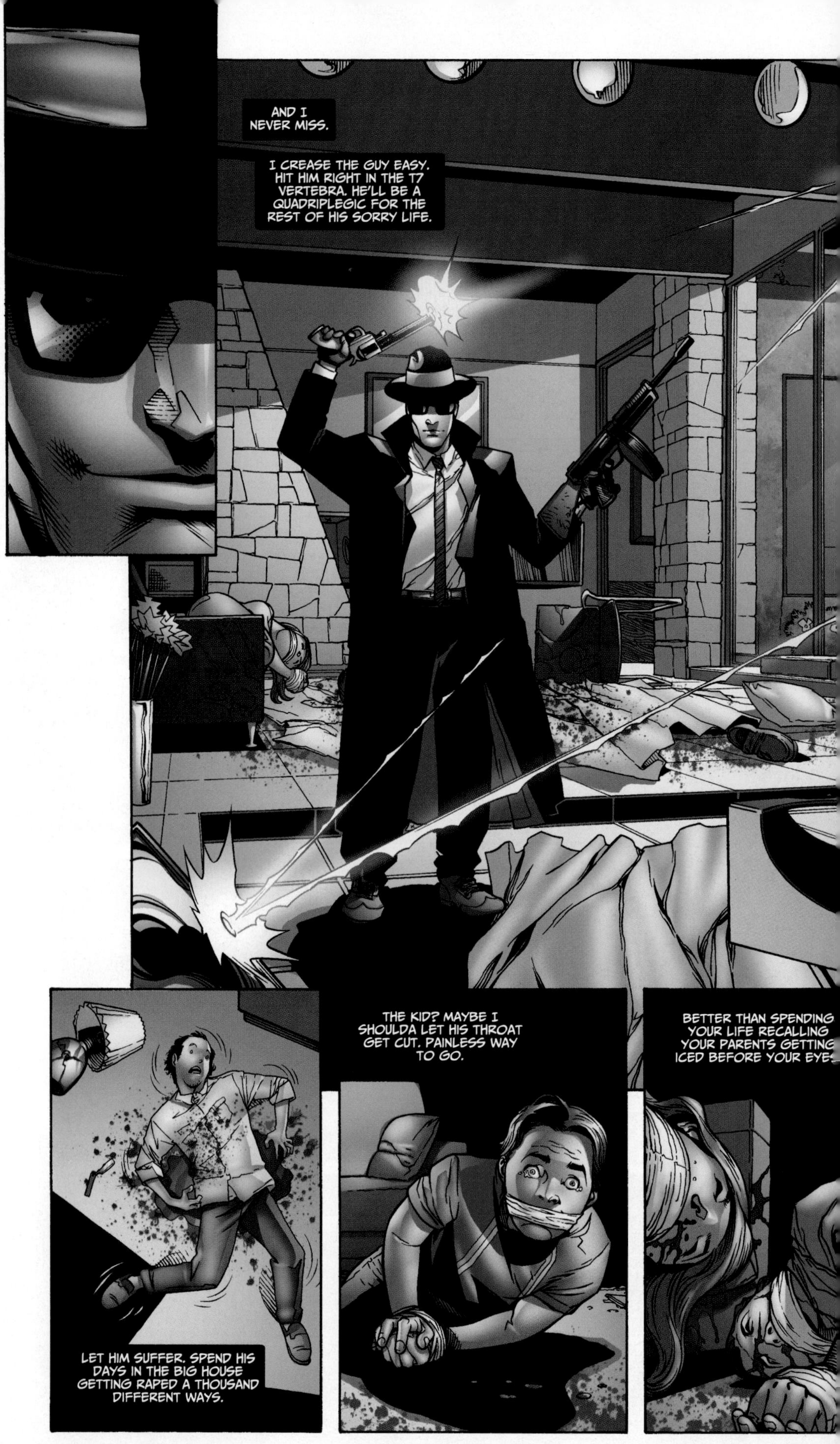
AND I NEVER MISS.
I CREASE THE GUY EASY. HIT HIM RIGHT IN THE T7 VERTEBRA. HE'LL BE A QUADRIPLEGIC FOR THE REST OF HIS SORRY LIFE.
LET HIM SUFFER. SPEND HIS DAYS IN THE BIG HOUSE GETTING RAPED A THOUSAND DIFFERENT WAYS.
THE KID? MAYBE I SHOULDA LET HIS THROAT GET CUT. PAINLESS WAY TO GO.
BETTER THAN SPENDING YOUR LIFE RECALLING YOUR PARENTS GETTING ICED BEFORE YOUR EYES

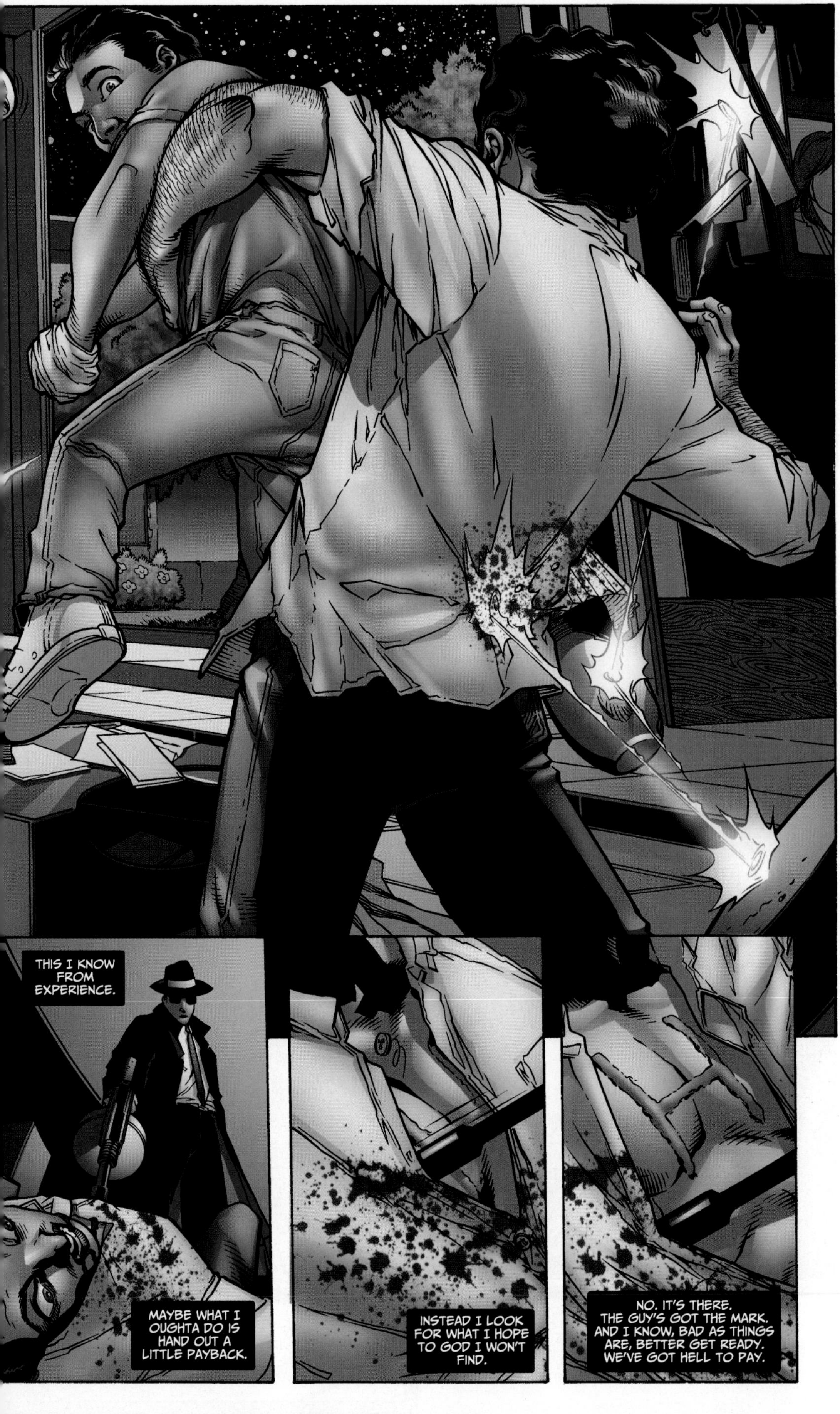
THIS I KNOW FROM EXPERIENCE.
MAYBE WHAT I OUGHTA DO IS HAND OUT A LITTLE PAYBACK.
INSTEAD I LOOK FOR WHAT I HOPE TO GOD I WON'T FIND.
NO. IT'S THERE. THE GUY'S GOT THE MARK. AND I KNOW, BAD AS THINGS ARE, BETTER GET READY. WE'VE GOT HELL TO PAY.

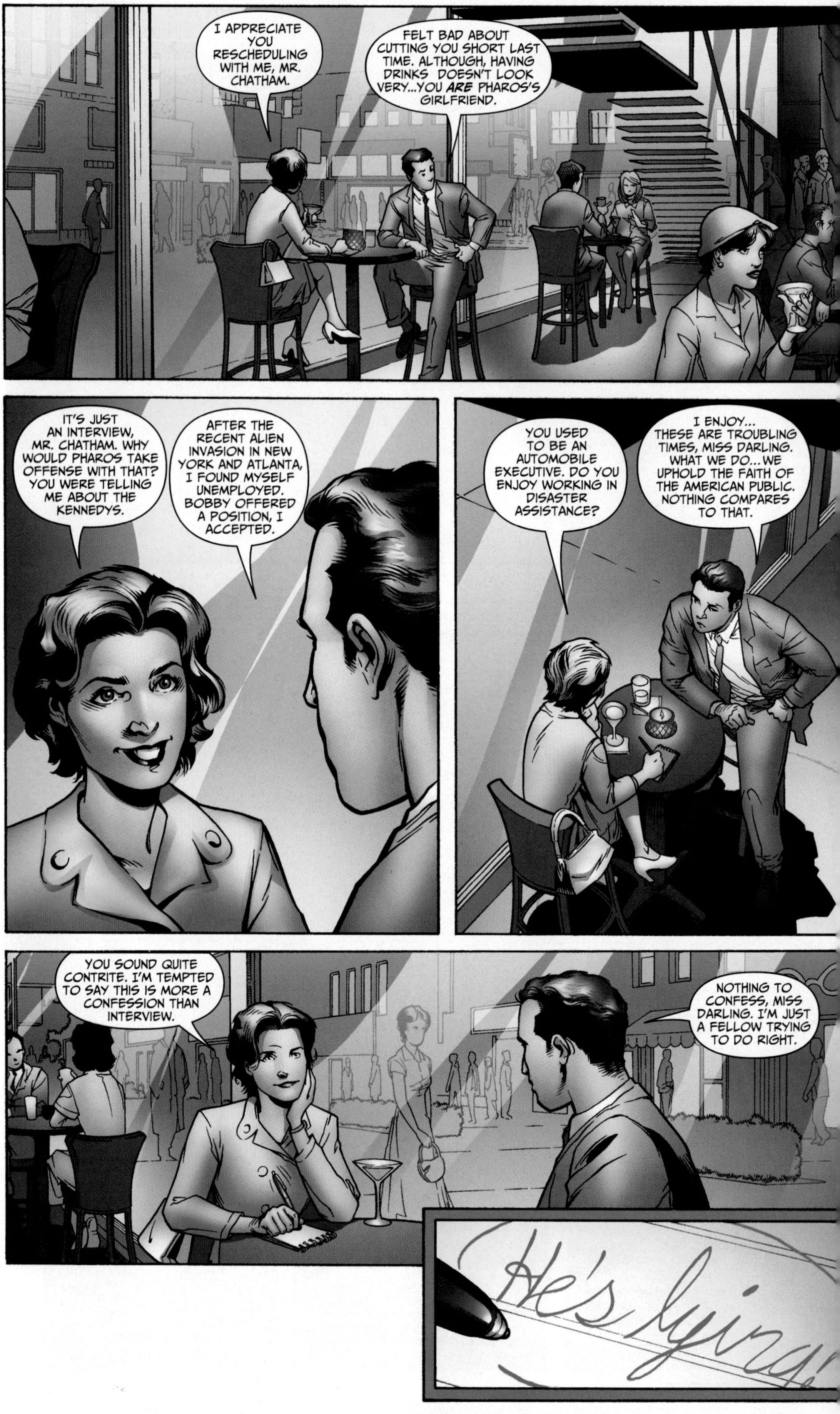
I APPRECIATE YOU RESCHEDULING WITH ME, MR. CHATHAM.
FELT BAD ABOUT CUTTING YOU SHORT LAST TIME. ALTHOUGH, HAVING DRINKS DOESN'T LOOK VERY...YOU ***ARE*** PHAROS'S GIRLFRIEND.
IT'S JUST AN INTERVIEW, MR. CHATHAM. WHY WOULD PHAROS TAKE OFFENSE WITH THAT? YOU WERE TELLING ME ABOUT THE KENNEDYS.
AFTER THE RECENT ALIEN INVASION IN NEW YORK AND ATLANTA, I FOUND MYSELF UNEMPLOYED. BOBBY OFFERED A POSITION, I ACCEPTED.
YOU USED TO BE AN AUTOMOBILE EXECUTIVE. DO YOU ENJOY WORKING IN DISASTER ASSISTANCE?
I ENJOY... THESE ARE TROUBLING TIMES, MISS DARLING. WHAT WE DO...WE UPHOLD THE FAITH OF THE AMERICAN PUBLIC. NOTHING COMPARES TO THAT.
YOU SOUND QUITE CONTRITE. I'M TEMPTED TO SAY THIS IS MORE A CONFESSION THAN INTERVIEW.
NOTHING TO CONFESS, MISS DARLING. I'M JUST A FELLOW TRYING TO DO RIGHT.
He's lying!

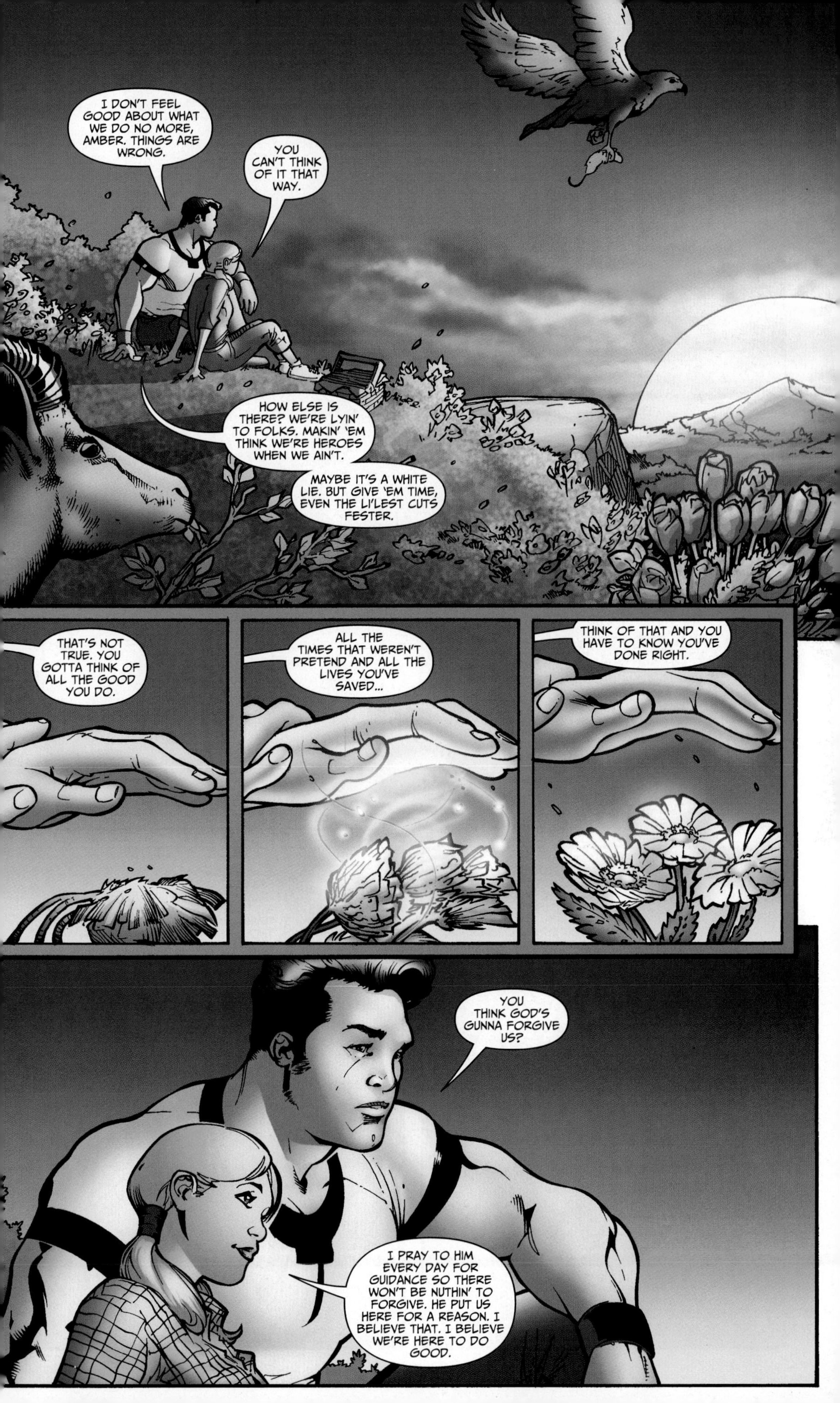

I DON'T FEEL GOOD ABOUT WHAT WE DO NO MORE, AMBER. THINGS ARE WRONG.
YOU CAN'T THINK OF IT THAT WAY.
HOW ELSE IS THERE? WE'RE LYIN' TO FOLKS. MAKIN' 'EM THINK WE'RE HEROES WHEN WE AIN'T.
MAYBE IT'S A WHITE LIE. BUT GIVE 'EM TIME, EVEN THE LI'LEST CUTS FESTER.
THAT'S NOT TRUE. YOU GOTTA THINK OF ALL THE GOOD YOU DO.
ALL THE TIMES THAT WEREN'T PRETEND AND ALL THE LIVES YOU'VE SAVED...
THINK OF THAT AND YOU HAVE TO KNOW YOU'VE DONE RIGHT.
YOU THINK GOD'S GUNNA FORGIVE US?
I PRAY TO HIM EVERY DAY FOR GUIDANCE SO THERE WON'T BE NUTHIN' TO FORGIVE. HE PUT US HERE FOR A REASON. I BELIEVE THAT. I BELIEVE WE'RE HERE TO DO GOOD.

LADIES AND GENTLEMEN, HUNT CALLOWAY. WELL, THE NEW AMERICAN HAS DONE IT AGAIN.

SAVED THE DAY. RESTORED O[U]R FAITH. JUST BEEN PLAIN SUPER.

FOLKS, AS A MOUTHPIECE OF TH[E] LIBERAL MEDIA I'M N[OT] TELLING YOU WHAT T[O] THINK. BUT IF I FOUND [OUT] THIS NEW AMERICAN FEL[LOW] WAS A FULL-ON JIG, C[OAL] SPOOKITY-SPOOK I'D L[OVE] HIM JUST AS MUCH AS IF [HE] WERE LILY, PORCELA[IN] WHITE!

CDC HQ WASHINGTON, DC

ARE YOU ALL RIGHT?

JUST DAY DREAMING.

THE TRAINING SESSION GOT YOU DOWN? DON'T PAY ANY MIND TO THAT MR. LUCKY. HE'S JUST JEALOUS.

THEY USED TO MAKE FUN OF ME ALL THE TIME BECAUSE I DON'T HAVE POWERS. WAS A CANDIDATE FOR GENE THERAPY, BUT, WELL, MY BODY WOULDN'T TAKE IT.

NOW I'M SORT OF LIKE ONE OF THOSE SPACE MONKEYS TESTING OUT ALL THOSE GIZMOS FOR NASA.

YOU'RE MORE THAN THAT.

IT'S OKAY, I KNOW I'M JUST A...NOT MUCH OF ANYTHING, REALLY. EVEN MY FAMILY THOUGHT I WAS A WASHOUT.

THEN I TOLD THEM I WAS THE WANDERER.

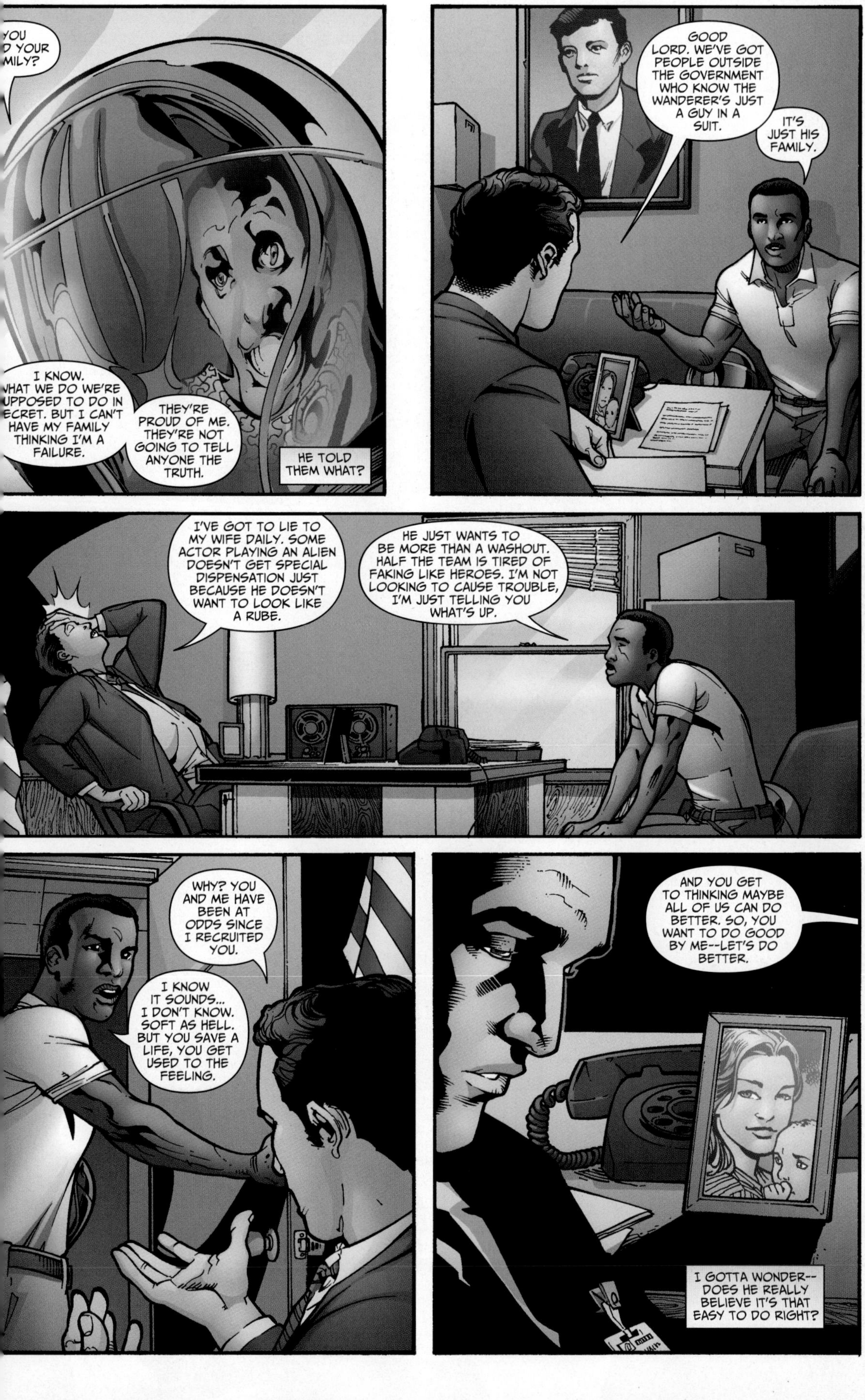

YOU
D YOUR
MILY?
I KNOW. WHAT WE DO WE'RE SUPPOSED TO DO IN ECRET. BUT I CAN'T HAVE MY FAMILY THINKING I'M A FAILURE.
THEY'RE PROUD OF ME. THEY'RE NOT GOING TO TELL ANYONE THE TRUTH.
HE TOLD THEM WHAT?
GOOD LORD. WE'VE GOT PEOPLE OUTSIDE THE GOVERNMENT WHO KNOW THE WANDERER'S JUST A GUY IN A SUIT.
IT'S JUST HIS FAMILY.
I'VE GOT TO LIE TO MY WIFE DAILY. SOME ACTOR PLAYING AN ALIEN DOESN'T GET SPECIAL DISPENSATION JUST BECAUSE HE DOESN'T WANT TO LOOK LIKE A RUBE.
HE JUST WANTS TO BE MORE THAN A WASHOUT. HALF THE TEAM IS TIRED OF FAKING LIKE HEROES. I'M NOT LOOKING TO CAUSE TROUBLE, I'M JUST TELLING YOU WHAT'S UP.
WHY? YOU AND ME HAVE BEEN AT ODDS SINCE I RECRUITED YOU.
I KNOW IT SOUNDS... I DON'T KNOW. SOFT AS HELL. BUT YOU SAVE A LIFE, YOU GET USED TO THE FEELING.
AND YOU GET TO THINKING MAYBE ALL OF US CAN DO BETTER. SO, YOU WANT TO DO GOOD BY ME--LET'S DO BETTER.
I GOTTA WONDER-- DOES HE REALLY BELIEVE IT'S THAT EASY TO DO RIGHT?

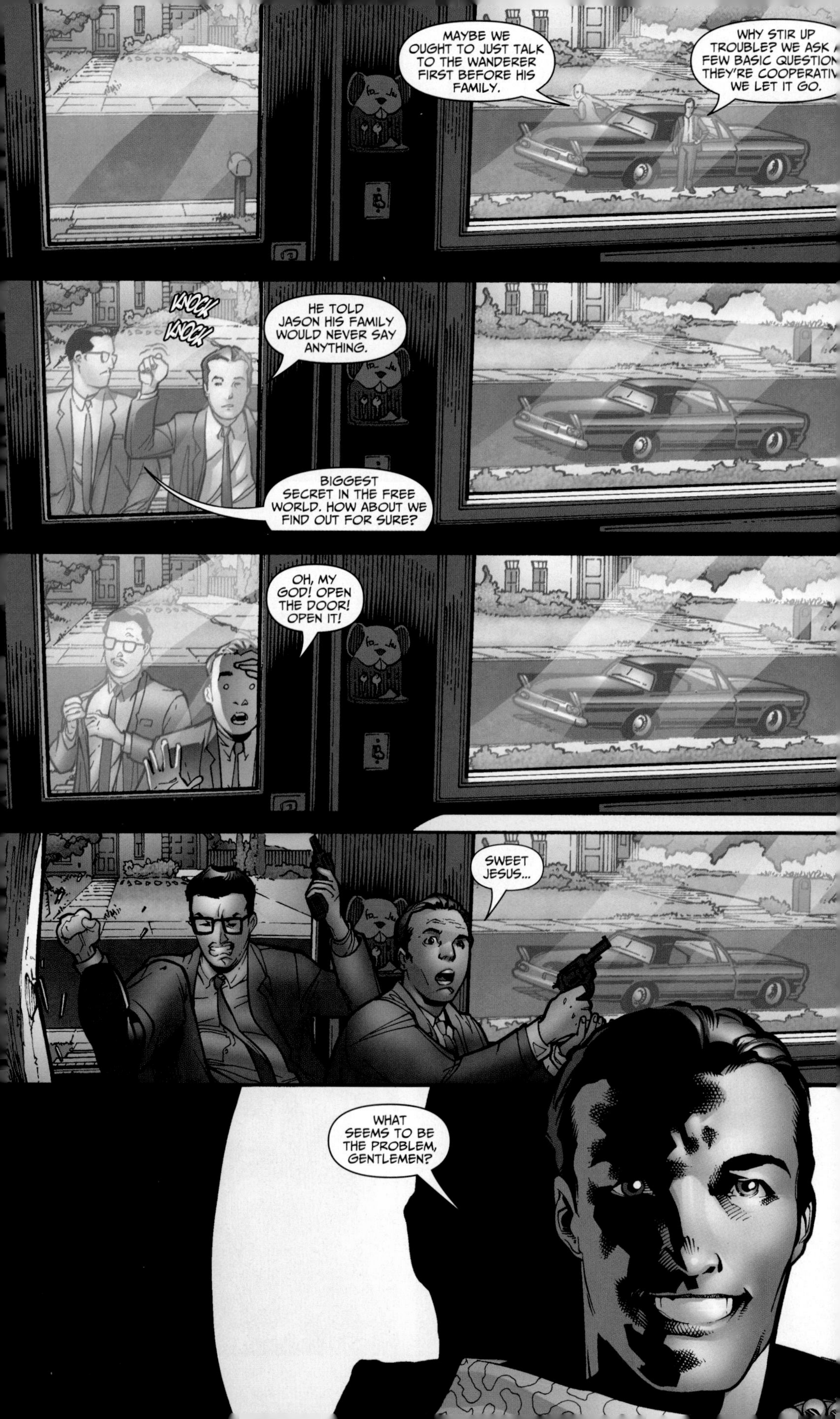
MAYBE WE OUGHT TO JUST TALK TO THE WANDERER FIRST BEFORE HIS FAMILY.
WHY STIR UP TROUBLE? WE ASK A FEW BASIC QUESTION THEY'RE COOPERATIV WE LET IT GO.
KNOCK KNOCK
HE TOLD JASON HIS FAMILY WOULD NEVER SAY ANYTHING.
BIGGEST SECRET IN THE FREE WORLD. HOW ABOUT WE FIND OUT FOR SURE?
OH, MY GOD! OPEN THE DOOR! OPEN IT!
SWEET JESUS...
WHAT SEEMS TO BE THE PROBLEM, GENTLEMEN?

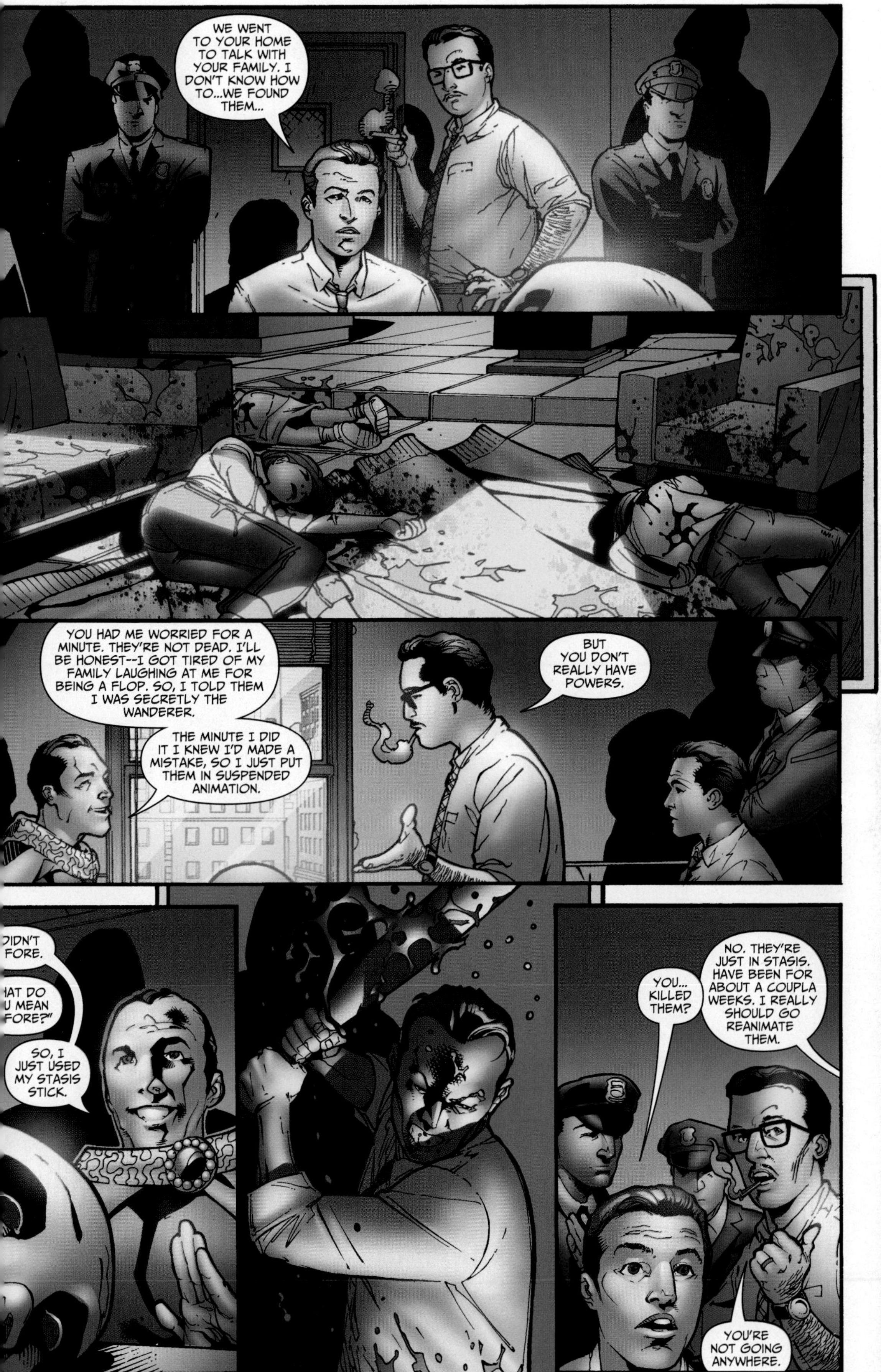
WE WENT TO YOUR HOME TO TALK WITH YOUR FAMILY. I DON'T KNOW HOW TO...WE FOUND THEM...
YOU HAD ME WORRIED FOR A MINUTE. THEY'RE NOT DEAD. I'LL BE HONEST--I GOT TIRED OF MY FAMILY LAUGHING AT ME FOR BEING A FLOP. SO, I TOLD THEM I WAS SECRETLY THE WANDERER.
THE MINUTE I DID IT I KNEW I'D MADE A MISTAKE, SO I JUST PUT THEM IN SUSPENDED ANIMATION.
BUT YOU DON'T REALLY HAVE POWERS.
SO, I JUST USED MY STASIS STICK.
YOU... KILLED THEM?
NO. THEY'RE JUST IN STASIS. HAVE BEEN FOR ABOUT A COUPLA WEEKS. I REALLY SHOULD GO REANIMATE THEM.
YOU'RE NOT GOING ANYWHERE.

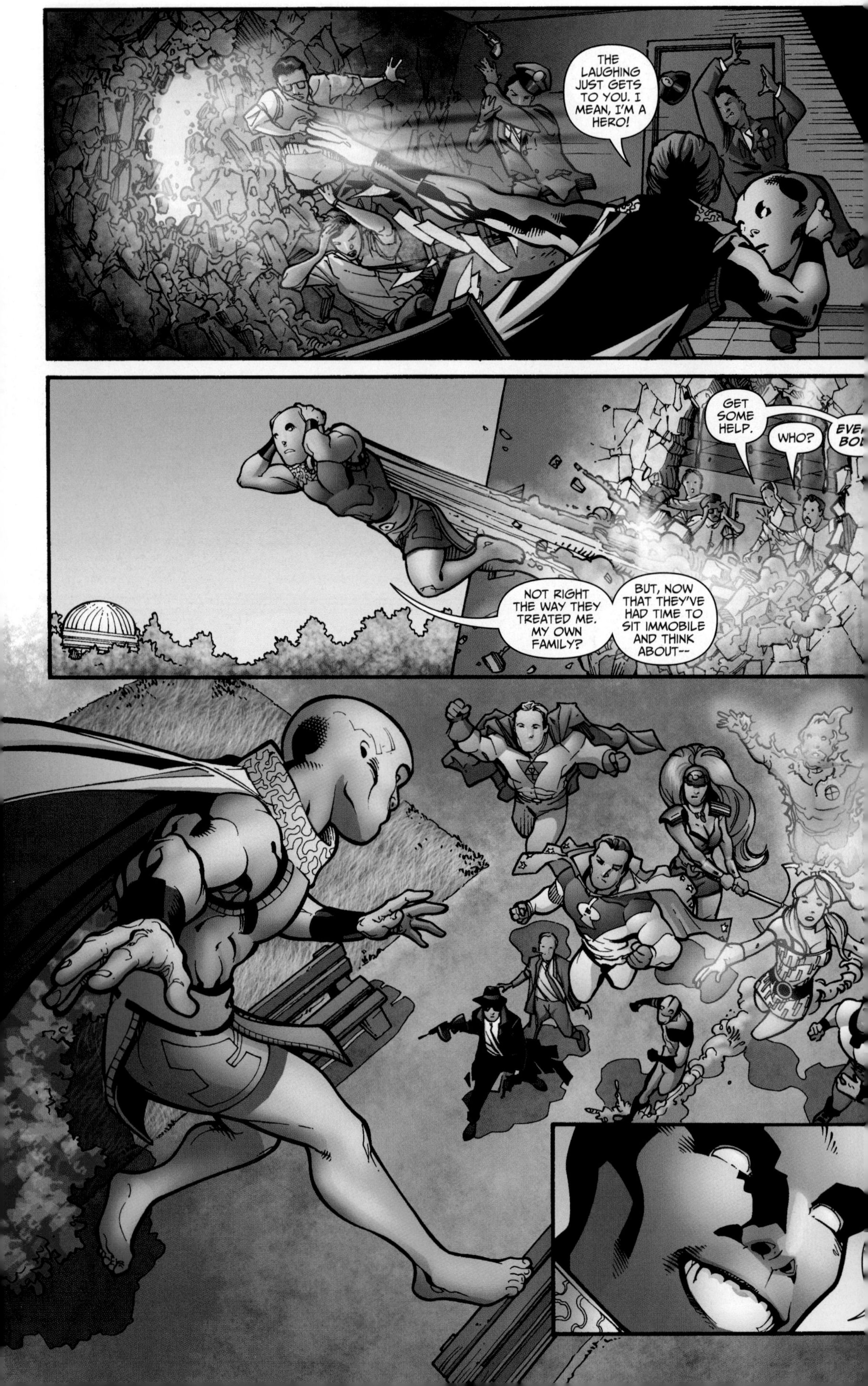
THE LAUGHING JUST GETS TO YOU. I MEAN, I'M A HERO!
GET SOME HELP.
WHO?
NOT RIGHT THE WAY THEY TREATED ME. MY OWN FAMILY?
BUT, NOW THAT THEY'VE HAD TIME TO SIT IMMOBILE AND THINK ABOUT--

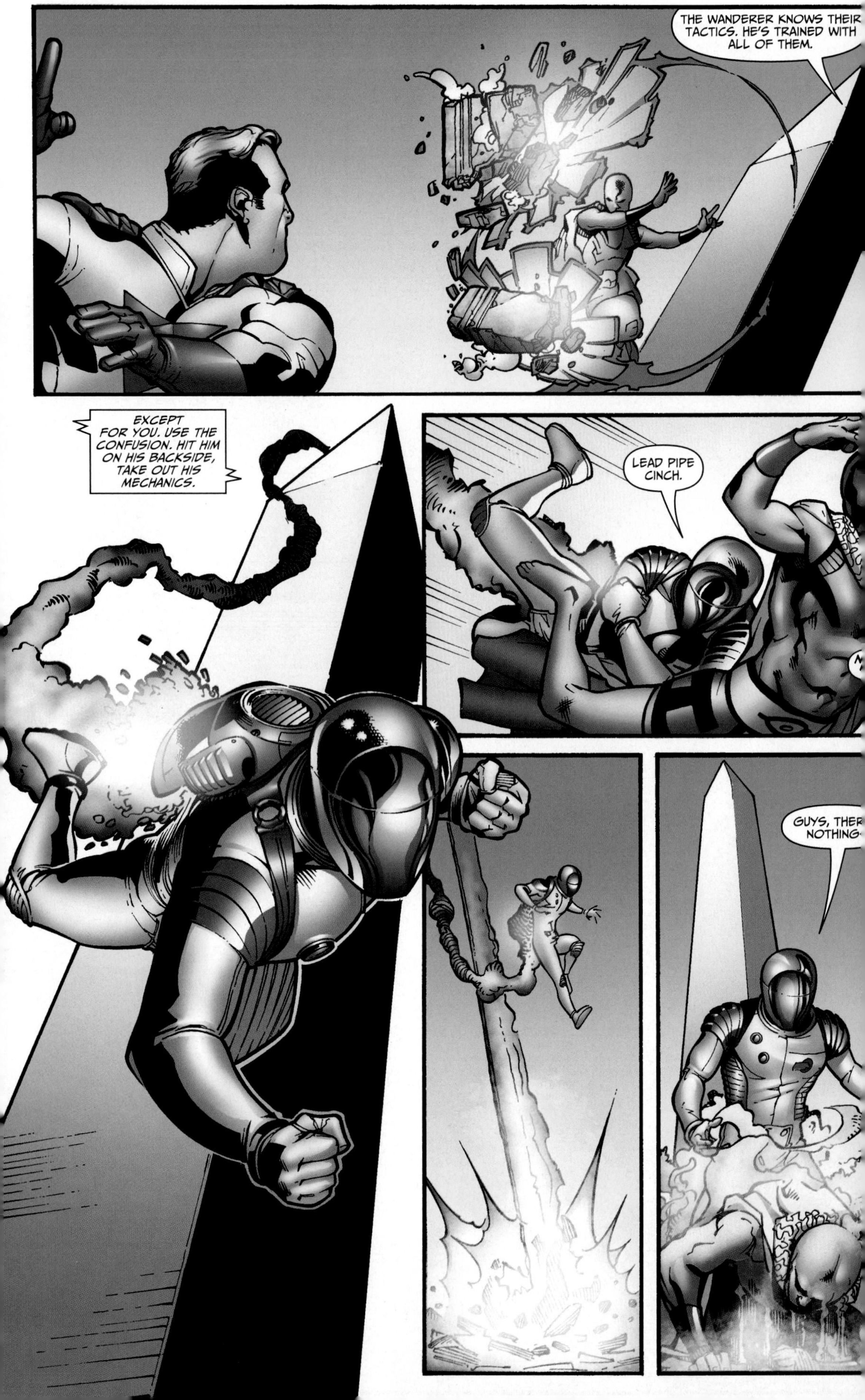

THE WANDERER KNOWS THEIR TACTICS. HE'S TRAINED WITH ALL OF THEM.
EXCEPT FOR YOU. USE THE CONFUSION. HIT HIM ON HIS BACKSIDE, TAKE OUT HIS MECHANICS.
LEAD PIPE CINCH.
GUYS, THER NOTHING

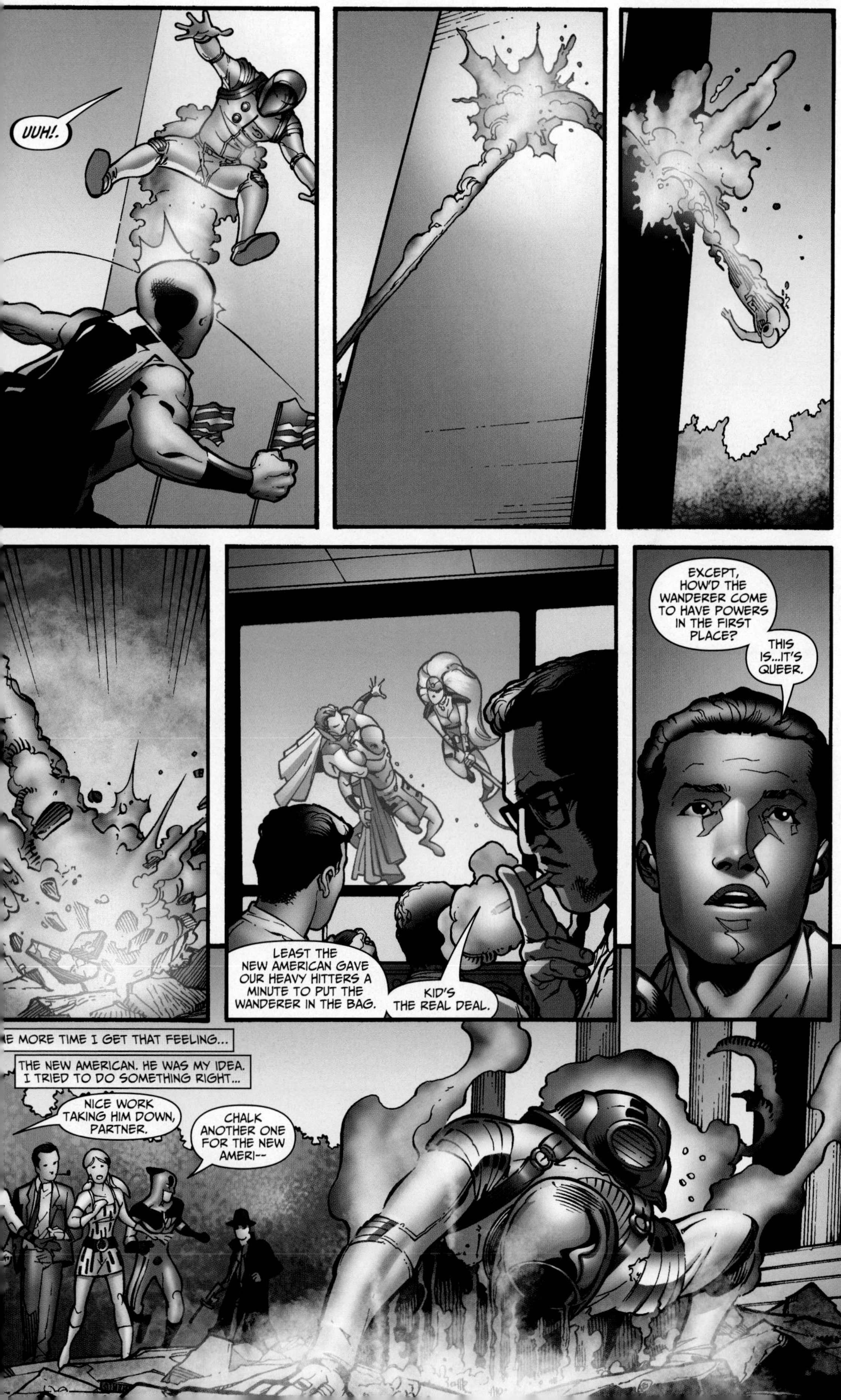
UUH!.
LEAST THE NEW AMERICAN GAVE OUR HEAVY HITTERS A MINUTE TO PUT THE WANDERER IN THE BAG.
KID'S THE REAL DEAL.
EXCEPT, HOW'D THE WANDERER COME TO HAVE POWERS IN THE FIRST PLACE?
THIS IS...IT'S QUEER.
E MORE TIME I GET THAT FEELING...
THE NEW AMERICAN. HE WAS MY IDEA. I TRIED TO DO SOMETHING RIGHT...
NICE WORK TAKING HIM DOWN, PARTNER.
CHALK ANOTHER ONE FOR THE NEW AMERI--

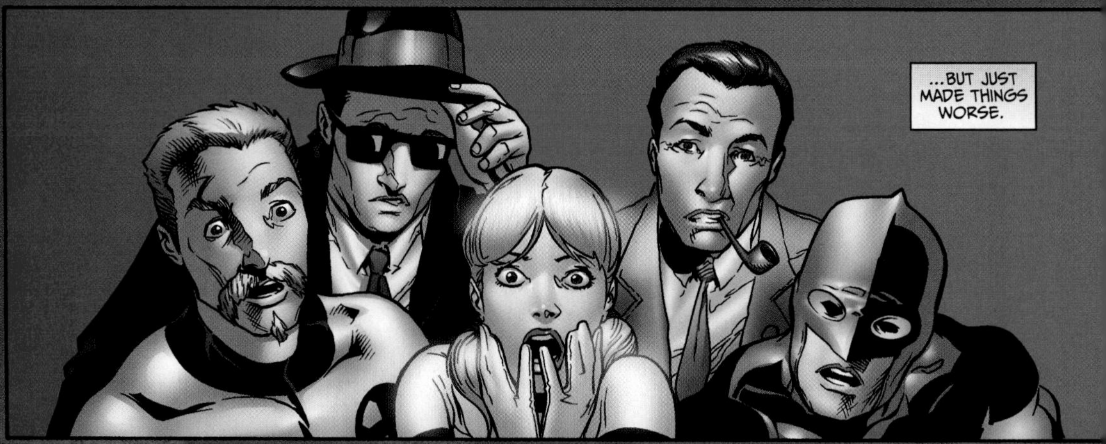
...BUT JUST MADE THINGS WORSE.
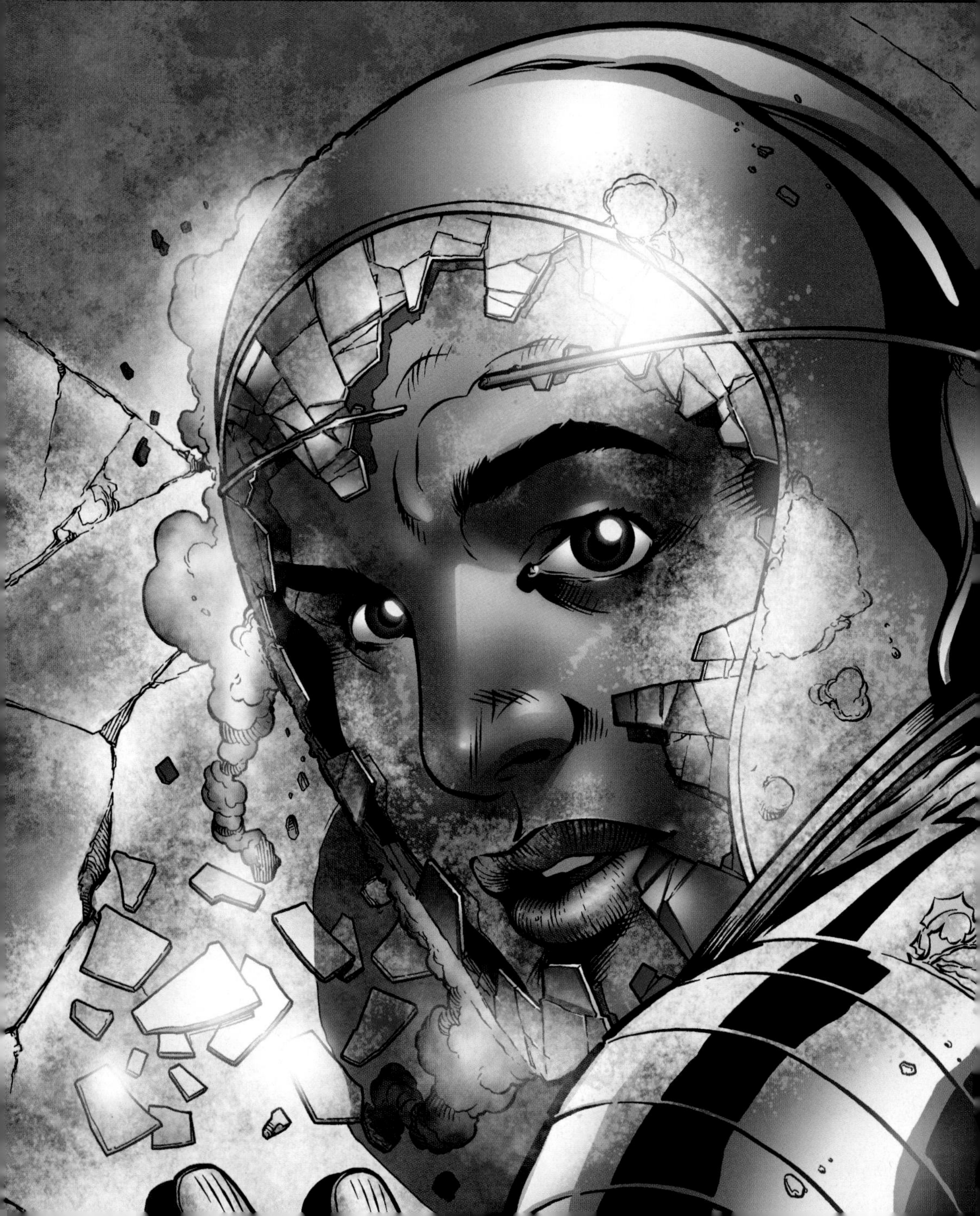

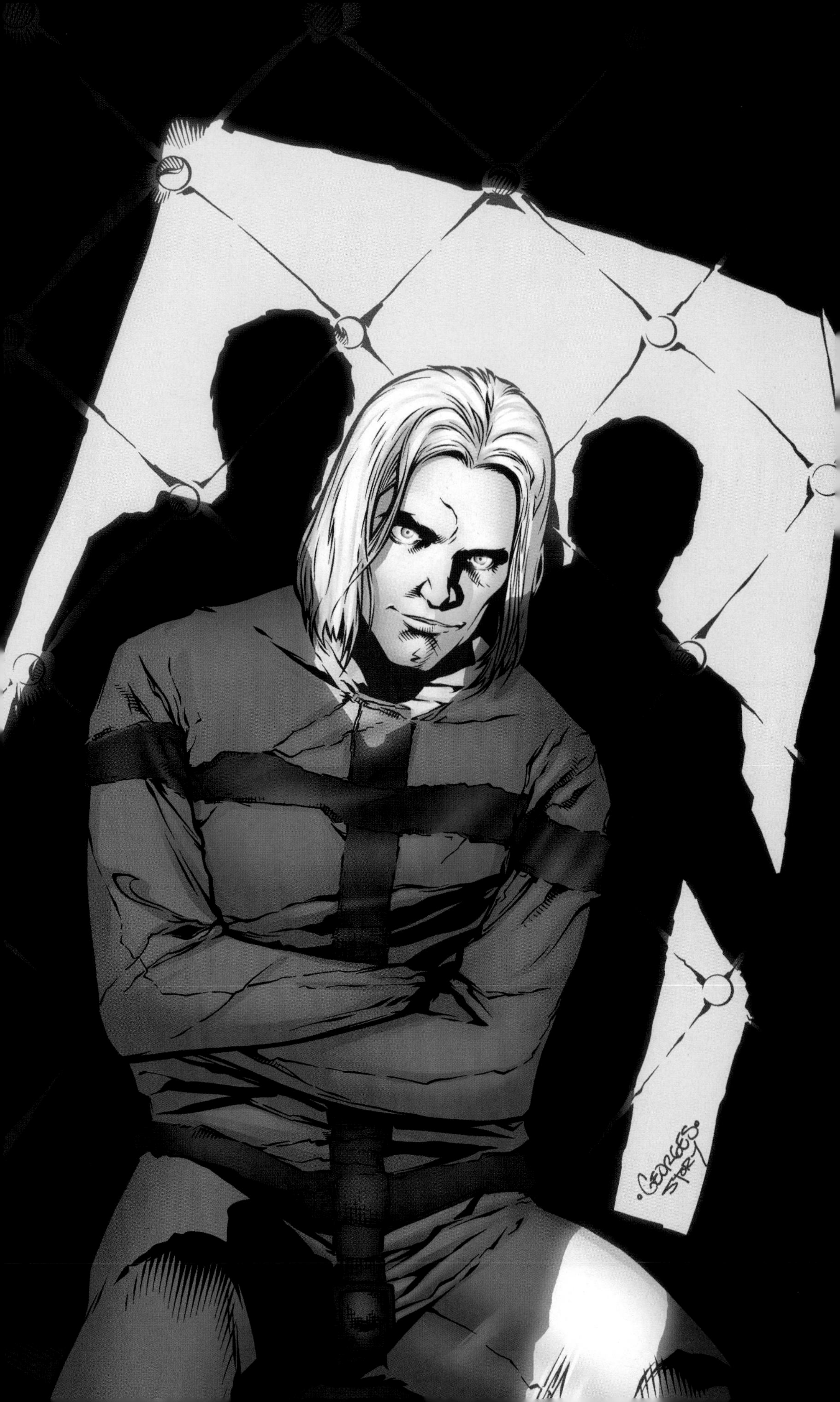
GEORGES STORY

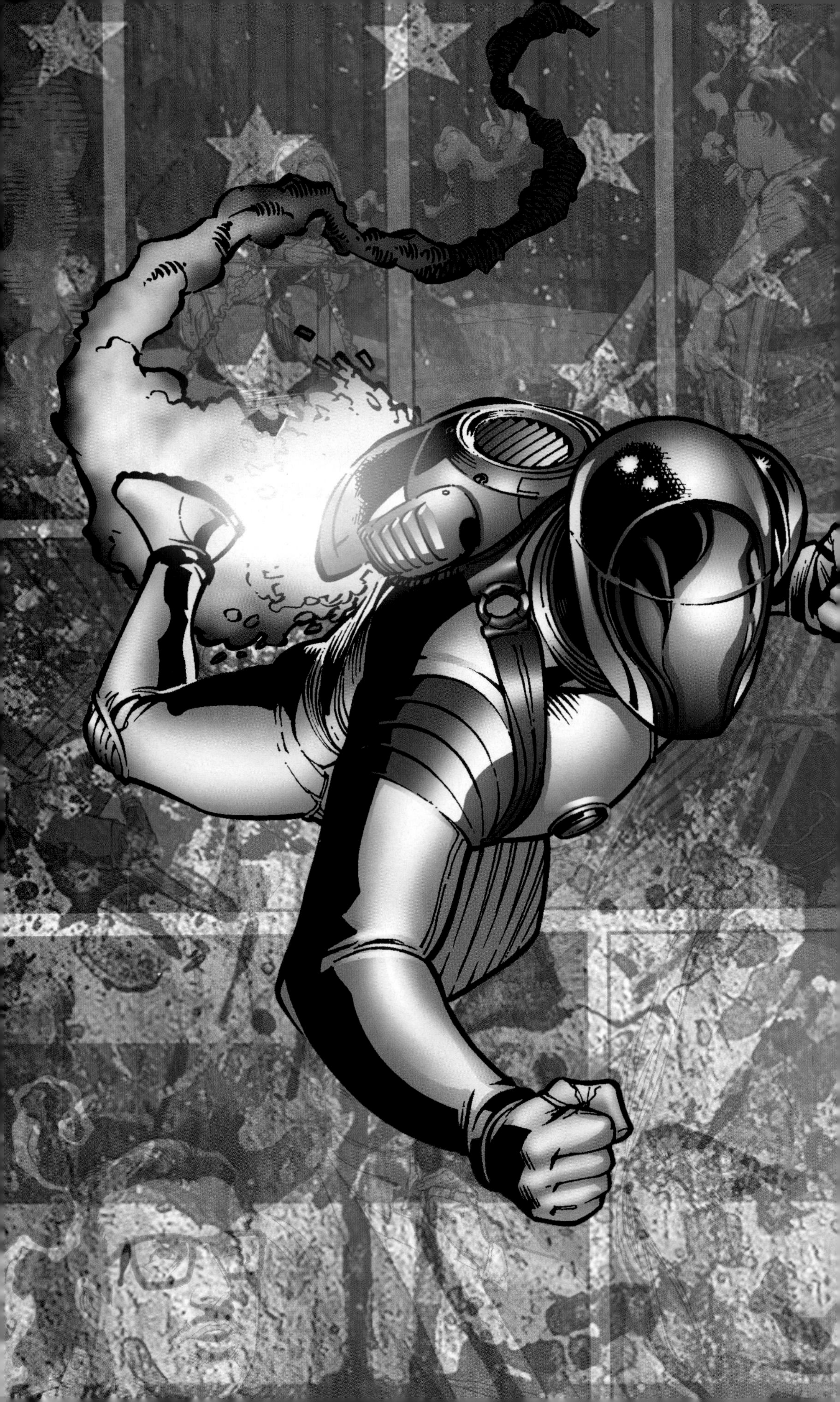

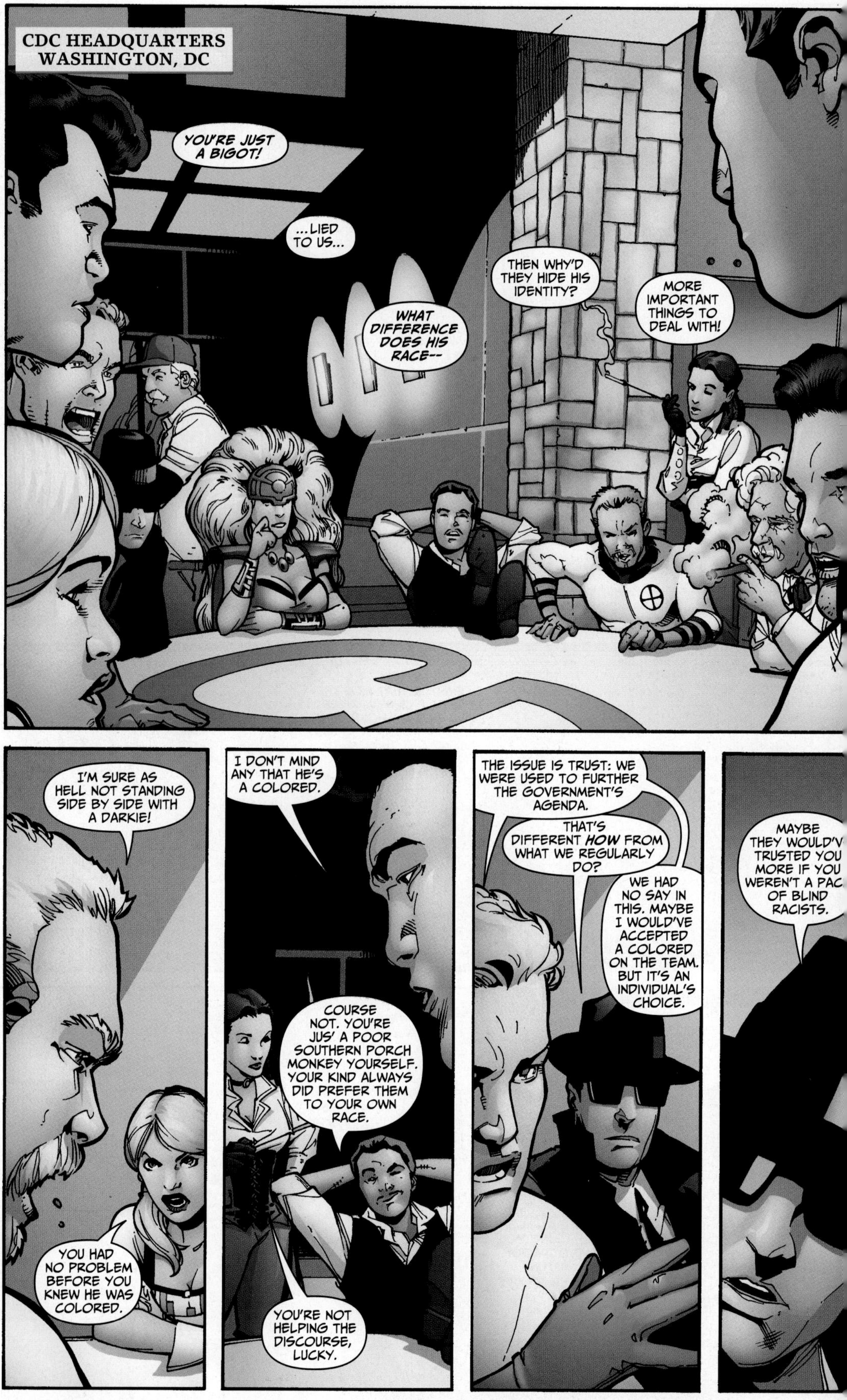
CDC HEADQUARTERS WASHINGTON, DC
YOU'RE JUST A BIGOT!
...LIED TO US...
WHAT DIFFERENCE DOES HIS RACE--
THEN WHY'D THEY HIDE HIS IDENTITY?
MORE IMPORTANT THINGS TO DEAL WITH!
I'M SURE AS HELL NOT STANDING SIDE BY SIDE WITH A DARKIE!
YOU HAD NO PROBLEM BEFORE YOU KNEW HE WAS COLORED.
I DON'T MIND ANY THAT HE'S A COLORED.
COURSE NOT. YOU'RE JUS' A POOR SOUTHERN PORCH MONKEY YOURSELF. YOUR KIND ALWAYS DID PREFER THEM TO YOUR OWN RACE.
YOU'RE NOT HELPING THE DISCOURSE, LUCKY.
THE ISSUE IS TRUST: WE WERE USED TO FURTHER THE GOVERNMENT'S AGENDA.
THAT'S DIFFERENT HOW FROM WHAT WE REGULARLY DO?
WE HAD NO SAY IN THIS. MAYBE I WOULD'VE ACCEPTED A COLORED ON THE TEAM. BUT IT'S AN INDIVIDUAL'S CHOICE.
MAYBE THEY WOULD'V TRUSTED YOU MORE IF YOU WEREN'T A PAC OF BLIND RACISTS.

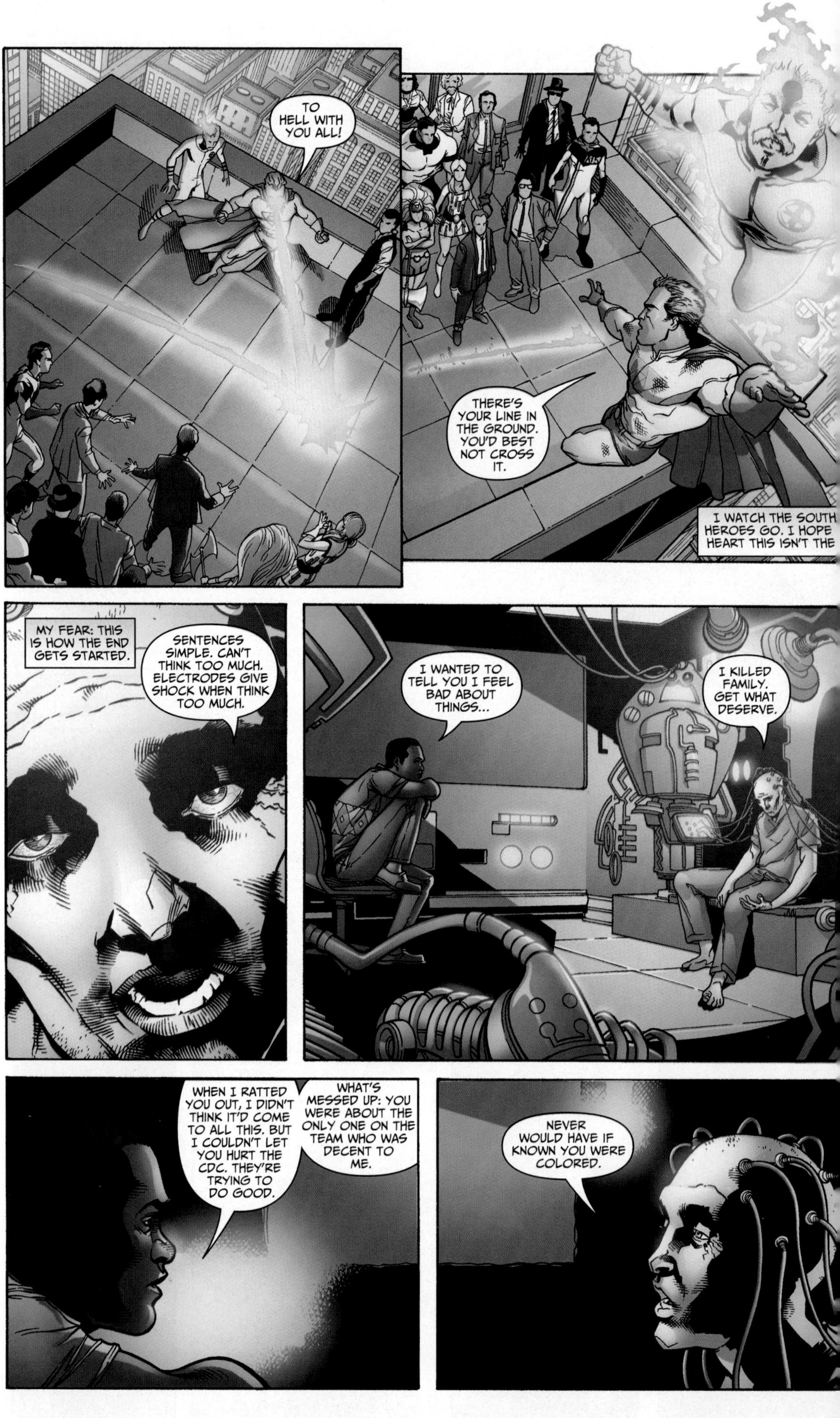
TO HELL WITH YOU ALL!
THERE'S YOUR LINE IN THE GROUND. YOU'D BEST NOT CROSS IT.
I WATCH THE SOUTH HEROES GO. I HOPE HEART THIS ISN'T THE
MY FEAR: THIS IS HOW THE END GETS STARTED.
SENTENCES SIMPLE. CAN'T THINK TOO MUCH. ELECTRODES GIVE SHOCK WHEN THINK TOO MUCH.
I WANTED TO TELL YOU I FEEL BAD ABOUT THINGS...
I KILLED FAMILY. GET WHAT DESERVE.
WHEN I RATTED YOU OUT, I DIDN'T THINK IT'D COME TO ALL THIS. BUT I COULDN'T LET YOU HURT THE CDC. THEY'RE TRYING TO DO GOOD.
WHAT'S MESSED UP: YOU WERE ABOUT THE ONLY ONE ON THE TEAM WHO WAS DECENT TO ME.
NEVER WOULD HAVE IF KNOWN YOU WERE COLORED.

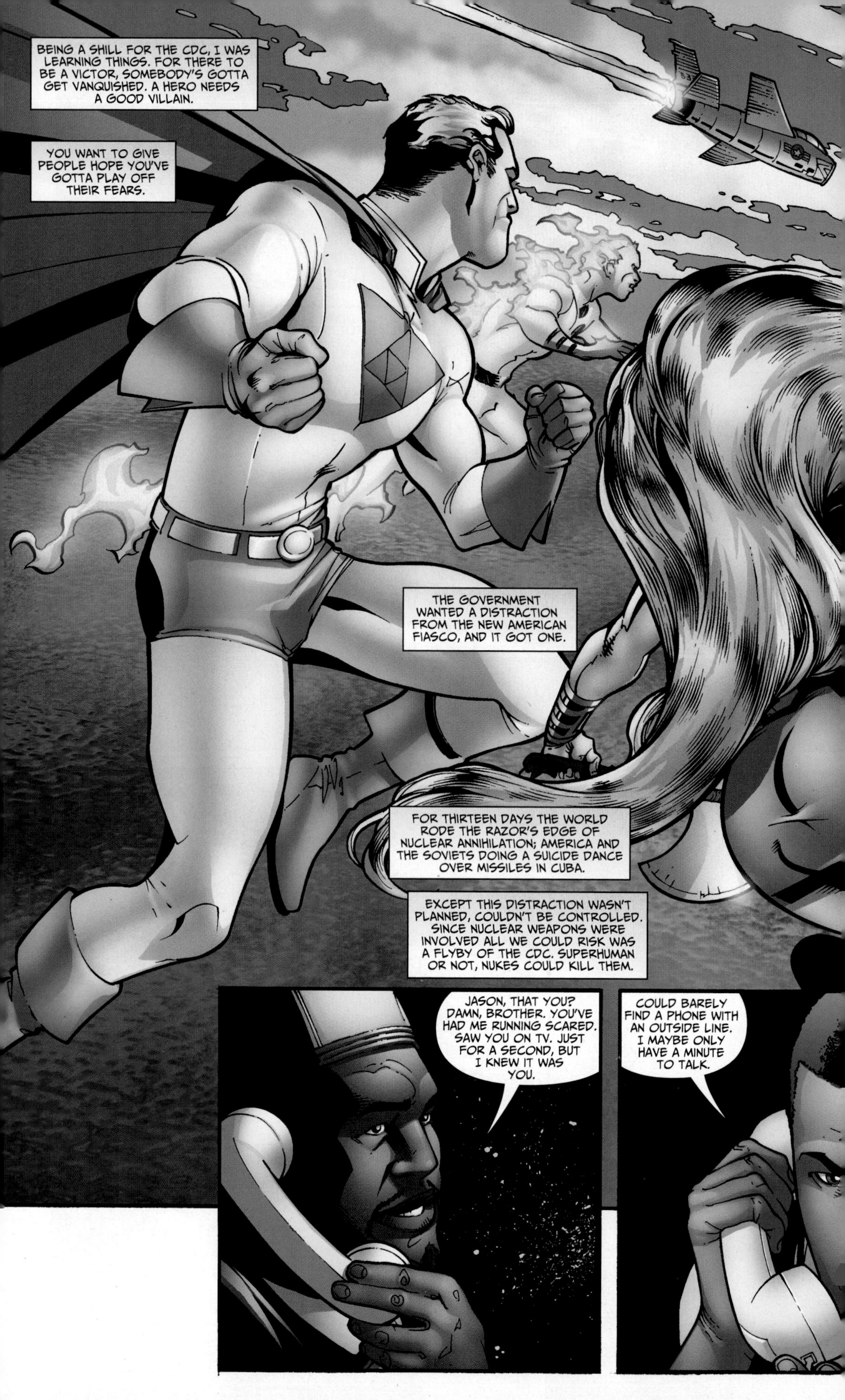
BEING A SHILL FOR THE CDC, I WAS LEARNING THINGS. FOR THERE TO BE A VICTOR, SOMEBODY'S GOTTA GET VANQUISHED. A HERO NEEDS A GOOD VILLAIN.
YOU WANT TO GIVE PEOPLE HOPE YOU'VE GOTTA PLAY OFF THEIR FEARS.
THE GOVERNMENT WANTED A DISTRACTION FROM THE NEW AMERICAN FIASCO, AND IT GOT ONE.
FOR THIRTEEN DAYS THE WORLD RODE THE RAZOR'S EDGE OF NUCLEAR ANNIHILATION; AMERICA AND THE SOVIETS DOING A SUICIDE DANCE OVER MISSILES IN CUBA.
EXCEPT THIS DISTRACTION WASN'T PLANNED, COULDN'T BE CONTROLLED. SINCE NUCLEAR WEAPONS WERE INVOLVED ALL WE COULD RISK WAS A FLYBY OF THE CDC. SUPERHUMAN OR NOT, NUKES COULD KILL THEM.
JASON, THAT YOU? DAMN, BROTHER. YOU'VE HAD ME RUNNING SCARED. SAW YOU ON TV. JUST FOR A SECOND, BUT I KNEW IT WAS YOU.
COULD BARELY FIND A PHONE WITH AN OUTSIDE LINE. I MAYBE ONLY HAVE A MINUTE TO TALK.

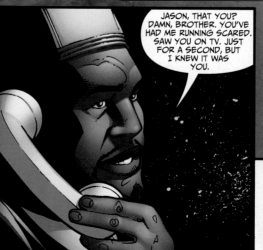

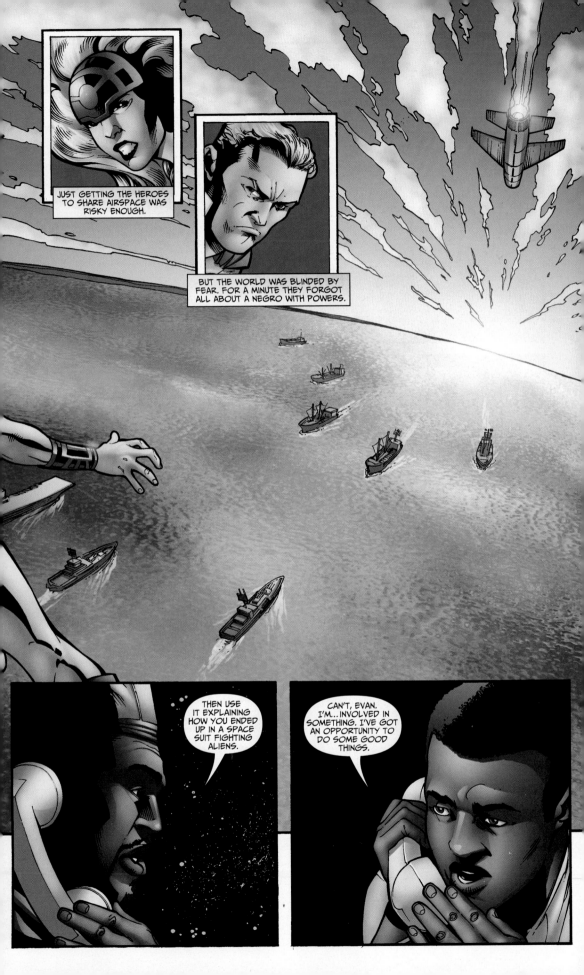

JUST GETTING THE HEROES TO SHARE AIRSPACE WAS RISKY ENOUGH.

BUT THE WORLD WAS BLINDED BY FEAR. FOR A MINUTE THEY FORGOT ALL ABOUT A NEGRO WITH POWERS.

THEN USE IT EXPLAINING HOW YOU ENDED UP IN A SPACE SUIT FIGHTING ALIENS.

CAN'T, EVAN. I'M...INVOLVED IN SOMETHING. I'VE GOT AN OPPORTUNITY TO DO SOME GOOD THINGS.

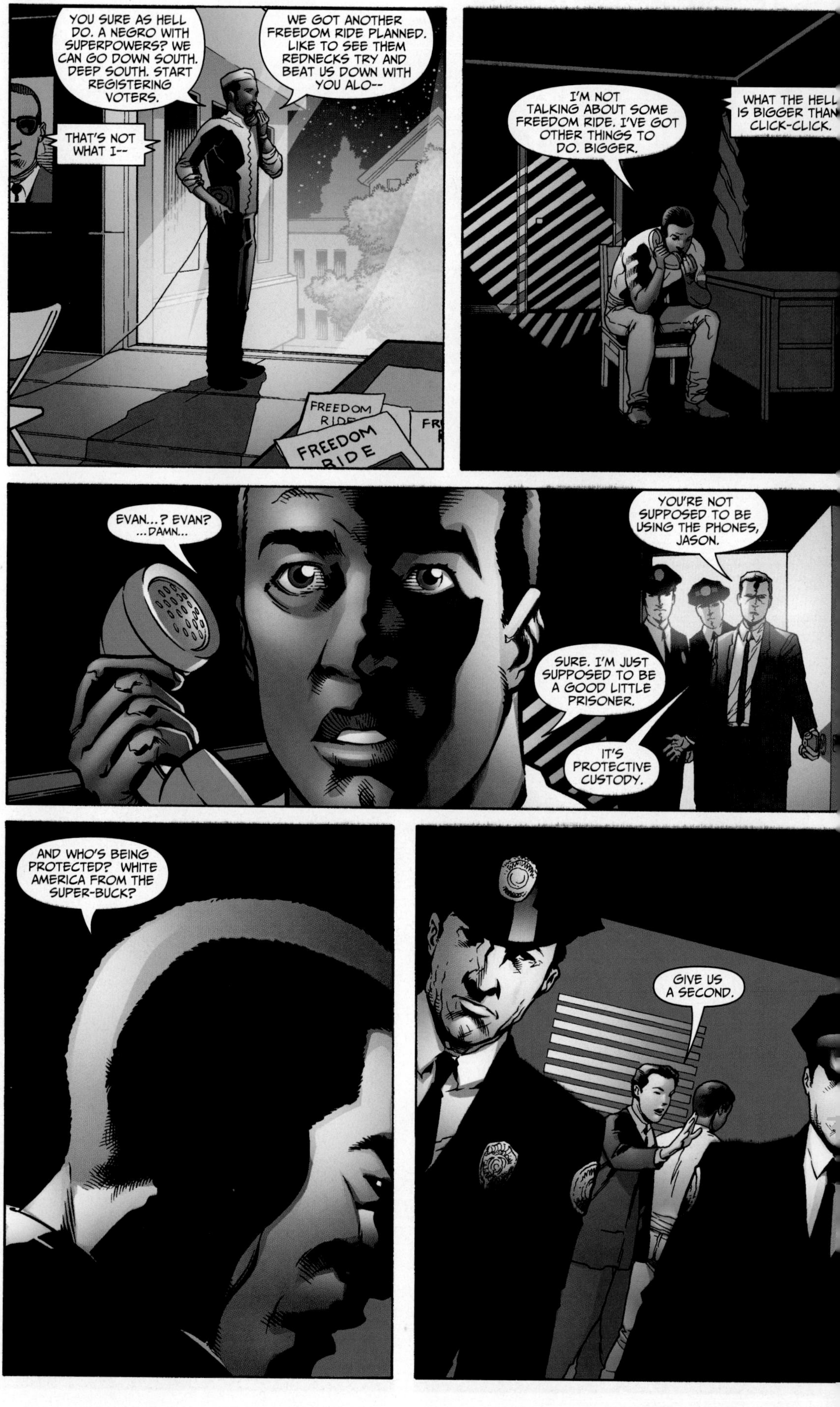

YOU SURE AS HELL DO. A NEGRO WITH SUPERPOWERS? WE CAN GO DOWN SOUTH. DEEP SOUTH. START REGISTERING VOTERS.
THAT'S NOT WHAT I--
WE GOT ANOTHER FREEDOM RIDE PLANNED. LIKE TO SEE THEM REDNECKS TRY AND BEAT US DOWN WITH YOU ALO--
FREEDOM RIDE
FREEDOM RIDE
I'M NOT TALKING ABOUT SOME FREEDOM RIDE. I'VE GOT OTHER THINGS TO DO. BIGGER.
WHAT THE HELL IS BIGGER THAN
CLICK-CLICK.
EVAN...? EVAN? ...DAMN...
YOU'RE NOT SUPPOSED TO BE USING THE PHONES, JASON.
SURE. I'M JUST SUPPOSED TO BE A GOOD LITTLE PRISONER.
IT'S PROTECTIVE CUSTODY.
AND WHO'S BEING PROTECTED? WHITE AMERICA FROM THE SUPER-BUCK?
GIVE US A SECOND.

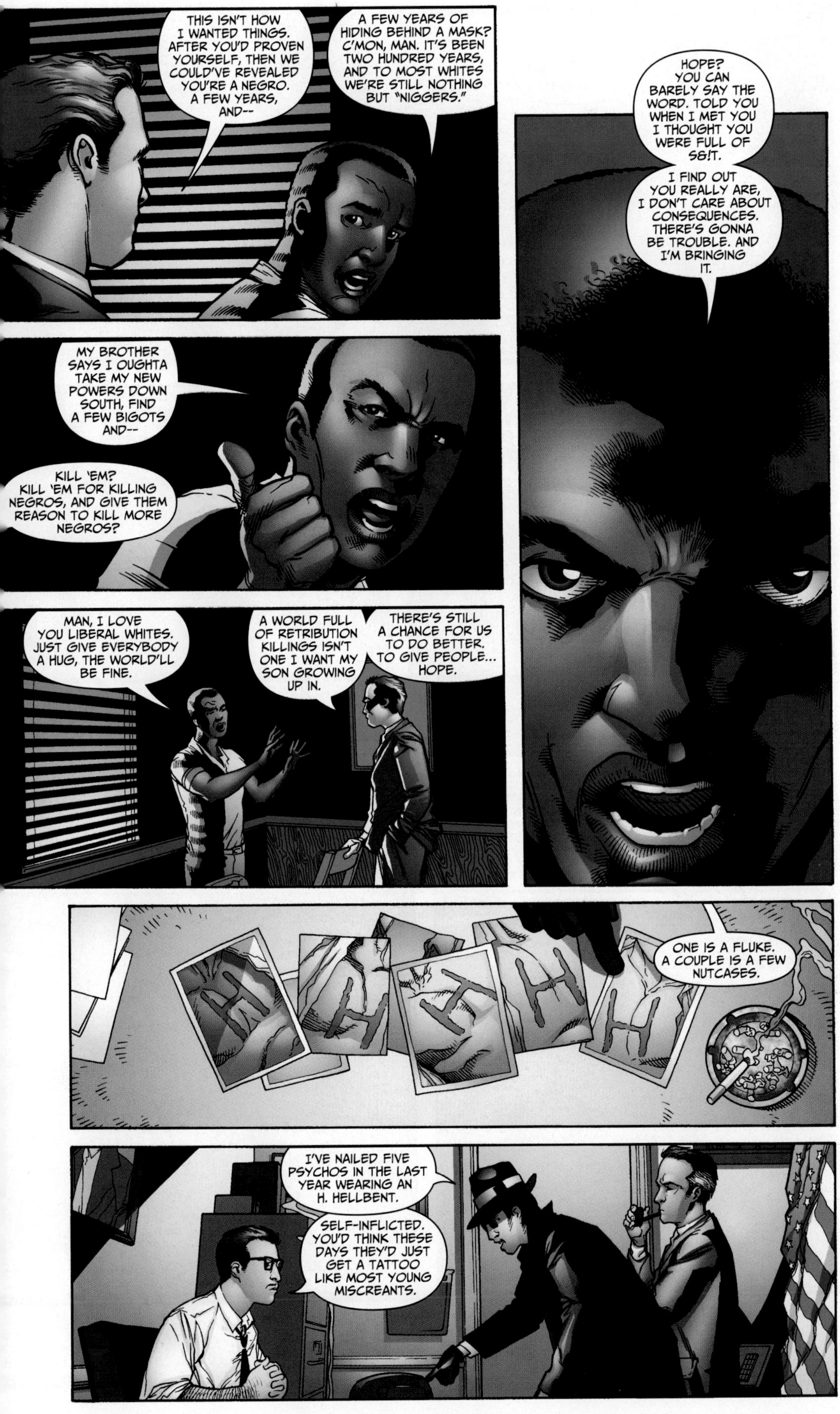
THIS ISN'T HOW I WANTED THINGS. AFTER YOU'D PROVEN YOURSELF, THEN WE COULD'VE REVEALED YOU'RE A NEGRO. A FEW YEARS, AND--
A FEW YEARS OF HIDING BEHIND A MASK? C'MON, MAN. IT'S BEEN TWO HUNDRED YEARS, AND TO MOST WHITES WE'RE STILL NOTHING BUT "NIGGERS."
MY BROTHER SAYS I OUGHTA TAKE MY NEW POWERS DOWN SOUTH, FIND A FEW BIGOTS AND--
KILL 'EM? KILL 'EM FOR KILLING NEGROS, AND GIVE THEM REASON TO KILL MORE NEGROS?
MAN, I LOVE YOU LIBERAL WHITES. JUST GIVE EVERYBODY A HUG, THE WORLD'LL BE FINE.
A WORLD FULL OF RETRIBUTION KILLINGS ISN'T ONE I WANT MY SON GROWING UP IN.
THERE'S STILL A CHANCE FOR US TO DO BETTER. TO GIVE PEOPLE... HOPE.
HOPE? YOU CAN BARELY SAY THE WORD. TOLD YOU WHEN I MET YOU I THOUGHT YOU WERE FULL OF S&!T.
I FIND OUT YOU REALLY ARE, I DON'T CARE ABOUT CONSEQUENCES. THERE'S GONNA BE TROUBLE. AND I'M BRINGING IT.
ONE IS A FLUKE. A COUPLE IS A FEW NUTCASES.
I'VE NAILED FIVE PSYCHOS IN THE LAST YEAR WEARING AN H. HELLBENT.
SELF-INFLICTED. YOU'D THINK THESE DAYS THEY'D JUST GET A TATTOO LIKE MOST YOUNG MISCREANTS.

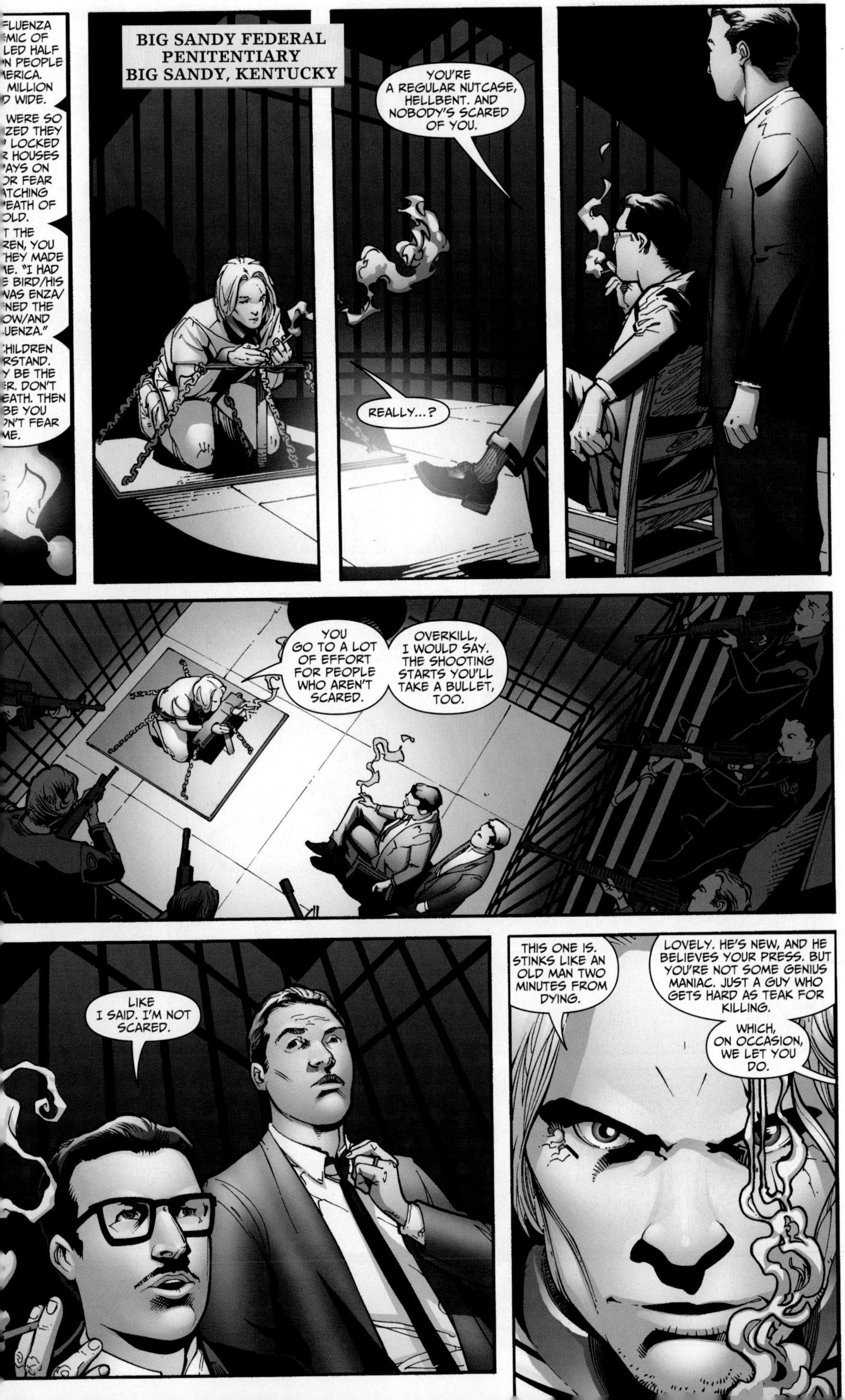

BIG SANDY FEDERAL PENITENTIARY
BIG SANDY, KENTUCKY
YOU'RE A REGULAR NUTCASE, HELLBENT. AND NOBODY'S SCARED OF YOU.
REALLY...?
YOU GO TO A LOT OF EFFORT FOR PEOPLE WHO AREN'T SCARED.
OVERKILL, I WOULD SAY. THE SHOOTING STARTS YOU'LL TAKE A BULLET, TOO.
LIKE I SAID. I'M NOT SCARED.
THIS ONE IS. STINKS LIKE AN OLD MAN TWO MINUTES FROM DYING.
LOVELY. HE'S NEW, AND HE BELIEVES YOUR PRESS. BUT YOU'RE NOT SOME GENIUS MANIAC. JUST A GUY WHO GETS HARD AS TEAK FOR KILLING.
WHICH, ON OCCASION, WE LET YOU DO.

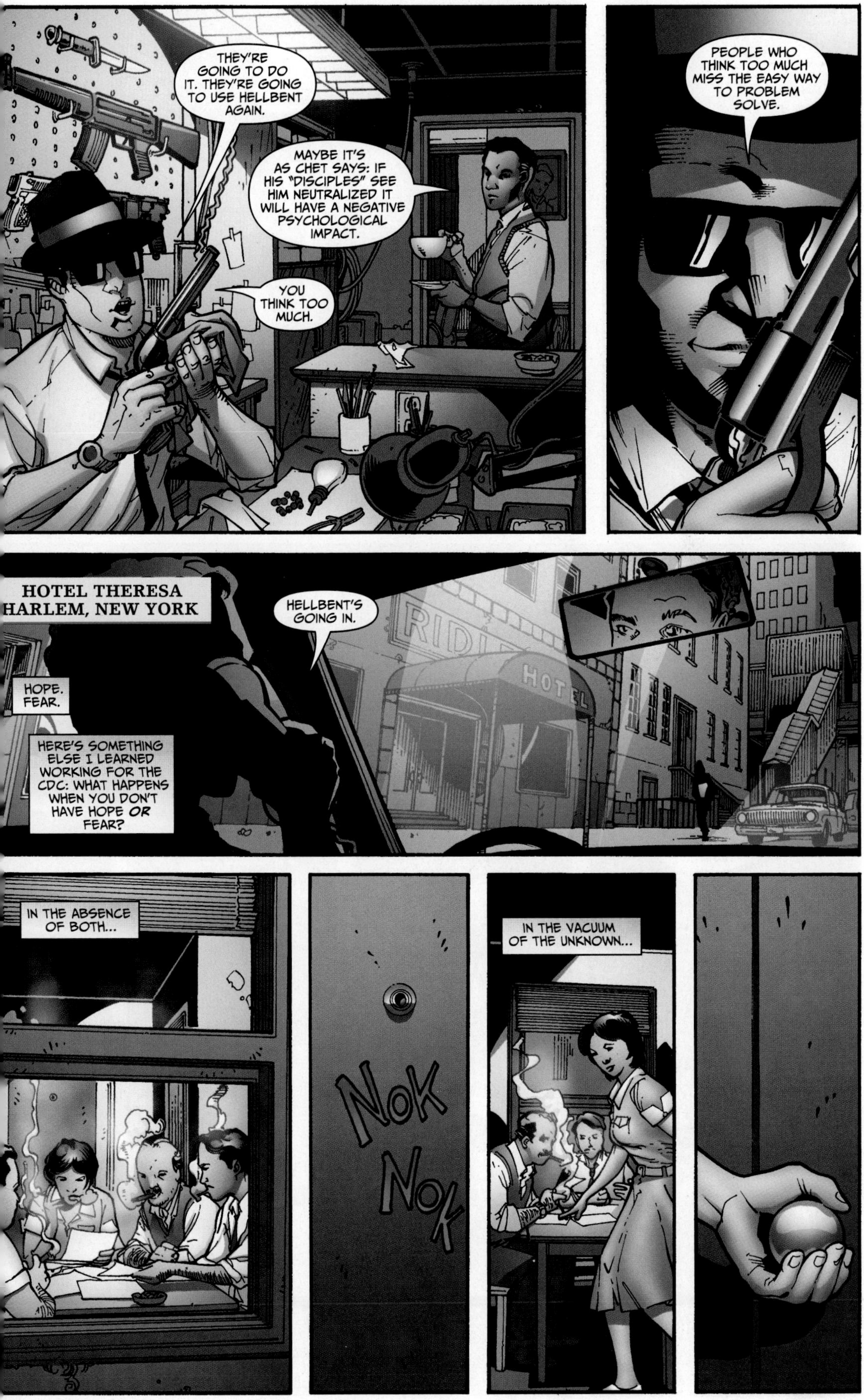
THEY'RE GOING TO DO IT. THEY'RE GOING TO USE HELLBENT AGAIN.
MAYBE IT'S AS CHET SAYS: IF HIS "DISCIPLES" SEE HIM NEUTRALIZED IT WILL HAVE A NEGATIVE PSYCHOLOGICAL IMPACT.
YOU THINK TOO MUCH.
PEOPLE WHO THINK TOO MUCH MISS THE EASY WAY TO PROBLEM SOLVE.
HOTEL THERESA
HARLEM, NEW YORK
HELLBENT'S GOING IN.
HOTEL
HOPE. FEAR.
HERE'S SOMETHING ELSE I LEARNED WORKING FOR THE CDC: WHAT HAPPENS WHEN YOU DON'T HAVE HOPE *OR* FEAR?
IN THE ABSENCE OF BOTH...
NOK NOK
IN THE VACUUM OF THE UNKNOWN...

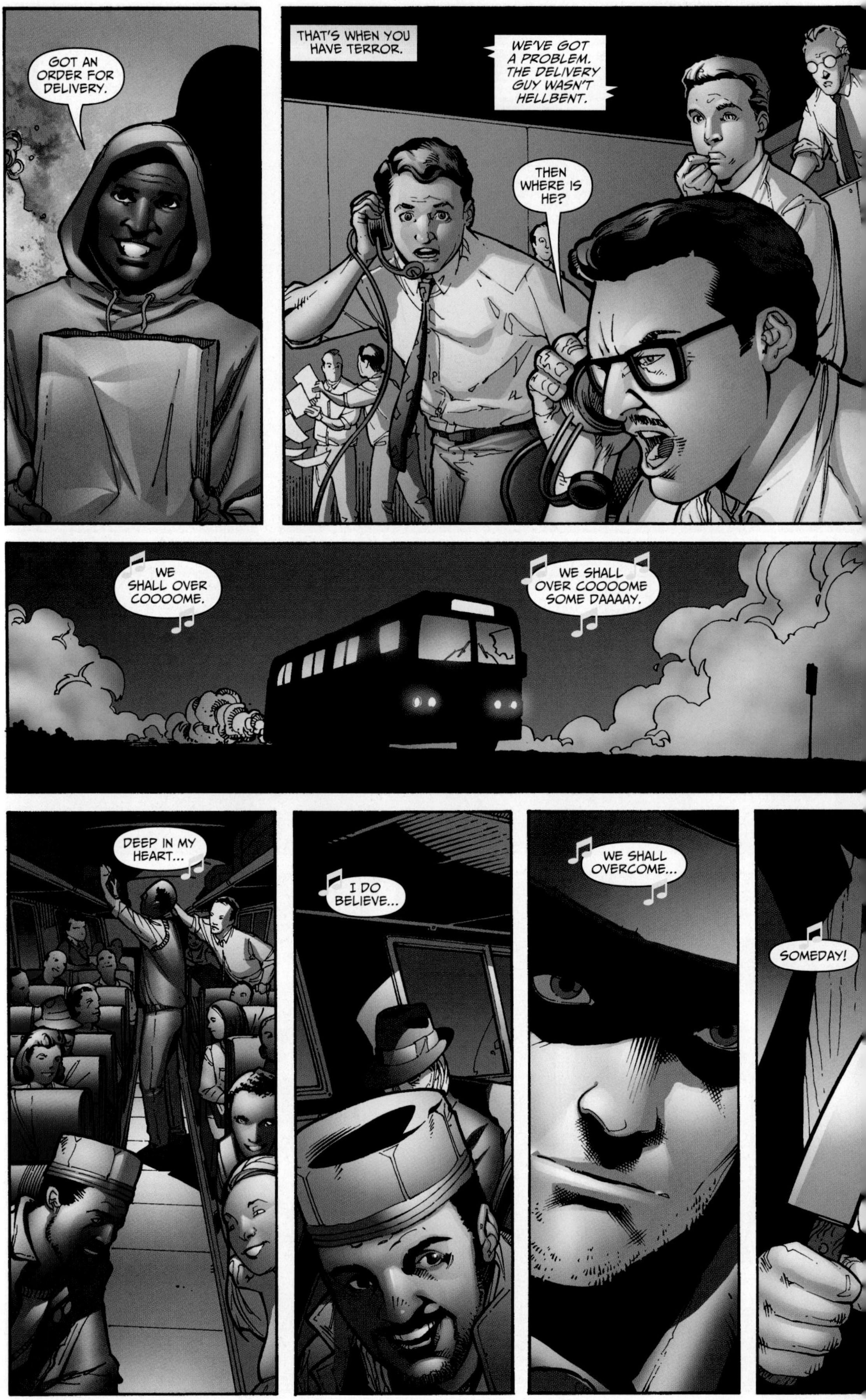
GOT AN ORDER FOR DELIVERY.
THAT'S WHEN YOU HAVE TERROR.
WE'VE GOT A PROBLEM. THE DELIVERY GUY WASN'T HELLBENT.
THEN WHERE IS HE?
WE SHALL OVER COOOOME.
WE SHALL OVER COOOOME SOME DAAAAY.
DEEP IN MY HEART...
I DO BELIEVE...
WE SHALL OVERCOME...
SOMEDAY!

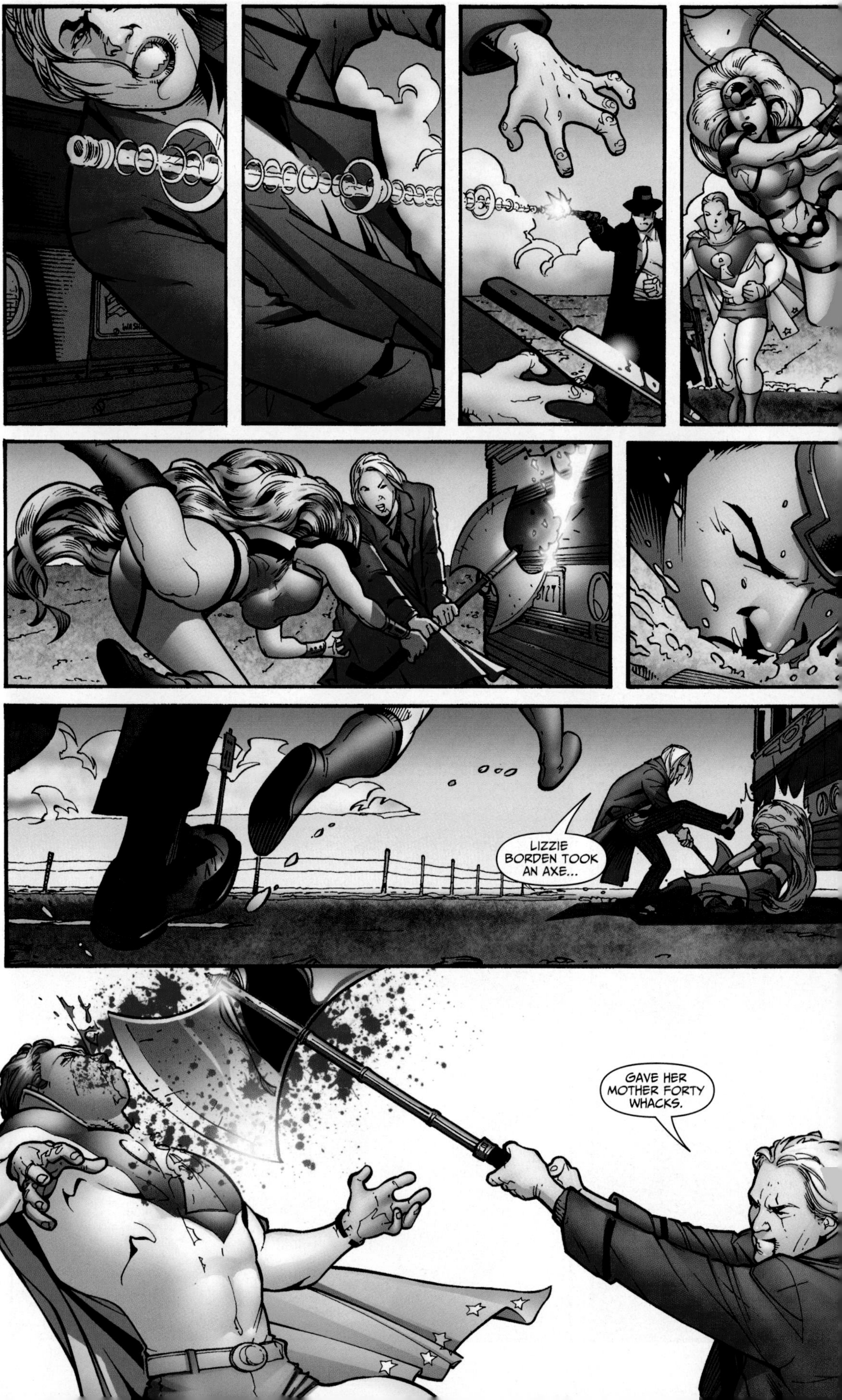
LIZZIE BORDEN TOOK AN AXE...
GAVE HER MOTHER FORTY WHACKS.

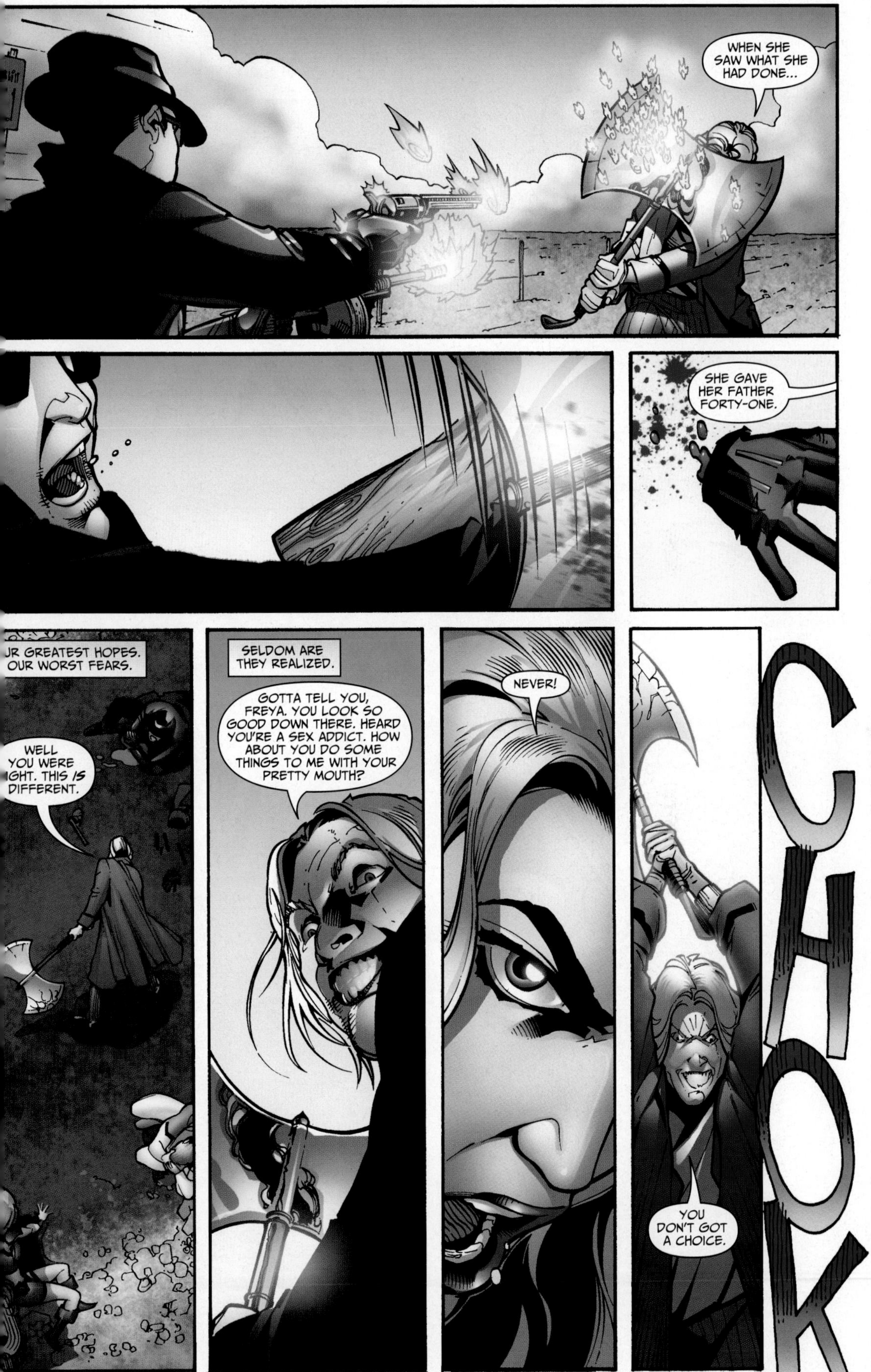
WHEN SHE SAW WHAT SHE HAD DONE...
SHE GAVE HER FATHER FORTY-ONE.
UR GREATEST HOPES. OUR WORST FEARS.
WELL YOU WERE IGHT. THIS IS DIFFERENT.
SELDOM ARE THEY REALIZED.
GOTTA TELL YOU, FREYA. YOU LOOK SO GOOD DOWN THERE. HEARD YOU'RE A SEX ADDICT. HOW ABOUT YOU DO SOME THINGS TO ME WITH YOUR PRETTY MOUTH?
NEVER!
YOU DON'T GOT A CHOICE.
CHOK

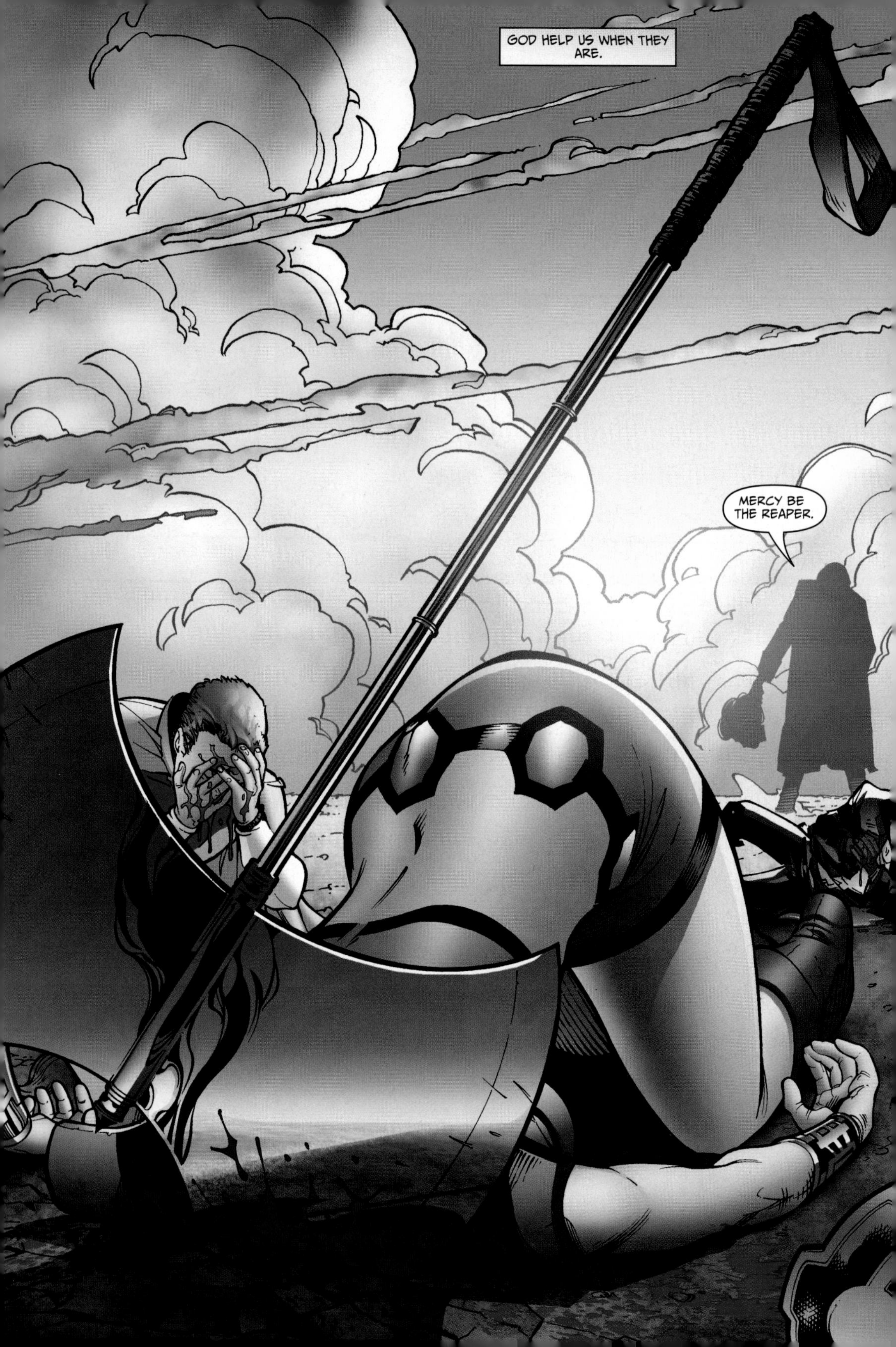
GOD HELP US WHEN THEY ARE.
MERCY BE THE REAPER.

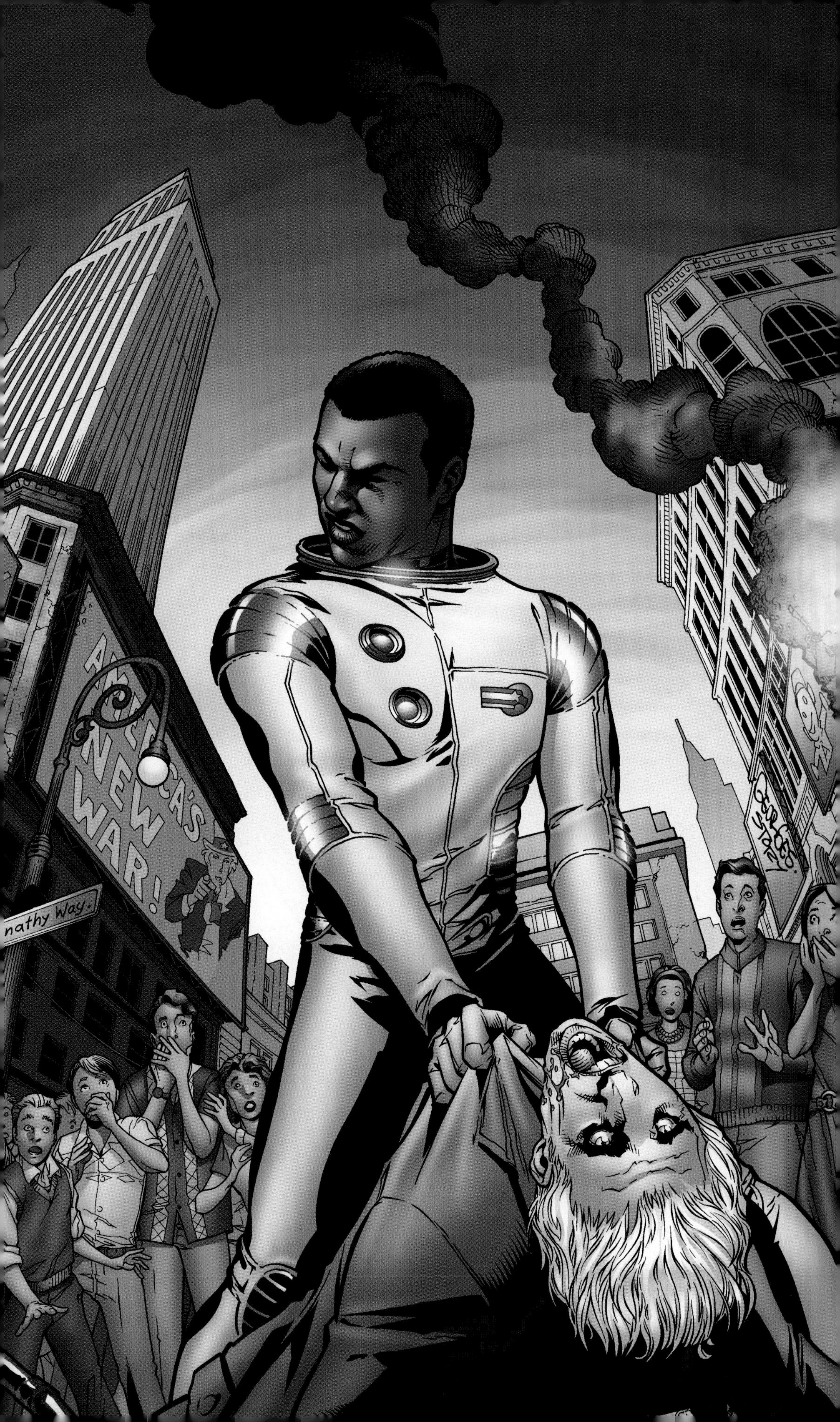
NEW WAR!
nathy Way.

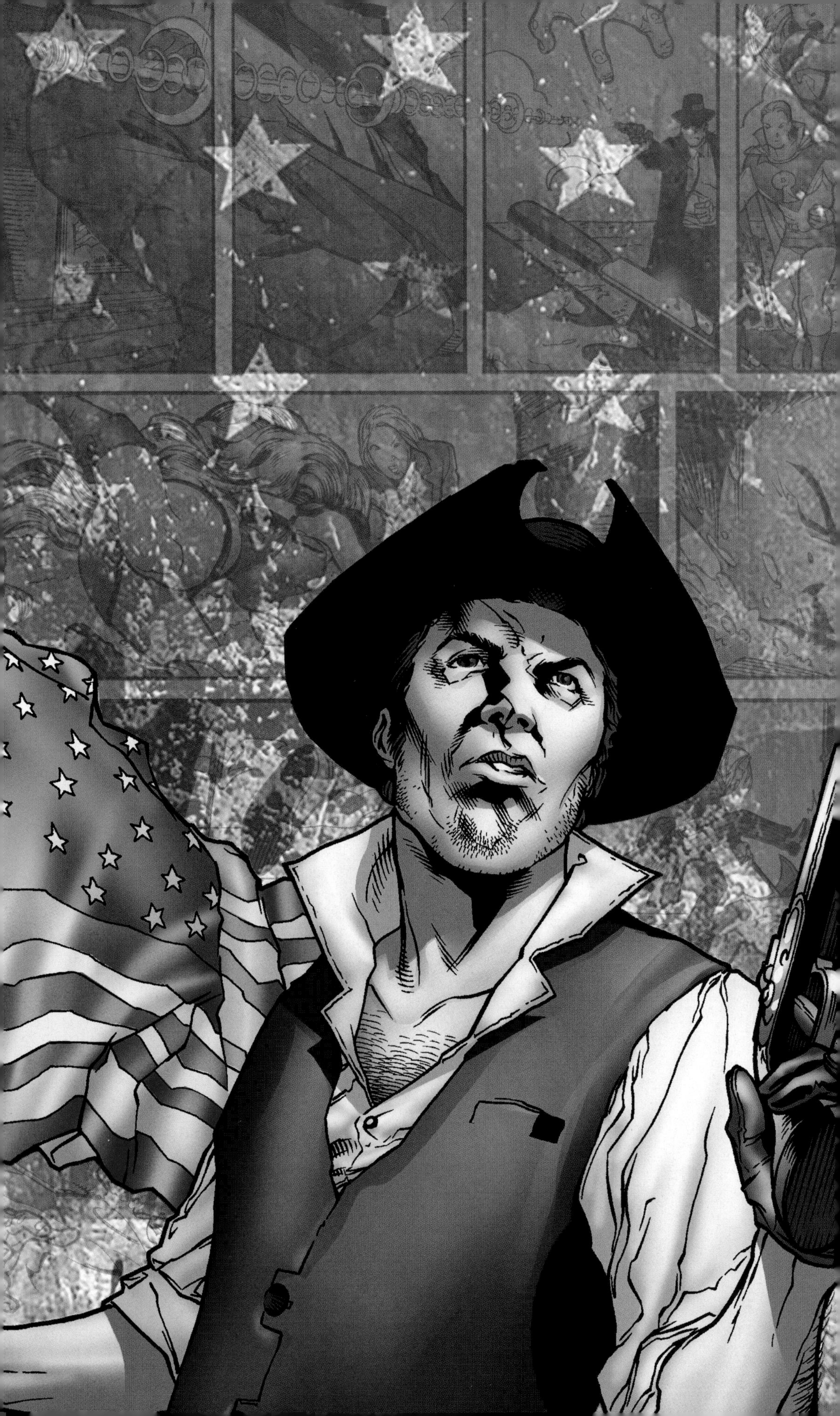

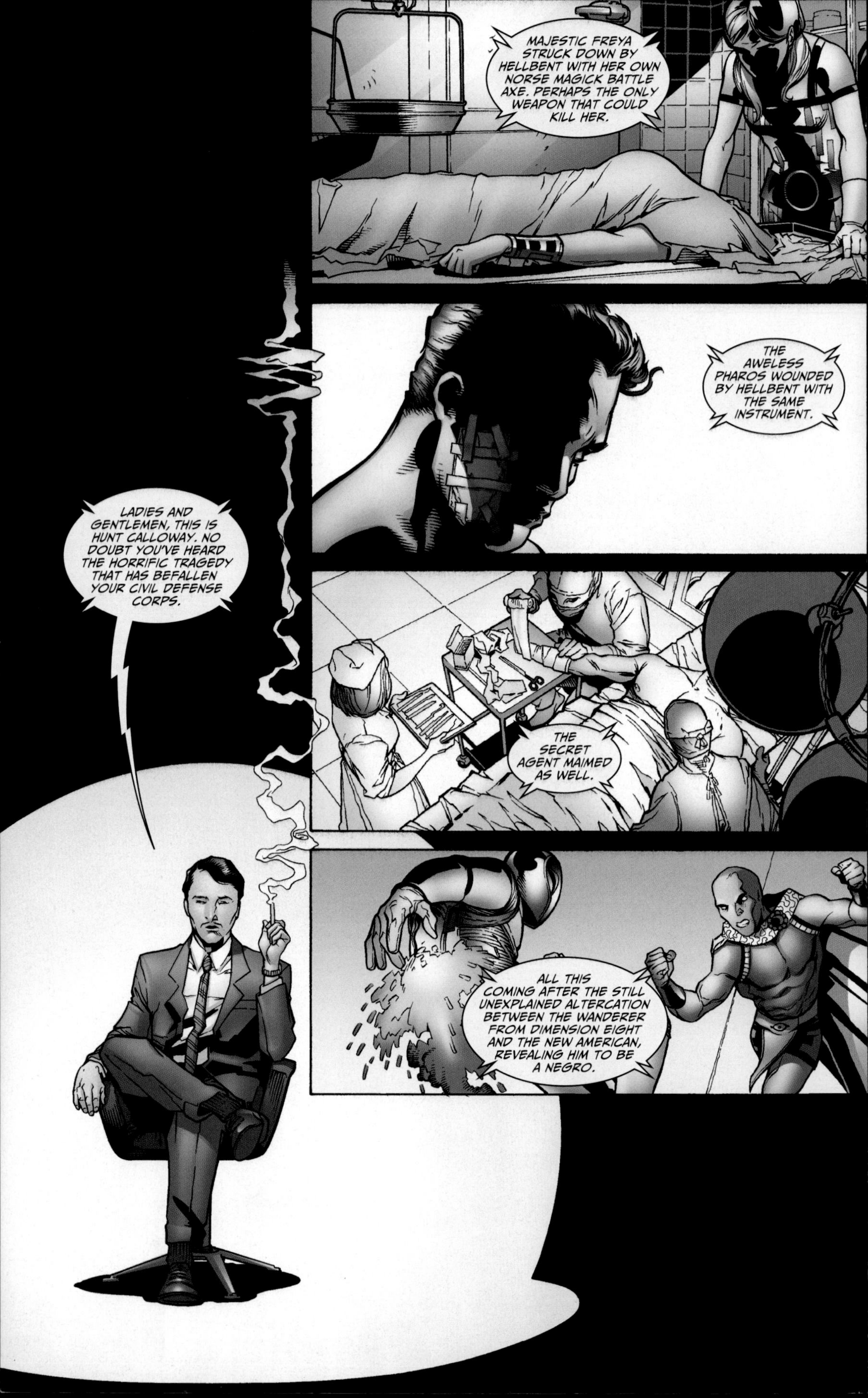
MAJESTIC FREYA STRUCK DOWN BY HELLBENT WITH HER OWN NORSE MAGICK BATTLE AXE. PERHAPS THE ONLY WEAPON THAT COULD KILL HER.
THE AWELESS PHAROS WOUNDED BY HELLBENT WITH THE SAME INSTRUMENT.
LADIES AND GENTLEMEN, THIS IS HUNT CALLOWAY. NO DOUBT YOU'VE HEARD THE HORRIFIC TRAGEDY THAT HAS BEFALLEN YOUR CIVIL DEFENSE CORPS.
THE SECRET AGENT MAIMED AS WELL.
ALL THIS COMING AFTER THE STILL UNEXPLAINED ALTERCATION BETWEEN THE WANDERER FROM DIMENSION EIGHT AND THE NEW AMERICAN, REVEALING HIM TO BE A NEGRO.

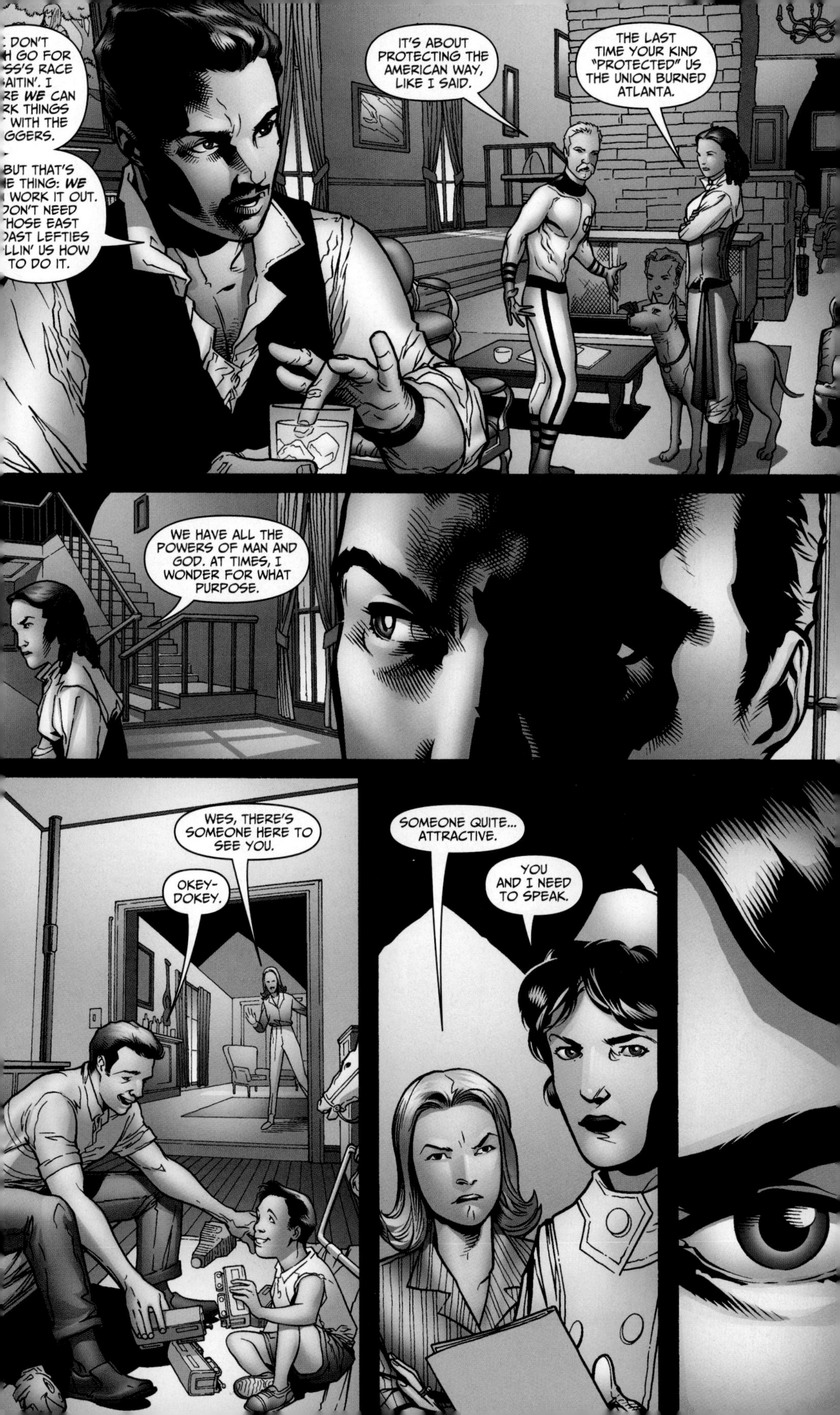
: DON'T H GO FOR SS'S RACE AITIN'. I RE WE CAN RK THINGS WITH THE GGERS.
BUT THAT'S E THING: WE WORK IT OUT. ON'T NEED HOSE EAST OAST LEFTIES LLIN' US HOW TO DO IT.
IT'S ABOUT PROTECTING THE AMERICAN WAY, LIKE I SAID.
THE LAST TIME YOUR KIND "PROTECTED" US THE UNION BURNED ATLANTA.
WE HAVE ALL THE POWERS OF MAN AND GOD. AT TIMES, I WONDER FOR WHAT PURPOSE.
WES, THERE'S SOMEONE HERE TO SEE YOU.
OKEY-DOKEY.
SOMEONE QUITE... ATTRACTIVE.
YOU AND I NEED TO SPEAK.

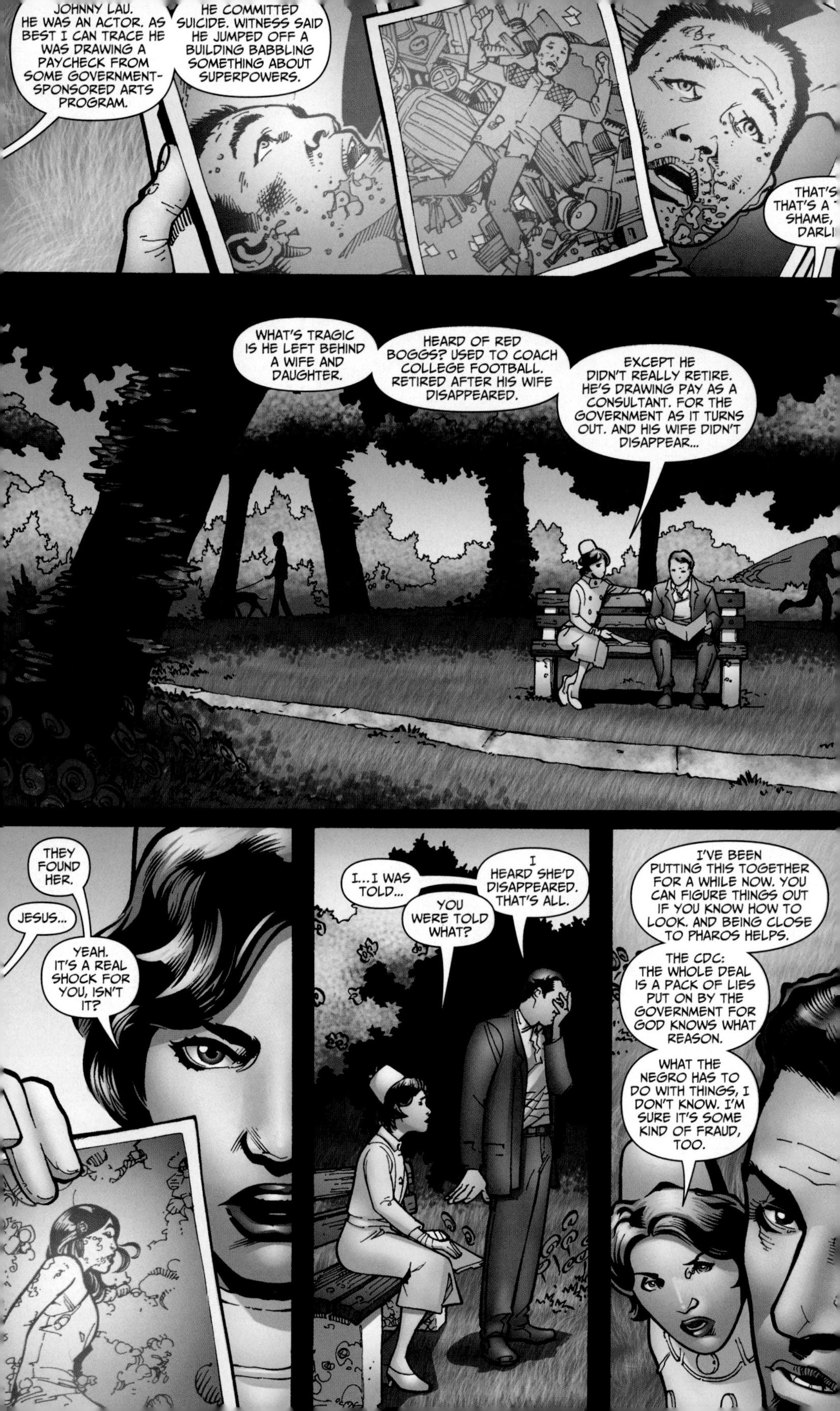
JOHNNY LAU. HE WAS AN ACTOR. AS BEST I CAN TRACE HE WAS DRAWING A PAYCHECK FROM SOME GOVERNMENT-SPONSORED ARTS PROGRAM.
HE COMMITTED SUICIDE. WITNESS SAID HE JUMPED OFF A BUILDING BABBLING SOMETHING ABOUT SUPERPOWERS.
THAT'S THAT'S A SHAME, DARLI
WHAT'S TRAGIC IS HE LEFT BEHIND A WIFE AND DAUGHTER.
HEARD OF RED BOGGS? USED TO COACH COLLEGE FOOTBALL. RETIRED AFTER HIS WIFE DISAPPEARED.
EXCEPT HE DIDN'T REALLY RETIRE. HE'S DRAWING PAY AS A CONSULTANT. FOR THE GOVERNMENT AS IT TURNS OUT. AND HIS WIFE DIDN'T DISAPPEAR...
THEY FOUND HER.
JESUS...
YEAH. IT'S A REAL SHOCK FOR YOU, ISN'T IT?
I...I WAS TOLD...
YOU WERE TOLD WHAT?
I HEARD SHE'D DISAPPEARED. THAT'S ALL.
I'VE BEEN PUTTING THIS TOGETHER FOR A WHILE NOW. YOU CAN FIGURE THINGS OUT IF YOU KNOW HOW TO LOOK. AND BEING CLOSE TO PHAROS HELPS.
THE CDC: THE WHOLE DEAL IS A PACK OF LIES PUT ON BY THE GOVERNMENT FOR GOD KNOWS WHAT REASON.
WHAT THE NEGRO HAS TO DO WITH THINGS, I DON'T KNOW. I'M SURE IT'S SOME KIND OF FRAUD, TOO.

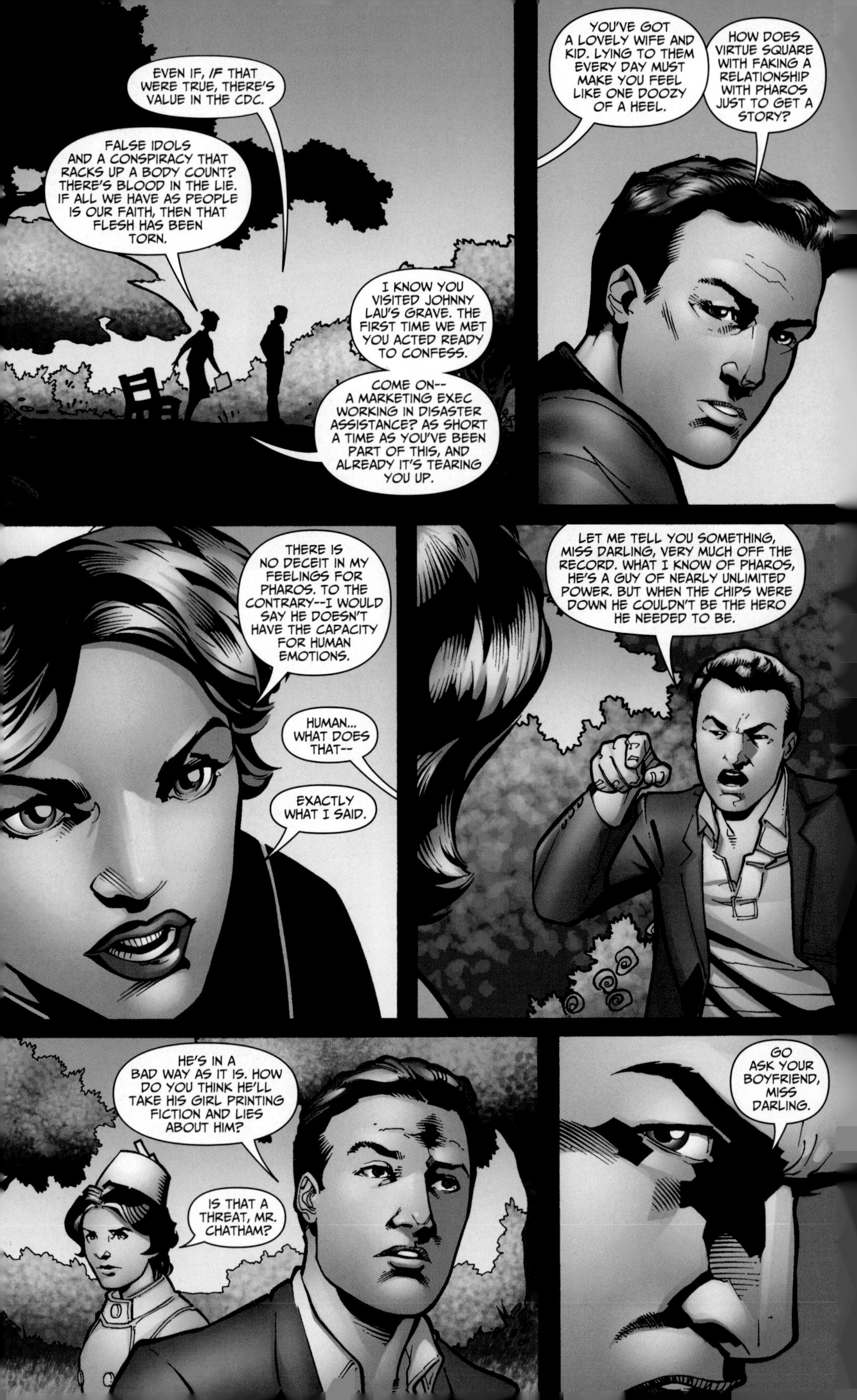
EVEN IF, IF THAT WERE TRUE, THERE'S VALUE IN THE CDC.
FALSE IDOLS AND A CONSPIRACY THAT RACKS UP A BODY COUNT? THERE'S BLOOD IN THE LIE. IF ALL WE HAVE AS PEOPLE IS OUR FAITH, THEN THAT FLESH HAS BEEN TORN.
I KNOW YOU VISITED JOHNNY LAU'S GRAVE. THE FIRST TIME WE MET YOU ACTED READY TO CONFESS.
COME ON-- A MARKETING EXEC WORKING IN DISASTER ASSISTANCE? AS SHORT A TIME AS YOU'VE BEEN PART OF THIS, AND ALREADY IT'S TEARING YOU UP.
YOU'VE GOT A LOVELY WIFE AND KID. LYING TO THEM EVERY DAY MUST MAKE YOU FEEL LIKE ONE DOOZY OF A HEEL.
HOW DOES VIRTUE SQUARE WITH FAKING A RELATIONSHIP WITH PHAROS JUST TO GET A STORY?
THERE IS NO DECEIT IN MY FEELINGS FOR PHAROS. TO THE CONTRARY--I WOULD SAY HE DOESN'T HAVE THE CAPACITY FOR HUMAN EMOTIONS.
HUMAN... WHAT DOES THAT--
EXACTLY WHAT I SAID.
LET ME TELL YOU SOMETHING, MISS DARLING, VERY MUCH OFF THE RECORD. WHAT I KNOW OF PHAROS, HE'S A GUY OF NEARLY UNLIMITED POWER. BUT WHEN THE CHIPS WERE DOWN HE COULDN'T BE THE HERO HE NEEDED TO BE.
HE'S IN A BAD WAY AS IT IS. HOW DO YOU THINK HE'LL TAKE HIS GIRL PRINTING FICTION AND LIES ABOUT HIM?
IS THAT A THREAT, MR. CHATHAM?
GO ASK YOUR BOYFRIEND, MISS DARLING.

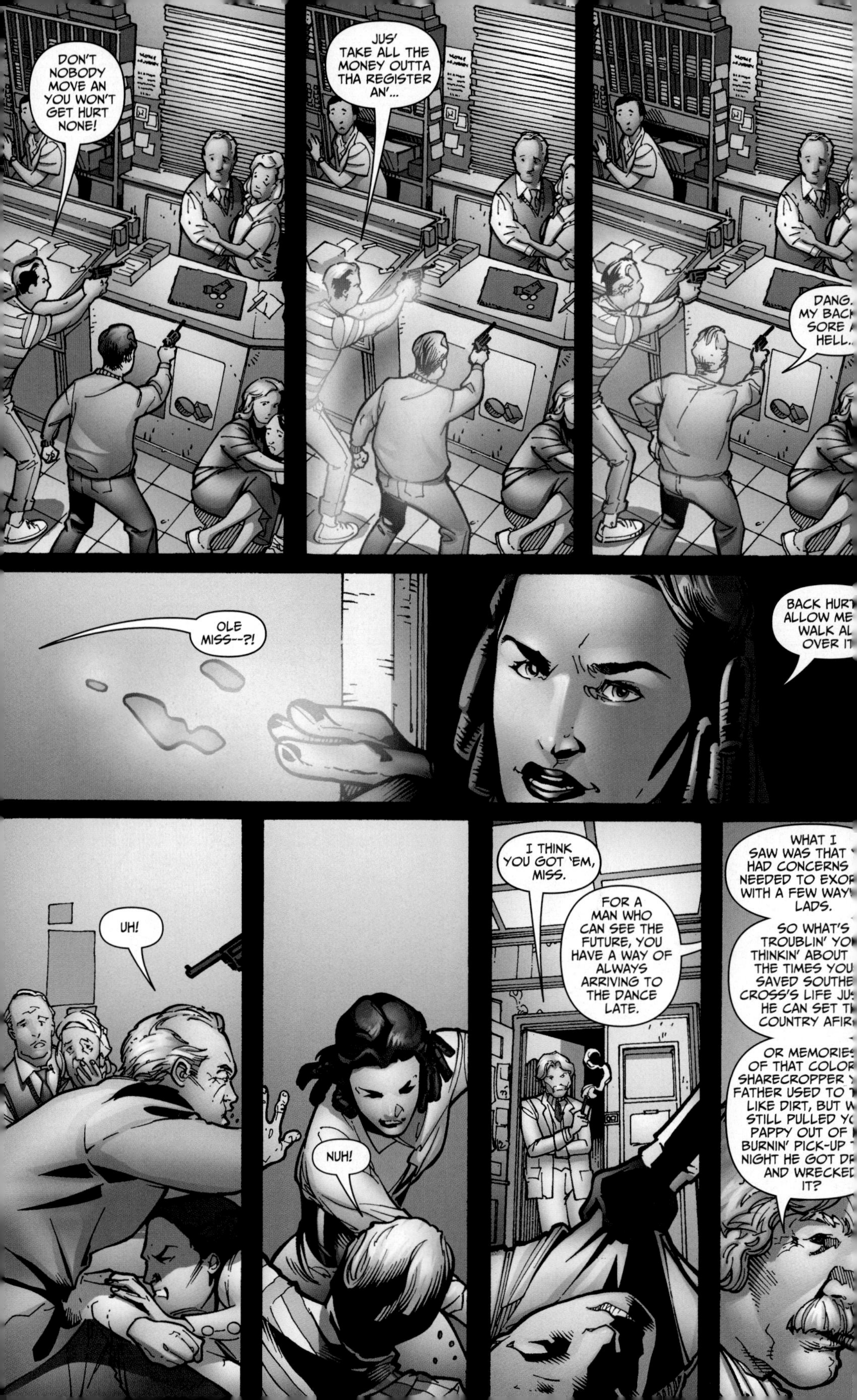
DON'T NOBODY MOVE AN YOU WON'T GET HURT NONE!
JUS' TAKE ALL THE MONEY OUTTA THA REGISTER AN'...
DANG. MY BACK SORE A HELL...
OLE MISS--?!
BACK HURT ALLOW ME WALK AL OVER IT
UH!
NUH!
I THINK YOU GOT 'EM, MISS.
FOR A MAN WHO CAN SEE THE FUTURE, YOU HAVE A WAY OF ALWAYS ARRIVING TO THE DANCE LATE.
WHAT I SAW WAS THAT HAD CONCERNS NEEDED TO EXOR WITH A FEW WAY LADS.
SO WHAT'S TROUBLIN' YO THINKIN' ABOUT THE TIMES YOU SAVED SOUTHE CROSS'S LIFE JUS HE CAN SET TH COUNTRY AFIR
OR MEMORIES OF THAT COLOR SHARECROPPER FATHER USED TO LIKE DIRT, BUT W STILL PULLED YO PAPPY OUT OF BURNIN' PICK-UP NIGHT HE GOT DR AND WRECKED IT?

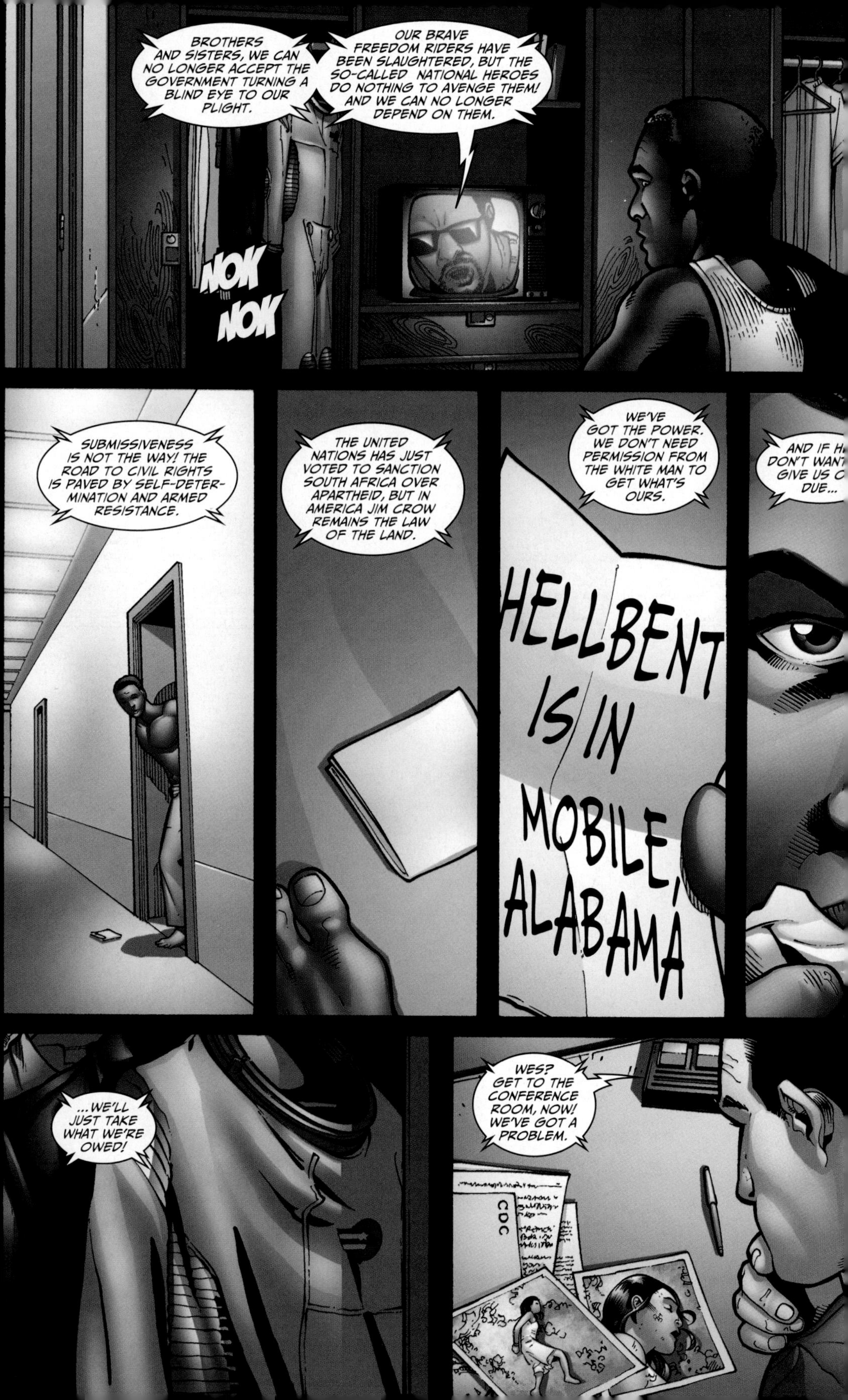
BROTHERS AND SISTERS, WE CAN NO LONGER ACCEPT THE GOVERNMENT TURNING A BLIND EYE TO OUR PLIGHT.
OUR BRAVE FREEDOM RIDERS HAVE BEEN SLAUGHTERED, BUT THE SO-CALLED NATIONAL HEROES DO NOTHING TO AVENGE THEM! AND WE CAN NO LONGER DEPEND ON THEM.
NOK NOK
SUBMISSIVENESS IS NOT THE WAY! THE ROAD TO CIVIL RIGHTS IS PAVED BY SELF-DETER-MINATION AND ARMED RESISTANCE.
THE UNITED NATIONS HAS JUST VOTED TO SANCTION SOUTH AFRICA OVER APARTHEID, BUT IN AMERICA JIM CROW REMAINS THE LAW OF THE LAND.
WE'VE GOT THE POWER. WE DON'T NEED PERMISSION FROM THE WHITE MAN TO GET WHAT'S OURS.
HELLBENT IS IN MOBILE, ALABAMA
AND IF H DON'T WANT GIVE US O DUE...
...WE'LL JUST TAKE WHAT WE'RE OWED!
WES? GET TO THE CONFERENCE ROOM, NOW! WE'VE GOT A PROBLEM.
CDC

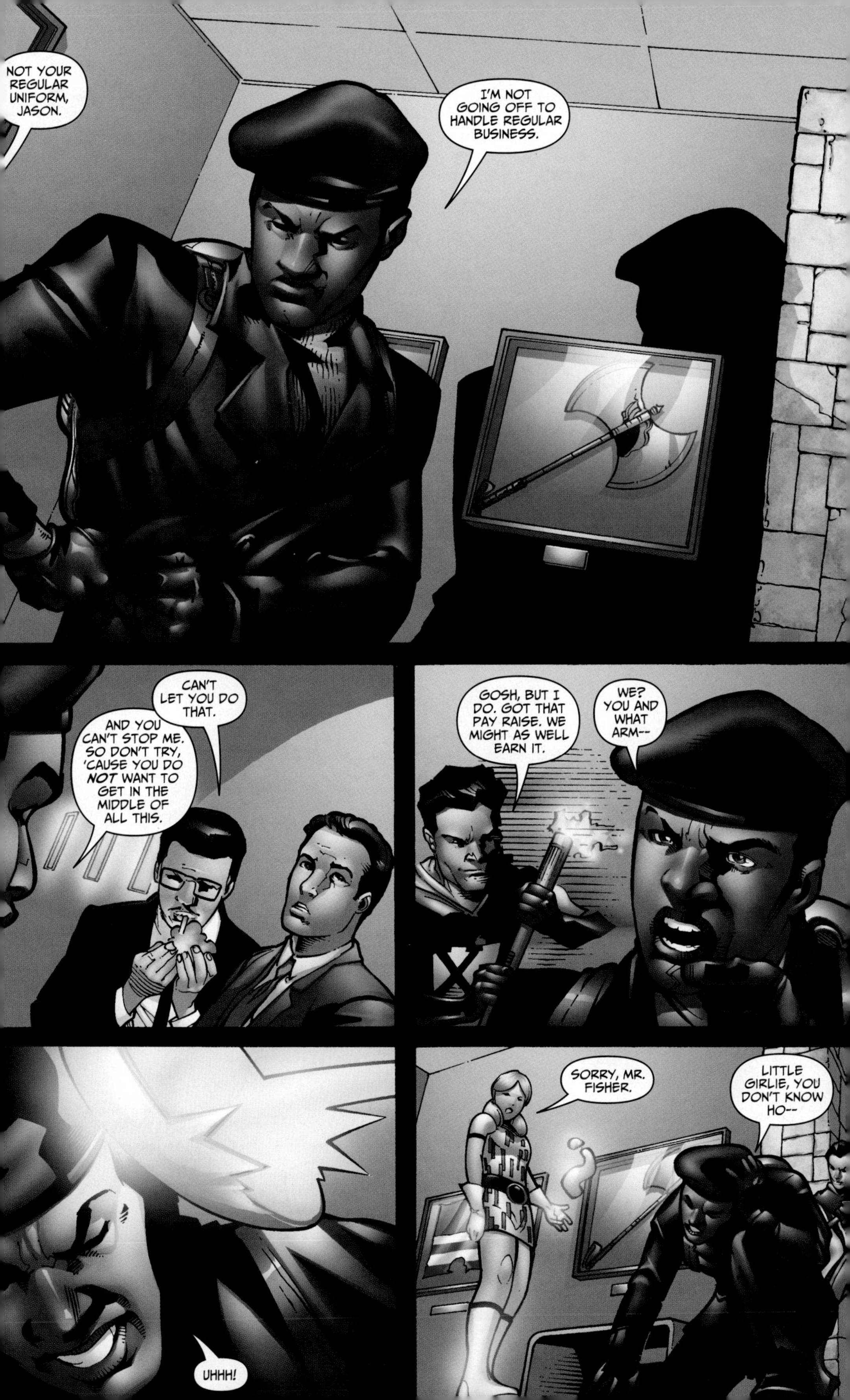

NOT YOUR REGULAR UNIFORM, JASON.
I'M NOT GOING OFF TO HANDLE REGULAR BUSINESS.
CAN'T LET YOU DO THAT.
AND YOU CAN'T STOP ME. SO DON'T TRY, 'CAUSE YOU DO NOT WANT TO GET IN THE MIDDLE OF ALL THIS.
GOSH, BUT I DO. GOT THAT PAY RAISE. WE MIGHT AS WELL EARN IT.
WE? YOU AND WHAT ARM--
UHHH!
SORRY, MR. FISHER.
LITTLE GIRLIE, YOU DON'T KNOW HO--

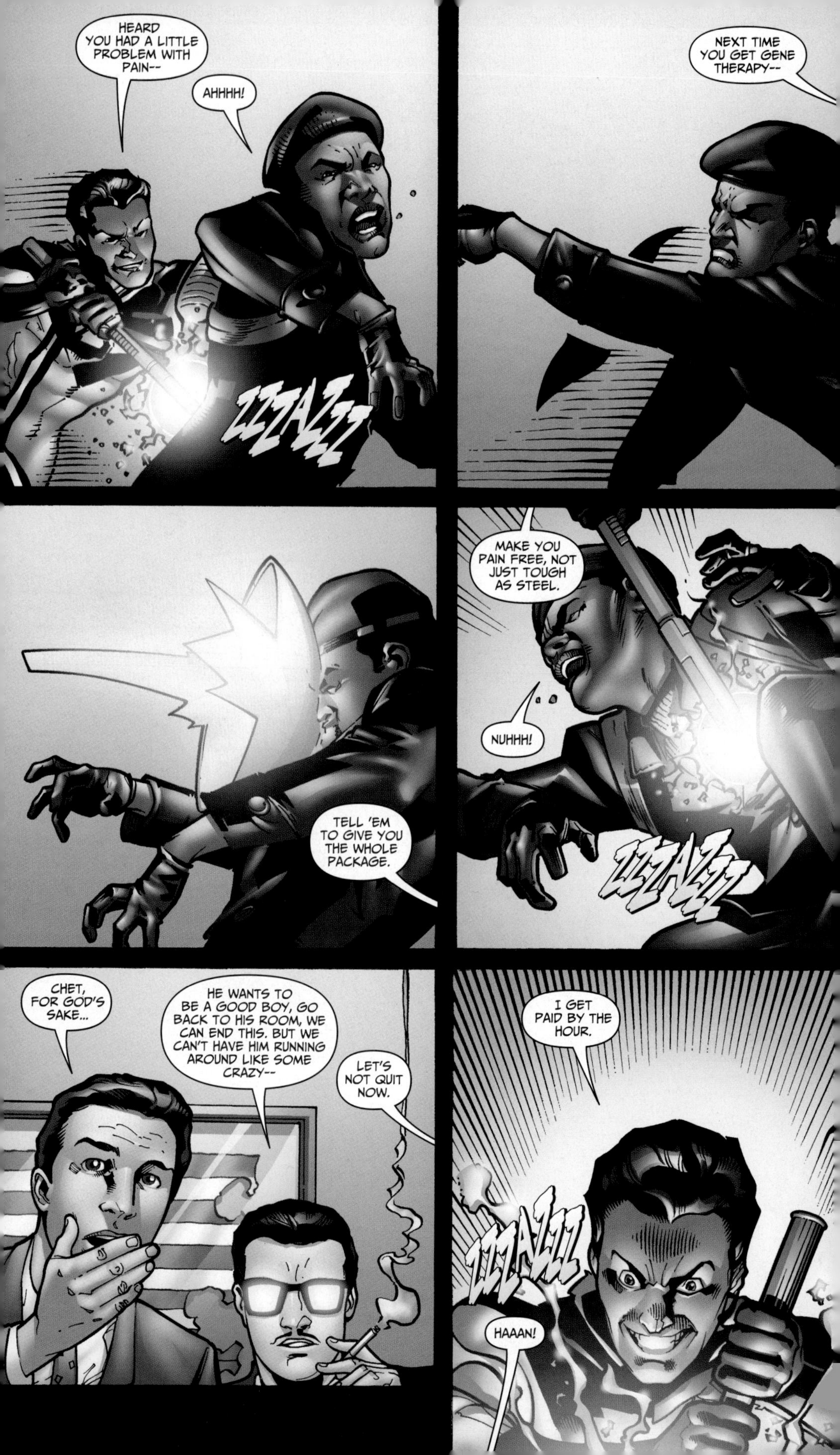
HEARD YOU HAD A LITTLE PROBLEM WITH PAIN--
AHHHH!
ZZZAZZZ
NEXT TIME YOU GET GENE THERAPY--
TELL 'EM TO GIVE YOU THE WHOLE PACKAGE.
MAKE YOU PAIN FREE, NOT JUST TOUGH AS STEEL.
NUHHH!
ZZZAZZZ
CHET, FOR GOD'S SAKE...
HE WANTS TO BE A GOOD BOY, GO BACK TO HIS ROOM, WE CAN END THIS. BUT WE CAN'T HAVE HIM RUNNING AROUND LIKE SOME CRAZY--
LET'S NOT QUIT NOW.
I GET PAID BY THE HOUR.
ZZZAZZZ
HAAAN!

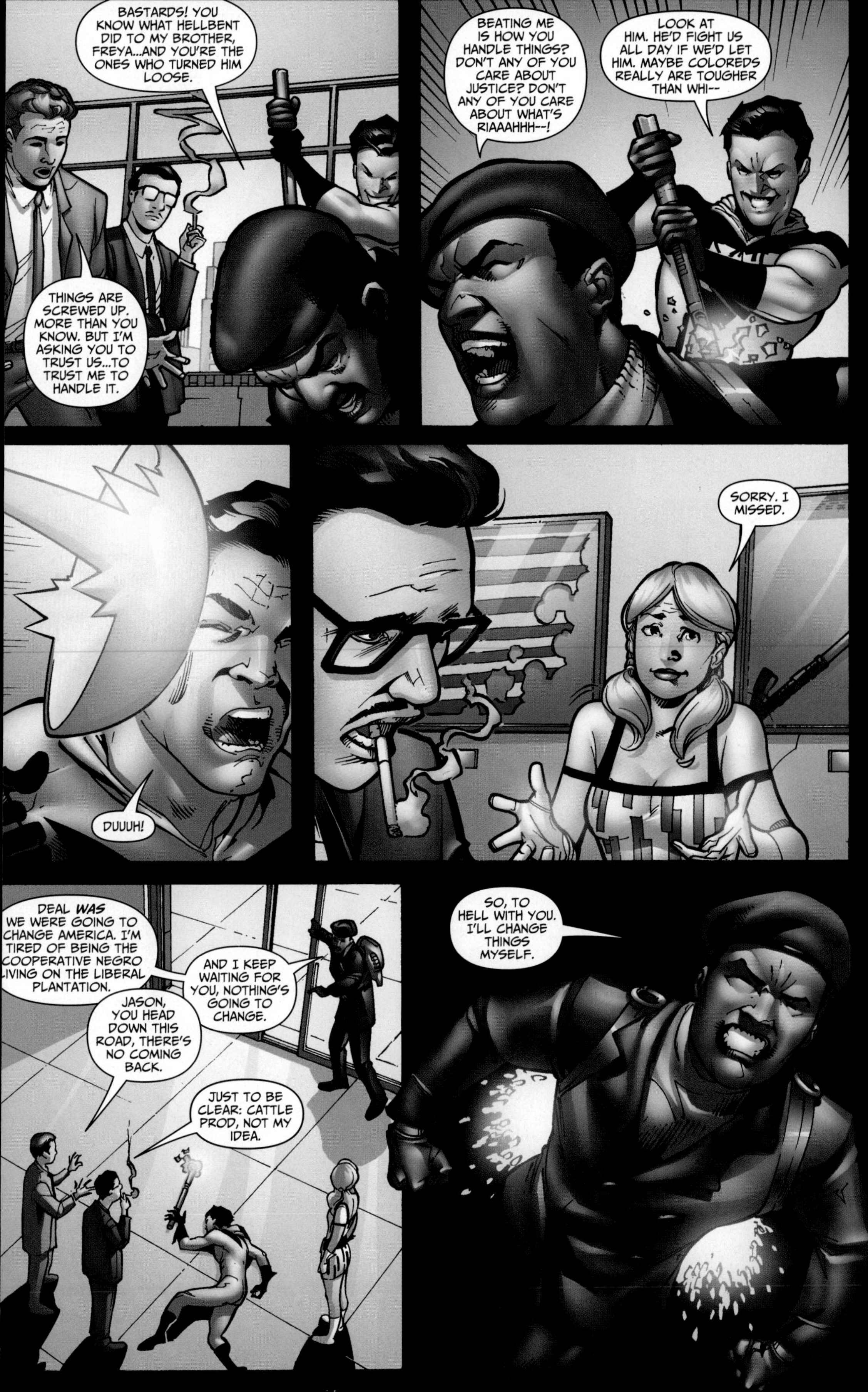
BASTARDS! YOU KNOW WHAT HELLBENT DID TO MY BROTHER, FREYA...AND YOU'RE THE ONES WHO TURNED HIM LOOSE.
THINGS ARE SCREWED UP. MORE THAN YOU KNOW. BUT I'M ASKING YOU TO TRUST US...TO TRUST ME TO HANDLE IT.
BEATING ME IS HOW YOU HANDLE THINGS? DON'T ANY OF YOU CARE ABOUT JUSTICE? DON'T ANY OF YOU CARE ABOUT WHAT'S RIAAAHHH--!
LOOK AT HIM. HE'D FIGHT US ALL DAY IF WE'D LET HIM. MAYBE COLOREDS REALLY ARE TOUGHER THAN WHI--
DUUUH!
SORRY. I MISSED.
DEAL *WAS* WE WERE GOING TO CHANGE AMERICA. I'M TIRED OF BEING THE COOPERATIVE NEGRO LIVING ON THE LIBERAL PLANTATION.
AND I KEEP WAITING FOR YOU, NOTHING'S GOING TO CHANGE.
JASON, YOU HEAD DOWN THIS ROAD, THERE'S NO COMING BACK.
JUST TO BE CLEAR: CATTLE PROD, NOT MY IDEA.
SO, TO HELL WITH YOU. I'LL CHANGE THINGS MYSELF.

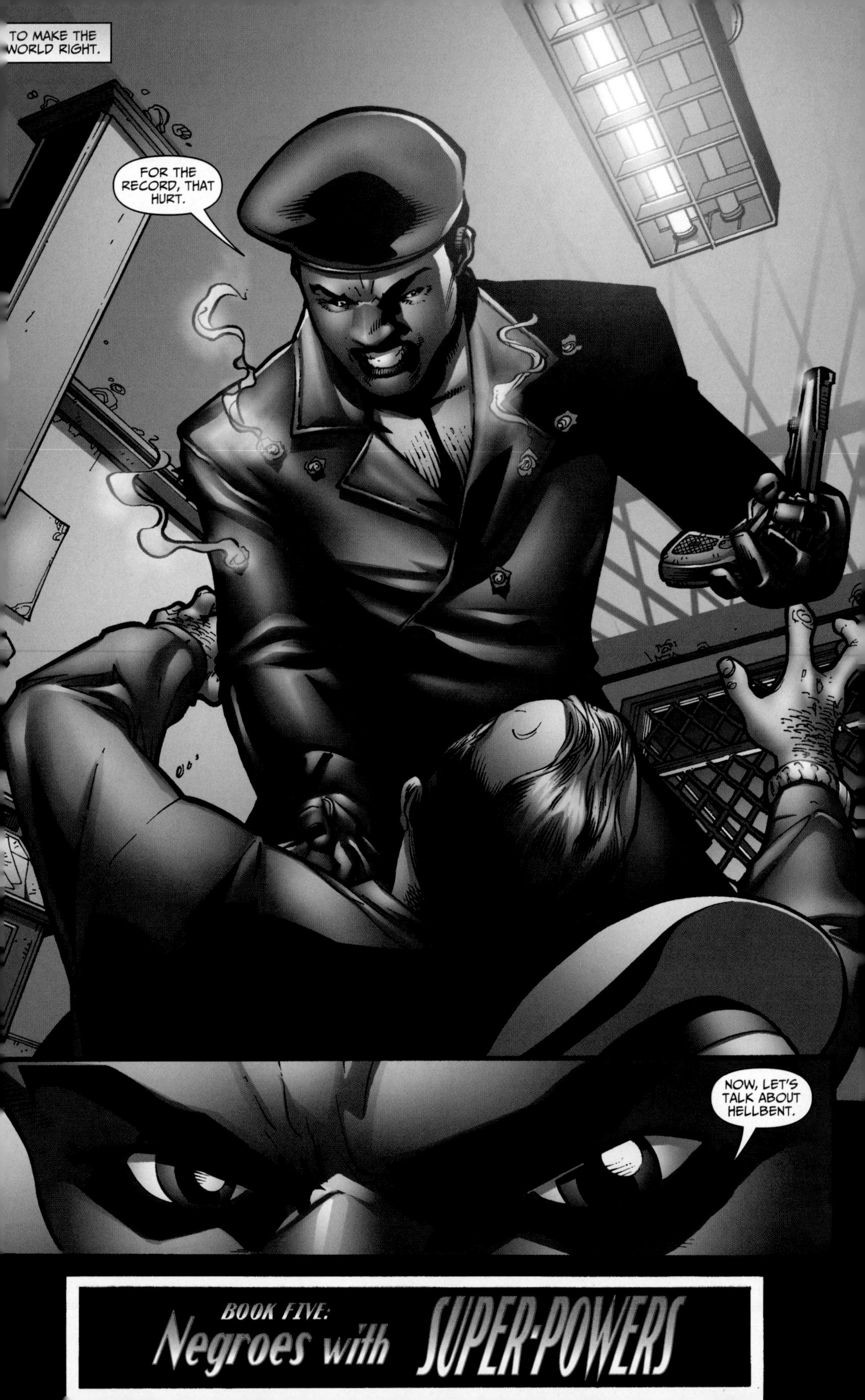
TO MAKE THE WORLD RIGHT.
FOR THE RECORD, THAT HURT.
NOW, LET'S TALK ABOUT HELLBENT.
BOOK FIVE:
Negroes with SUPER-POWERS

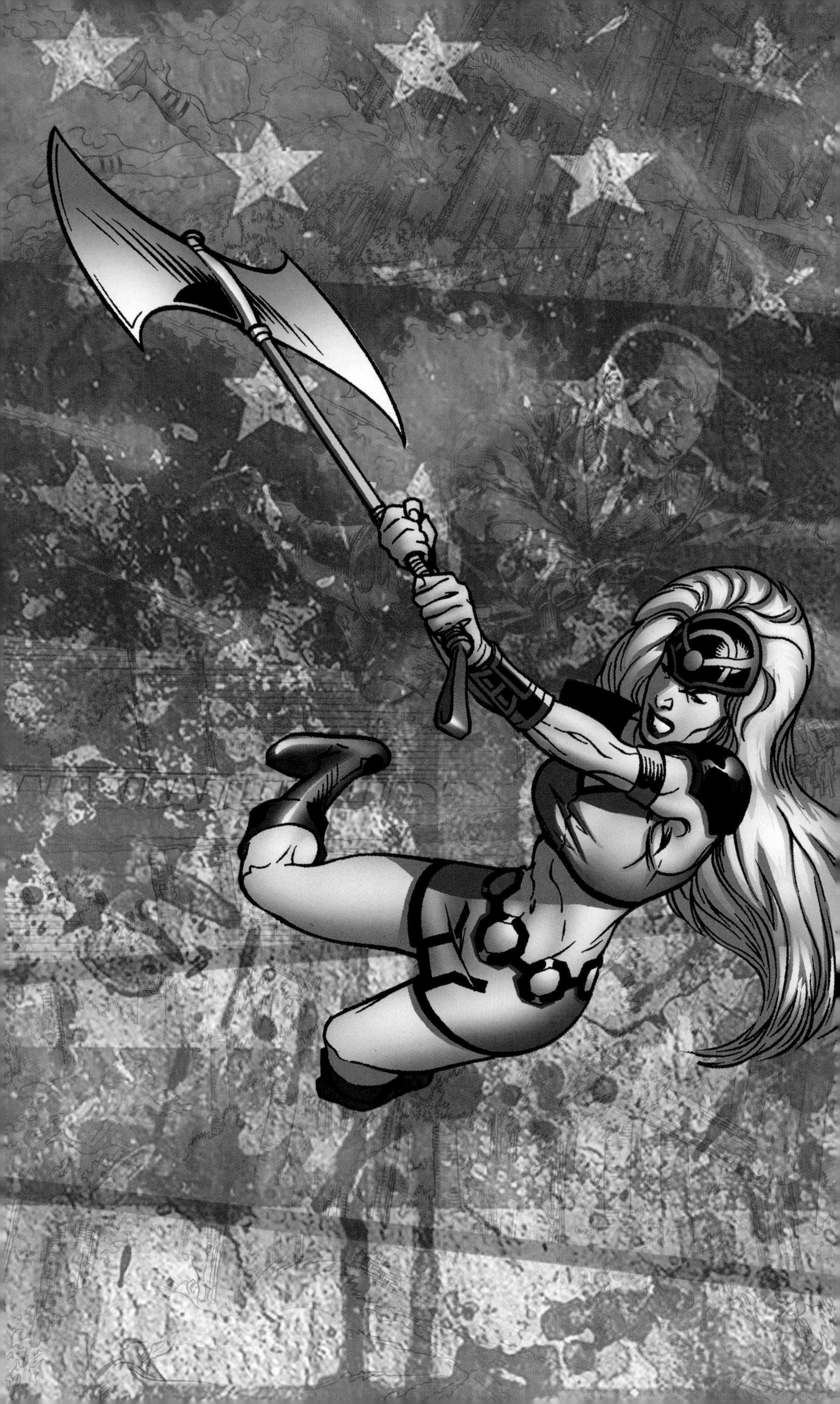

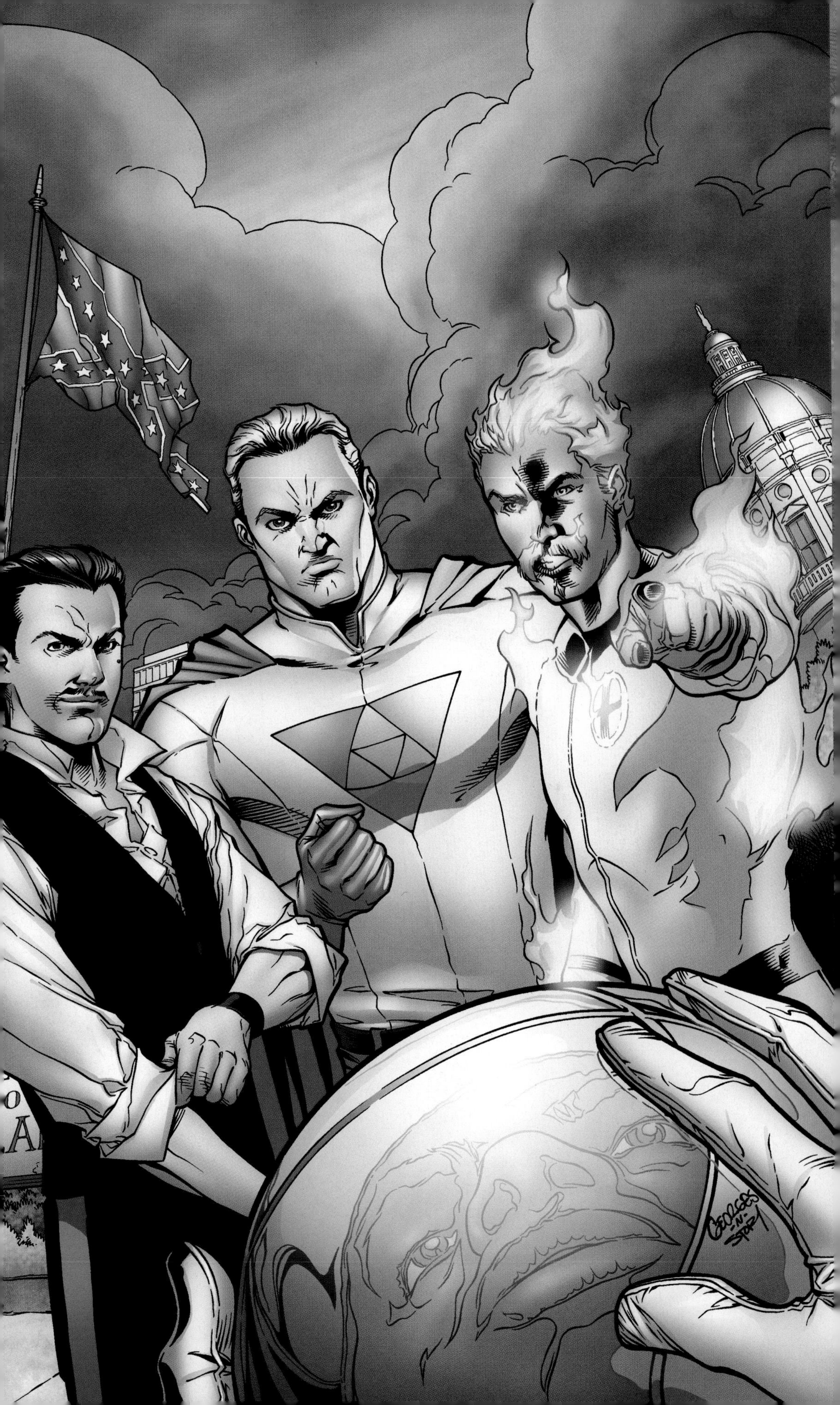

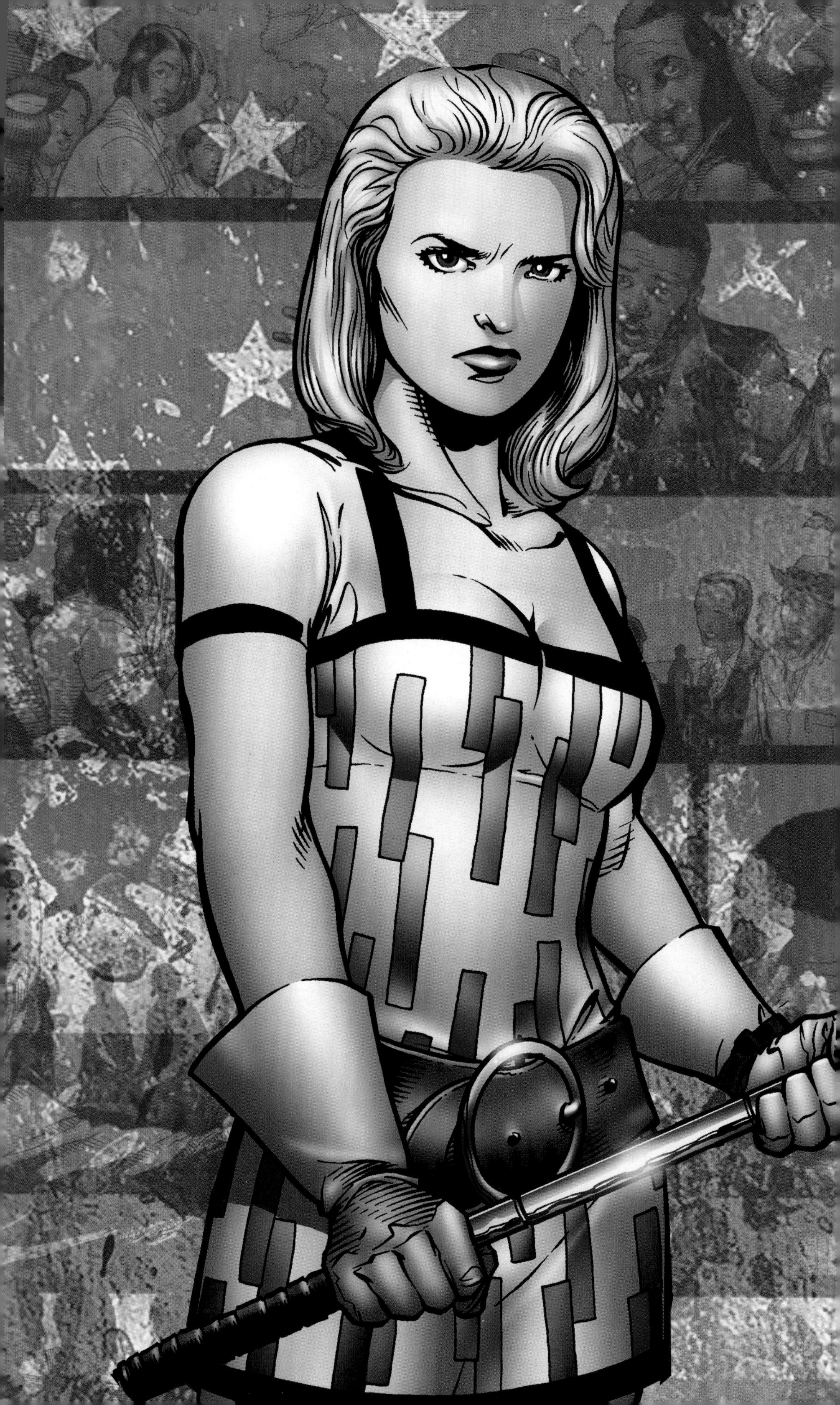

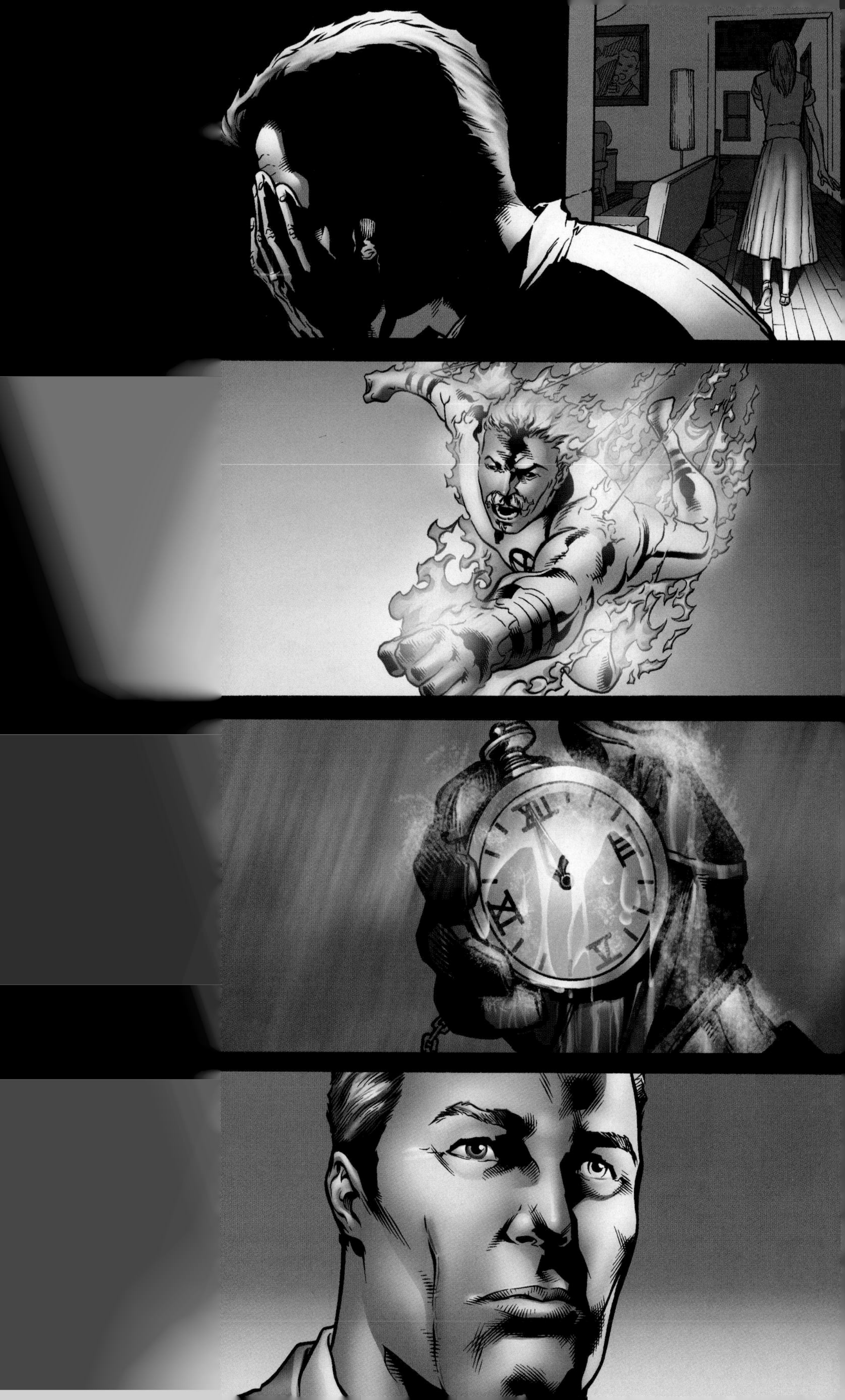

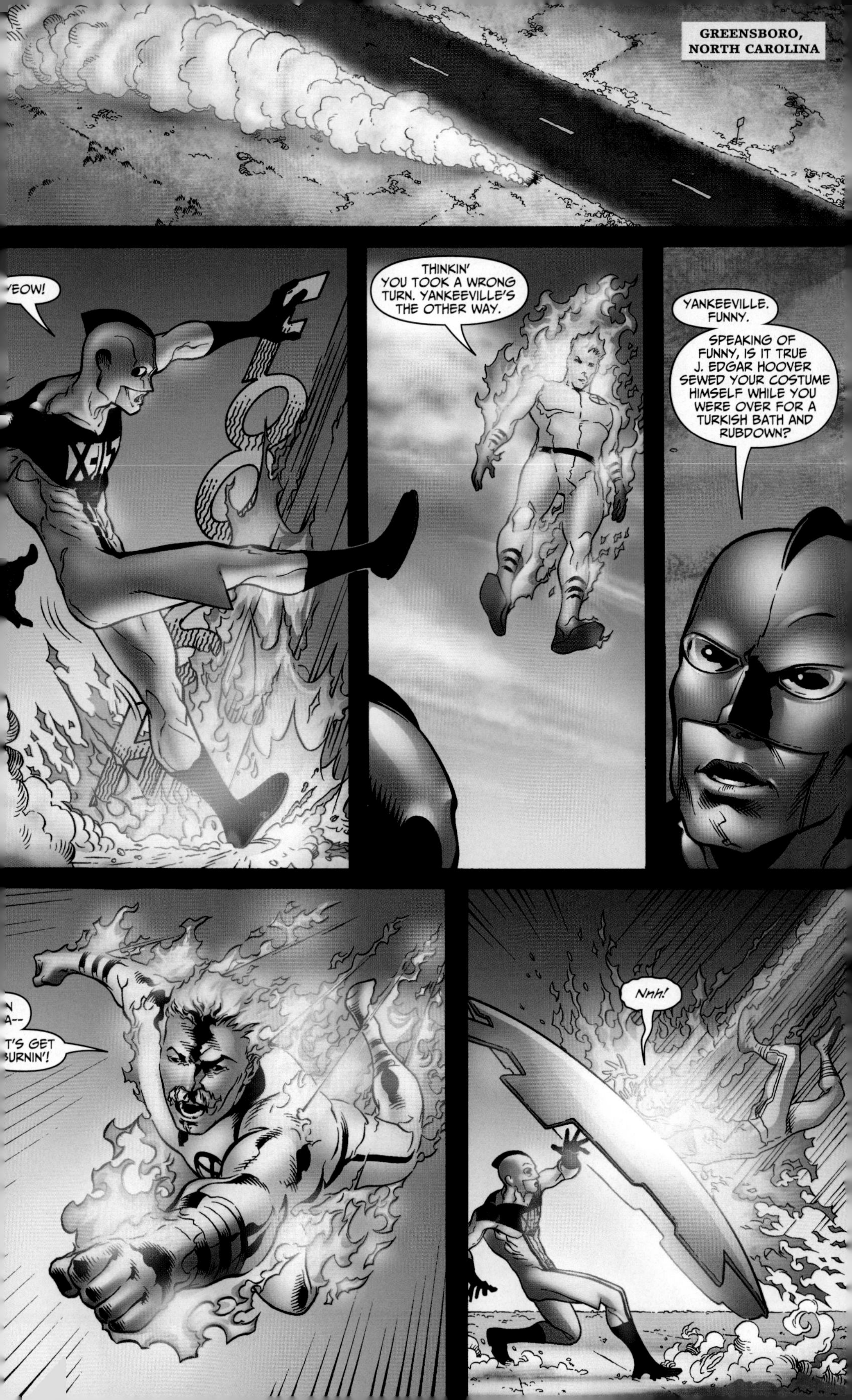
GREENSBORO, NORTH CAROLINA
THINKIN' YOU TOOK A WRONG TURN. YANKEEVILLE'S THE OTHER WAY.
YANKEEVILLE. FUNNY.
SPEAKING OF FUNNY, IS IT TRUE J. EDGAR HOOVER SEWED YOUR COSTUME HIMSELF WHILE YOU WERE OVER FOR A TURKISH BATH AND RUBDOWN?
Nnh!

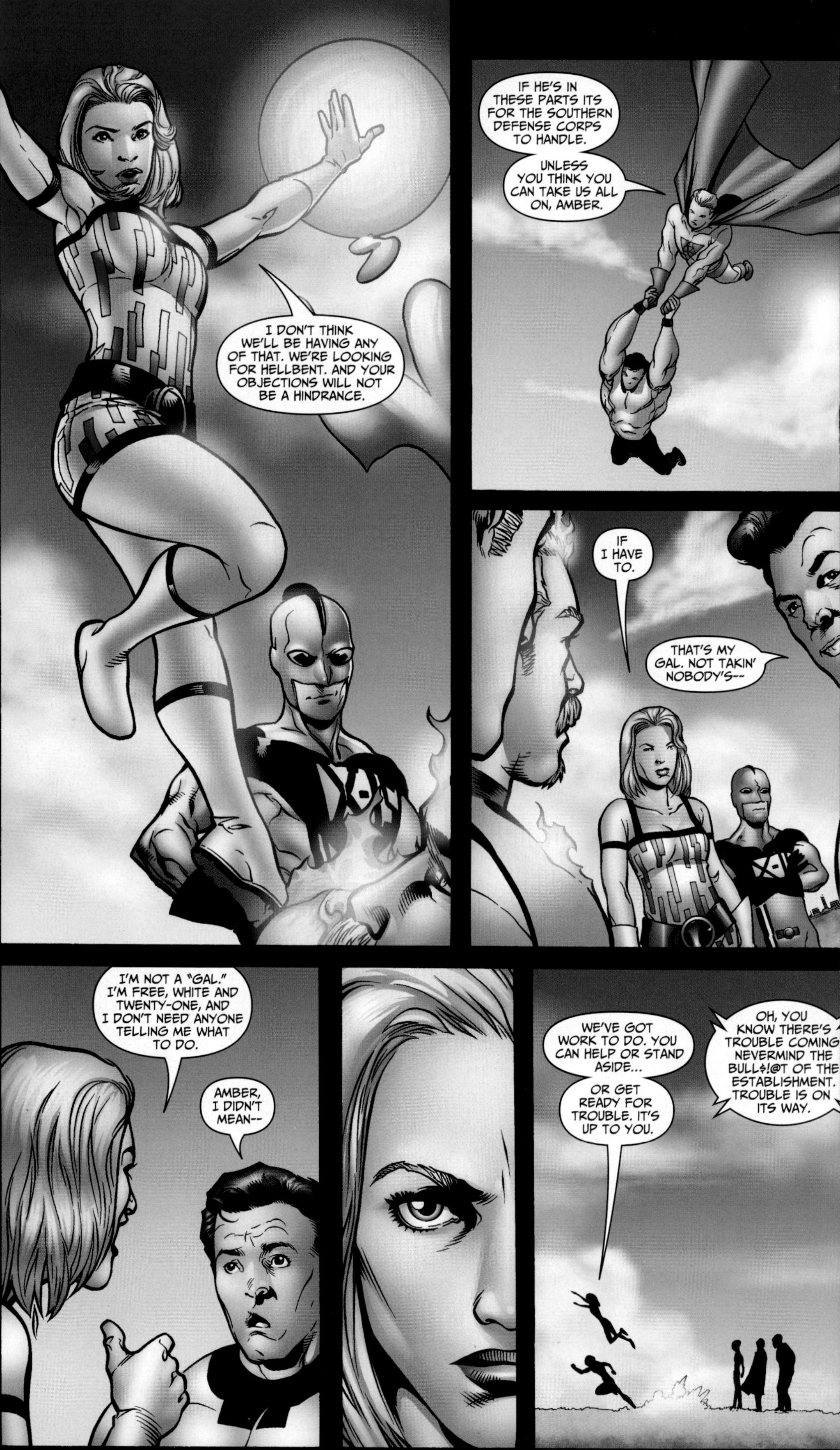
I DON'T THINK WE'LL BE HAVING ANY OF THAT. WE'RE LOOKING FOR HELLBENT. AND YOUR OBJECTIONS WILL NOT BE A HINDRANCE.
IF HE'S IN THESE PARTS ITS FOR THE SOUTHERN DEFENSE CORPS TO HANDLE.
UNLESS YOU THINK YOU CAN TAKE US ALL ON, AMBER.
IF I HAVE TO.
THAT'S MY GAL. NOT TAKIN' NOBODY'S--
I'M NOT A "GAL." I'M FREE, WHITE AND TWENTY-ONE, AND I DON'T NEED ANYONE TELLING ME WHAT TO DO.
AMBER, I DIDN'T MEAN--
WE'VE GOT WORK TO DO. YOU CAN HELP OR STAND ASIDE...
OR GET READY FOR TROUBLE. IT'S UP TO YOU.
OH, YOU KNOW THERE'S TROUBLE COMING NEVERMIND THE BULL$!@T OF THE ESTABLISHMENT. TROUBLE IS ON ITS WAY.

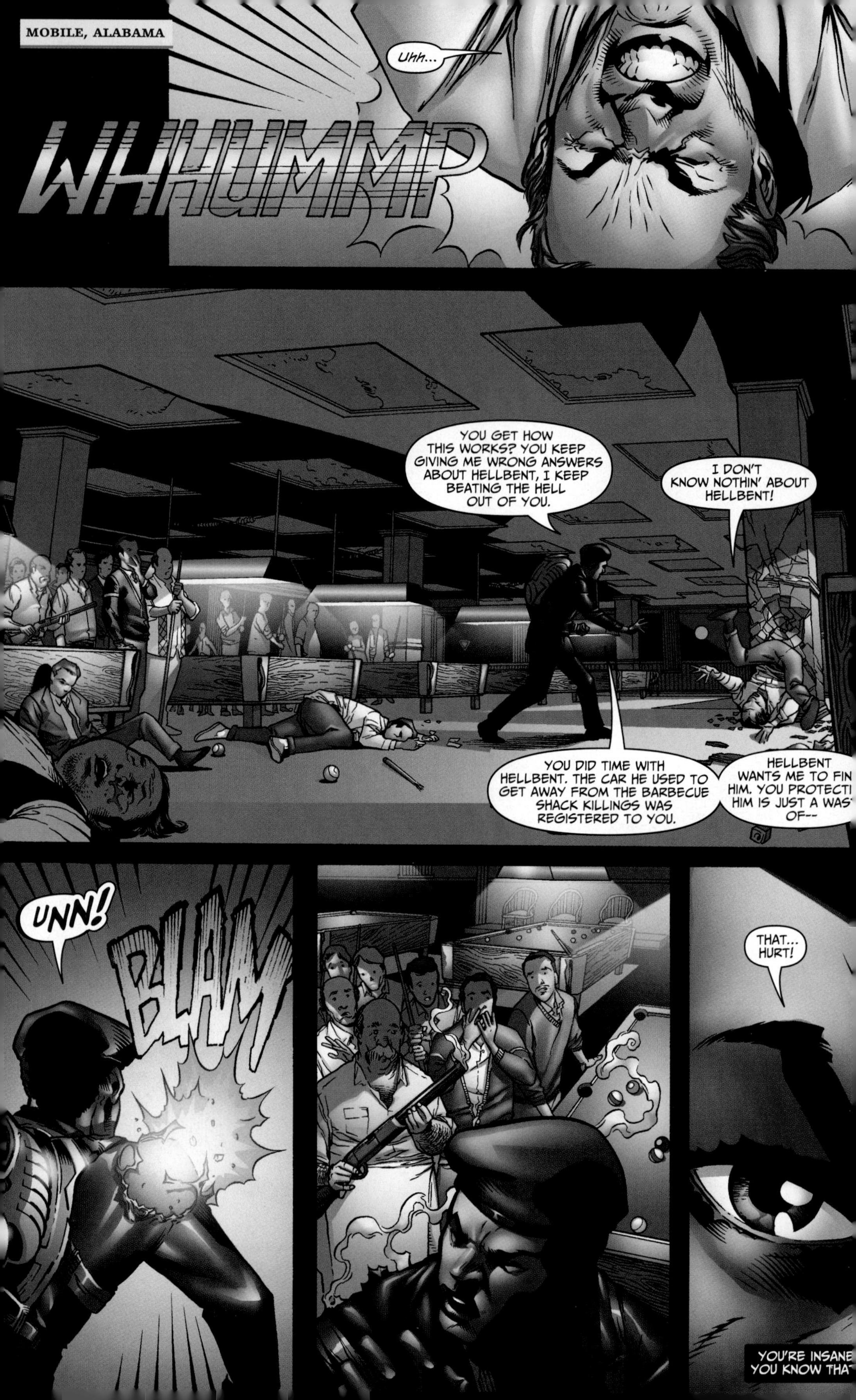
MOBILE, ALABAMA
Uhh...
WHHUMMP
YOU GET HOW THIS WORKS? YOU KEEP GIVING ME WRONG ANSWERS ABOUT HELLBENT, I KEEP BEATING THE HELL OUT OF YOU.
I DON'T KNOW NOTHIN' ABOUT HELLBENT!
YOU DID TIME WITH HELLBENT. THE CAR HE USED TO GET AWAY FROM THE BARBECUE SHACK KILLINGS WAS REGISTERED TO YOU.
HELLBENT WANTS ME TO FIN HIM. YOU PROTECTI HIM IS JUST A WAS OF--
UNN!
BLAM
THAT... HURT!
YOU'RE INSANE YOU KNOW THA

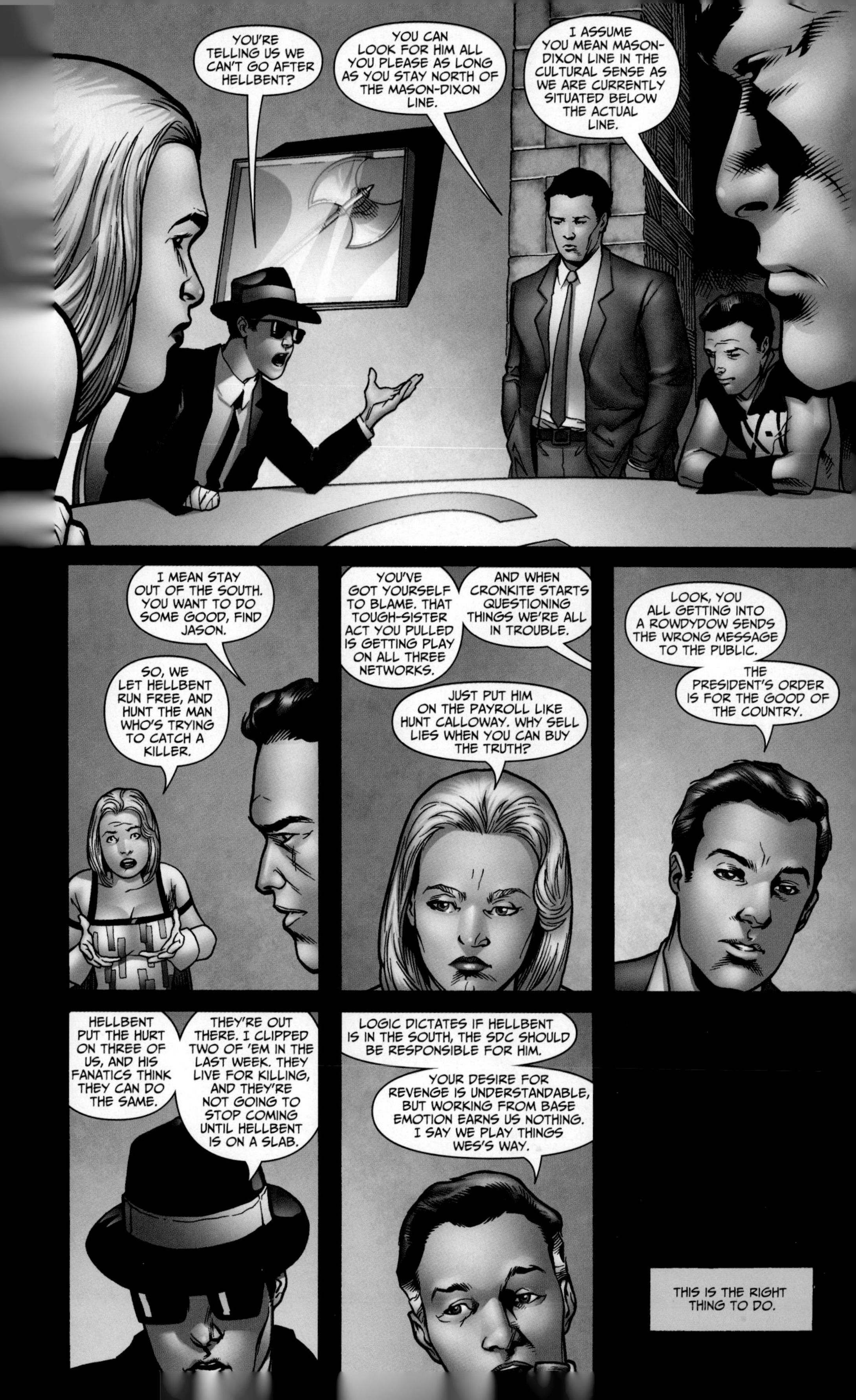

YOU'RE TELLING US WE CAN'T GO AFTER HELLBENT?
YOU CAN LOOK FOR HIM ALL YOU PLEASE AS LONG AS YOU STAY NORTH OF THE MASON-DIXON LINE.
I ASSUME YOU MEAN MASON-DIXON LINE IN THE CULTURAL SENSE AS WE ARE CURRENTLY SITUATED BELOW THE ACTUAL LINE.
I MEAN STAY OUT OF THE SOUTH. YOU WANT TO DO SOME GOOD, FIND JASON.
SO, WE LET HELLBENT RUN FREE, AND HUNT THE MAN WHO'S TRYING TO CATCH A KILLER.
YOU'VE GOT YOURSELF TO BLAME. THAT TOUGH-SISTER ACT YOU PULLED IS GETTING PLAY ON ALL THREE NETWORKS.
AND WHEN CRONKITE STARTS QUESTIONING THINGS WE'RE ALL IN TROUBLE.
JUST PUT HIM ON THE PAYROLL LIKE HUNT CALLOWAY. WHY SELL LIES WHEN YOU CAN BUY THE TRUTH?
LOOK, YOU ALL GETTING INTO A ROWDYDOW SENDS THE WRONG MESSAGE TO THE PUBLIC.
THE PRESIDENT'S ORDER IS FOR THE GOOD OF THE COUNTRY.
HELLBENT PUT THE HURT ON THREE OF US, AND HIS FANATICS THINK THEY CAN DO THE SAME.
THEY'RE OUT THERE. I CLIPPED TWO OF 'EM IN THE LAST WEEK. THEY LIVE FOR KILLING, AND THEY'RE NOT GOING TO STOP COMING UNTIL HELLBENT IS ON A SLAB.
LOGIC DICTATES IF HELLBENT IS IN THE SOUTH, THE SDC SHOULD BE RESPONSIBLE FOR HIM.
YOUR DESIRE FOR REVENGE IS UNDERSTANDABLE, BUT WORKING FROM BASE EMOTION EARNS US NOTHING. I SAY WE PLAY THINGS WES'S WAY.
THIS IS THE RIGHT THING TO DO.

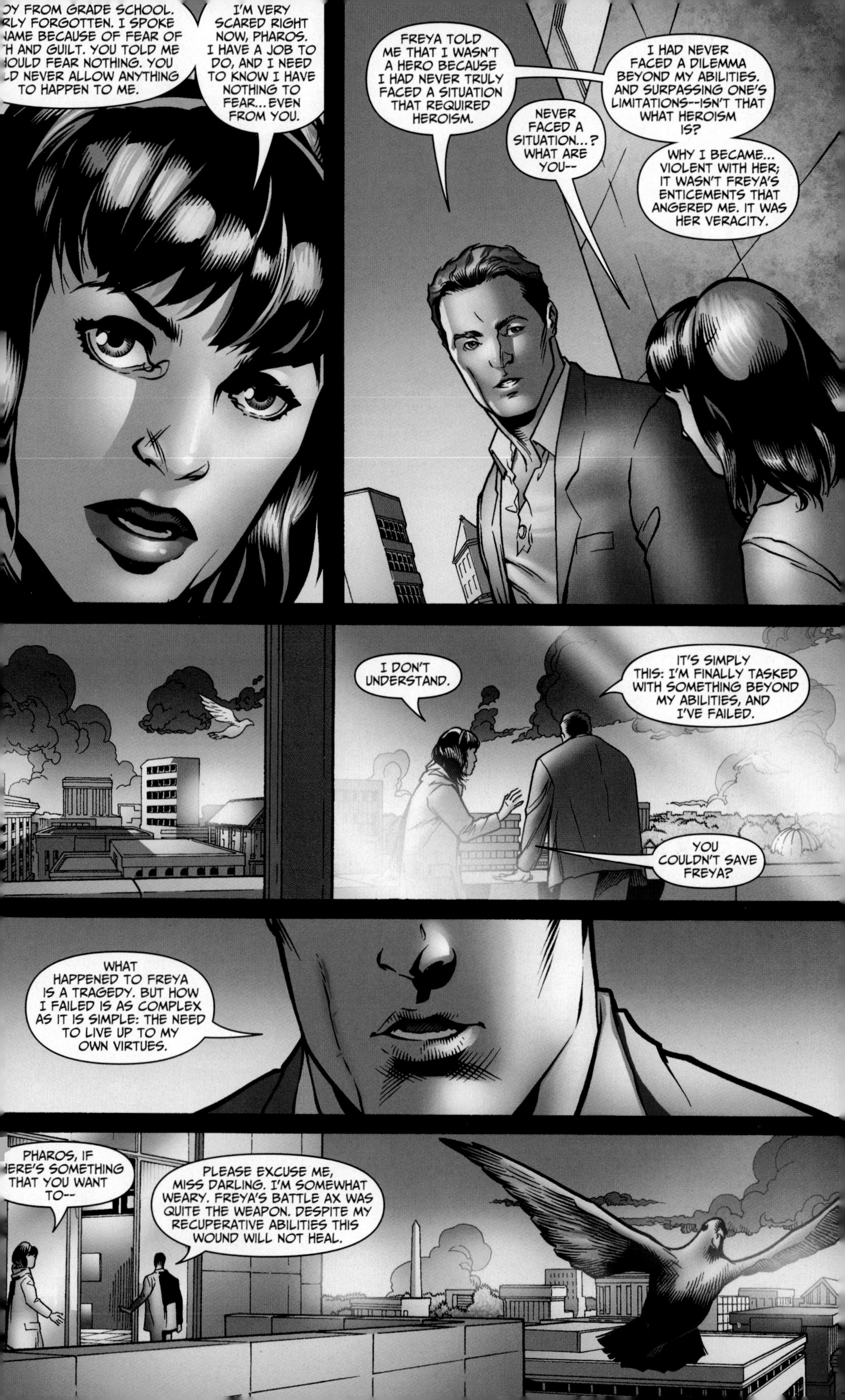

OY FROM GRADE SCHOOL. RLY FORGOTTEN. I SPOKE NAME BECAUSE OF FEAR OF TH AND GUILT. YOU TOLD ME HOULD FEAR NOTHING. YOU LD NEVER ALLOW ANYTHING TO HAPPEN TO ME.
I'M VERY SCARED RIGHT NOW, PHAROS. I HAVE A JOB TO DO, AND I NEED TO KNOW I HAVE NOTHING TO FEAR...EVEN FROM YOU.
FREYA TOLD ME THAT I WASN'T A HERO BECAUSE I HAD NEVER TRULY FACED A SITUATION THAT REQUIRED HEROISM.
I HAD NEVER FACED A DILEMMA BEYOND MY ABILITIES. AND SURPASSING ONE'S LIMITATIONS--ISN'T THAT WHAT HEROISM IS?
NEVER FACED A SITUATION...? WHAT ARE YOU--
WHY I BECAME... VIOLENT WITH HER; IT WASN'T FREYA'S ENTICEMENTS THAT ANGERED ME. IT WAS HER VERACITY.
I DON'T UNDERSTAND.
IT'S SIMPLY THIS: I'M FINALLY TASKED WITH SOMETHING BEYOND MY ABILITIES, AND I'VE FAILED.
YOU COULDN'T SAVE FREYA?
WHAT HAPPENED TO FREYA IS A TRAGEDY. BUT HOW I FAILED IS AS COMPLEX AS IT IS SIMPLE: THE NEED TO LIVE UP TO MY OWN VIRTUES.
PHAROS, IF HERE'S SOMETHING THAT YOU WANT TO--
PLEASE EXCUSE ME, MISS DARLING. I'M SOMEWHAT WEARY. FREYA'S BATTLE AX WAS QUITE THE WEAPON. DESPITE MY RECUPERATIVE ABILITIES THIS WOUND WILL NOT HEAL.

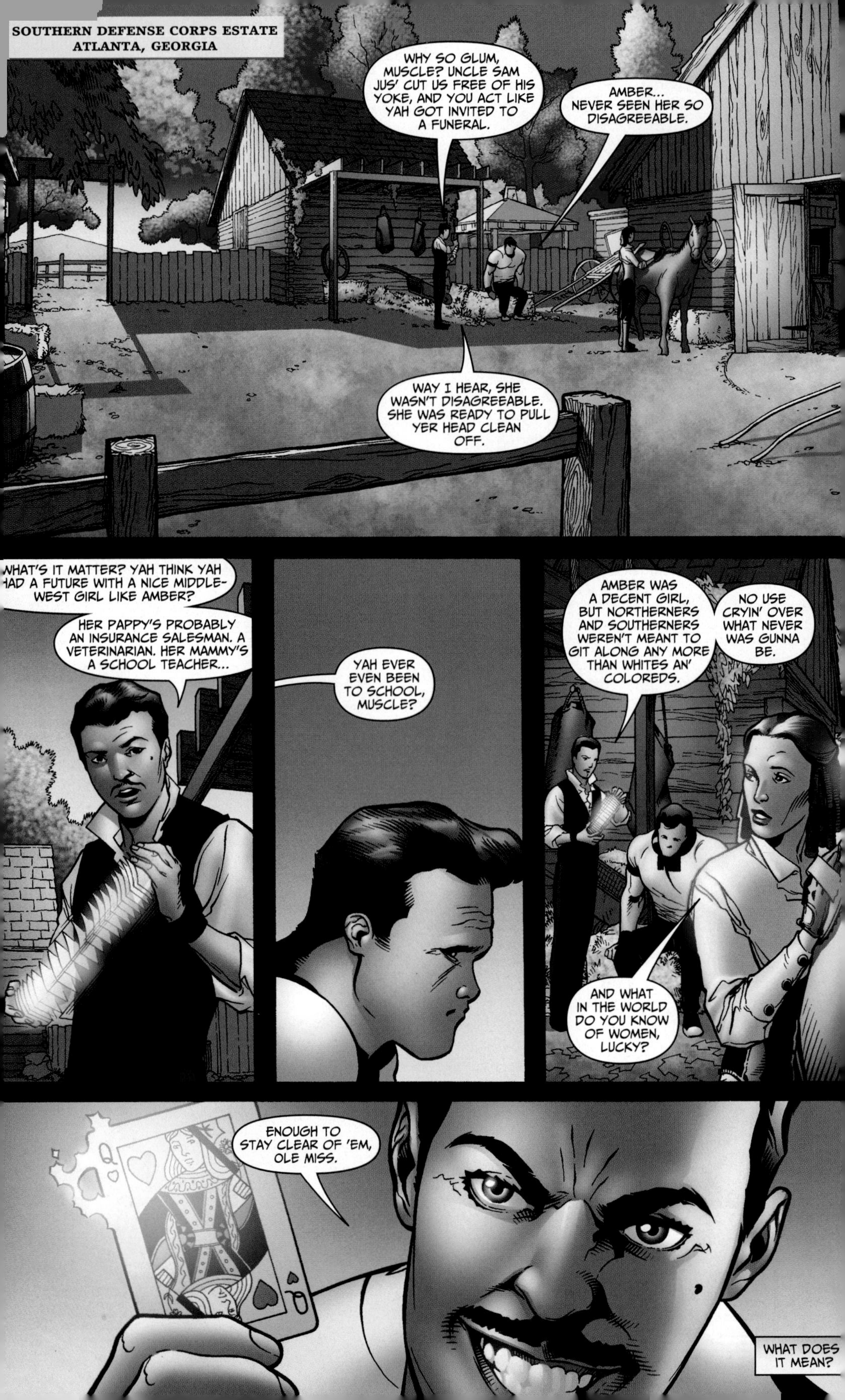
SOUTHERN DEFENSE CORPS ESTATE
ATLANTA, GEORGIA
WHY SO GLUM, MUSCLE? UNCLE SAM JUS' CUT US FREE OF HIS YOKE, AND YOU ACT LIKE YAH GOT INVITED TO A FUNERAL.
AMBER... NEVER SEEN HER SO DISAGREEABLE.
WAY I HEAR, SHE WASN'T DISAGREEABLE. SHE WAS READY TO PULL YER HEAD CLEAN OFF.
WHAT'S IT MATTER? YAH THINK YAH HAD A FUTURE WITH A NICE MIDDLE-WEST GIRL LIKE AMBER?
HER PAPPY'S PROBABLY AN INSURANCE SALESMAN. A VETERINARIAN. HER MAMMY'S A SCHOOL TEACHER...
YAH EVER EVEN BEEN TO SCHOOL, MUSCLE?
AMBER WAS A DECENT GIRL, BUT NORTHERNERS AND SOUTHERNERS WEREN'T MEANT TO GIT ALONG ANY MORE THAN WHITES AN' COLOREDS.
NO USE CRYIN' OVER WHAT NEVER WAS GUNNA BE.
AND WHAT IN THE WORLD DO YOU KNOW OF WOMEN, LUCKY?
ENOUGH TO STAY CLEAR OF 'EM, OLE MISS.
WHAT DOES IT MEAN?

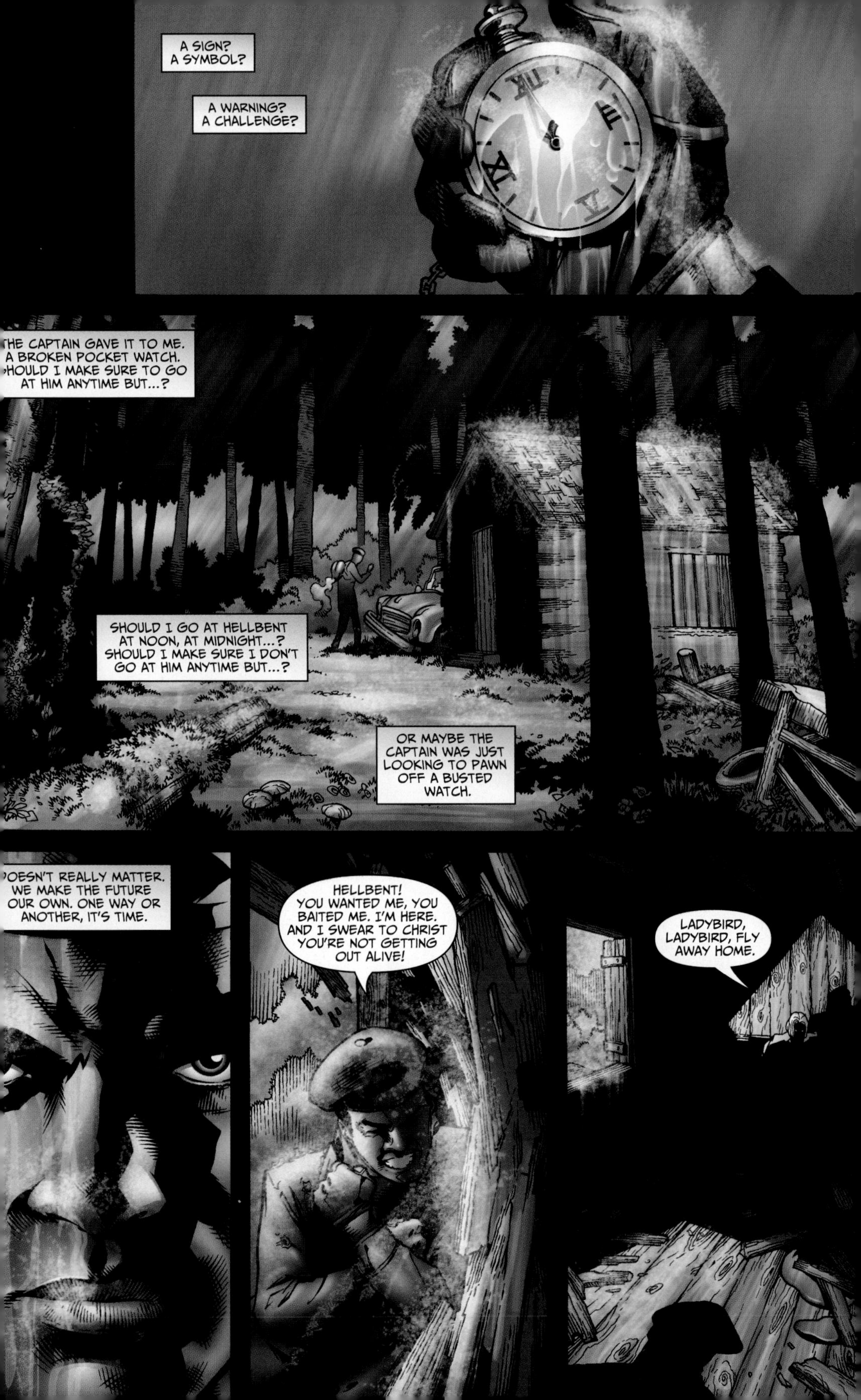
A SIGN?
A SYMBOL?
A WARNING?
A CHALLENGE?
THE CAPTAIN GAVE IT TO ME. A BROKEN POCKET WATCH. SHOULD I MAKE SURE TO GO AT HIM ANYTIME BUT...?
SHOULD I GO AT HELLBENT AT NOON, AT MIDNIGHT...? SHOULD I MAKE SURE I DON'T GO AT HIM ANYTIME BUT...?
OR MAYBE THE CAPTAIN WAS JUST LOOKING TO PAWN OFF A BUSTED WATCH.
DOESN'T REALLY MATTER. WE MAKE THE FUTURE OUR OWN. ONE WAY OR ANOTHER, IT'S TIME.
HELLBENT! YOU WANTED ME, YOU BAITED ME. I'M HERE. AND I SWEAR TO CHRIST YOU'RE NOT GETTING OUT ALIVE!
LADYBIRD, LADYBIRD, FLY AWAY HOME.

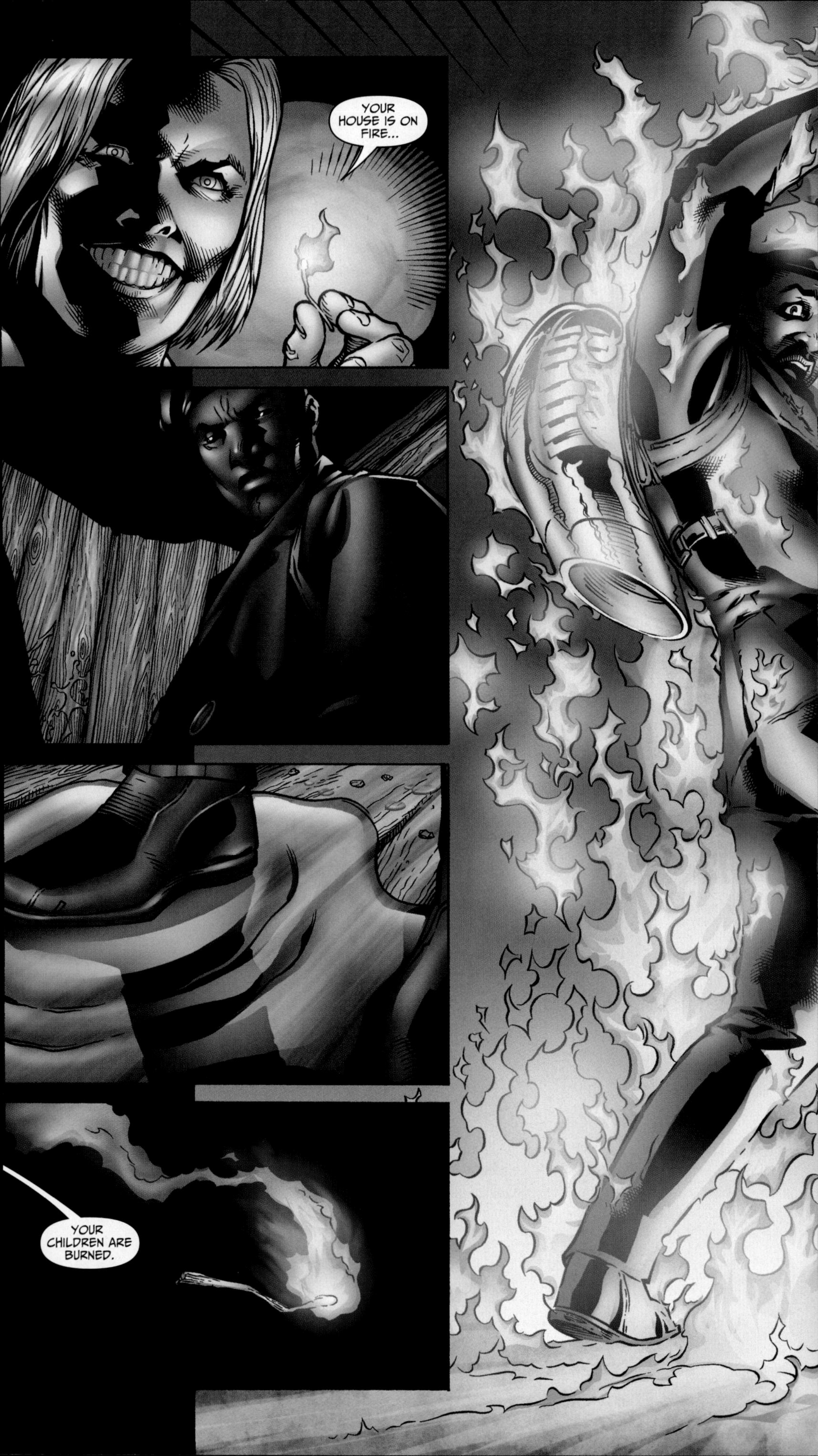
YOUR HOUSE IS ON FIRE...
YOUR CHILDREN ARE BURNED.

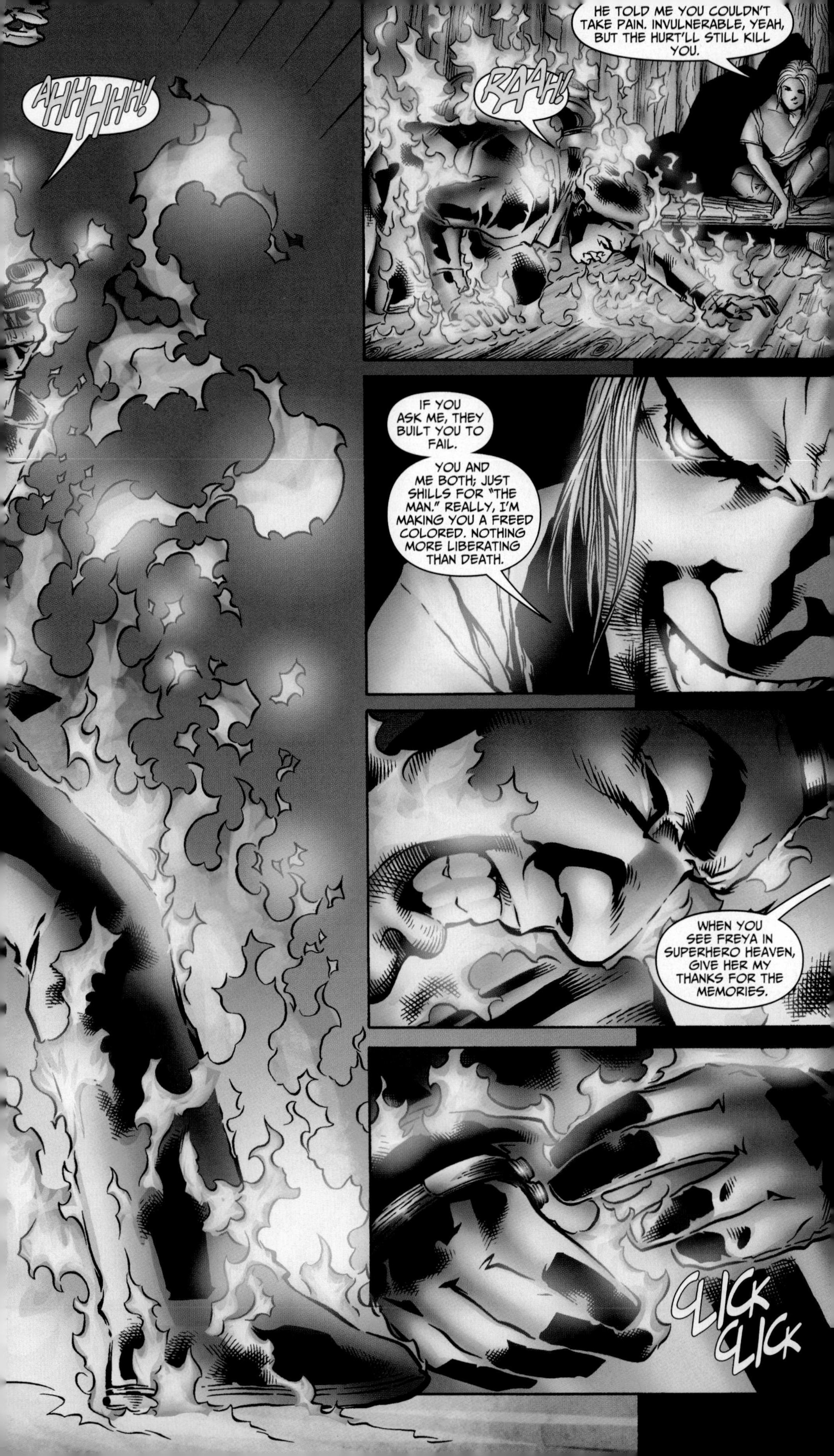
AHHHHH!
HE TOLD ME YOU COULDN'T TAKE PAIN. INVULNERABLE, YEAH, BUT THE HURT'LL STILL KILL YOU.
RAAH!
IF YOU ASK ME, THEY BUILT YOU TO FAIL.
YOU AND ME BOTH; JUST SHILLS FOR "THE MAN." REALLY, I'M MAKING YOU A FREED COLORED. NOTHING MORE LIBERATING THAN DEATH.
WHEN YOU SEE FREYA IN SUPERHERO HEAVEN, GIVE HER MY THANKS FOR THE MEMORIES.
CLICK
CLICK

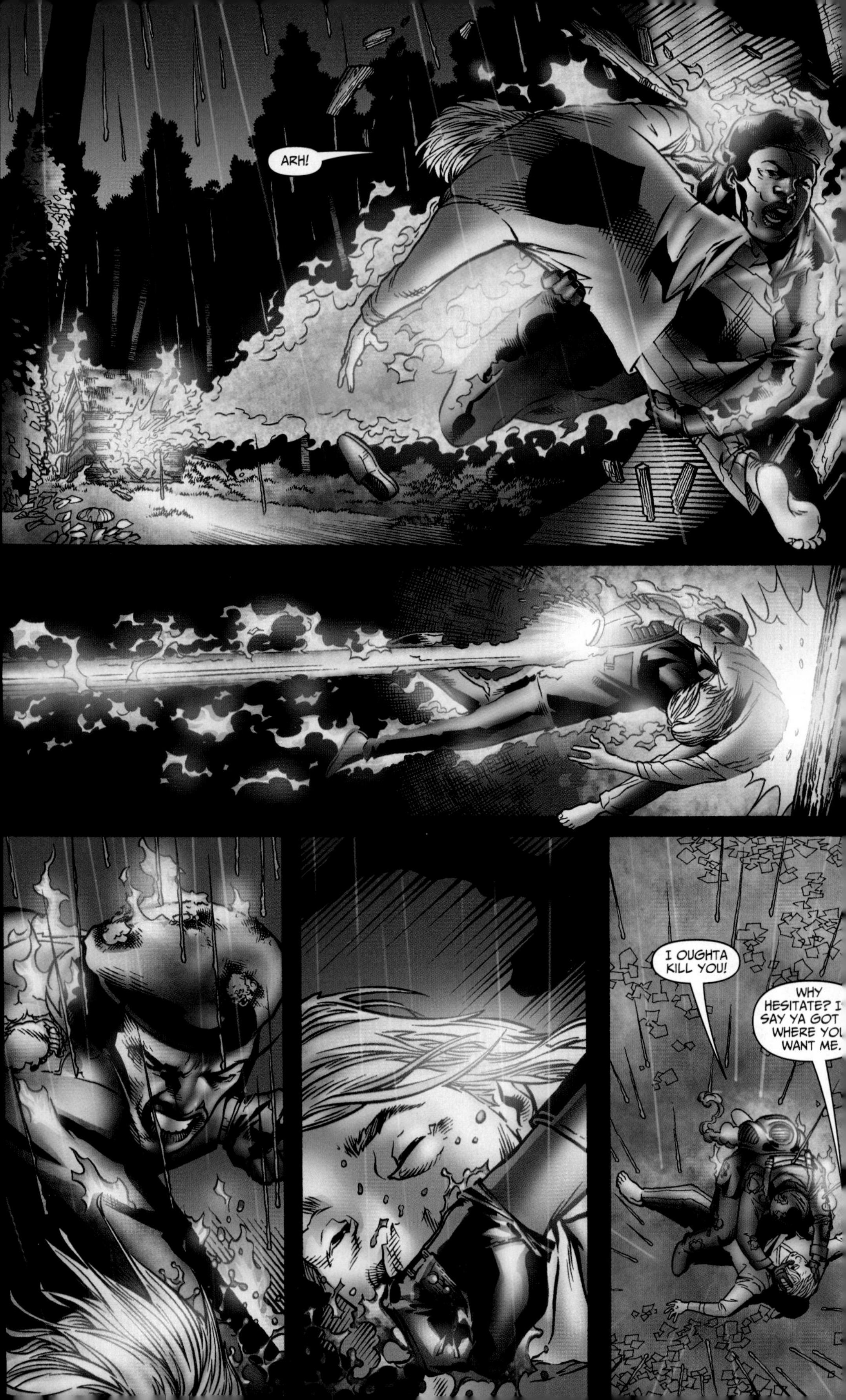
ARH!
I OUGHTA KILL YOU!
WHY HESITATE? I' SAY YA GOT WHERE YOU WANT ME.

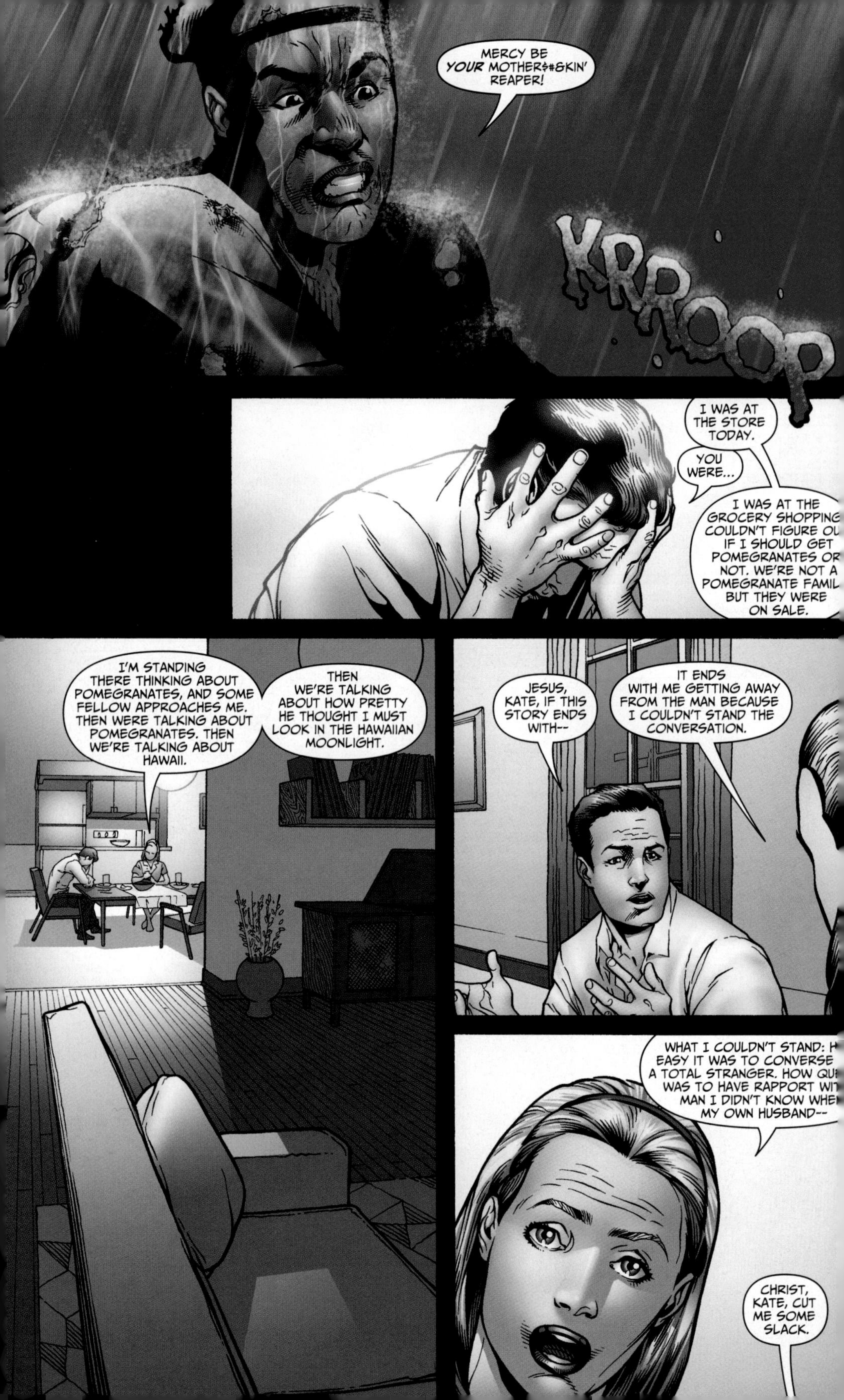
MERCY BE *YOUR* MOTHER$#&KIN' REAPER!
KRROOOP
I WAS AT THE STORE TODAY.
YOU WERE...
I WAS AT THE GROCERY SHOPPING COULDN'T FIGURE OU IF I SHOULD GET POMEGRANATES OR NOT. WE'RE NOT A POMEGRANATE FAMIL BUT THEY WERE ON SALE.
I'M STANDING THERE THINKING ABOUT POMEGRANATES, AND SOME FELLOW APPROACHES ME. THEN WERE TALKING ABOUT POMEGRANATES. THEN WE'RE TALKING ABOUT HAWAII.
THEN WE'RE TALKING ABOUT HOW PRETTY HE THOUGHT I MUST LOOK IN THE HAWAIIAN MOONLIGHT.
JESUS, KATE, IF THIS STORY ENDS WITH--
IT ENDS WITH ME GETTING AWAY FROM THE MAN BECAUSE I COULDN'T STAND THE CONVERSATION.
WHAT I COULDN'T STAND: H EASY IT WAS TO CONVERSE A TOTAL STRANGER. HOW QU WAS TO HAVE RAPPORT WIT MAN I DIDN'T KNOW WHE MY OWN HUSBAND--
CHRIST, KATE, CUT ME SOME SLACK.

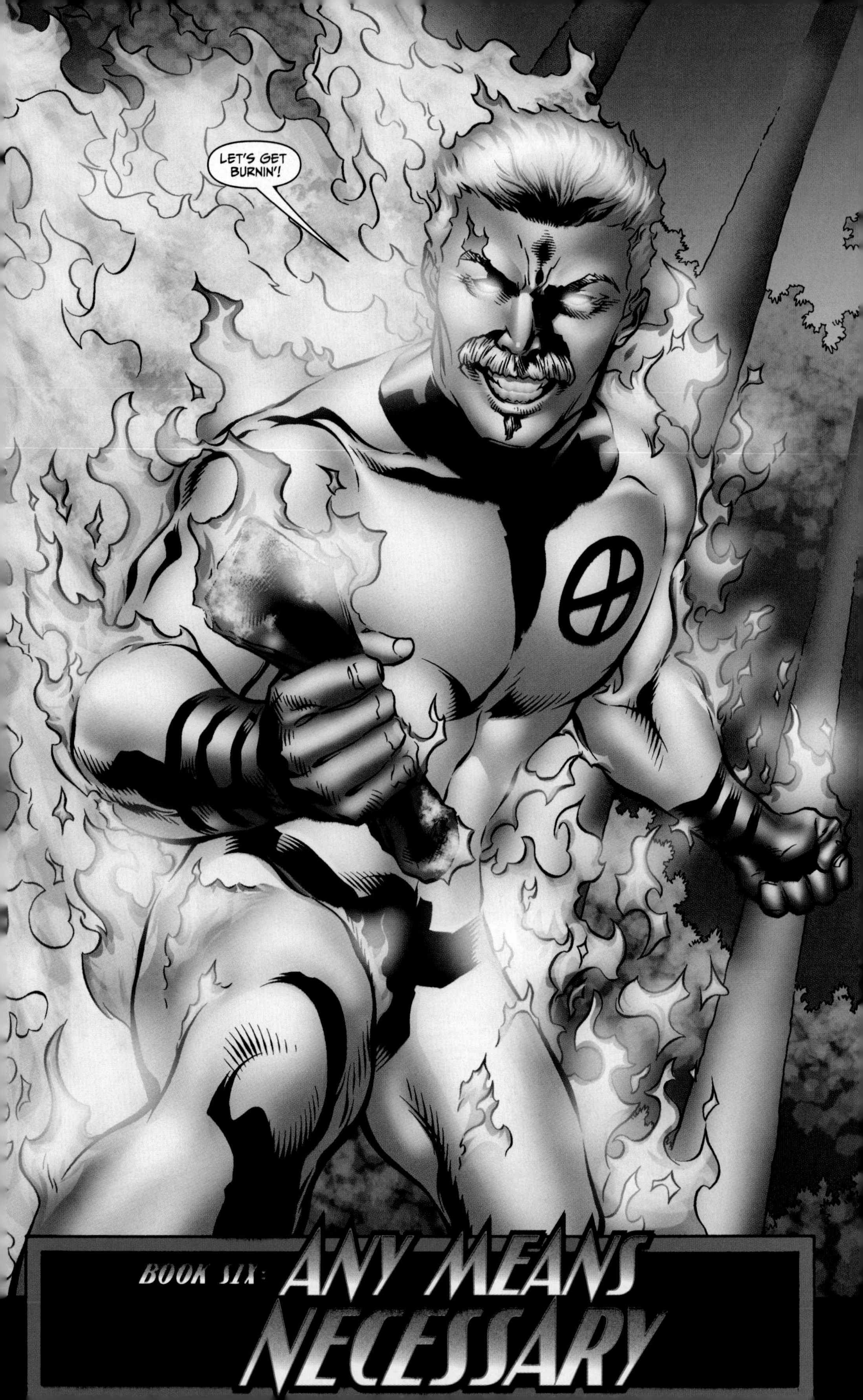
LET'S GET BURNIN'!
BOOK SIX: ANY MEANS NECESSARY

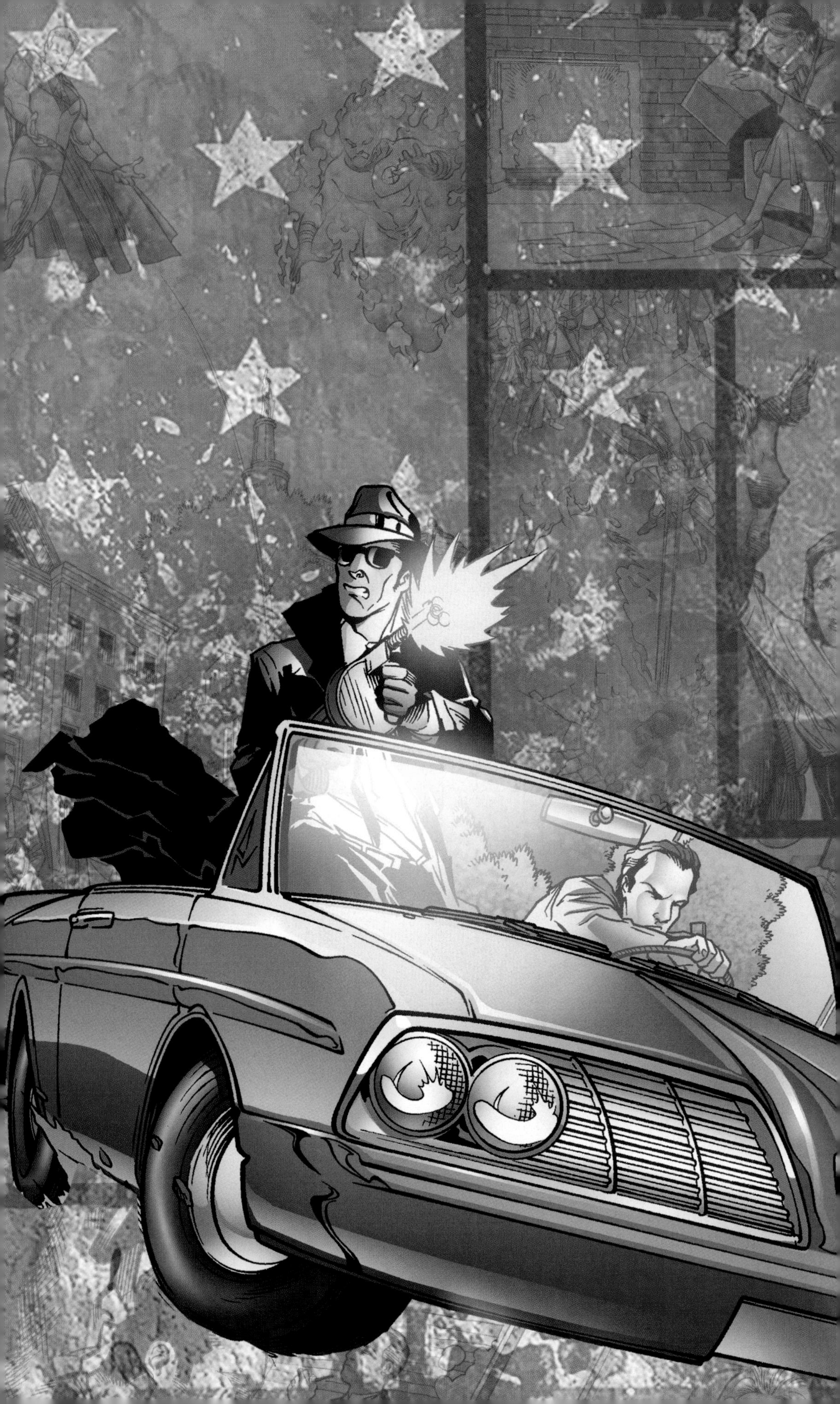

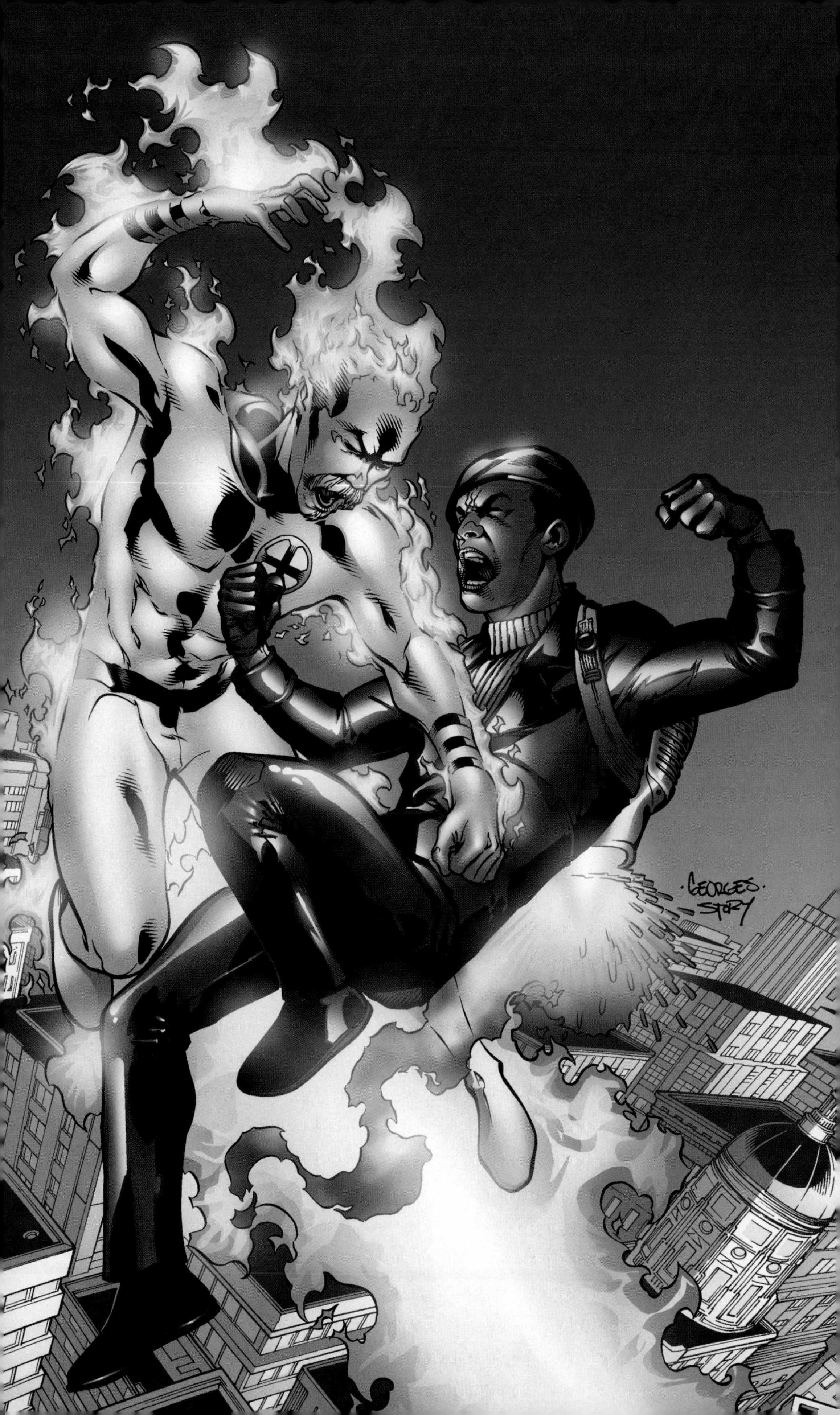
·GEORGES·
STORY

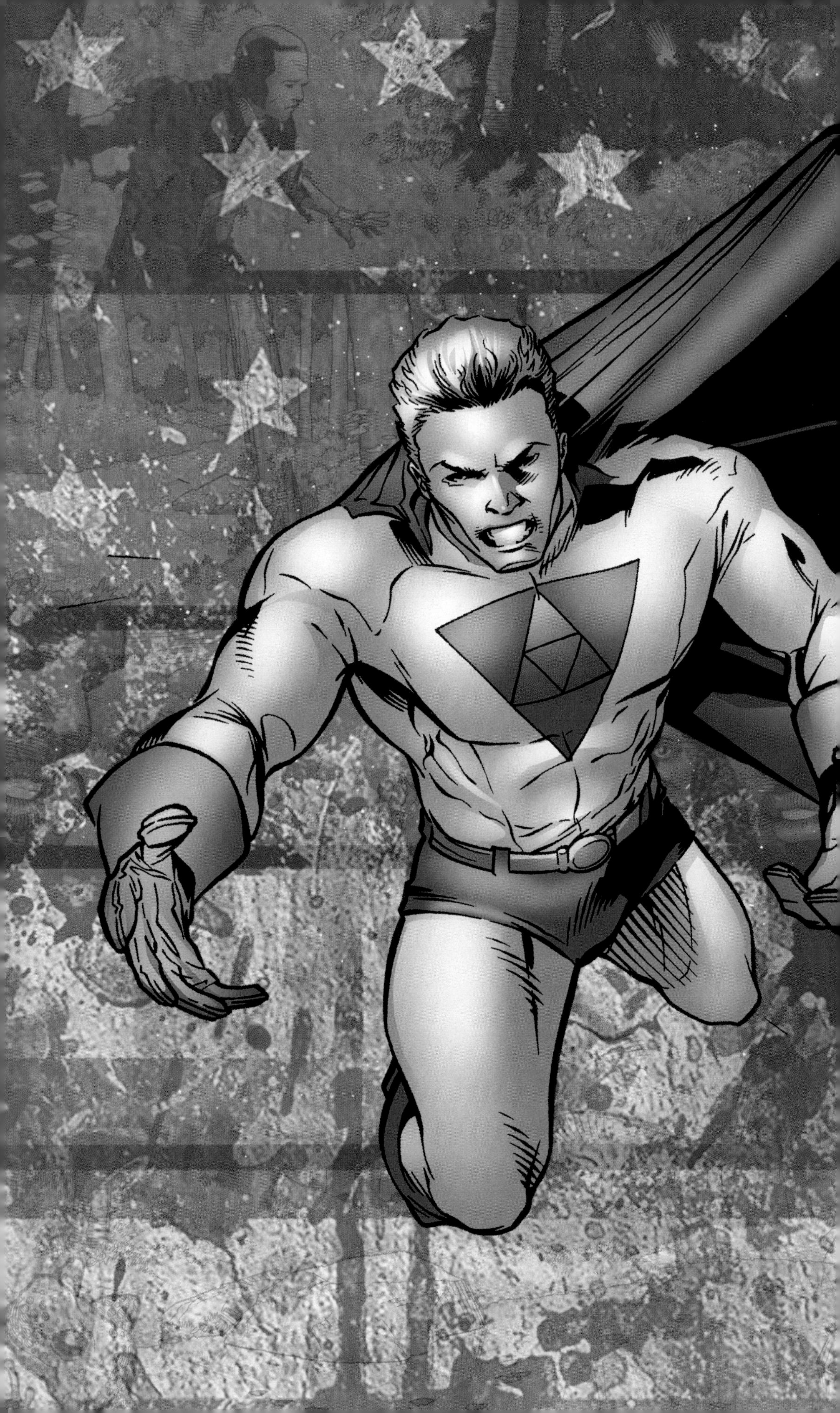

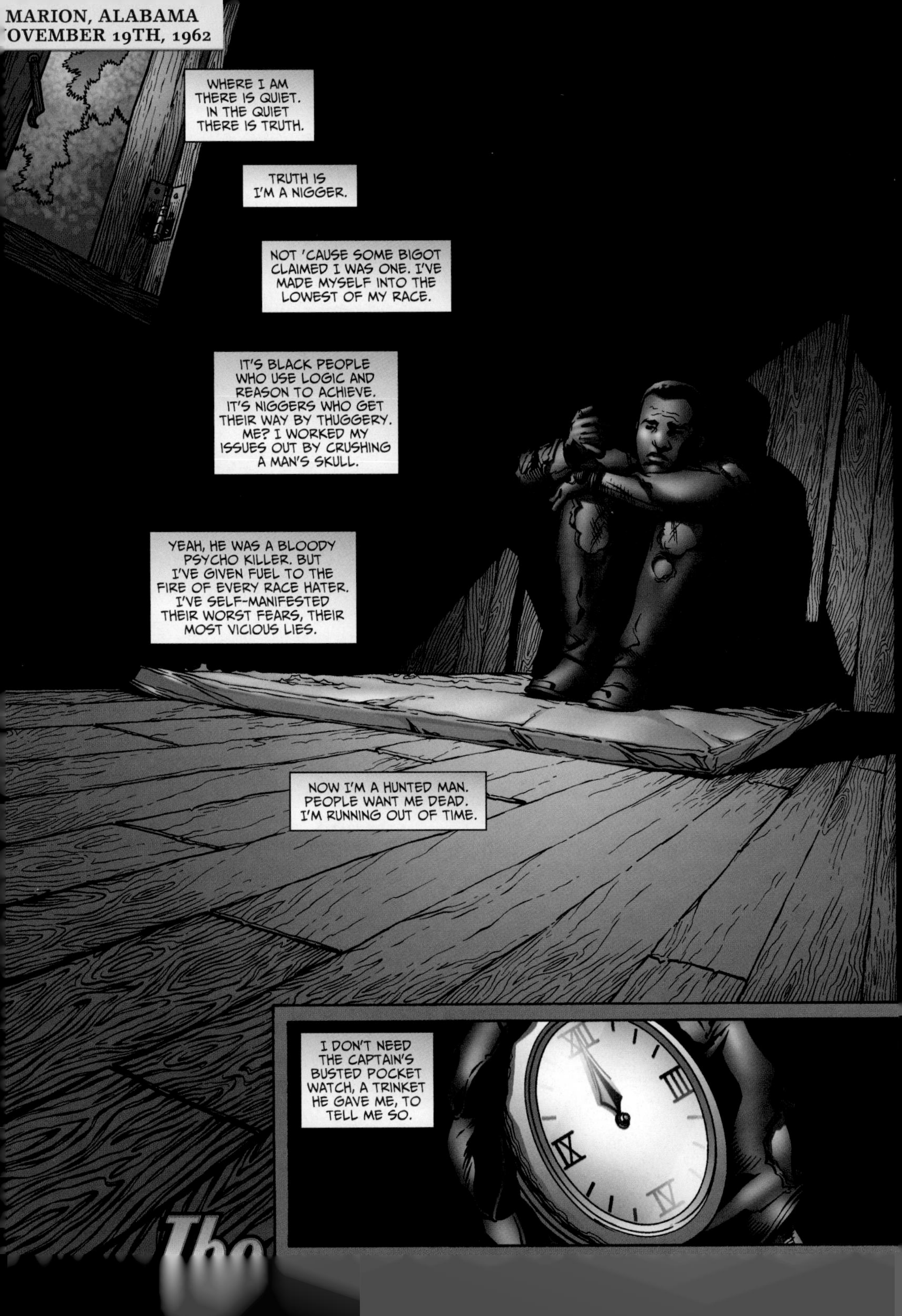
MARION, ALABAMA
'OVEMBER 19TH, 1962
WHERE I AM THERE IS QUIET. IN THE QUIET THERE IS TRUTH.
TRUTH IS I'M A NIGGER.
NOT 'CAUSE SOME BIGOT CLAIMED I WAS ONE. I'VE MADE MYSELF INTO THE LOWEST OF MY RACE.
IT'S BLACK PEOPLE WHO USE LOGIC AND REASON TO ACHIEVE. IT'S NIGGERS WHO GET THEIR WAY BY THUGGERY. ME? I WORKED MY ISSUES OUT BY CRUSHING A MAN'S SKULL.
YEAH, HE WAS A BLOODY PSYCHO KILLER. BUT I'VE GIVEN FUEL TO THE FIRE OF EVERY RACE HATER. I'VE SELF-MANIFESTED THEIR WORST FEARS, THEIR MOST VICIOUS LIES.
NOW I'M A HUNTED MAN. PEOPLE WANT ME DEAD. I'M RUNNING OUT OF TIME.
I DON'T NEED THE CAPTAIN'S BUSTED POCKET WATCH, A TRINKET HE GAVE ME, TO TELL ME SO.

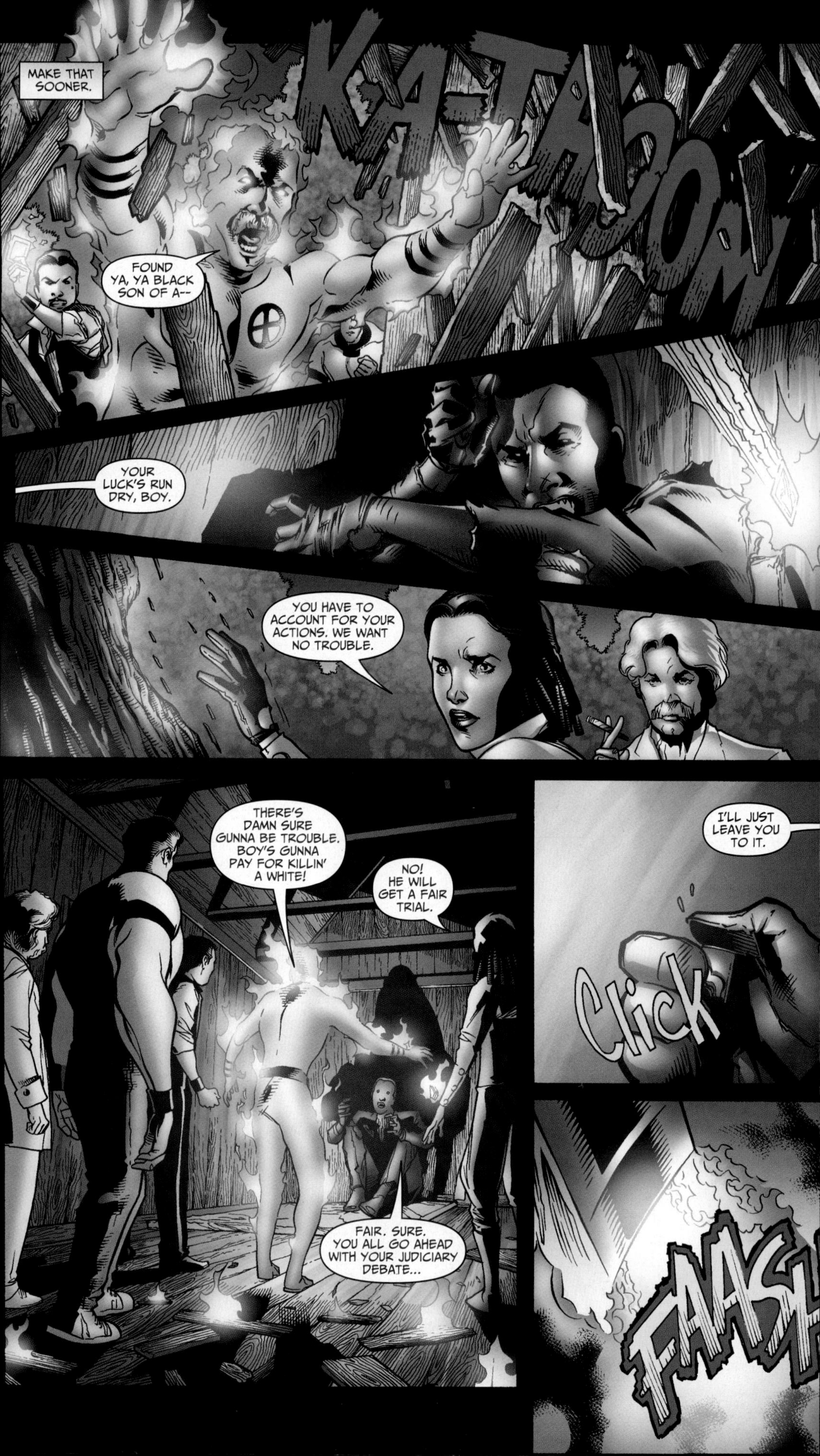
MAKE THAT SOONER.
KA-TA-BOOM
FOUND YA, YA BLACK SON OF A--
YOUR LUCK'S RUN DRY, BOY.
YOU HAVE TO ACCOUNT FOR YOUR ACTIONS. WE WANT NO TROUBLE.
THERE'S DAMN SURE GUNNA BE TROUBLE. BOY'S GUNNA PAY FOR KILLIN' A WHITE!
NO! HE WILL GET A FAIR TRIAL.
FAIR. SURE. YOU ALL GO AHEAD WITH YOUR JUDICIARY DEBATE...
I'LL JUST LEAVE YOU TO IT.
CLICK
FAASH

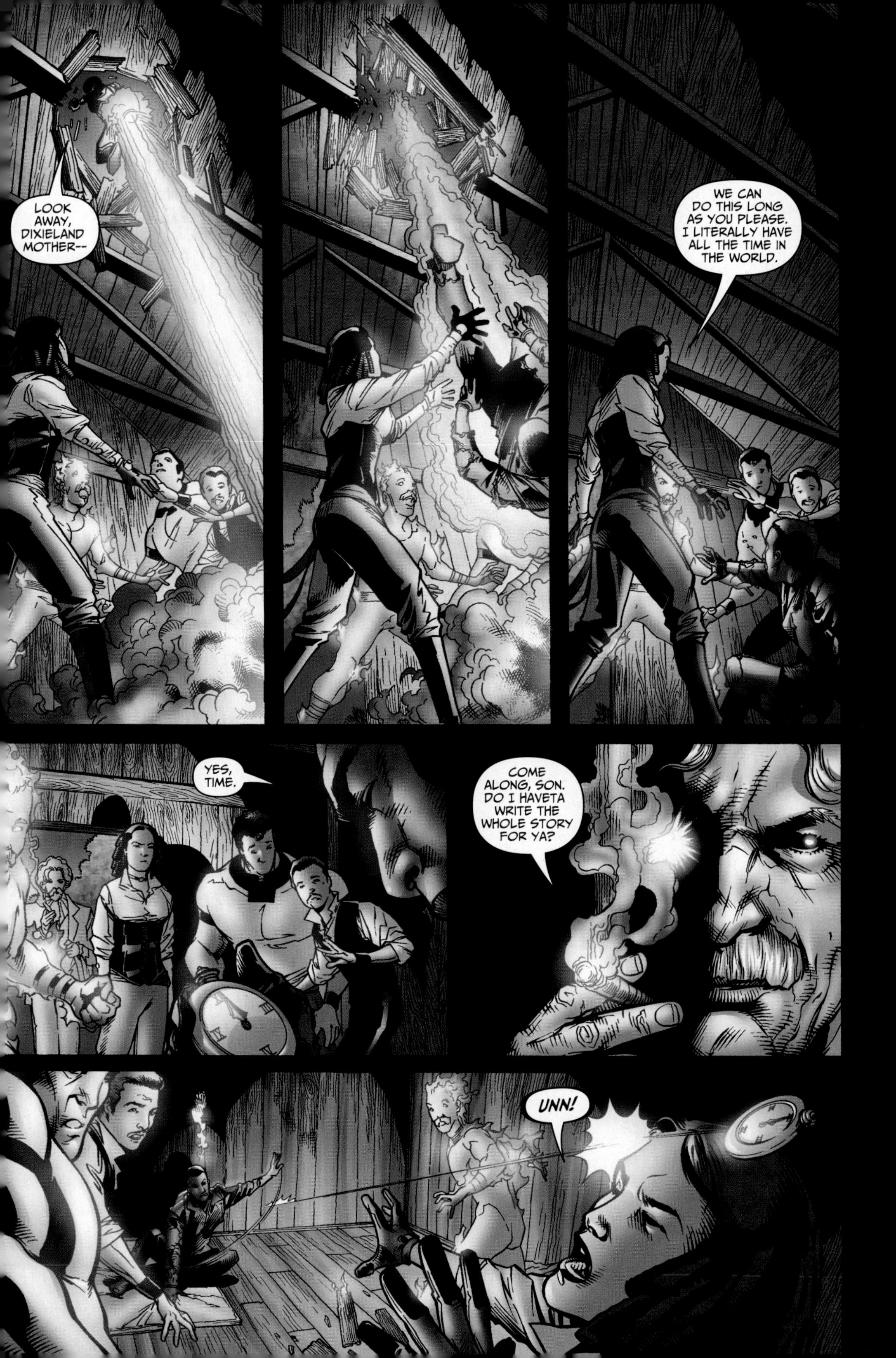
LOOK AWAY, DIXIELAND MOTHER--
WE CAN DO THIS LONG AS YOU PLEASE. I LITERALLY HAVE ALL THE TIME IN THE WORLD.
YES, TIME.
COME ALONG, SON. DO I HAVETA WRITE THE WHOLE STORY FOR YA?
UNN!

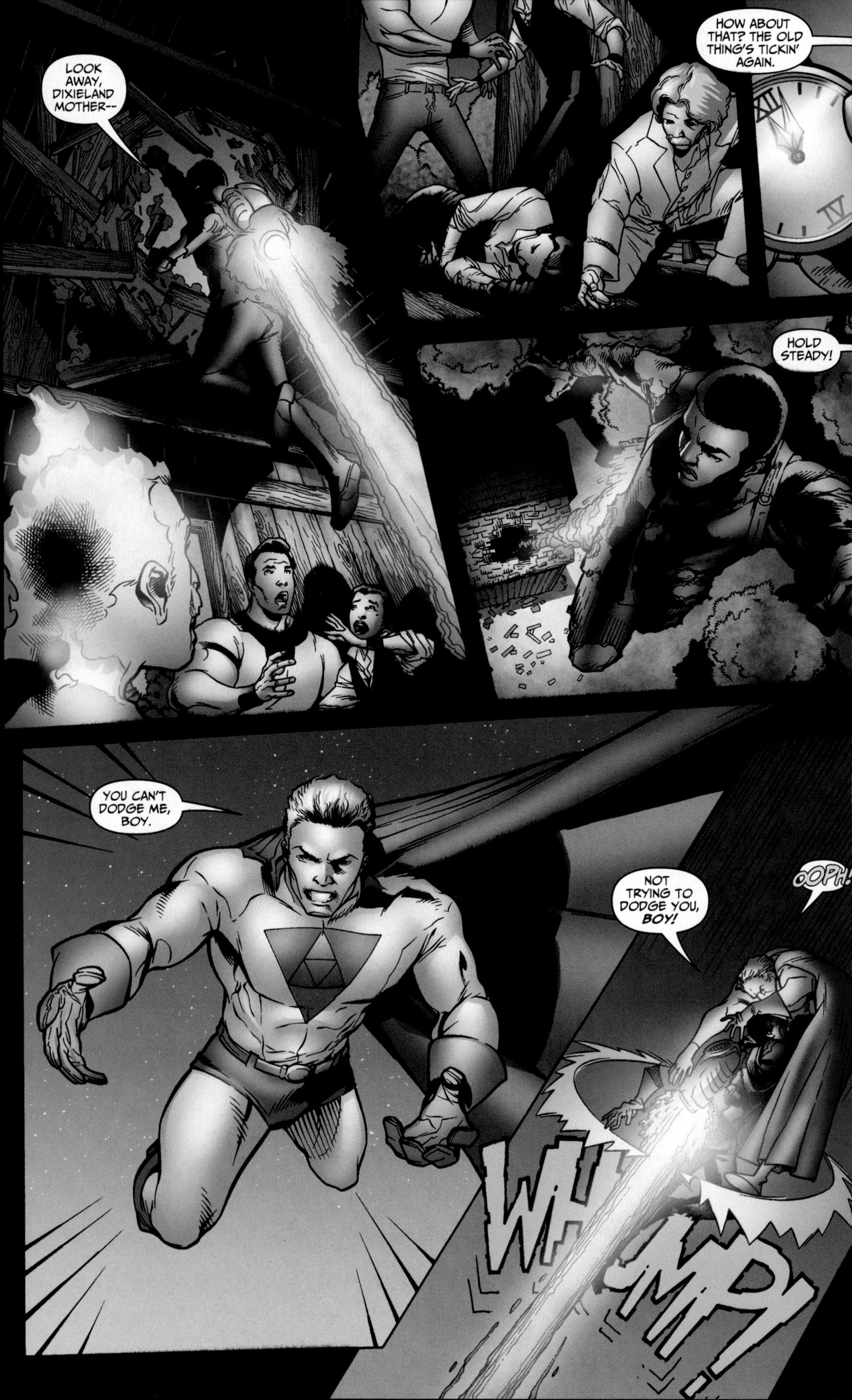

LOOK AWAY, DIXIELAND MOTHER--
HOW ABOUT THAT? THE OLD THING'S TICKIN' AGAIN.
HOLD STEADY!
YOU CAN'T DODGE ME, BOY.
NOT TRYING TO DODGE YOU, BOY!
OOPH!
WHUMP!

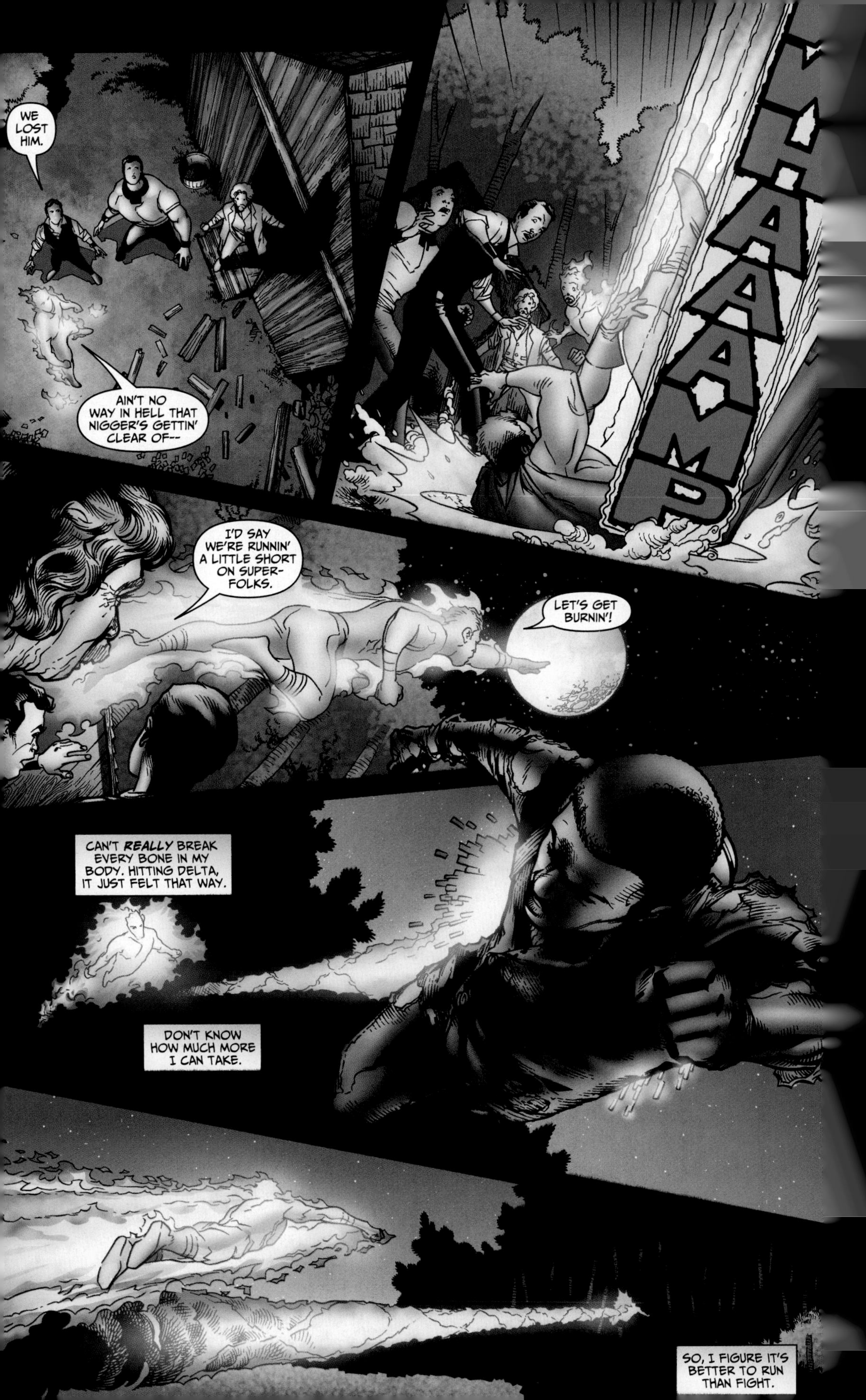
WE LOST HIM.
AIN'T NO WAY IN HELL THAT NIGGER'S GETTIN' CLEAR OF--
HAAAAMP
I'D SAY WE'RE RUNNIN' A LITTLE SHORT ON SUPER-FOLKS.
LET'S GET BURNIN'!
CAN'T *REALLY* BREAK EVERY BONE IN MY BODY. HITTING DELTA, IT JUST FELT THAT WAY.
DON'T KNOW HOW MUCH MORE I CAN TAKE.
SO, I FIGURE IT'S BETTER TO RUN THAN FIGHT.

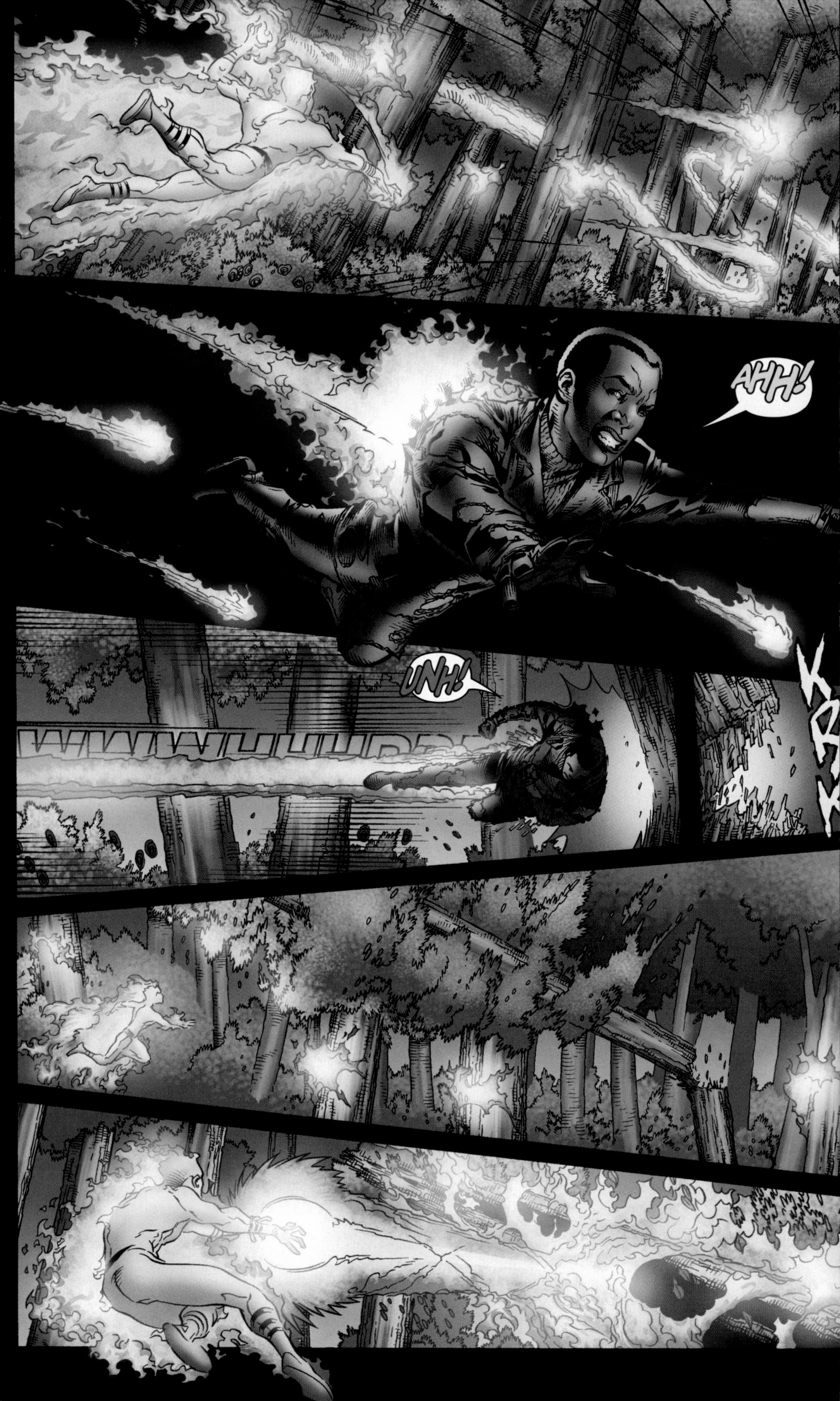
AHH!
UNH!

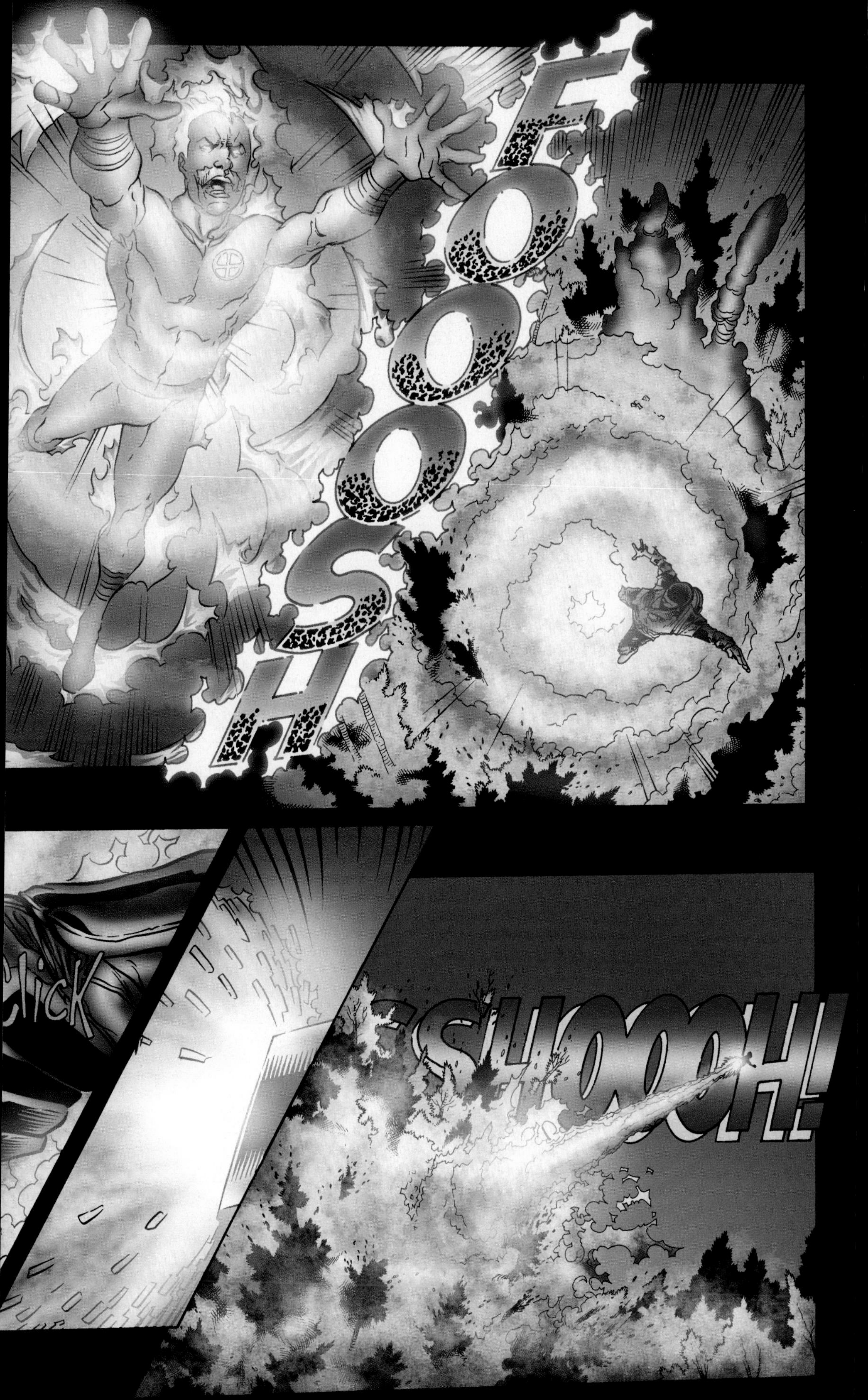
FOOOSH
CLICK
SHOOOH!

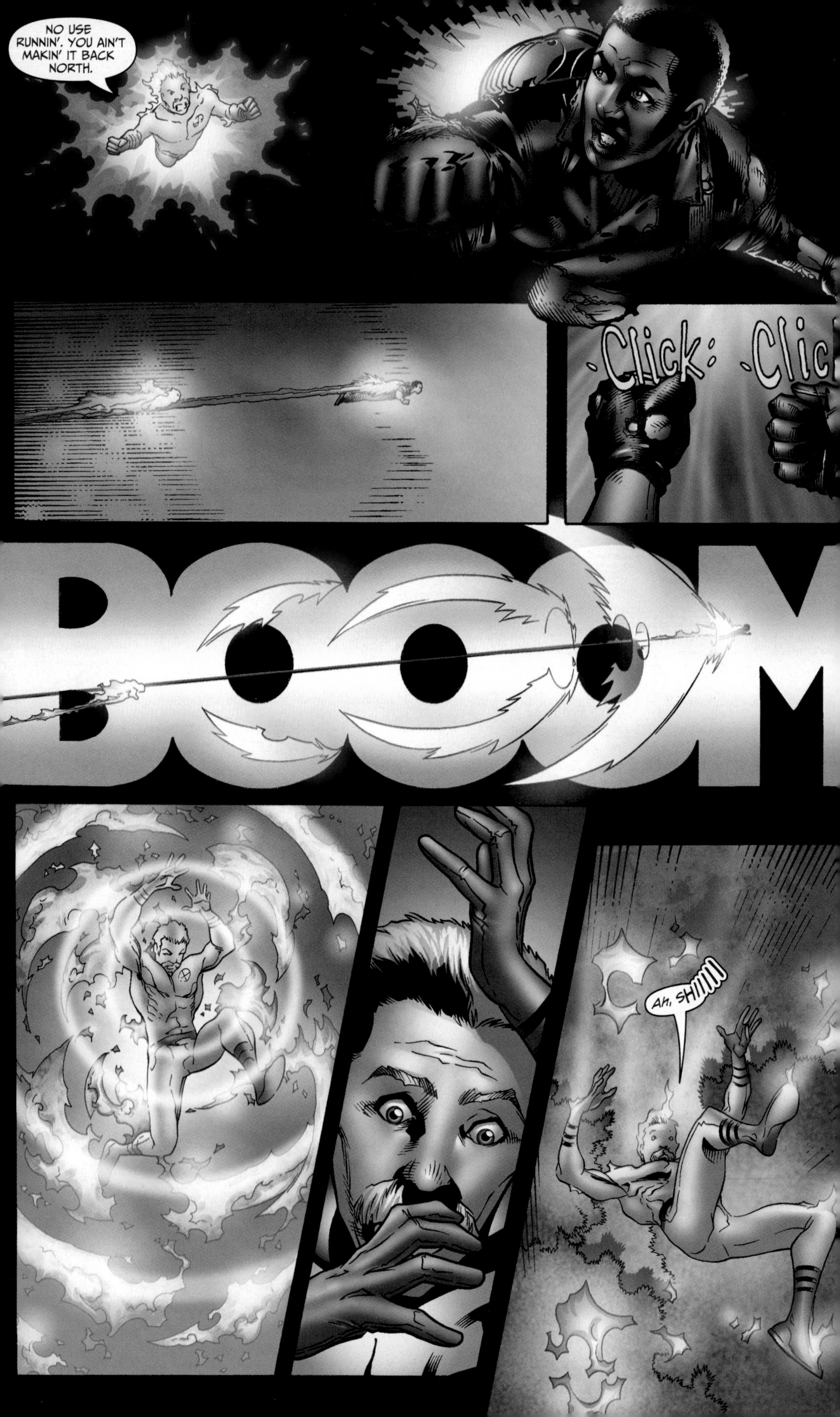
NO USE RUNNIN'. YOU AIN'T MAKIN' IT BACK NORTH.
Click: Click
BOOOM
Ah, SHIIIII

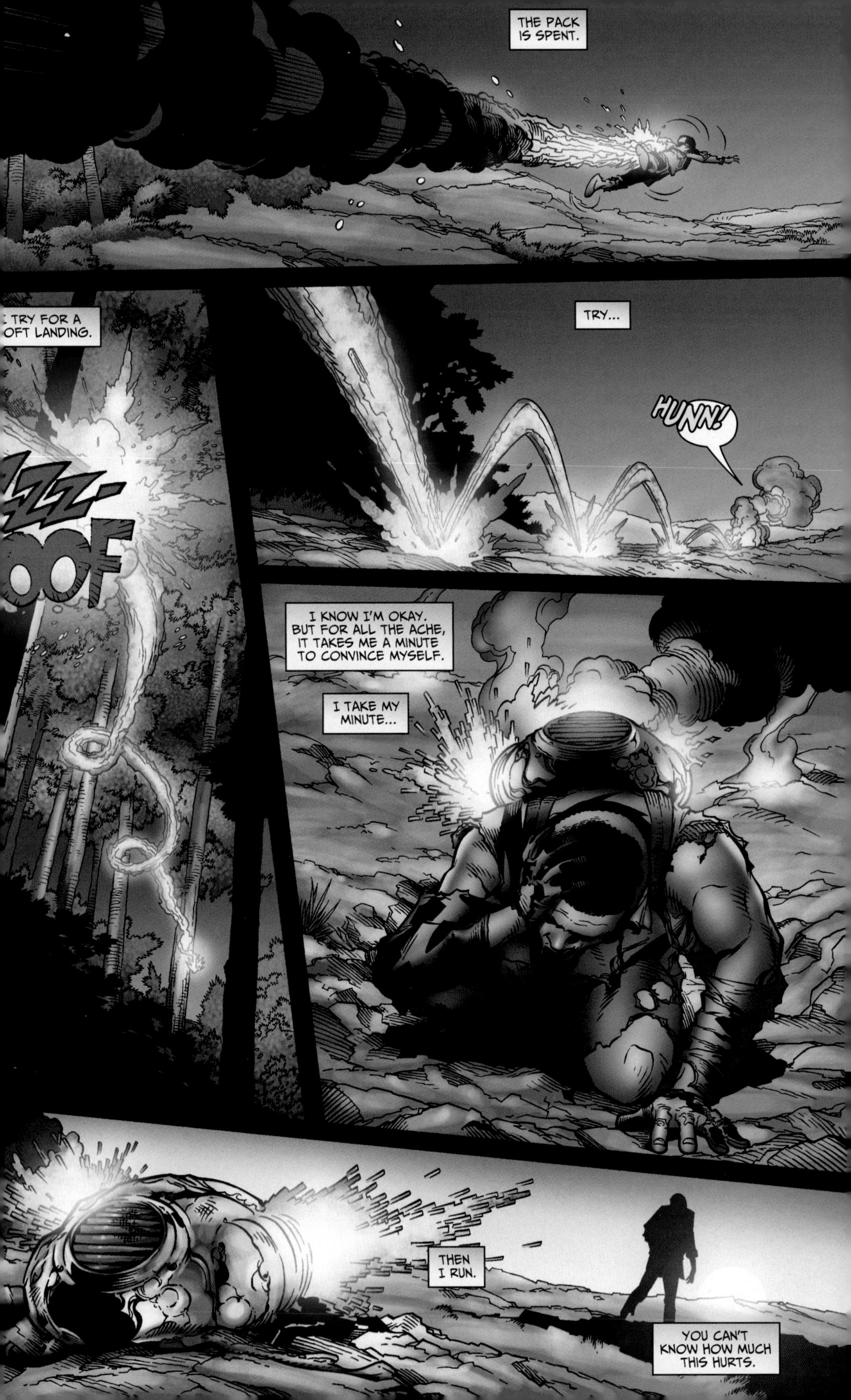
THE PACK IS SPENT.
TRY FOR A
OFT LANDING.
TRY...
HUNN!
I KNOW I'M OKAY. BUT FOR ALL THE ACHE, IT TAKES ME A MINUTE TO CONVINCE MYSELF.
I TAKE MY MINUTE...
THEN I RUN.
YOU CAN'T KNOW HOW MUCH THIS HURTS.

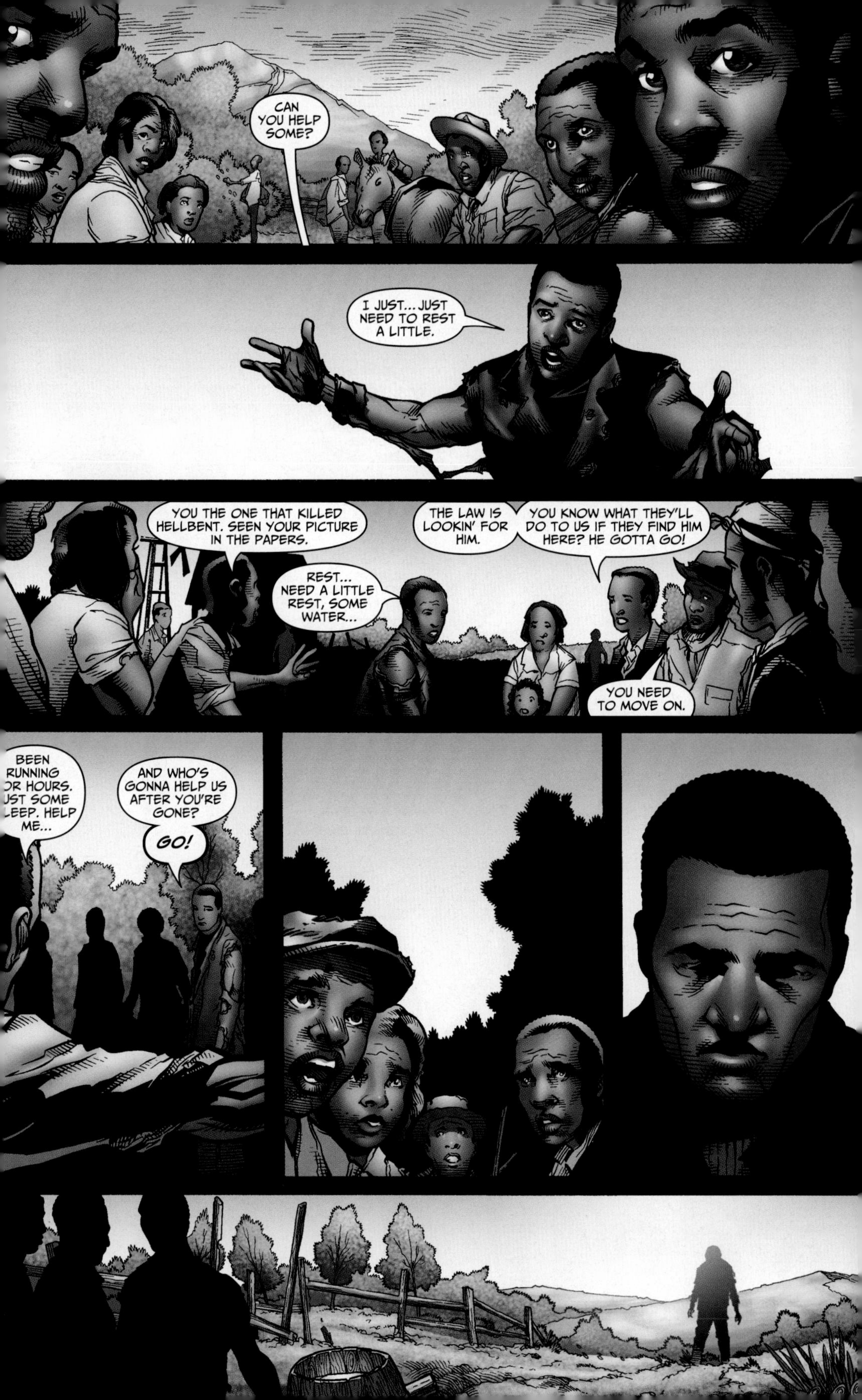
CAN YOU HELP SOME?
I JUST... JUST NEED TO REST A LITTLE.
YOU THE ONE THAT KILLED HELLBENT. SEEN YOUR PICTURE IN THE PAPERS.
REST... NEED A LITTLE REST, SOME WATER...
THE LAW IS LOOKIN' FOR HIM.
YOU KNOW WHAT THEY'LL DO TO US IF THEY FIND HIM HERE? HE GOTTA GO!
YOU NEED TO MOVE ON.
BEEN RUNNING OR HOURS. UST SOME LEEP. HELP ME...
AND WHO'S GONNA HELP US AFTER YOU'RE GONE?
GO!

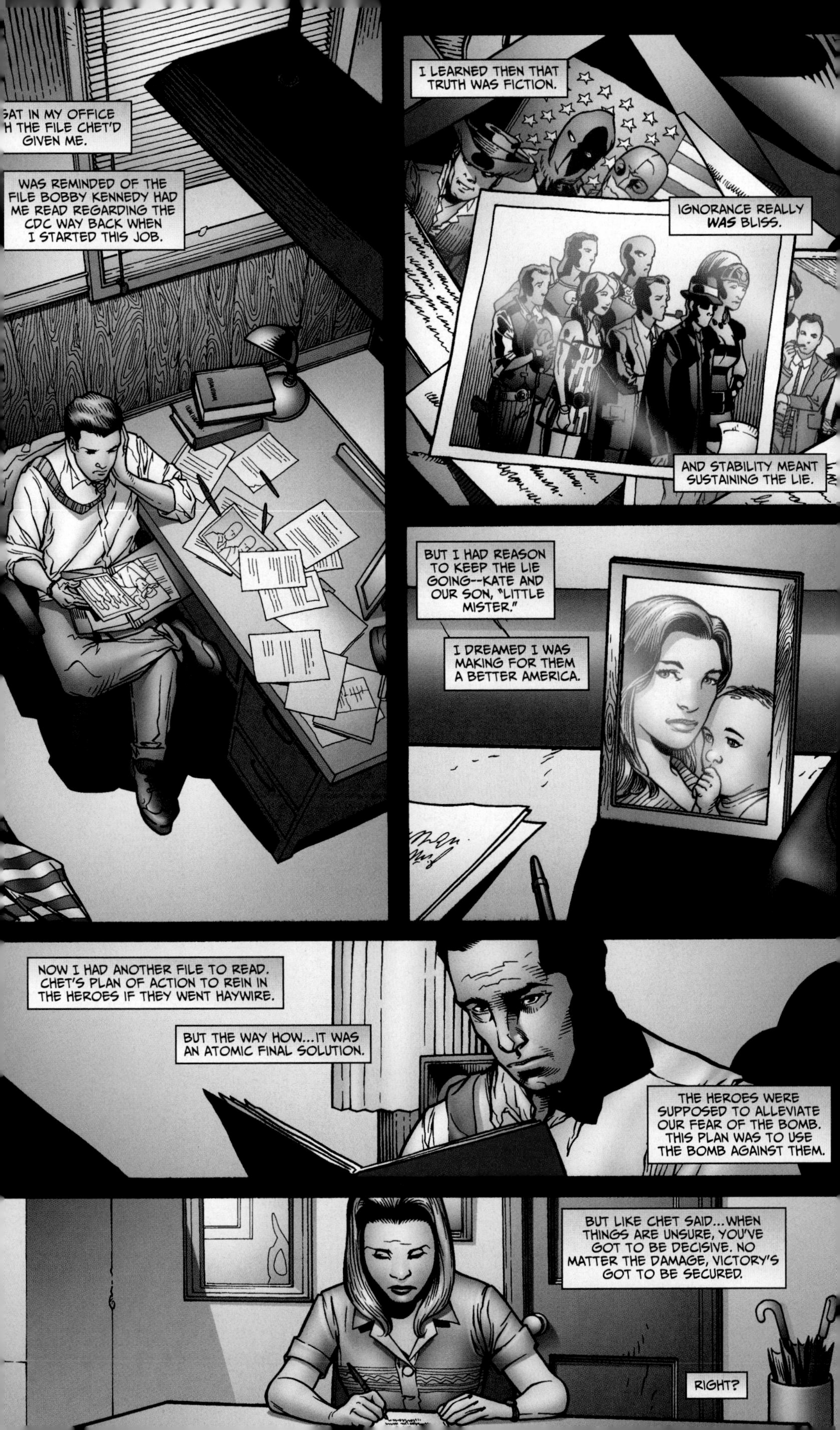

SAT IN MY OFFICE
H THE FILE CHET'D GIVEN ME.
WAS REMINDED OF THE FILE BOBBY KENNEDY HAD ME READ REGARDING THE CDC WAY BACK WHEN I STARTED THIS JOB.
I LEARNED THEN THAT TRUTH WAS FICTION.
IGNORANCE REALLY WAS BLISS.
AND STABILITY MEANT SUSTAINING THE LIE.
BUT I HAD REASON TO KEEP THE LIE GOING--KATE AND OUR SON, "LITTLE MISTER."
I DREAMED I WAS MAKING FOR THEM A BETTER AMERICA.
NOW I HAD ANOTHER FILE TO READ. CHET'S PLAN OF ACTION TO REIN IN THE HEROES IF THEY WENT HAYWIRE.
BUT THE WAY HOW...IT WAS AN ATOMIC FINAL SOLUTION.
THE HEROES WERE SUPPOSED TO ALLEVIATE OUR FEAR OF THE BOMB. THIS PLAN WAS TO USE THE BOMB AGAINST THEM.
BUT LIKE CHET SAID...WHEN THINGS ARE UNSURE, YOU'VE GOT TO BE DECISIVE. NO MATTER THE DAMAGE, VICTORY'S GOT TO BE SECURED.
RIGHT?

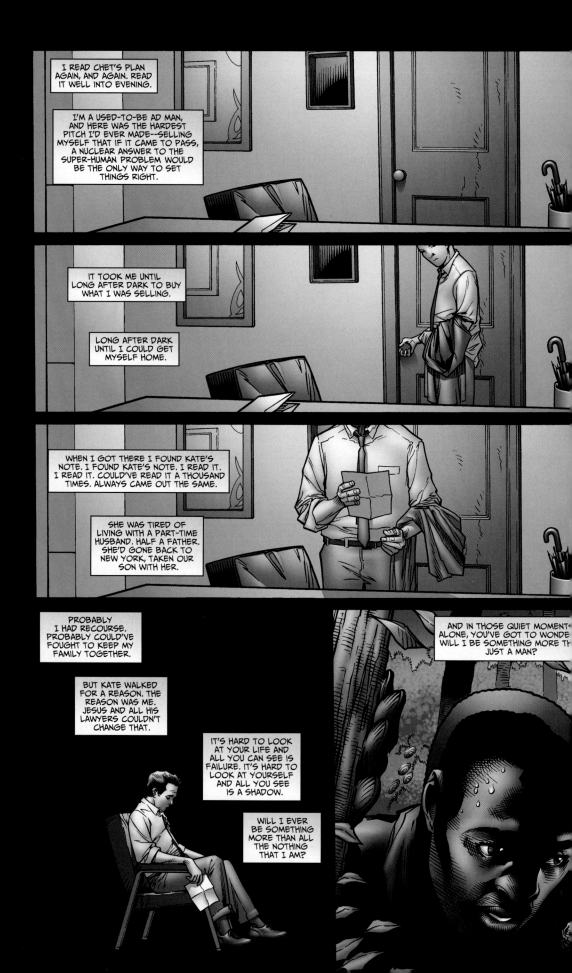

I READ CHET'S PLAN AGAIN, AND AGAIN. READ IT WELL INTO EVENING.

I'M A USED-TO-BE AD MAN, AND HERE WAS THE HARDEST PITCH I'D EVER MADE--SELLING MYSELF THAT IF IT CAME TO PASS, A NUCLEAR ANSWER TO THE SUPER-HUMAN PROBLEM WOULD BE THE ONLY WAY TO SET THINGS RIGHT.

IT TOOK ME UNTIL LONG AFTER DARK TO BUY WHAT I WAS SELLING.

LONG AFTER DARK UNTIL I COULD GET MYSELF HOME.

WHEN I GOT THERE I FOUND KATE'S NOTE. I FOUND KATE'S NOTE. I READ IT. I READ IT. COULD'VE READ IT A THOUSAND TIMES. ALWAYS CAME OUT THE SAME.

SHE WAS TIRED OF LIVING WITH A PART-TIME HUSBAND. HALF A FATHER. SHE'D GONE BACK TO NEW YORK, TAKEN OUR SON WITH HER.

PROBABLY I HAD RECOURSE. PROBABLY COULD'VE FOUGHT TO KEEP MY FAMILY TOGETHER.

BUT KATE WALKED FOR A REASON. THE REASON WAS ME. JESUS AND ALL HIS LAWYERS COULDN'T CHANGE THAT.

IT'S HARD TO LOOK AT YOUR LIFE AND ALL YOU CAN SEE IS FAILURE. IT'S HARD TO LOOK AT YOURSELF AND ALL YOU SEE IS A SHADOW.

WILL I EVER BE SOMETHING MORE THAN ALL THE NOTHING THAT I AM?

AND IN THOSE QUIET MOMENTS ALONE, YOU'VE GOT TO WONDER WILL I BE SOMETHING MORE THAN JUST A MAN?

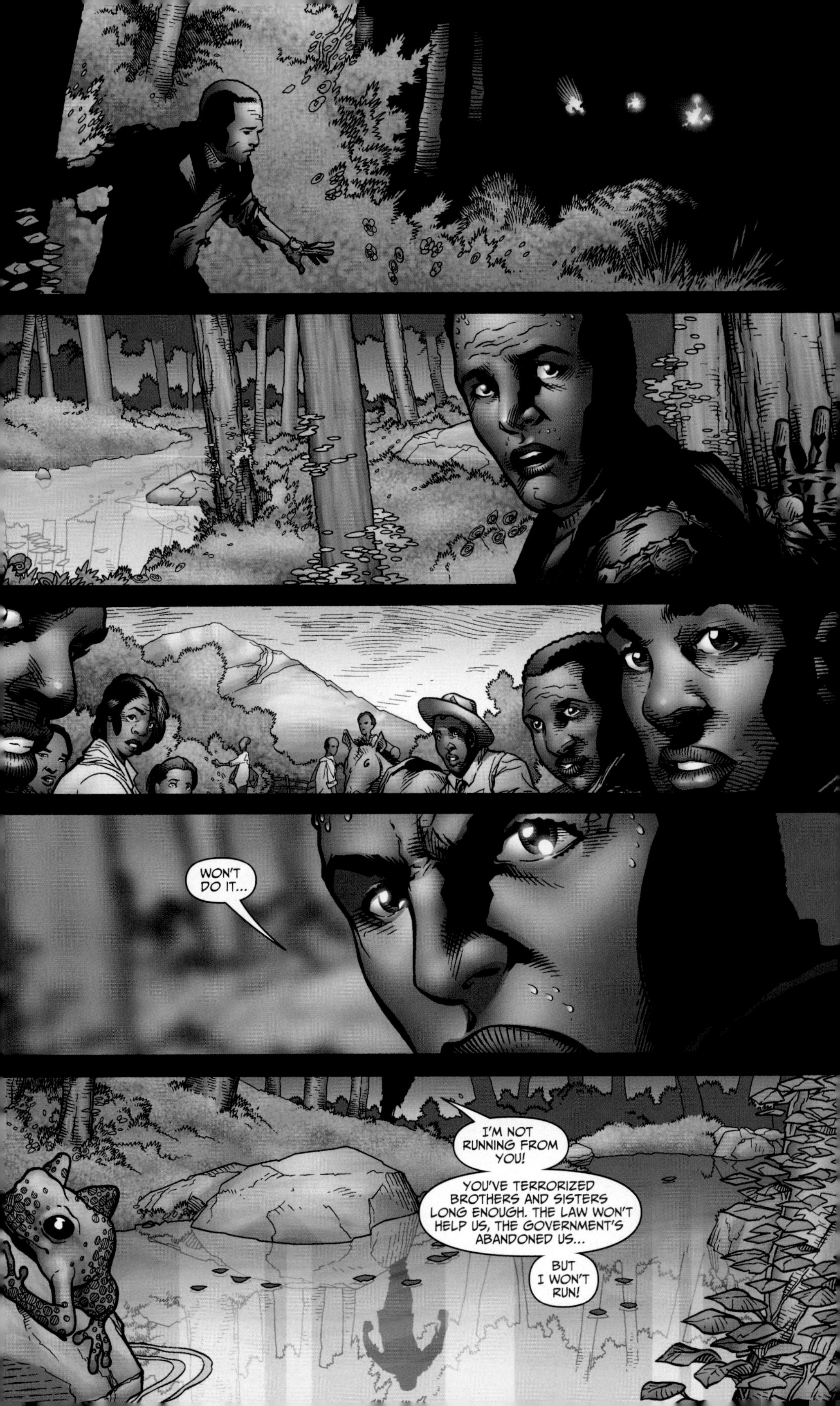
WON'T DO IT...
I'M NOT RUNNING FROM YOU!
YOU'VE TERRORIZED BROTHERS AND SISTERS LONG ENOUGH. THE LAW WON'T HELP US, THE GOVERNMENT'S ABANDONED US...
BUT I WON'T RUN!

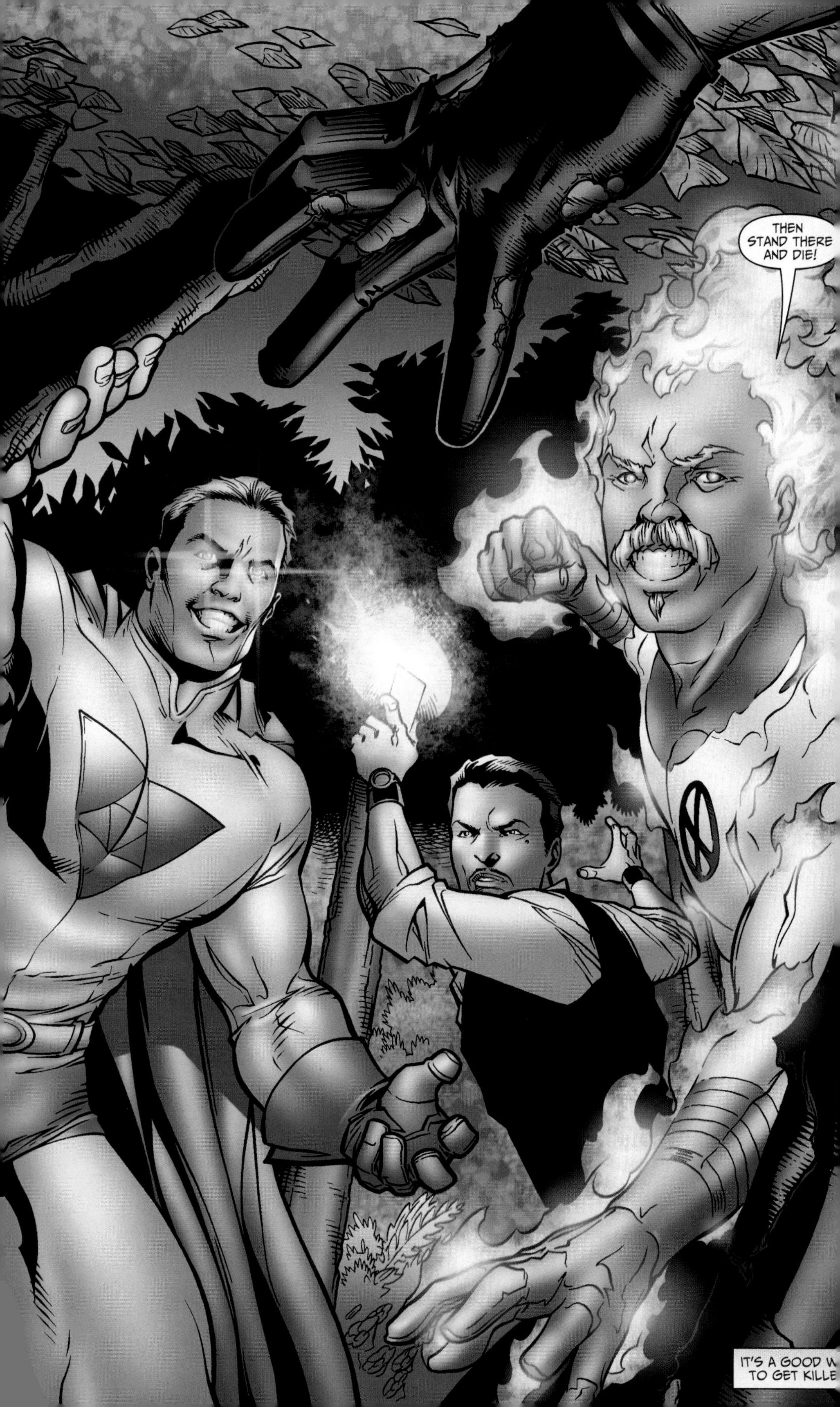
THEN STAND THERE AND DIE!
IT'S A GOOD W
TO GET KILLE

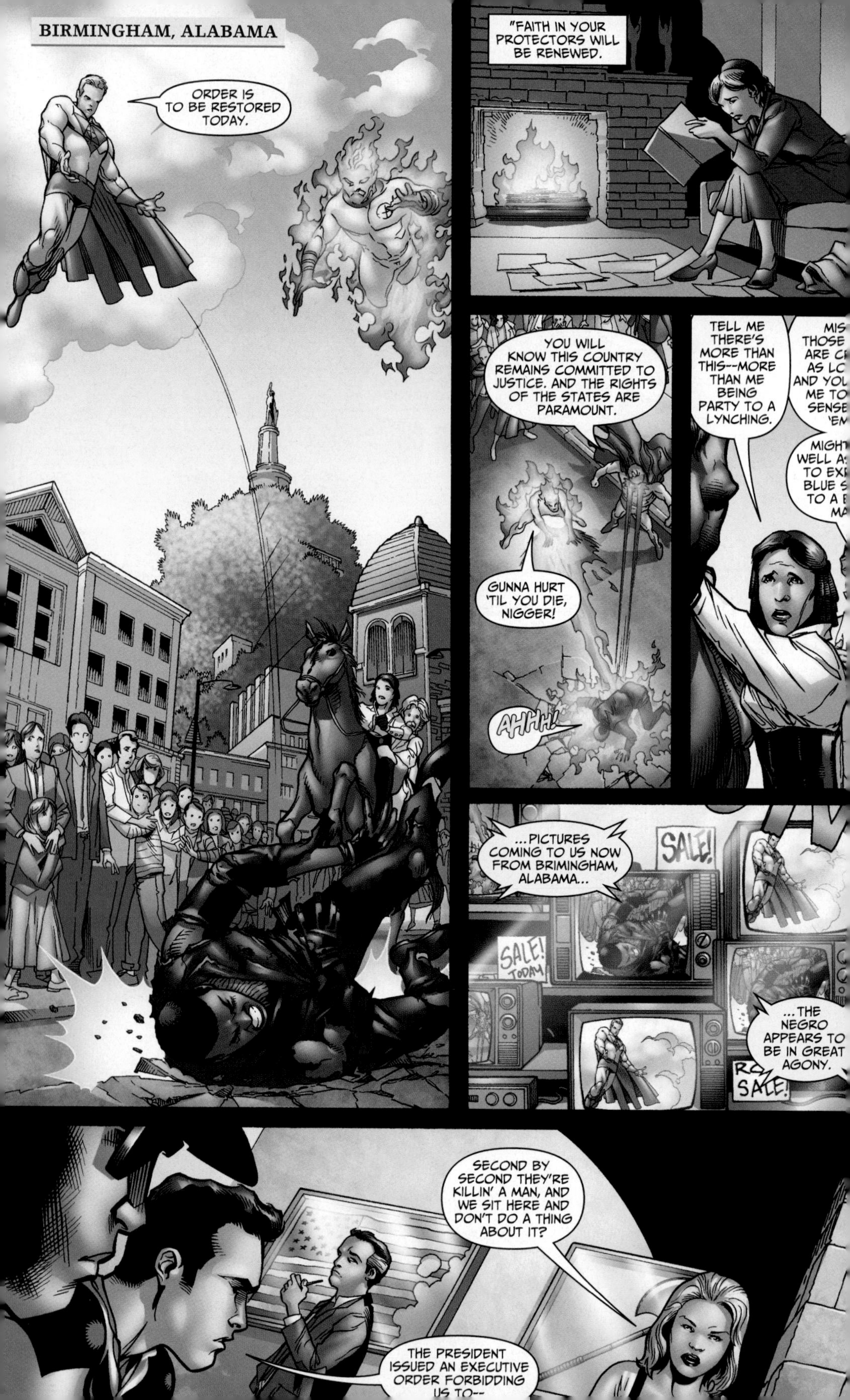
BIRMINGHAM, ALABAMA
ORDER IS TO BE RESTORED TODAY.
"FAITH IN YOUR PROTECTORS WILL BE RENEWED.
YOU WILL KNOW THIS COUNTRY REMAINS COMMITTED TO JUSTICE. AND THE RIGHTS OF THE STATES ARE PARAMOUNT.
GUNNA HURT 'TIL YOU DIE, NIGGER!
AHHH!
TELL ME THERE'S MORE THAN THIS--MORE THAN ME BEING PARTY TO A LYNCHING.
...PICTURES COMING TO US NOW FROM BRIMINGHAM, ALABAMA...
SALE!
SALE! TODAY
...THE NEGRO APPEARS TO BE IN GREAT AGONY.
SALE!
SECOND BY SECOND THEY'RE KILLIN' A MAN, AND WE SIT HERE AND DON'T DO A THING ABOUT IT?
THE PRESIDENT ISSUED AN EXECUTIVE ORDER FORBIDDING US TO--

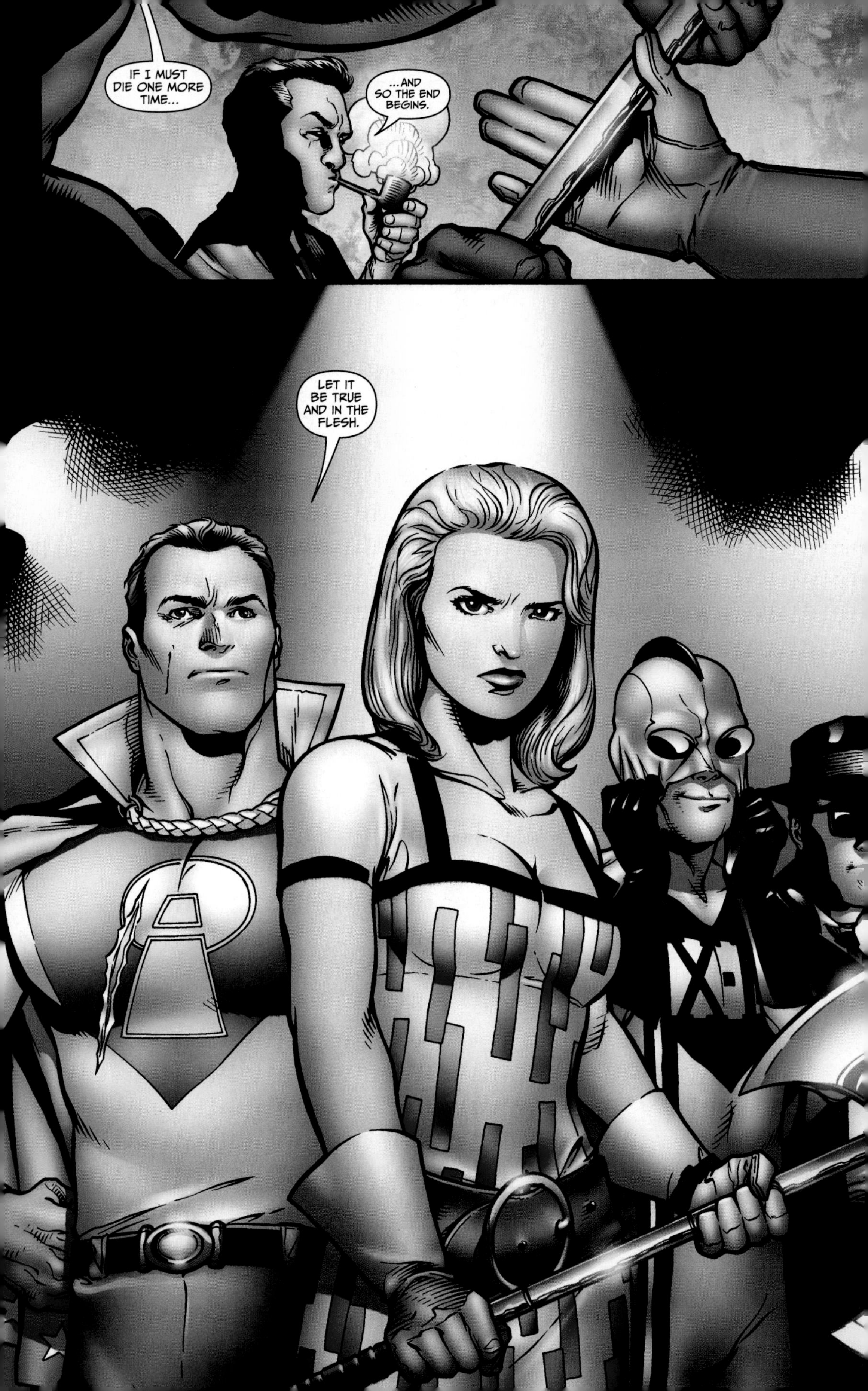
IF I MUST DIE ONE MORE TIME...
...AND SO THE END BEGINS.
LET IT BE TRUE AND IN THE FLESH.

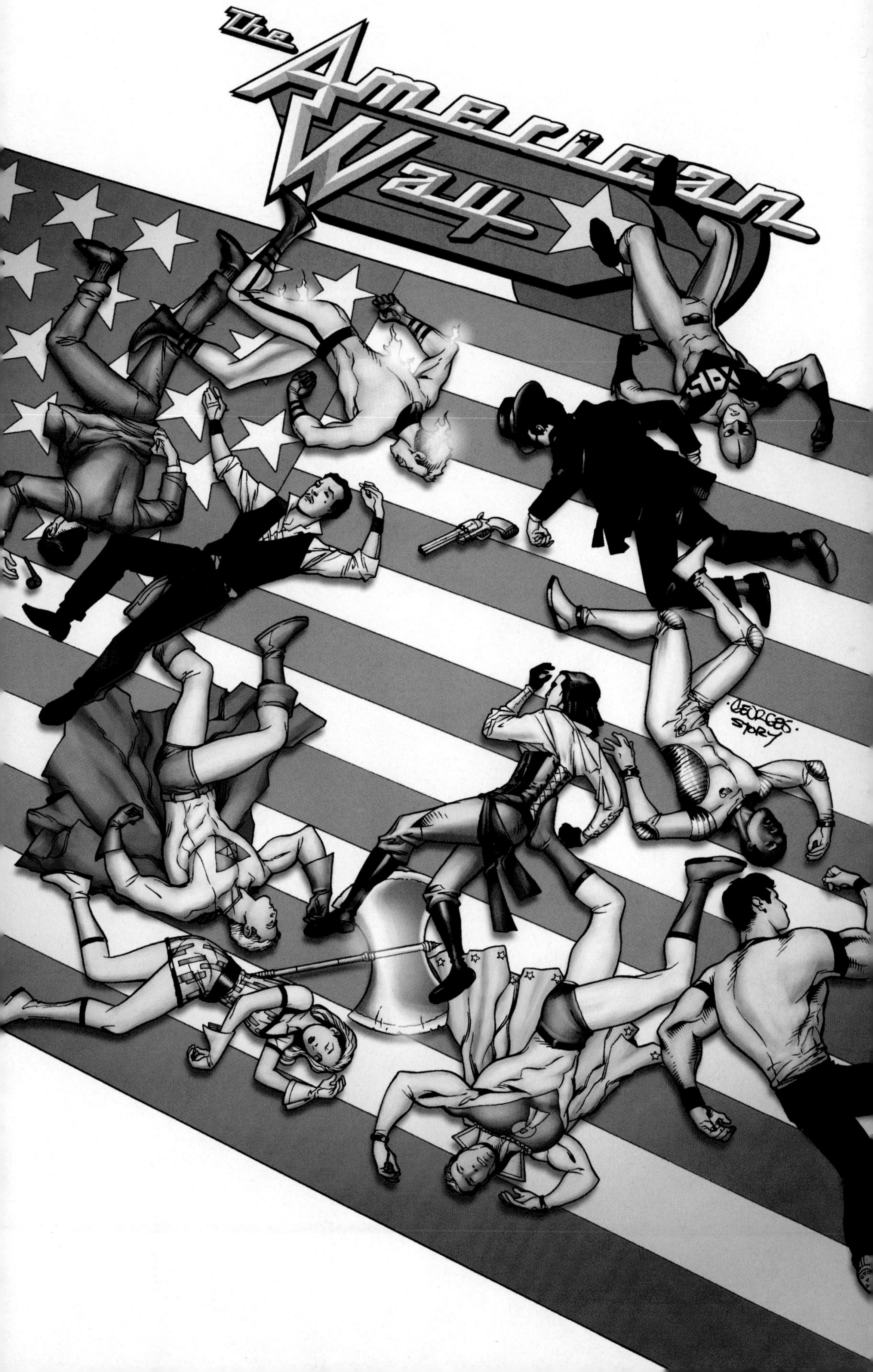
The American Way
GEORGES STORY

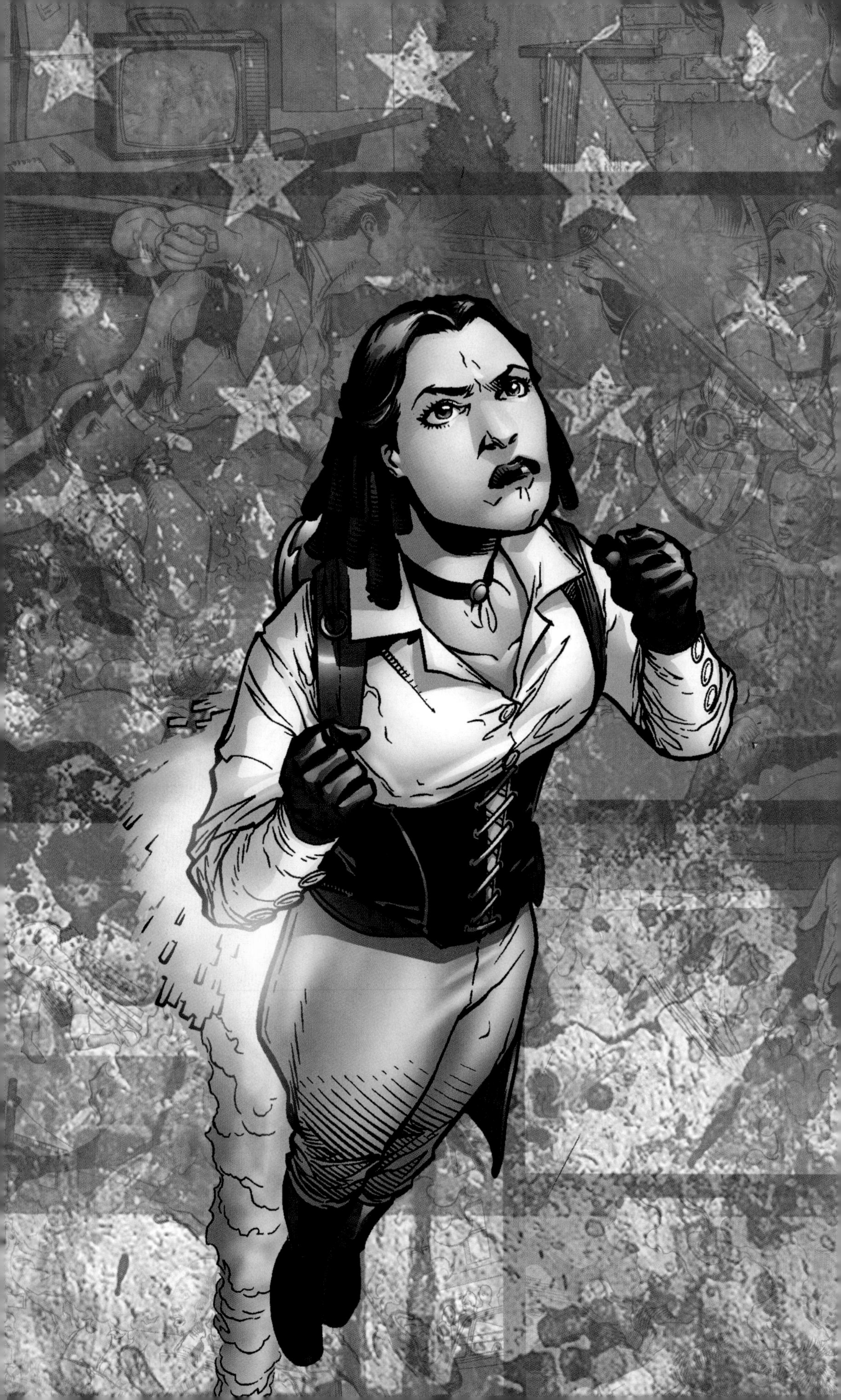

THE WOODS IN ALABAMA LAYS
BODY. THAT'S ALL THE BODY
ES, LAY IN THE WOODS, 'CAUSE
T OF ITS HEAD IS TOO CRUSHED
R IT TO DO ANYTHING ELSE.

NEVERMIND HE WAS A HOMICIDAL
GENIUS, NOT EVEN HELLBENT COULD
FIGURE A WAY AROUND DEATH.

AND WHILE HE LAYS DEAD,
THE NEW AMERICAN--THE
HERO I "CREATED," THE
GUY WHO WAS GOING
TO UNITE THE COUNTRY--
BURNS.

AND, OH YEAH,
MY WIFE LEFT
ME AND TOOK
OUR KID WITH HER.
BUT, COMPARED
TO THE END
OF MY DREAM
OF CRUSHING
RACE HATE IN
AMERICA,
PERSONAL
PROBLEMS
ARE AN ASIDE.

SO, HERE WE ARE.
OUR PROSPECTS
MISERABLE.
THE PROMISE OF
THE PRESIDENT'S
NEW GENERATION
WRECKED.

AND WHAT BURNS
WITH HIM: AMERICA'S
HOPE. FAITH.

AND IN THAT WOODS
IN ALABAMA WHAT'S LEFT
OF HELLBENT'S HEAD--
I THINK IT'S SMILING

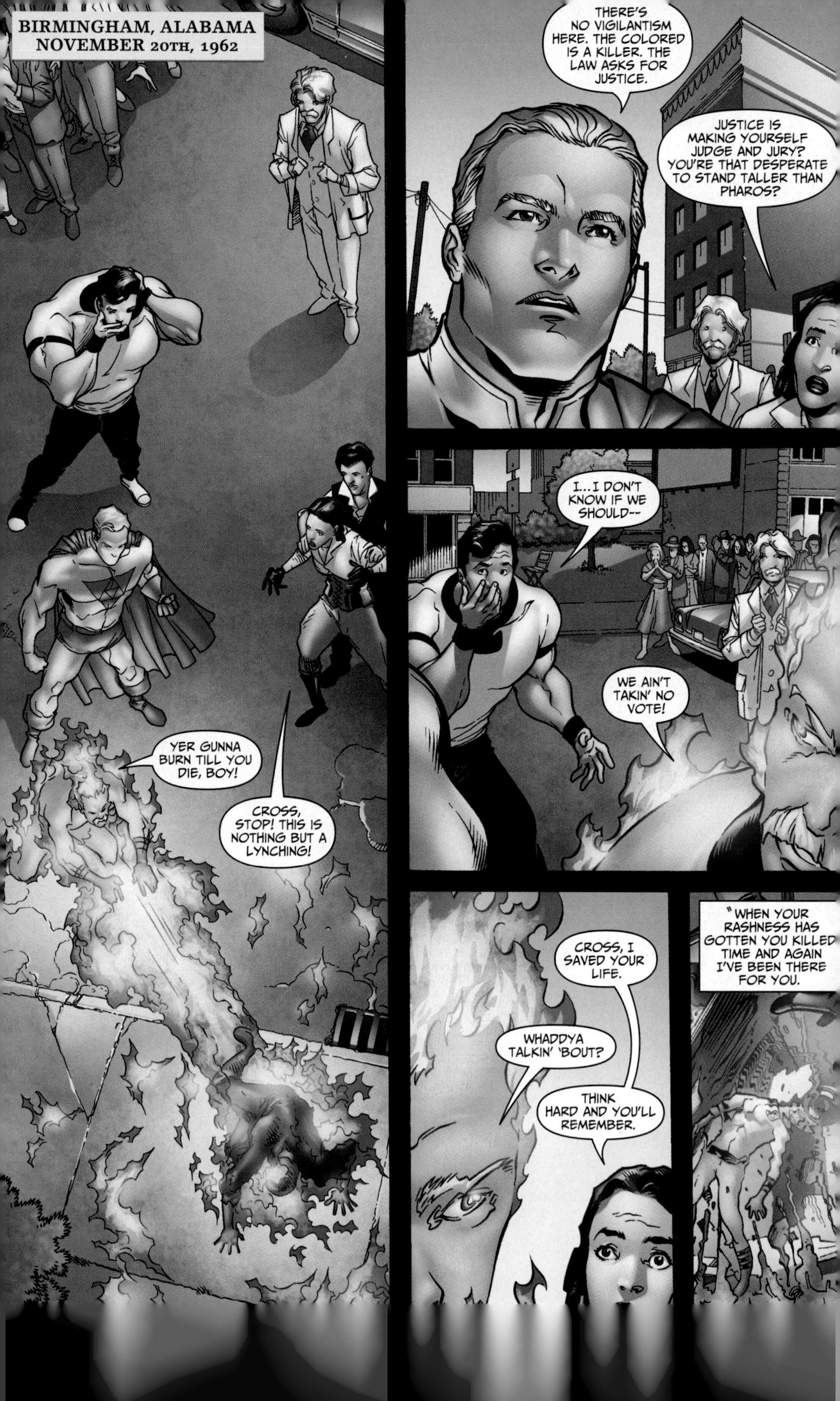
BIRMINGHAM, ALABAMA
NOVEMBER 20TH, 1962
YER GUNNA BURN TILL YOU DIE, BOY!
CROSS, STOP! THIS IS NOTHING BUT A LYNCHING!
THERE'S NO VIGILANTISM HERE. THE COLORED IS A KILLER. THE LAW ASKS FOR JUSTICE.
JUSTICE IS MAKING YOURSELF JUDGE AND JURY? YOU'RE THAT DESPERATE TO STAND TALLER THAN PHAROS?
I...I DON'T KNOW IF WE SHOULD--
WE AIN'T TAKIN' NO VOTE!
CROSS, I SAVED YOUR LIFE.
WHADDYA TALKIN' 'BOUT?
THINK HARD AND YOU'LL REMEMBER.
"WHEN YOUR RASHNESS HAS GOTTEN YOU KILLED TIME AND AGAIN I'VE BEEN THERE FOR YOU.

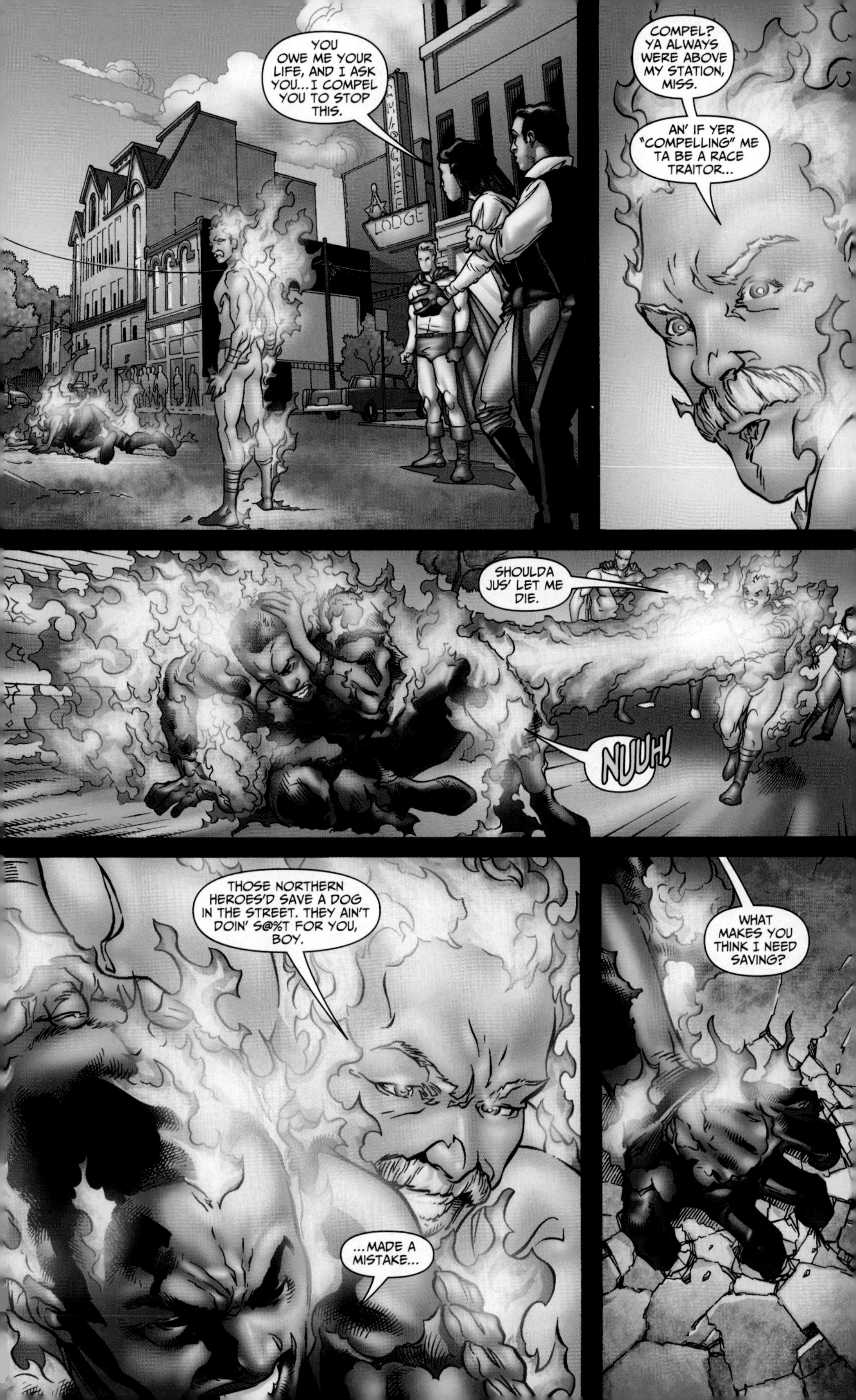
YOU OWE ME YOUR LIFE, AND I ASK YOU... I COMPEL YOU TO STOP THIS.
LODGE
COMPEL? YA ALWAYS WERE ABOVE MY STATION, MISS.
AN' IF YER "COMPELLING" ME TA BE A RACE TRAITOR...
SHOULDA JUS' LET ME DIE.
NUUH!
THOSE NORTHERN HEROES'D SAVE A DOG IN THE STREET. THEY AIN'T DOIN' S@%T FOR YOU, BOY.
...MADE A MISTAKE...
WHAT MAKES YOU THINK I NEED SAVING?

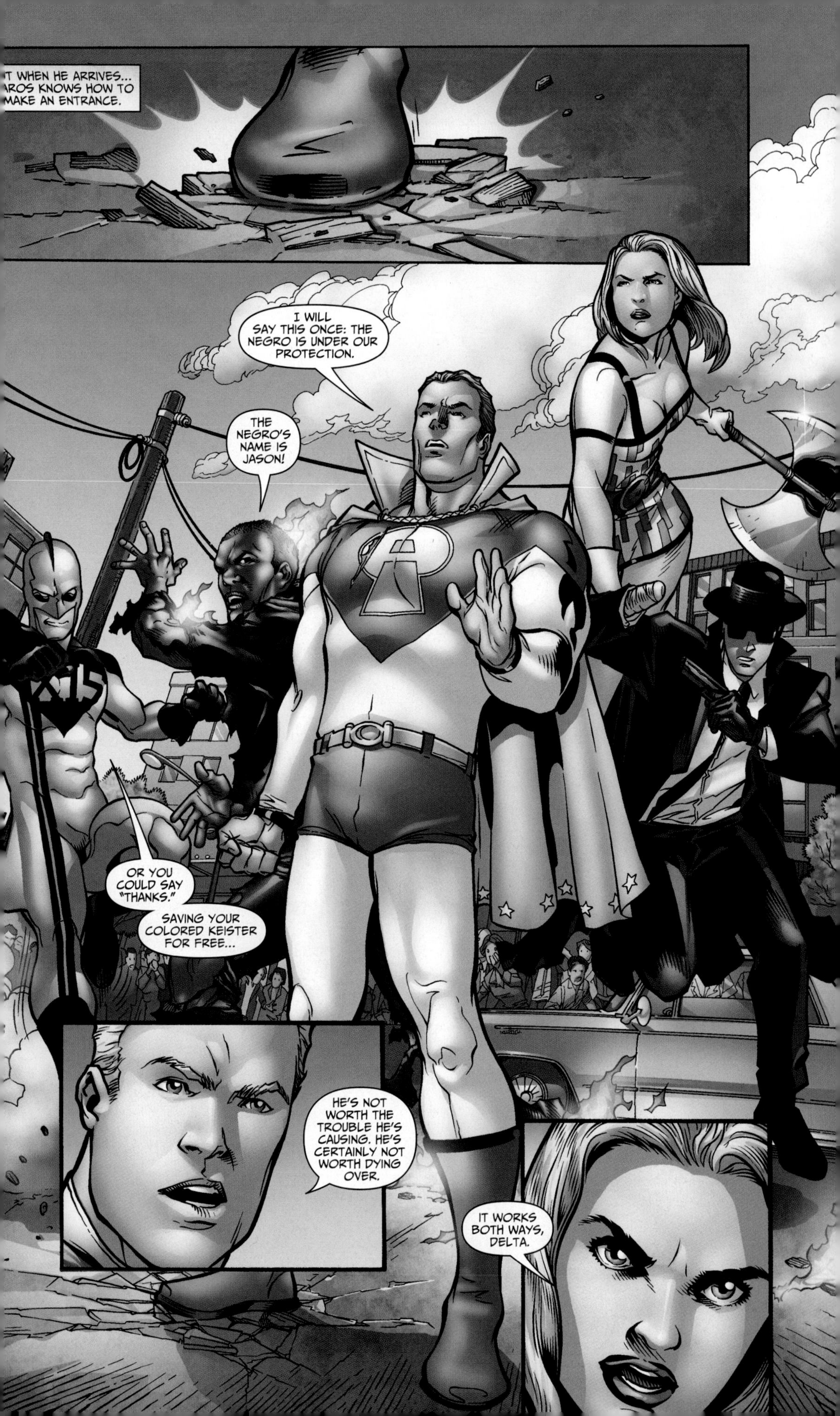
...T WHEN HE ARRIVES... ...AROS KNOWS HOW TO MAKE AN ENTRANCE.
I WILL SAY THIS ONCE: THE NEGRO IS UNDER OUR PROTECTION.
THE NEGRO'S NAME IS JASON!
OR YOU COULD SAY "THANKS."
SAVING YOUR COLORED KEISTER FOR FREE...
HE'S NOT WORTH THE TROUBLE HE'S CAUSING. HE'S CERTAINLY NOT WORTH DYING OVER.
IT WORKS BOTH WAYS, DELTA.

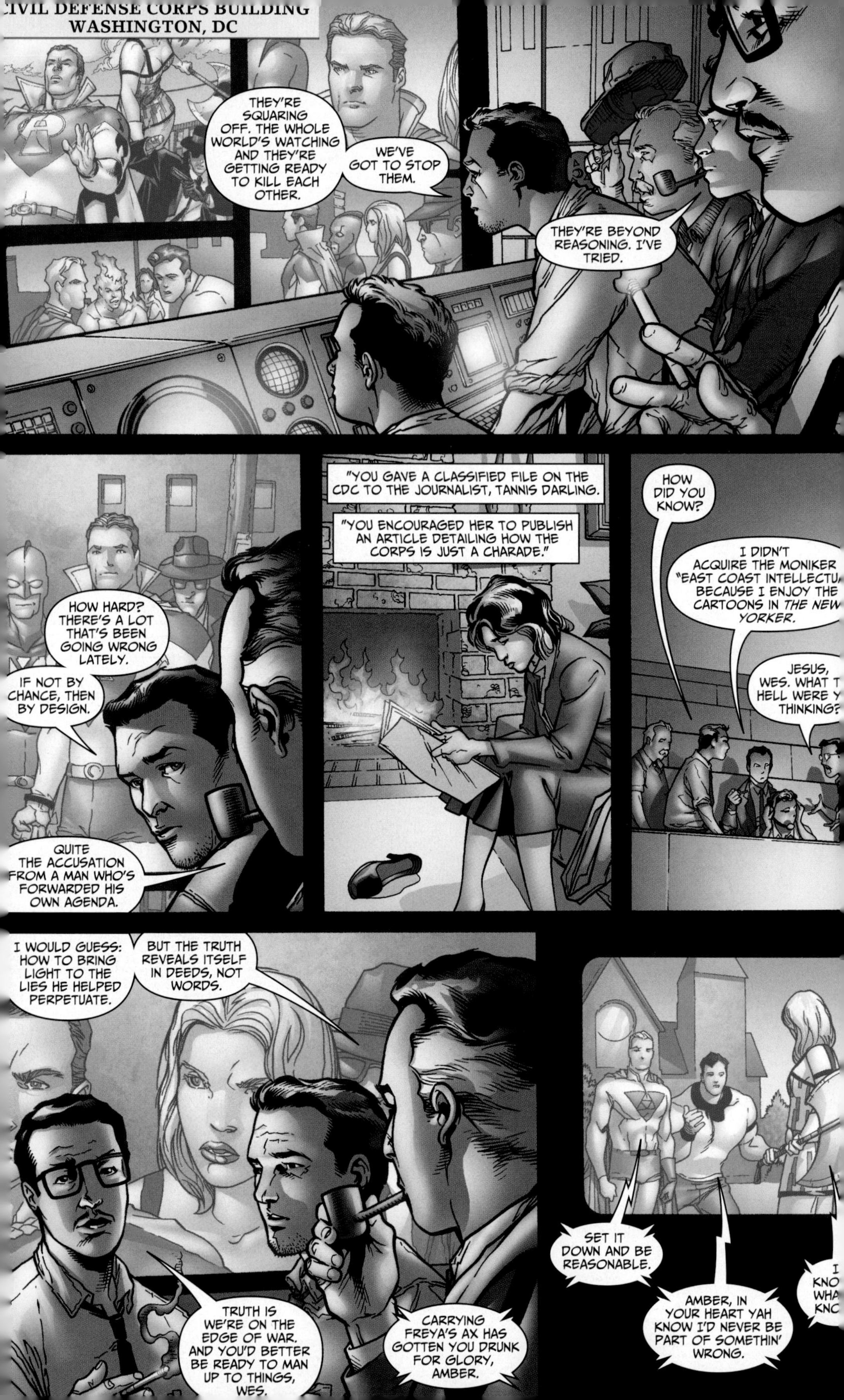
CIVIL DEFENSE CORPS BUILDING WASHINGTON, DC
THEY'RE SQUARING OFF. THE WHOLE WORLD'S WATCHING AND THEY'RE GETTING READY TO KILL EACH OTHER.
WE'VE GOT TO STOP THEM.
THEY'RE BEYOND REASONING. I'VE TRIED.
HOW HARD? THERE'S A LOT THAT'S BEEN GOING WRONG LATELY.
IF NOT BY CHANCE, THEN BY DESIGN.
QUITE THE ACCUSATION FROM A MAN WHO'S FORWARDED HIS OWN AGENDA.
"YOU GAVE A CLASSIFIED FILE ON THE CDC TO THE JOURNALIST, TANNIS DARLING.
"YOU ENCOURAGED HER TO PUBLISH AN ARTICLE DETAILING HOW THE CORPS IS JUST A CHARADE."
HOW DID YOU KNOW?
I DIDN'T ACQUIRE THE MONIKER "EAST COAST INTELLECTU BECAUSE I ENJOY THE CARTOONS IN *THE NEW YORKER*.
JESUS, WES. WHAT T HELL WERE Y THINKING?
I WOULD GUESS: HOW TO BRING LIGHT TO THE LIES HE HELPED PERPETUATE.
BUT THE TRUTH REVEALS ITSELF IN DEEDS, NOT WORDS.
TRUTH IS WE'RE ON THE EDGE OF WAR. AND YOU'D BETTER BE READY TO MAN UP TO THINGS, WES.
CARRYING FREYA'S AX HAS GOTTEN YOU DRUNK FOR GLORY, AMBER.
SET IT DOWN AND BE REASONABLE.
AMBER, IN YOUR HEART YAH KNOW I'D NEVER BE PART OF SOMETHIN' WRONG.
I KNO WHA KNO

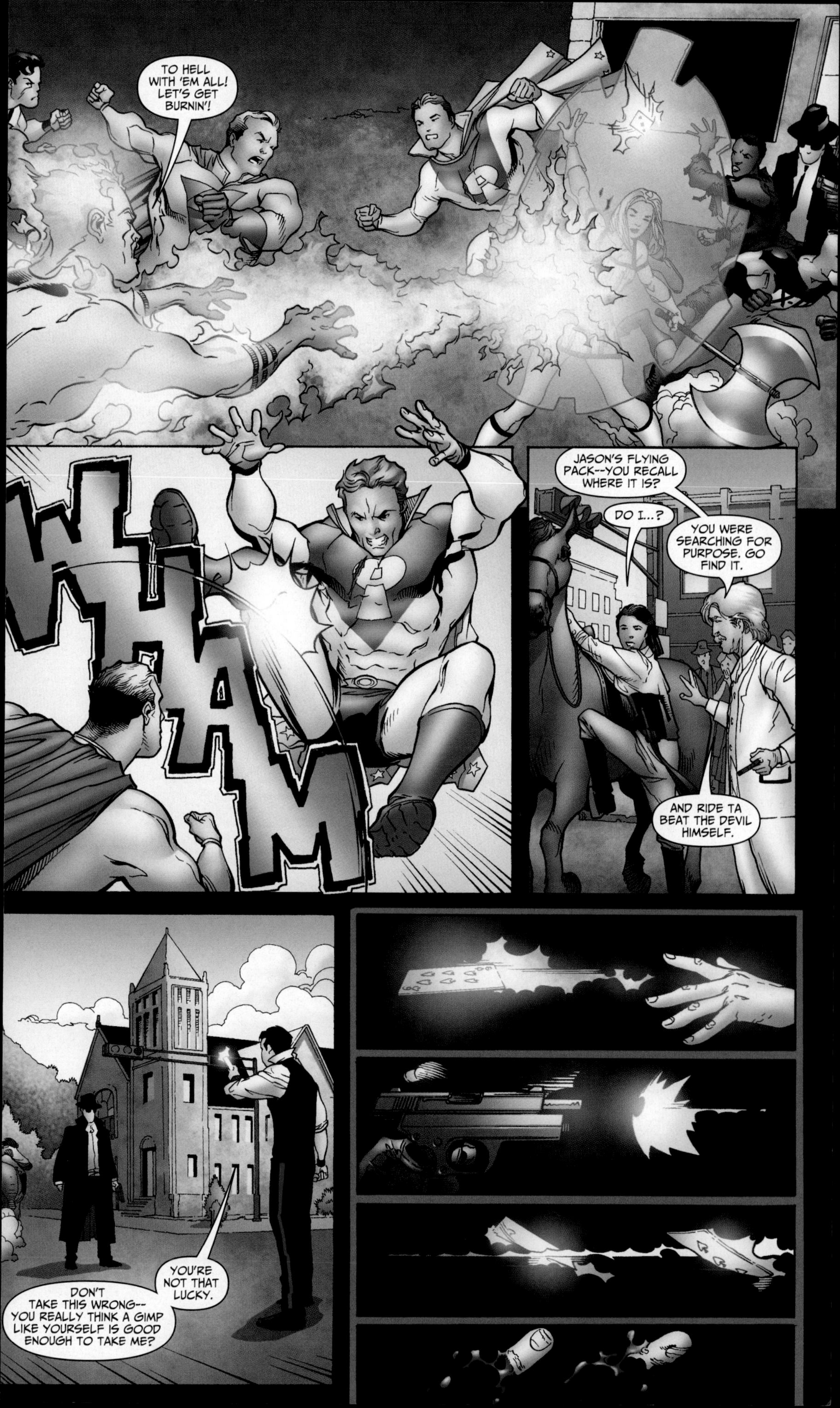
TO HELL WITH 'EM ALL! LET'S GET BURNIN'!
JASON'S FLYING PACK--YOU RECALL WHERE IT IS?
DO I...?
YOU WERE SEARCHING FOR PURPOSE. GO FIND IT.
AND RIDE TA BEAT THE DEVIL HIMSELF.
DON'T TAKE THIS WRONG-- YOU REALLY THINK A GIMP LIKE YOURSELF IS GOOD ENOUGH TO TAKE ME?
YOU'RE NOT THAT LUCKY.

ACROSS AMERICA WE HUDDLE AROUND "THE BOX." WE WATCH ON TRANSCONTINENTAL COAXIAL CABLE AND ALL ASK: IF THIS IS THE BEST OF US...

...SWEET JESUS...

...WHAT DOES THEIR PETTINESS SAY ABOUT ALL OF US?

WE WONDER: WHEN THE CHIPS ARE DOWN...

CAN ANY OF US RISE UP, TAKE RESPONSIBILITY? DO AS WE'RE SUPPOSED TO?

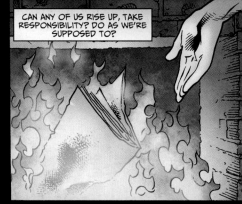

ARE THERE ANY PROSPE FOR MANKIND?

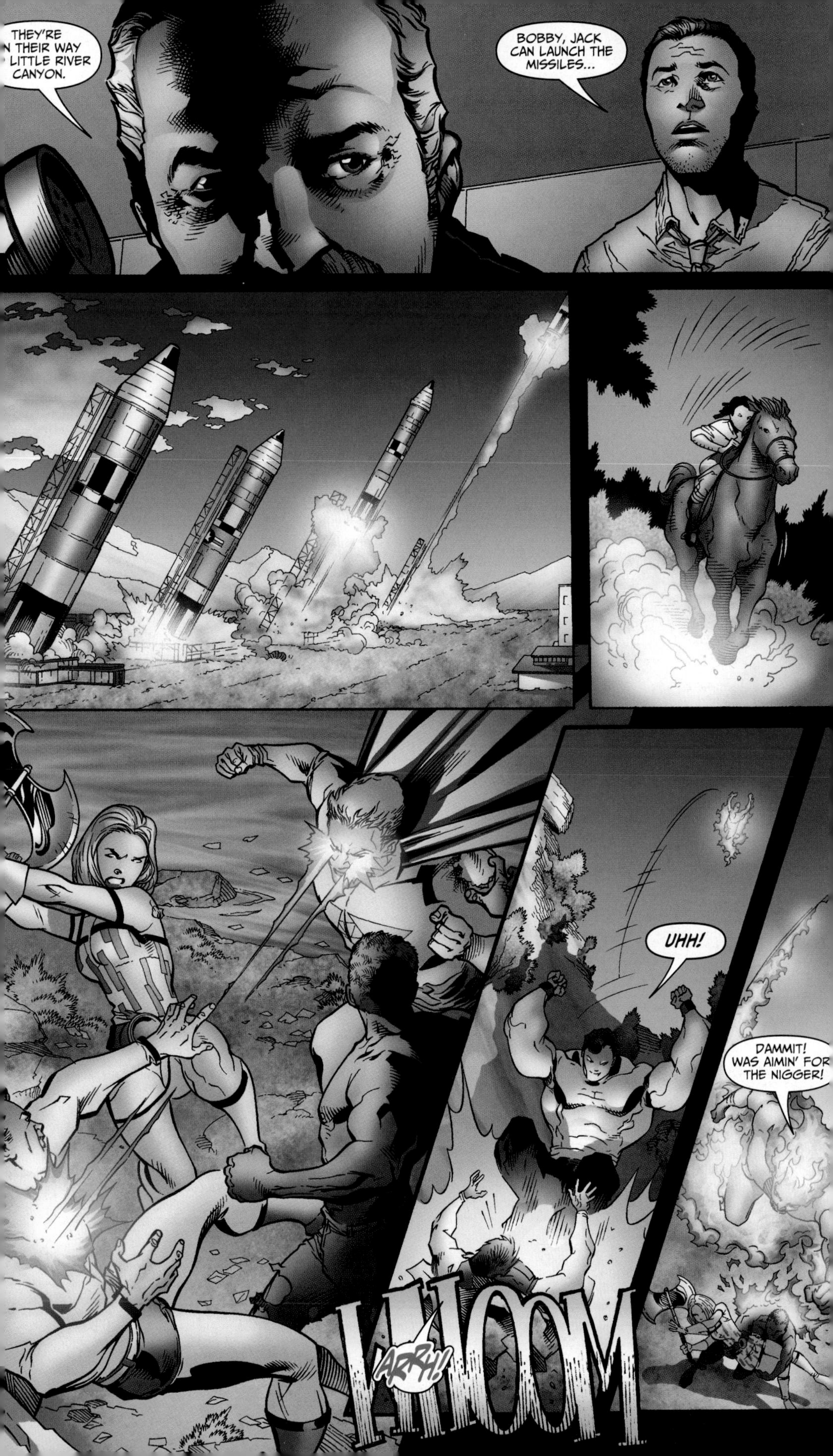
THEY'RE N THEIR WAY LITTLE RIVER CANYON.
BOBBY, JACK CAN LAUNCH THE MISSILES...
UHH!
DAMMIT! WAS AIMIN' FOR THE NIGGER!
VHOOM
ARRH!

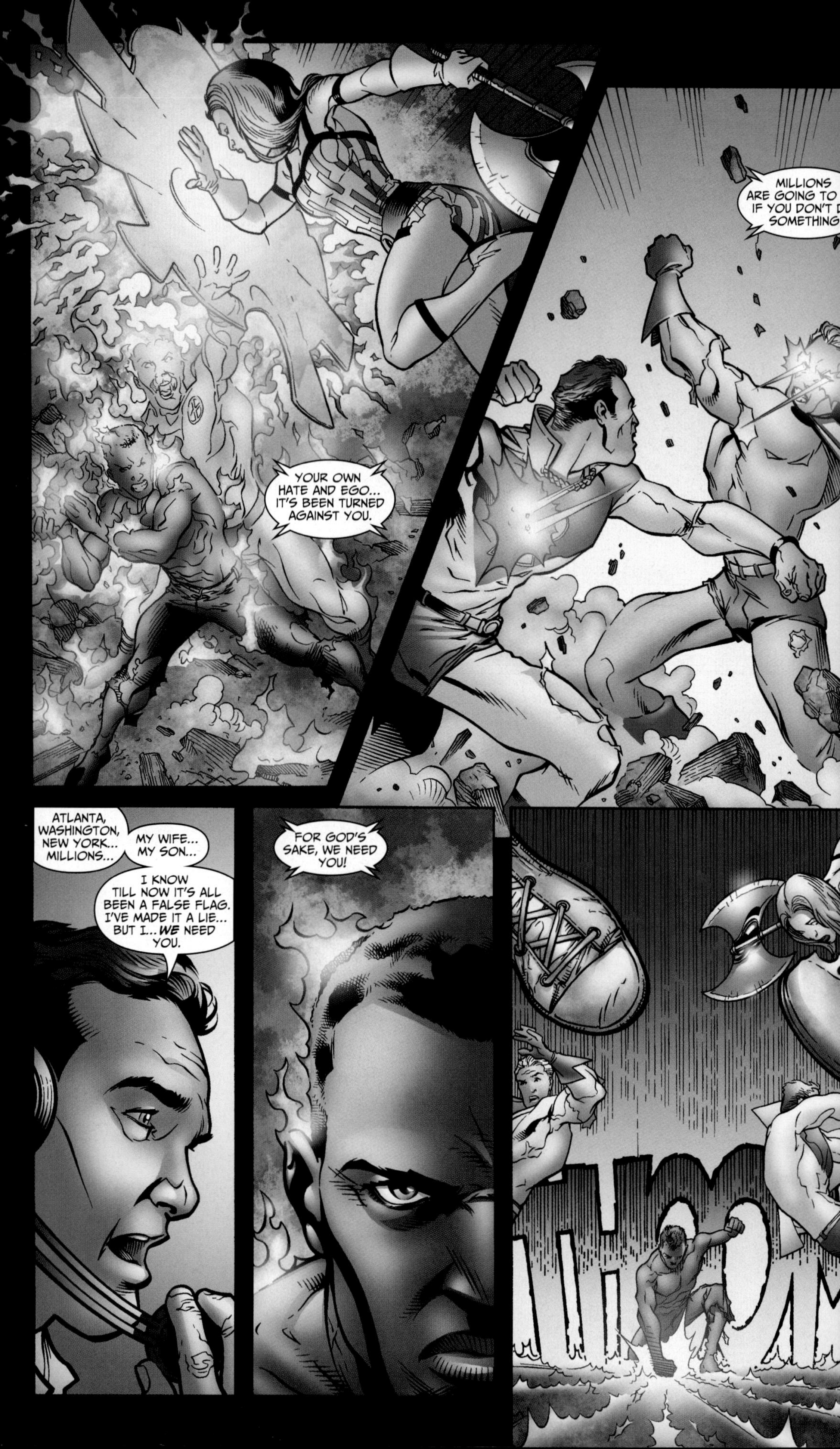
YOUR OWN HATE AND EGO... IT'S BEEN TURNED AGAINST YOU.
MILLIONS ARE GOING TO
IF YOU DON'T
SOMETHING
ATLANTA, WASHINGTON, NEW YORK... MILLIONS...
MY WIFE... MY SON...
I KNOW TILL NOW IT'S ALL BEEN A FALSE FLAG. I'VE MADE IT A LIE... BUT I... WE NEED YOU.
FOR GOD'S SAKE, WE NEED YOU!

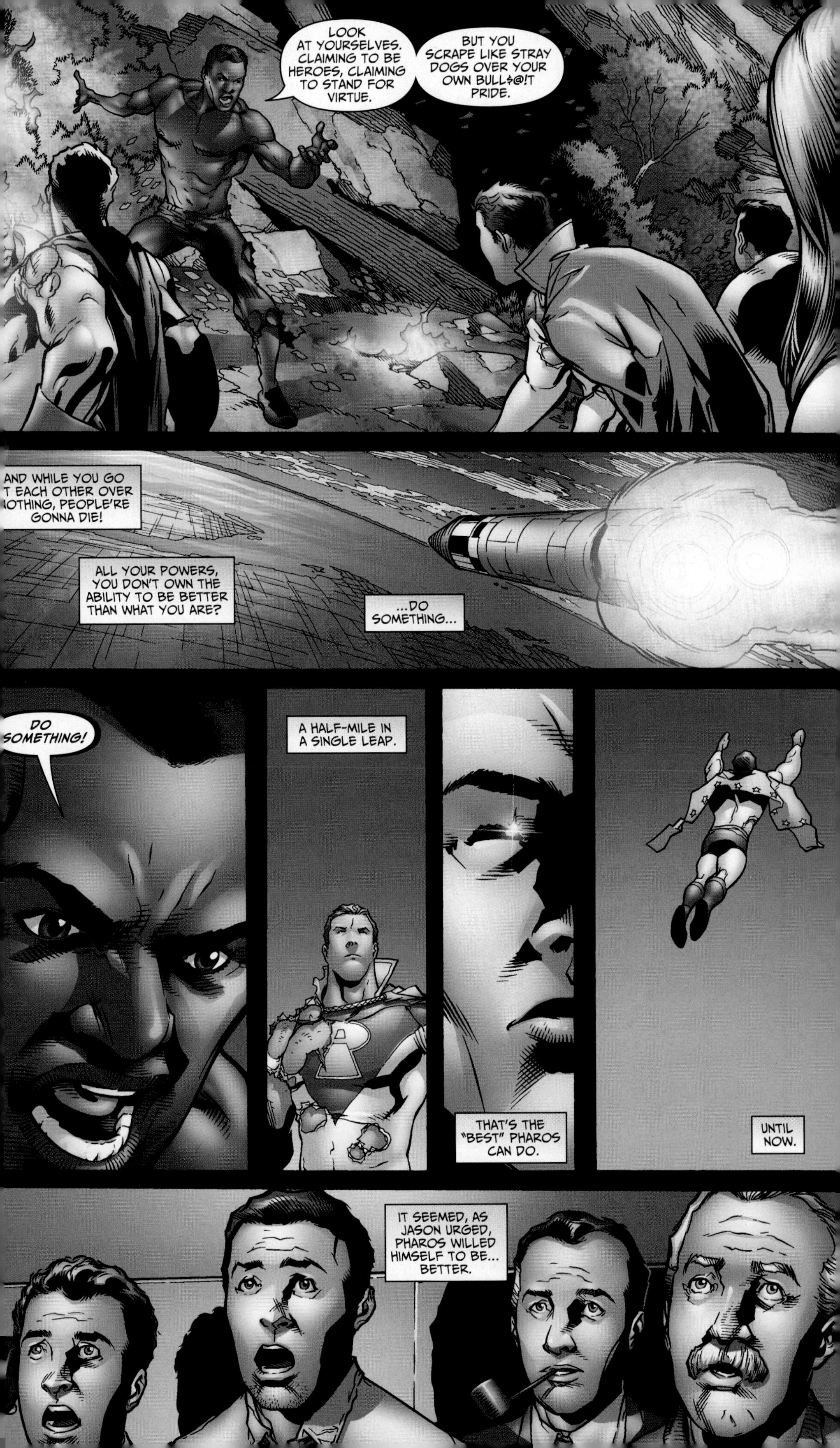
LOOK AT YOURSELVES. CLAIMING TO BE HEROES, CLAIMING TO STAND FOR VIRTUE.
BUT YOU SCRAPE LIKE STRAY DOGS OVER YOUR OWN BULL$@!T PRIDE.
AND WHILE YOU GO AT EACH OTHER OVER NOTHING, PEOPLE'RE GONNA DIE!
ALL YOUR POWERS, YOU DON'T OWN THE ABILITY TO BE BETTER THAN WHAT YOU ARE?
...DO SOMETHING...
DO SOMETHING!
A HALF-MILE IN A SINGLE LEAP.
THAT'S THE "BEST" PHAROS CAN DO.
UNTIL NOW.
IT SEEMED, AS JASON URGED, PHAROS WILLED HIMSELF TO BE... BETTER.

BUT IN TRUTH: HUMAN NATURE IS A CONSTANT. PEOPLE DO NOT CHANGE.

THEY BECOME MORE OF WHAT THEY ARE.

SOM
ASCE

OTHERS DEVOLVE IN THEIR MALICIOUSNESS.

WE AIN'T DONE!

I AIN'T BUYIN' ANY LIES ABOUT NO MISSILES!

OLE MISS?

I HEAR YOU, CAPTAIN.

YOU'RE WONDERIN' WHY I SENT YOU TO FIND A BUSTED-UP FLYIN' PACK.

GOTTA FIGURE, ABILITIES LIKE YOURS, IF YOU CAN MAKE THINGS OLD...

STANDS TO REASON YOU CAN MAKE 'EM NEW AGAIN.

THE BIRDS ARE CLOSING ON WASHINGTON AND MANHATTAN.

THEY WILL DETONAT TWENTY THOUS FEET.

SOMETHING ELSE JUST TOOK TO THE SKY!

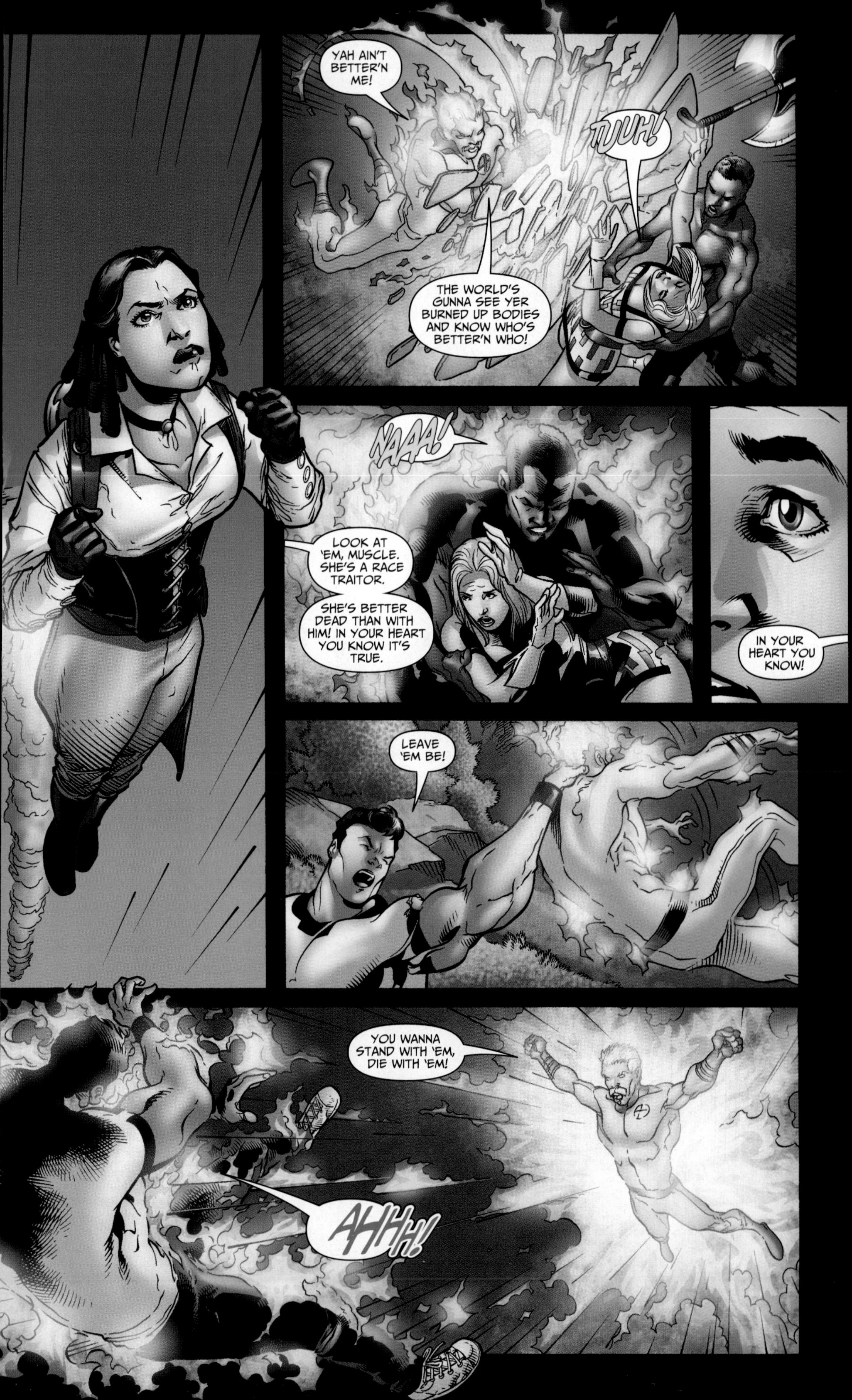
YAH AIN'T BETTER'N ME!
TUUH!
THE WORLD'S GUNNA SEE YER BURNED UP BODIES AND KNOW WHO'S BETTER'N WHO!
NAAA!
LOOK AT 'EM, MUSCLE. SHE'S A RACE TRAITOR.
SHE'S BETTER DEAD THAN WITH HIM! IN YOUR HEART YOU KNOW IT'S TRUE.
IN YOUR HEART YOU KNOW!
LEAVE 'EM BE!
YOU WANNA STAND WITH 'EM, DIE WITH 'EM!
AHHH!

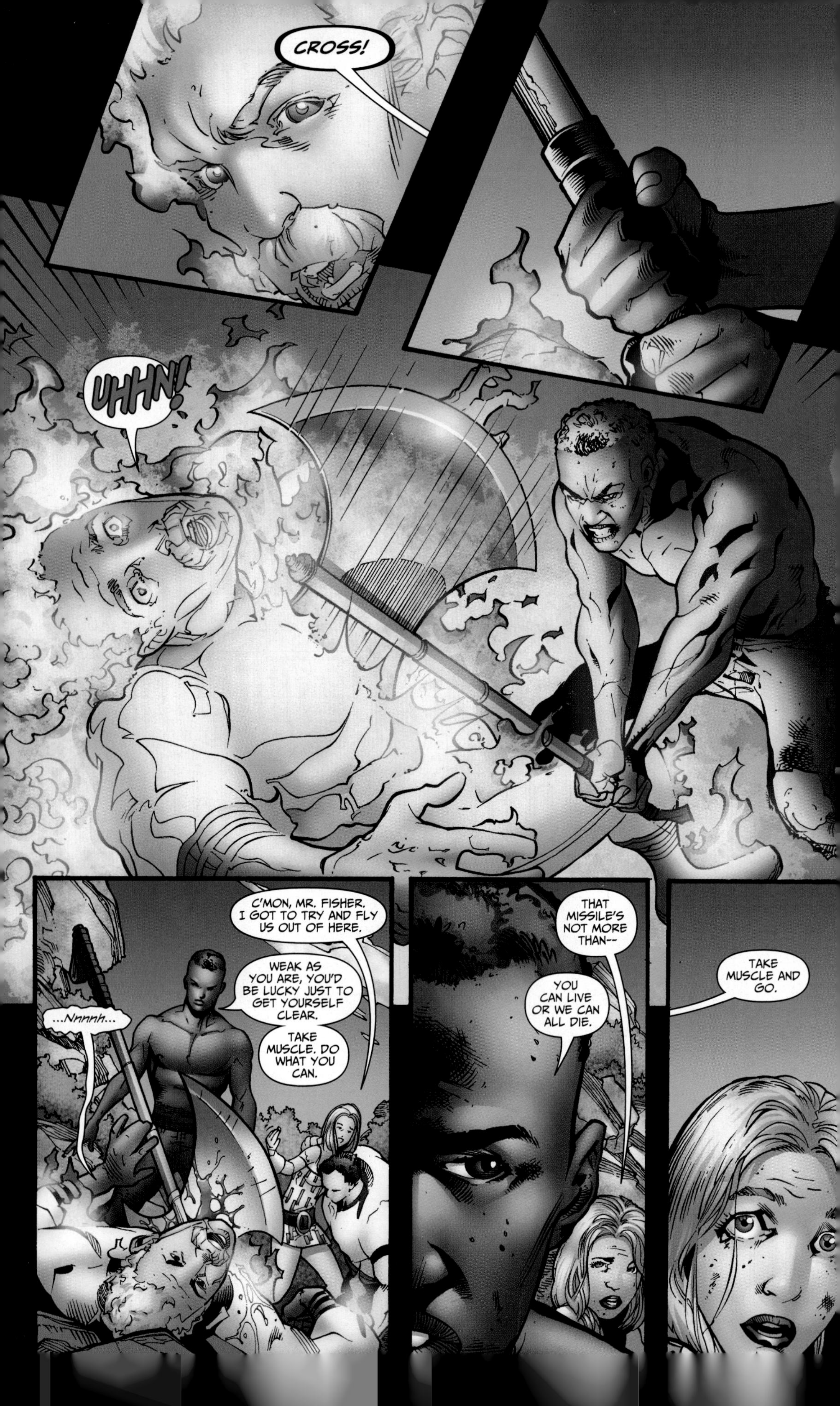
CROSS!
UHHN!
C'MON, MR. FISHER. I GOT TO TRY AND FLY US OUT OF HERE.
WEAK AS YOU ARE, YOU'D BE LUCKY JUST TO GET YOURSELF CLEAR.
TAKE MUSCLE. DO WHAT YOU CAN.
...Nnnnh...
THAT MISSILE'S NOT MORE THAN--
YOU CAN LIVE OR WE CAN ALL DIE.
TAKE MUSCLE AND GO.

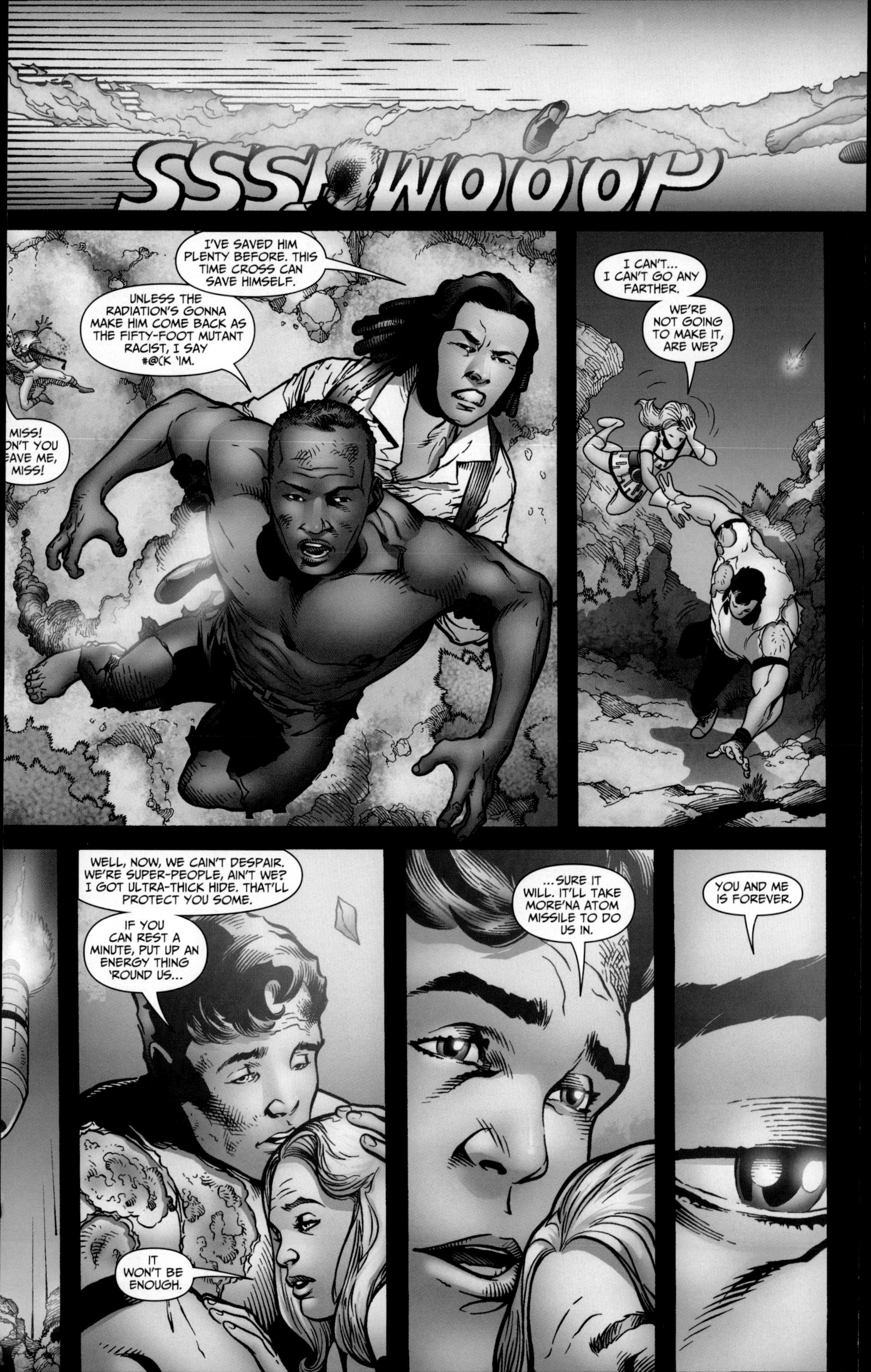
SSSHWOOOP
I'VE SAVED HIM PLENTY BEFORE. THIS TIME CROSS CAN SAVE HIMSELF.
UNLESS THE RADIATION'S GONNA MAKE HIM COME BACK AS THE FIFTY-FOOT MUTANT RACIST, I SAY #@CK 'IM.
MISS! ON'T YOU EAVE ME, MISS!
I CAN'T... I CAN'T GO ANY FARTHER.
WE'RE NOT GOING TO MAKE IT, ARE WE?
WELL, NOW, WE CAIN'T DESPAIR. WE'RE SUPER-PEOPLE, AIN'T WE? I GOT ULTRA-THICK HIDE. THAT'LL PROTECT YOU SOME.
IF YOU CAN REST A MINUTE, PUT UP AN ENERGY THING 'ROUND US...
IT WON'T BE ENOUGH.
...SURE IT WILL. IT'LL TAKE MORE'NA ATOM MISSILE TO DO US IN.
YOU AND ME IS FOREVER.

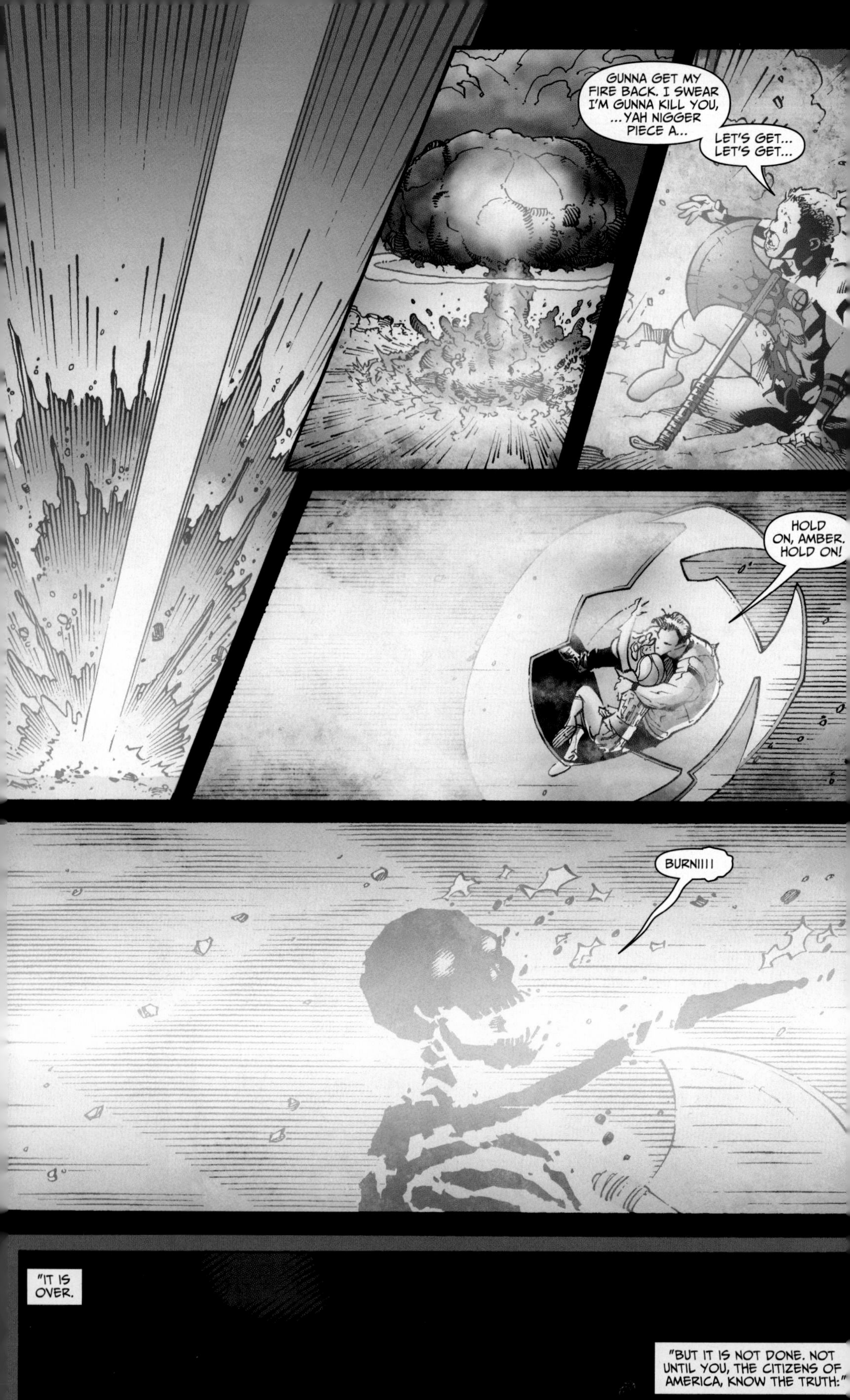
GUNNA GET MY FIRE BACK. I SWEAR I'M GUNNA KILL YOU, ...YAH NIGGER PIECE A...
LET'S GET... LET'S GET...
HOLD ON, AMBER. HOLD ON!
BURNIIII
"IT IS OVER.
"BUT IT IS NOT DONE. NOT UNTIL YOU, THE CITIZENS OF AMERICA, KNOW THE TRUTH:"

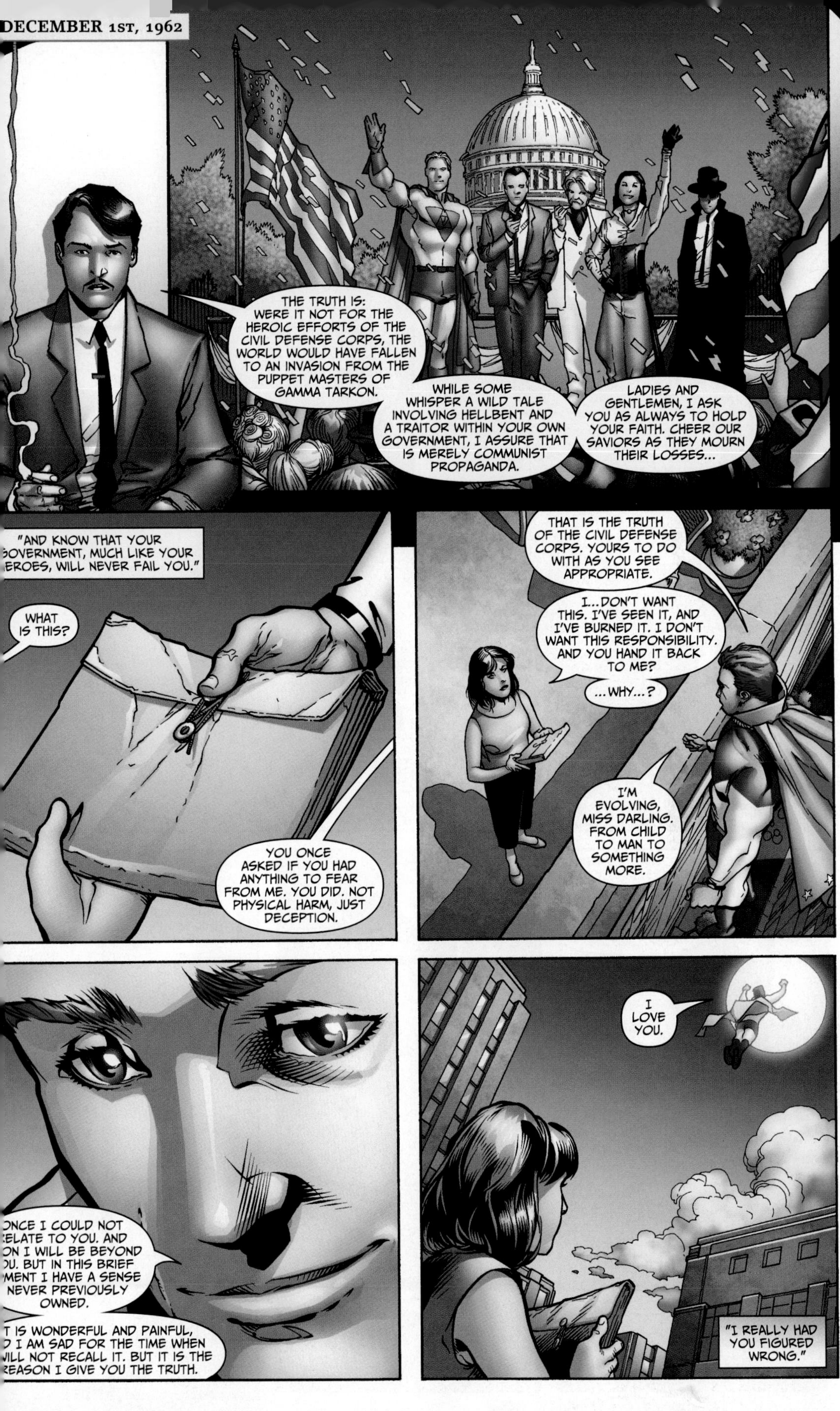
DECEMBER 1ST, 1962
THE TRUTH IS: WERE IT NOT FOR THE HEROIC EFFORTS OF THE CIVIL DEFENSE CORPS, THE WORLD WOULD HAVE FALLEN TO AN INVASION FROM THE PUPPET MASTERS OF GAMMA TARKON.
WHILE SOME WHISPER A WILD TALE INVOLVING HELLBENT AND A TRAITOR WITHIN YOUR OWN GOVERNMENT, I ASSURE THAT IS MERELY COMMUNIST PROPAGANDA.
LADIES AND GENTLEMEN, I ASK YOU AS ALWAYS TO HOLD YOUR FAITH. CHEER OUR SAVIORS AS THEY MOURN THEIR LOSSES...
"AND KNOW THAT YOUR GOVERNMENT, MUCH LIKE YOUR HEROES, WILL NEVER FAIL YOU."
WHAT IS THIS?
YOU ONCE ASKED IF YOU HAD ANYTHING TO FEAR FROM ME. YOU DID. NOT PHYSICAL HARM, JUST DECEPTION.
THAT IS THE TRUTH OF THE CIVIL DEFENSE CORPS. YOURS TO DO WITH AS YOU SEE APPROPRIATE.
I...DON'T WANT THIS. I'VE SEEN IT, AND I'VE BURNED IT. I DON'T WANT THIS RESPONSIBILITY. AND YOU HAND IT BACK TO ME?
...WHY...?
I'M EVOLVING, MISS DARLING. FROM CHILD TO MAN TO SOMETHING MORE.
ONCE I COULD NOT RELATE TO YOU. AND ON I WILL BE BEYOND OU. BUT IN THIS BRIEF MENT I HAVE A SENSE NEVER PREVIOUSLY OWNED.
T IS WONDERFUL AND PAINFUL, D I AM SAD FOR THE TIME WHEN ILL NOT RECALL IT. BUT IT IS THE REASON I GIVE YOU THE TRUTH.
I LOVE YOU.
"I REALLY HAD YOU FIGURED WRONG."

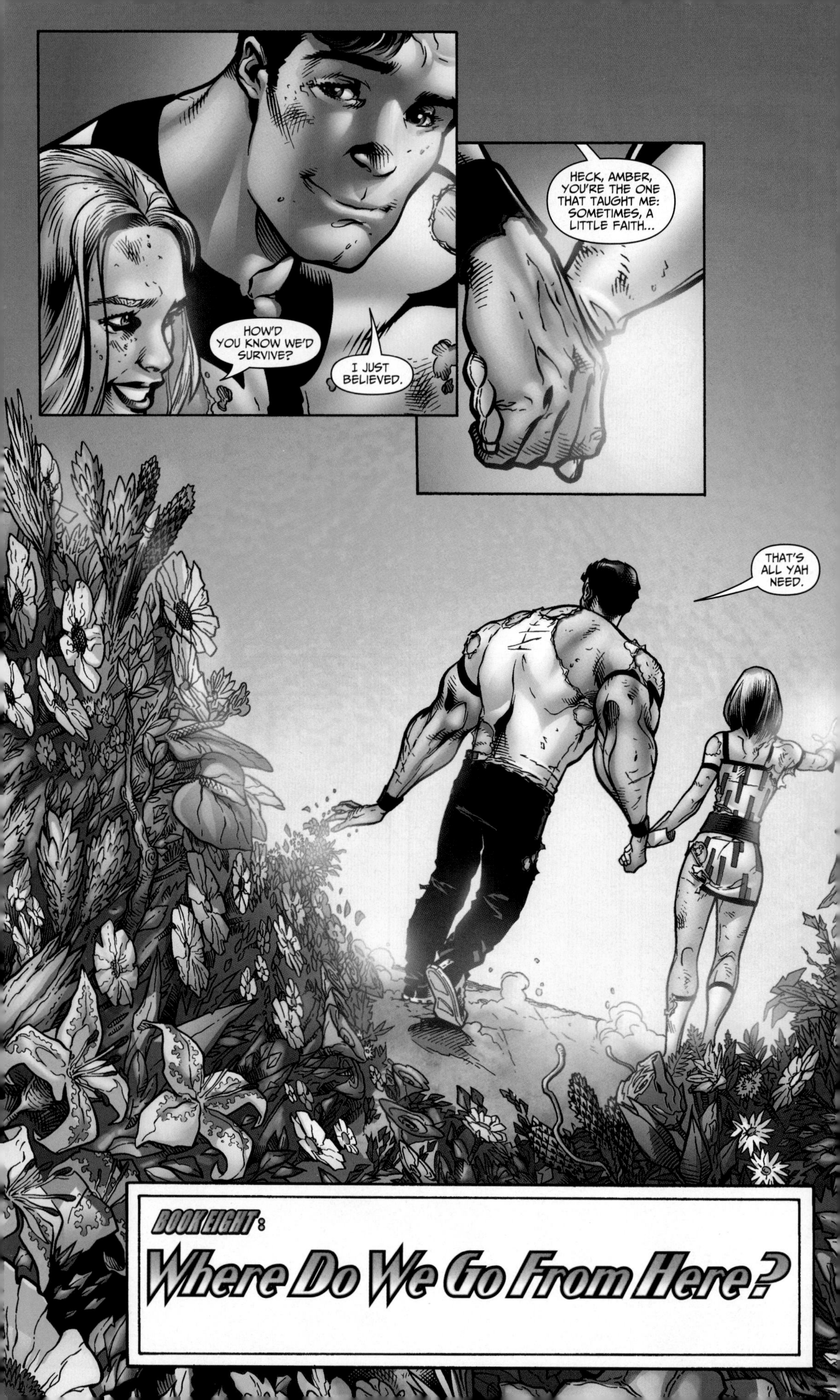
HOW'D YOU KNOW WE'D SURVIVE?
I JUST BELIEVED.
HECK, AMBER, YOU'RE THE ONE THAT TAUGHT ME: SOMETIMES, A LITTLE FAITH...
THAT'S ALL YAH NEED.
BOOK EIGHT:
Where Do We Go From Here?

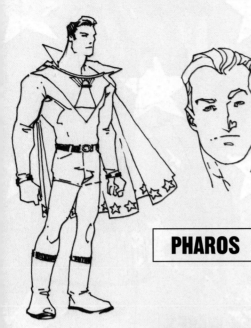

Character sketches by Georges Jeanty

PHAROS

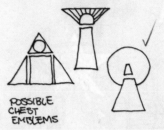

POSSIBLE
CHEST
EMBLEMS

CIVIL DEFENSE CORPS

HEAD DRESS

OPTIONAL CAPE

FREYA

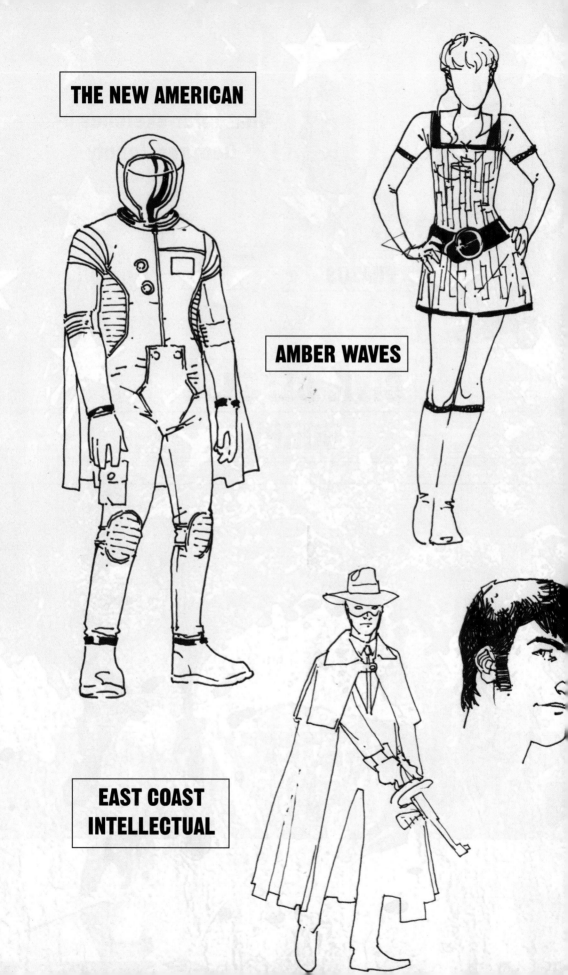

THE NEW AMERICAN

AMBER WAVES

EAST COAST
INTELLECTUAL

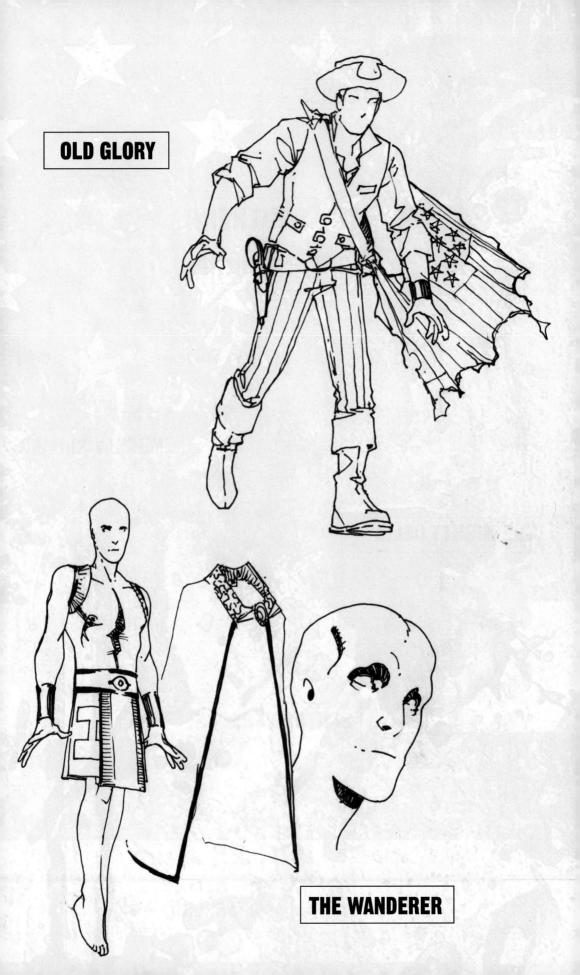

OLD GLORY

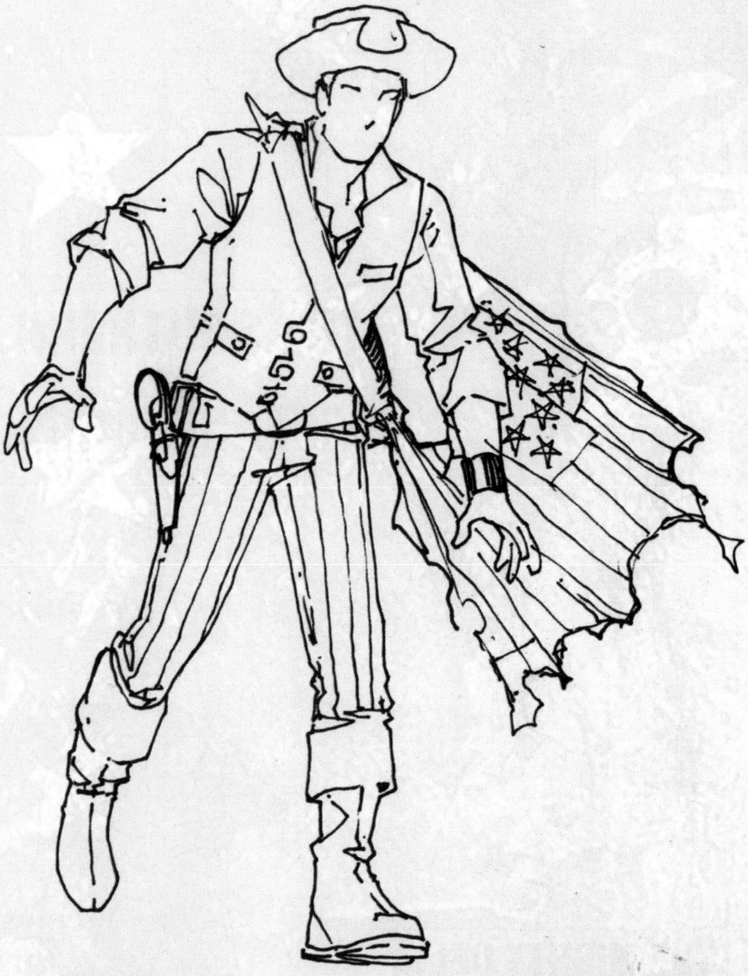

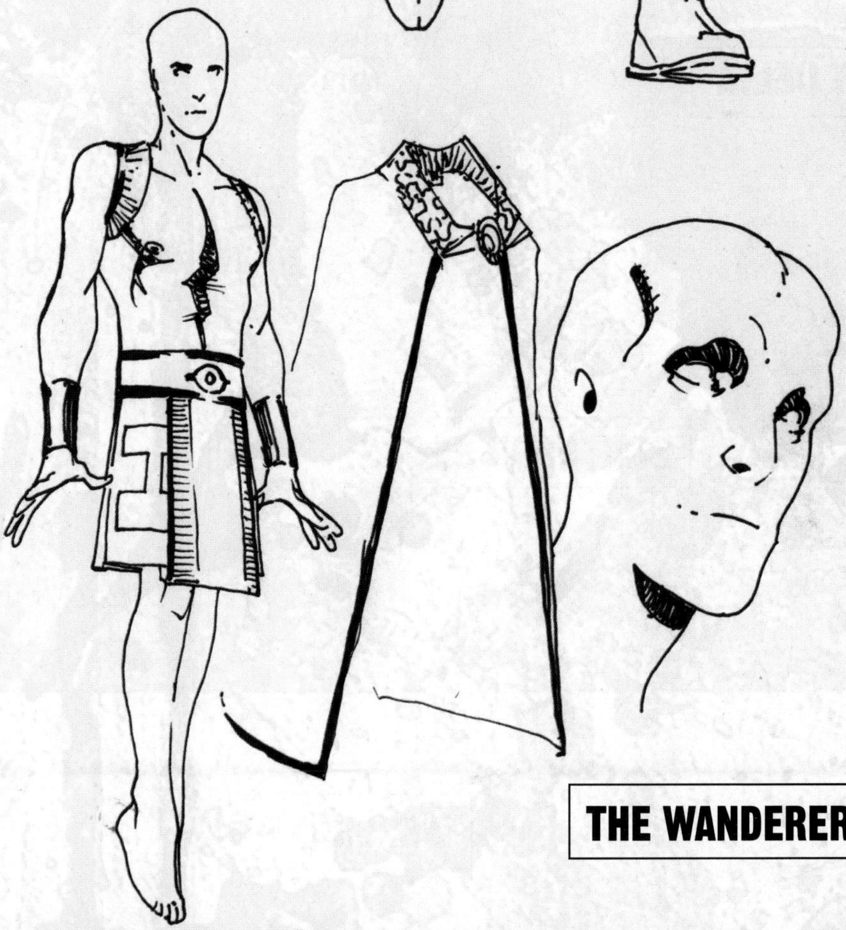

THE WANDERER

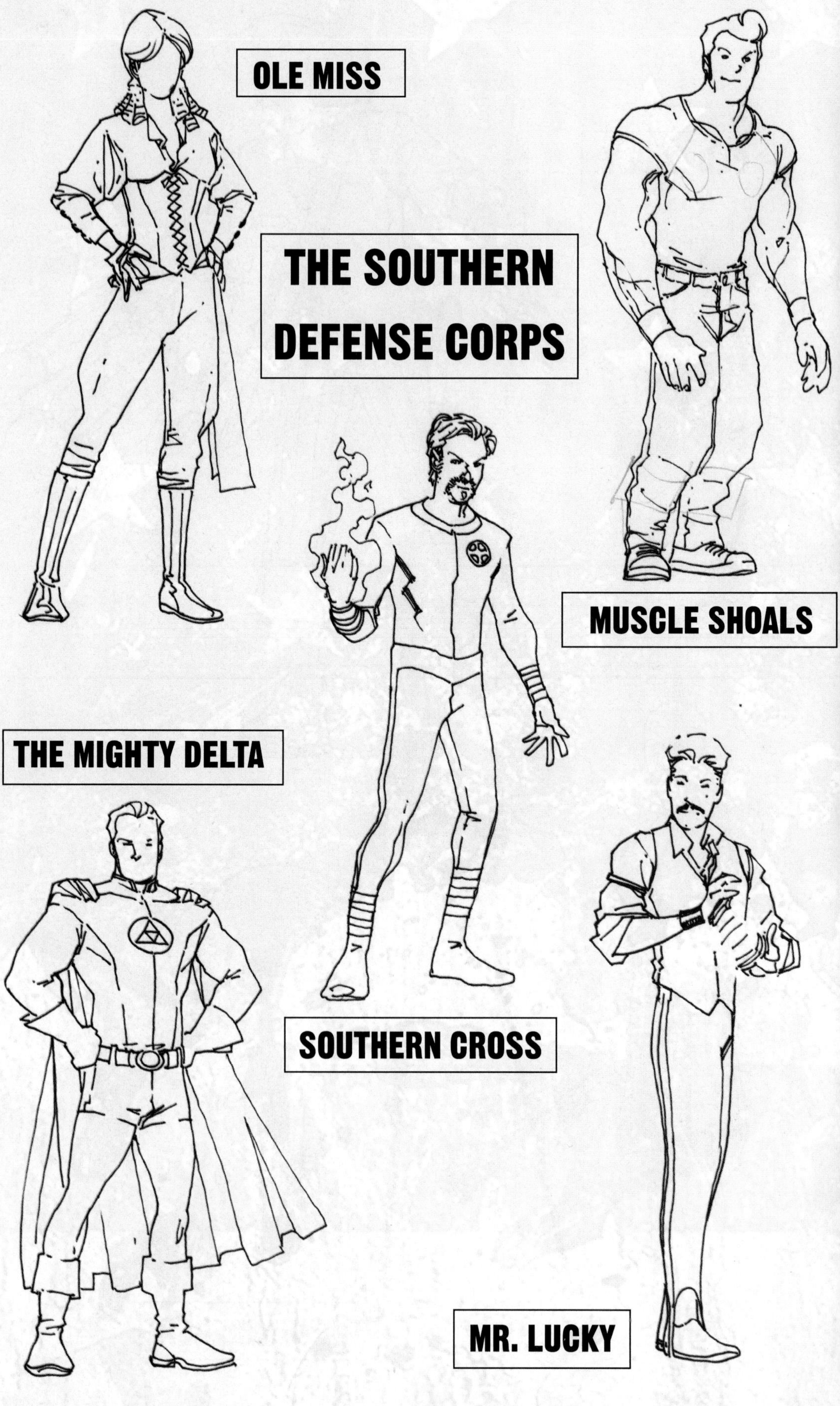
OLE MISS
THE SOUTHERN DEFENSE CORPS
MUSCLE SHOALS
THE MIGHTY DELTA
SOUTHERN CROSS
MR. LUCKY

Cover Sketches by Georges Jeanty

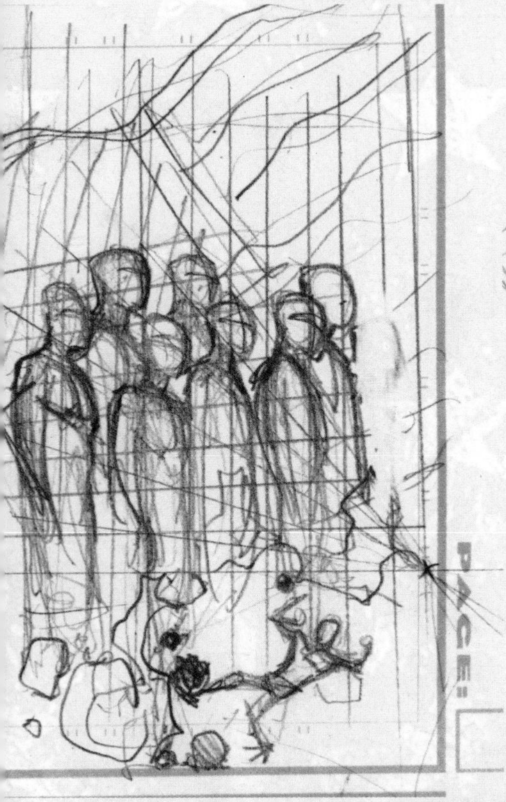

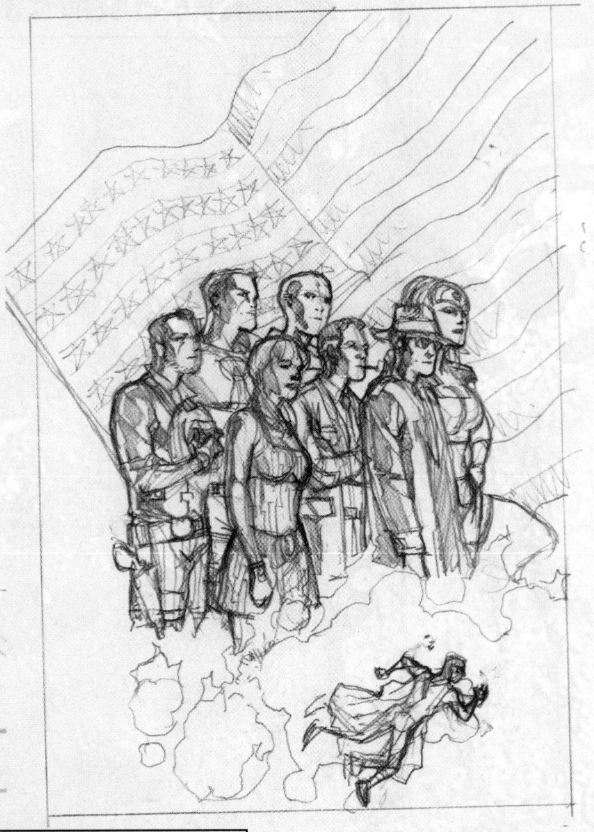

American Way # 1 cover sketches

American Way # 2 cover sketches

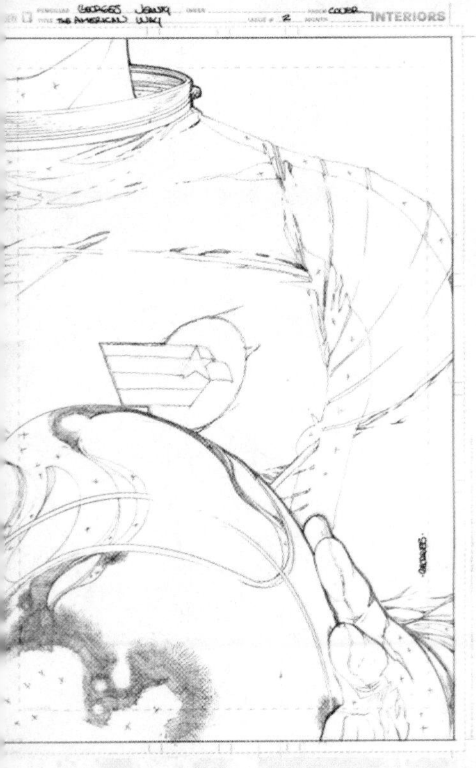
GEORGES JEANTY
THE AMERICAN WAY
COVER
2
INTERIORS

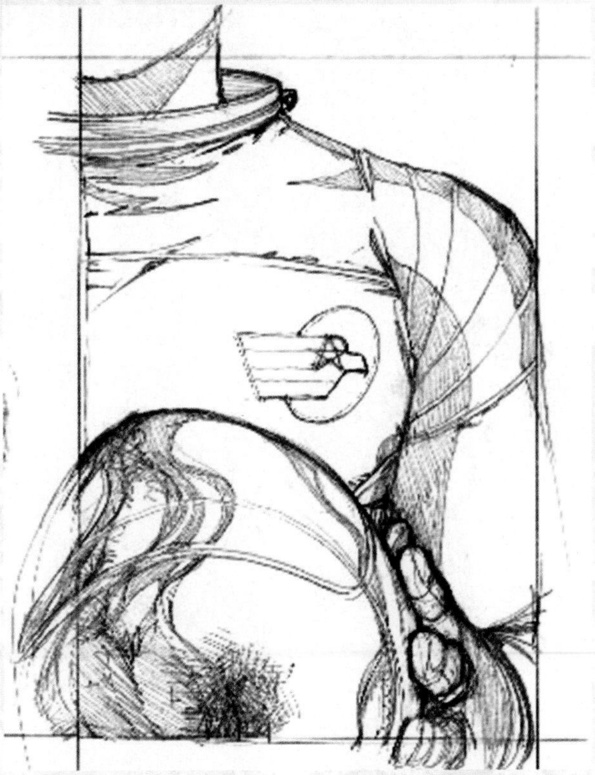

American Way # 3 cover sketches

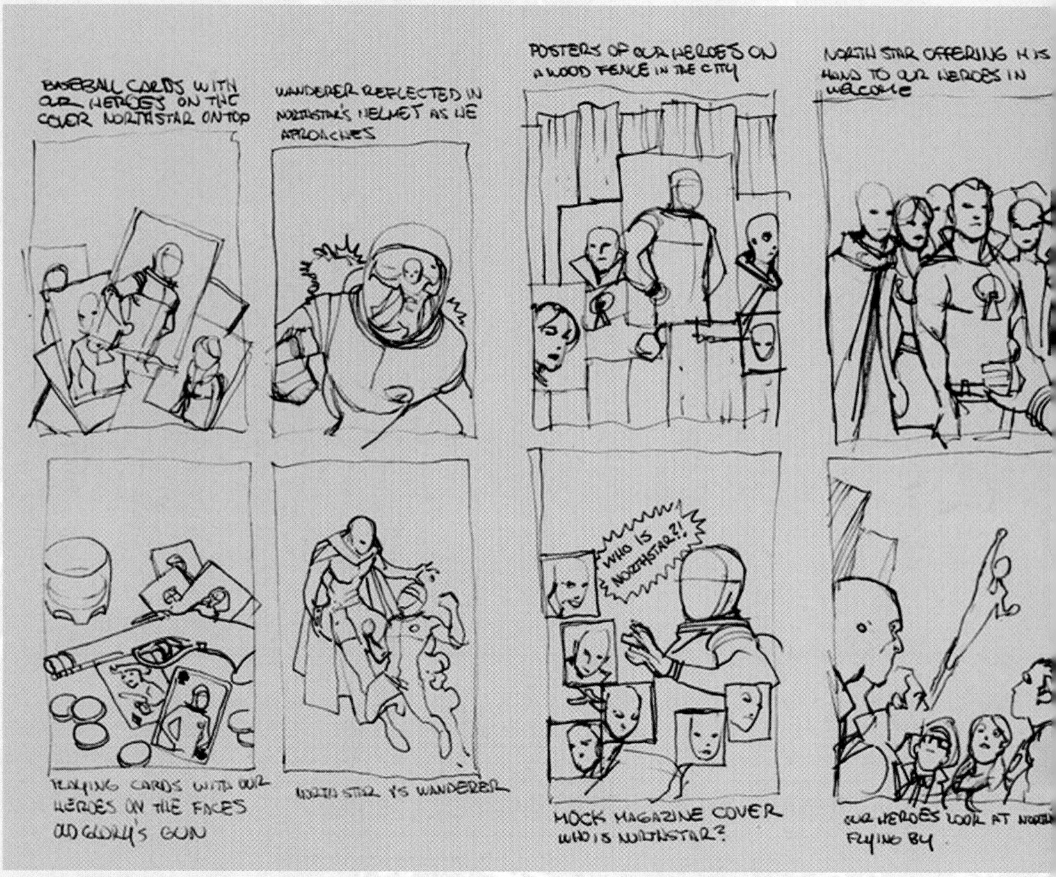
BASEBALL CARDS WITH OUR HEROES ON THE COVER NORTHSTAR ON TOP
WANDERER REFLECTED IN NORTHSTAR'S HELMET AS HE APROACHES
POSTERS OF OUR HEROES ON A WOOD FENCE IN THE CITY
NORTH STAR OFFERING HIS HAND TO OUR HEROES IN WELCOME
PLAYING CARDS WITH OUR HEROES ON THE FACES OLD GLORY'S GUN
NORTH STAR VS WANDERER
WHO IS NORTHSTAR?!
MOCK MAGAZINE COVER WHO IS NORTHSTAR?
OUR HEROES LOOK AT NORTH
FLYING BY

American Way # 4 cover sketches

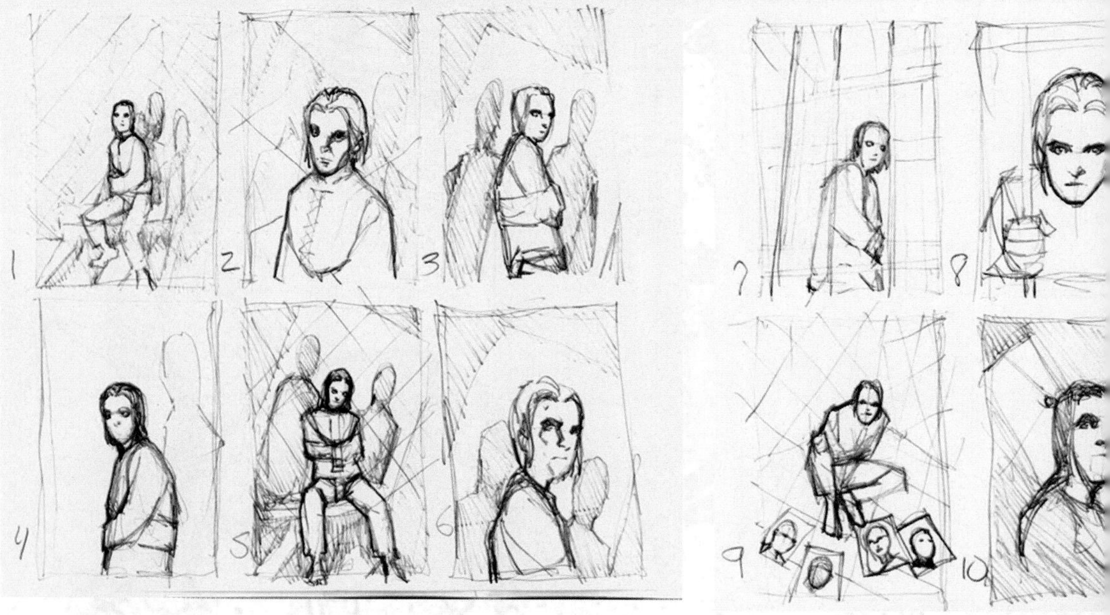
1
2
3
4
5
6
7
8
9
10

American Way # 5 cover sketches

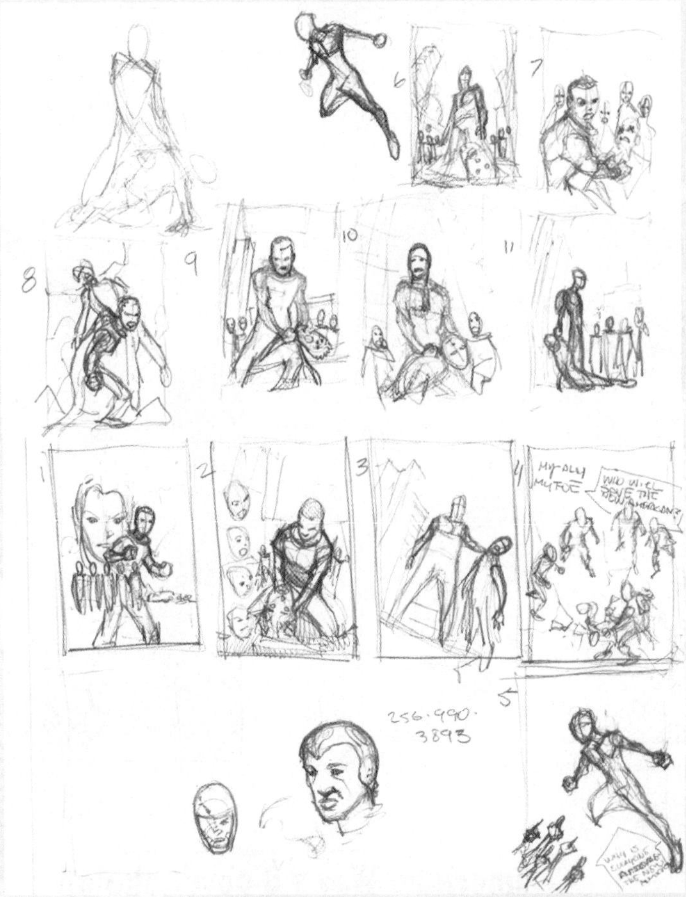
MY ALLY
MY FOE
256·990·
3893

American Way # 6 cover sketches

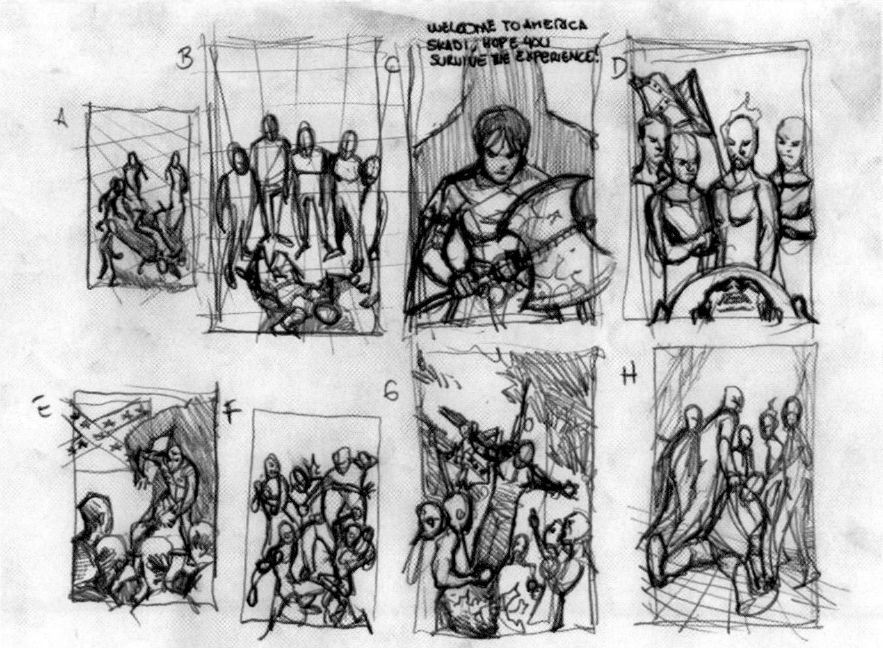
WELCOME TO AMERICA
SKADI, HOPE YOU
SURVIVE THE EXPERIENCE!

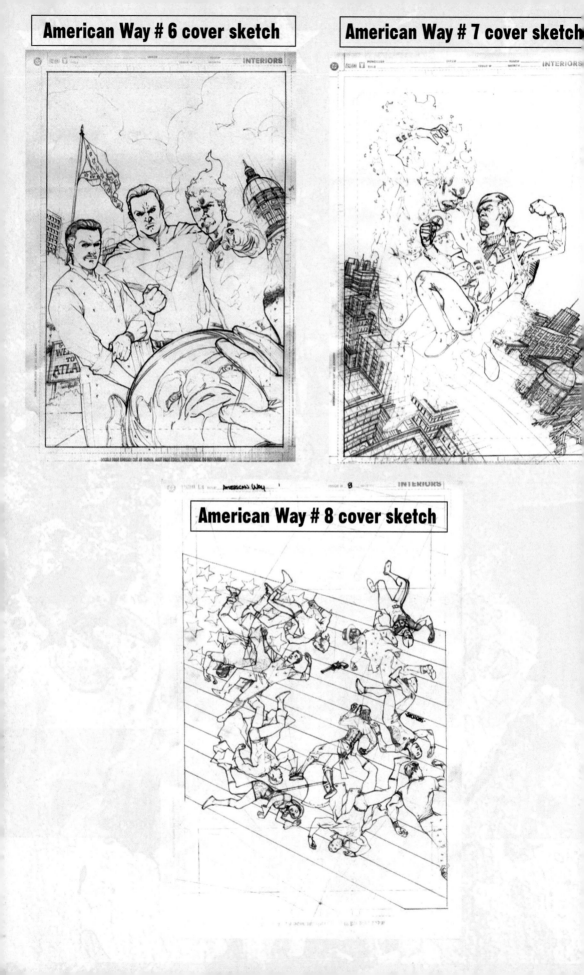

American Way # 6 cover sketch

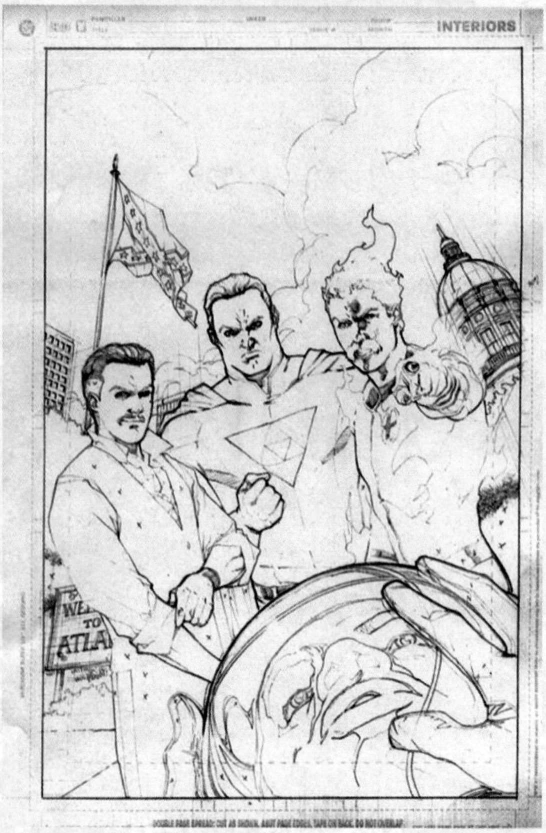
INTERIORS

American Way # 7 cover sketch

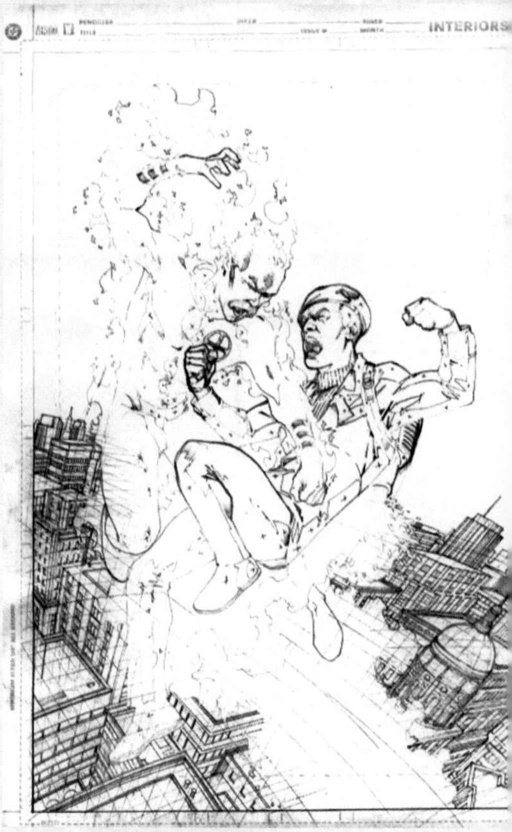
INTERIORS

American Way # 8 cover sketch

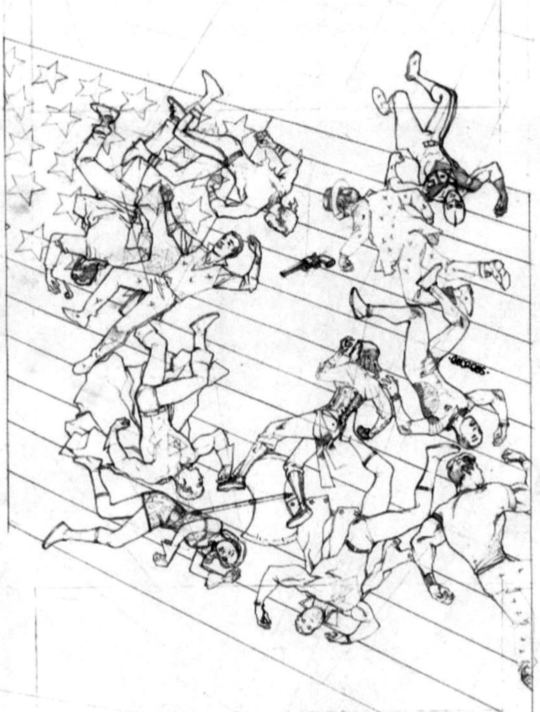